Teacher's Edition

PRENTICE HALL
SCIENCE EXPLORER

Environmental Science

PRENTICE HALL
Needham, Massachusetts
Upper Saddle River, New Jersey
Glenview, Illinois

ISBN 0-13-4345673

4 5 6 7 8 9 10   03 02 01 00

PRENTICE HALL
SCIENCE EXPLORER
GET READY FOR A CONTENT-RICH, HANDS-ON EXPLORATION!
15 Books In All
PRENTICE HALL SCIENCE EXPLORER Earth's Waters
PRENTICE HALL SCIENCE EXPLORER Motion, Forces and Energy
PRENTICE HALL SCIENCE EXPLORER Animals

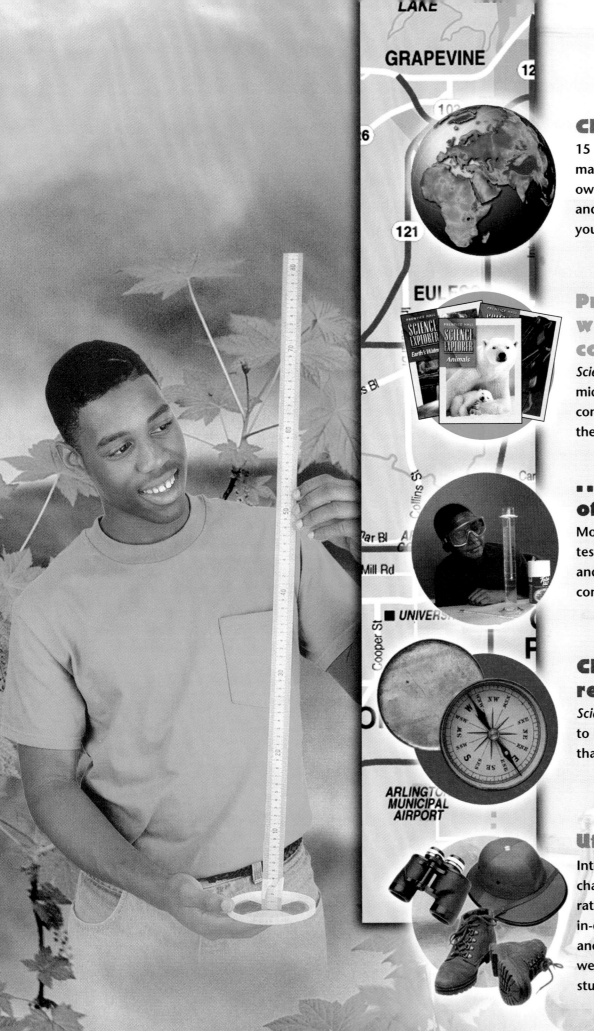

Chart your own course.

15 motivational hardcover books make it easy for you to create your own curriculum; meet local, state, and national guidelines; and teach your favorite topics in depth.

Prepare your students with rich, motivating content...

Science Explorer is crafted for today's middle grades student, with accessible content and in-depth coverage of all the important concepts.

...and a wide variety of inquiry activities.

Motivational student- and teacher-tested activities reinforce key concepts and allow students to explore science concepts for themselves.

Check your compass regularly.

Science Explorer gives you more ways to regularly check student performance than any other program available.

Utilize a variety of tools.

Integrated science sections in every chapter and Interdisciplinary Explorations in every book allow you to make in-depth connections to other sciences and disciplines. Plus, you will find a wealth of additional tools to set your students on a successful course.

Chart the course you want with 15 motivating books that easily match your curriculum.

Each book in the series contains:
- Integrated Science sections in every chapter
- Interdisciplinary Explorations for team teaching at the end of each book
- Comprehensive skills practice and application—assuring that you meet the National Science Education Standards and your local and state standards

For custom binding options, see your local sales representative.

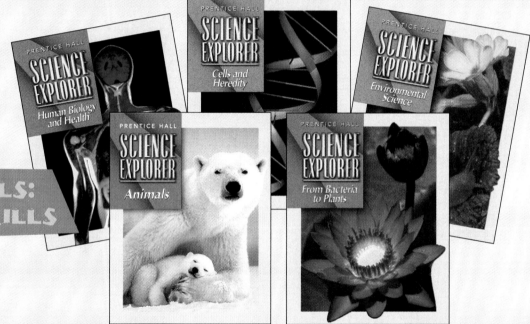

EXPLORATION TOOLS: BASIC PROCESS SKILLS

Observing

Measuring

Calculating

Classifying

Predicting

Inferring

Graphing

Creating data tables

Communicating

LIFE SCIENCE TITLES

From Bacteria to Plants
1 Living Things
2 Viruses and Bacteria
3 Protists and Fungi
4 Introduction to Plants
5 Seed Plants

Animals
1 Sponges, Cnidarians, and Worms
2 Mollusks, Arthropods, and Echinoderms
3 Fishes, Amphibians, and Reptiles
4 Birds and Mammals
5 Animal Behavior

Cells and Heredity
1 Cell Structure and Function
2 Cell Processes and Energy
3 Genetics: The Science of Heredity
4 Modern Genetics
5 Changes Over Time

Human Biology and Health
1 Healthy Body Systems
2 Bones, Muscles, and Skin
3 Food and Digestion
4 Circulation
5 Respiration and Excretion
6 Fighting Disease
7 The Nervous System
8 The Endocrine System and Reproduction

Environmental Science
1 Populations and Communities
2 Ecosystems and Biomes
3 Living Resources
4 Land and Soil Resources
5 Air and Water Resources
6 Energy Resources

 Integrated Science sections in every chapter

Posing questions

Forming operational definitions

Developing hypotheses

Controlling variables

Interpreting data

Interpreting graphs

Making models

Drawing conclusions

Designing experiments

EARTH SCIENCE TITLES

Inside Earth
1 Plate Tectonics
2 Earthquakes
3 Volcanoes
4 Minerals
5 Rocks

Earth's Changing Surface
1 Mapping Earth's Surface
2 Weathering and
  Soil Formation
3 Erosion and Deposition
4 A Trip Through
  Geologic Time

Earth's Waters
1 Earth: The Water Planet
2 Fresh Water
3 Freshwater Resources
4 Ocean Motions
5 Ocean Zones

Weather and Climate
1 The Atmosphere
2 Weather Factors
3 Weather Patterns
4 Climate and
  Climate Change

Astronomy
1 Earth, Moon, and Sun
2 The Solar System
3 Stars, Galaxies, and
  the Universe

PHYSICAL SCIENCE TITLES

Chemical Building Blocks
1 An Introduction to Matter
2 Changes in Matter
3 Elements and the Periodic
  Table
4 Carbon Chemistry

Chemical Interactions
1 Chemical Reactions
2 Atoms and Bonding
3 Acids, Bases, and Solutions
4 Exploring Materials

Motion, Forces, and Energy
1 Motion
2 Forces
3 Forces in Fluids
4 Work and Machines
5 Energy and Power
6 Thermal Energy and Heat

Electricity and Magnetism
1 Magnetism and
  Electromagnetism
2 Electric Charges
  and Current
3 Electricity and
  Magnetism at Work
4 Electronics

Sound and Light
1 Characteristics of Waves
2 Sound
3 The Electromagnetic
  Spectrum
4 Light

*Integrated Science sections
in every chapter*

Place your students in the role of science explorer through a variety of inquiry activities.

Motivational student- and teacher-tested activities reinforce key concepts and allow students to explore science concepts for themselves. More than 350 activities are provided for each book in the Student Edition, Teacher's Edition, Teaching Resources, Integrated Science Lab Manual, Inquiry Skills Activity Book, Interactive Student Tutorial CD-ROM, and *Science Explorer* Web Site.

STUDENT EDITION ACTIVITIES

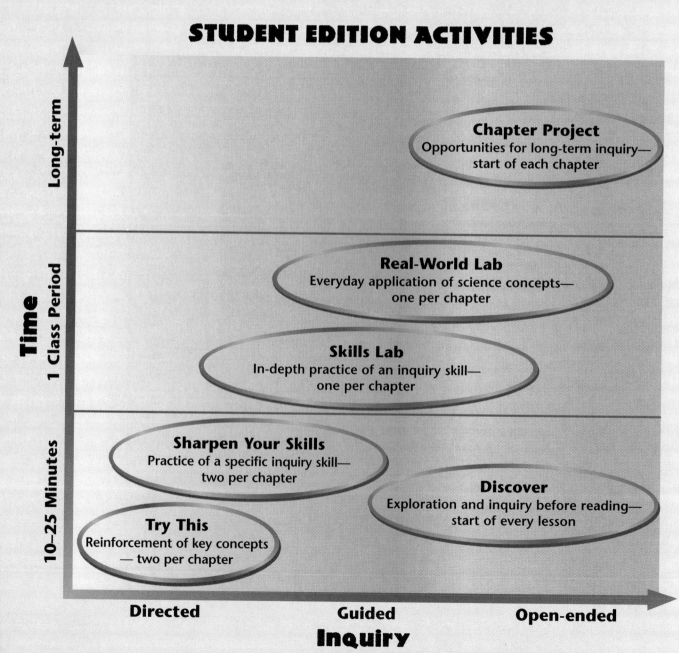

Time

Long-term

Chapter Project
Opportunities for long-term inquiry—
start of each chapter

1 Class Period

Real-World Lab
Everyday application of science concepts—
one per chapter

Skills Lab
In-depth practice of an inquiry skill—
one per chapter

10–25 Minutes

Sharpen Your Skills
Practice of a specific inquiry skill—
two per chapter

Discover
Exploration and inquiry before reading—
start of every lesson

Try This
Reinforcement of key concepts
— two per chapter

Directed   Guided   Open-ended

Inquiry

Check your compass regularly with integrated assessment tools.

Prepare for state exams with traditional and performance-based assessment.

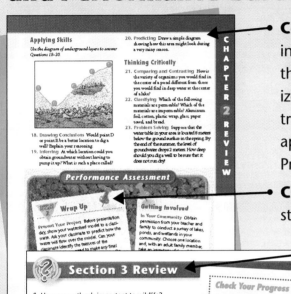

- **Comprehensive Chapter Reviews** include a wide range of question types that students will encounter on standardized tests. Types include multiple choice, enhanced true/false, concept mastery, visual thinking, skill application, and critical thinking. Also includes Chapter Project "Wrap Up."

- **Chapter Projects** contain rubrics that allow you to easily assess student progress.

- **Section Reviews** provide "Check your Progress" opportunities for the Chapter Project, as well as review questions for the section.

Additional *Science Explorer* **assessment resources:**

- **Assessment Resources with CD-ROM**

- **Resource Pro® with Planning Express® CD-ROM**

- **Standardized Test Practice Book**

- **On-line review activities** at www.phschool.com
  See page T9 for complete product descriptions.

Self-assessment opportunities help students keep themselves on course.

- **Caption Questions** throughout the text assess critical thinking skills.

- **Checkpoint Questions** give students an immediate content check as new concepts are presented.

- **Interactive Student Tutorial CD-ROM** provides students with electronic self-tests, review activities, and Exploration activities.

- **Got It! Video Quizzes** motivate and challenge students with engaging animations and interactive questions.

- **www.science-explorer.phschool.com** provides additional support and on-line test prep.

Utilize a wide variety of tools.

Easy-to-manage, book-specific teaching resources

15 Teaching Resource Packages, each containing a Student Edition, Teacher's Edition, Teaching Resources with Color Transparencies, Guided Reading Audiotape, Materials Kit Order form, and Correlation to the National Science Education Standards.

15 Teacher's Editions with a three-step lesson plan—*Engage/Explore, Facilitate,* and *Assess*—that is ideal for reaching all students. Chapter planning charts make it easy to find resources, as well as to plan for block scheduling and team teaching.

15 Teaching Resource Books with Color Transparencies offer complete support organized by chapter to make it easy for you to find what you need—when you need it.

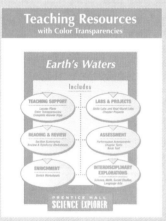

15 Guided Reading Audiotapes (English and Spanish) provide section summaries for students who need additional support.

15 Explorer Videotapes allow students to explore concepts through spectacular short videos containing computer animations. Available in Spanish.

Program-wide print resources

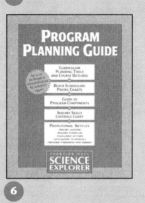

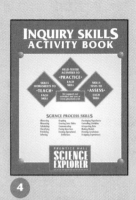

1. **Materials Kits**—Prentice Hall and Science Kit, Inc. have collaborated to develop a Consumable Kit and Nonconsumable Kit for each book. Ordering software makes it easy to customize!

2&3. **Integrated Science Laboratory Manual with Teacher's Edition**—74 in-depth labs covering the entire curriculum, with complete teaching support.

4. **Inquiry Skills Activity Book**—additional activities to teach, practice, and assess a wide range of inquiry skills.

5. **Student-Centered Science Activities**—five activity books for the Northeast, Southeast, Midwest, Southwest, and West.

6. **Program Planning Guide**—course outlines, block scheduling pacing charts, correlations, and more.

7. **Product Testing Activities by *Consumer Reports*—**19 student-oriented testing activities turn students into real-world explorers.

Additional print resources...
8. **Reading in the Content Area**—with Literature Connections
9. **Standardized Test Practice**—review and self-tests to prepare for statewide exams.
10. **15 Prentice Hall Interdisciplinary Explorations**
11. **How to Assess Student Work**
12. **How to Manage Instruction in the Block**
13. ***Cobblestone, Odyssey, Calliope,* and *Faces* Magazines**

Program-wide technology resources

1. **Resource Pro® CD-ROM**—the ultimate management tool with easy access to blackline masters and lab activities for all 15 books. Planning Express® software lets you customize lesson plans by day, week, month, and year. Also includes Computer Test Bank software.

2. **Assessment Resources with CD-ROM**—*Computer Test Bank* software with Dial-A-Test® provides you with unparalleled flexibility in creating tests.

3. *Science Explorer* **Web Site**—activities and teaching resources for every chapter at www.science-explorer.phschool.com

4. **Interactive Student Tutorial CD-ROMs**—provide students with self-tests, helpful hints, and Explorations. Tests are scored instantly and provide complete explanations to all answers.

5. **An Odyssey of Discovery CD-ROMs**—interactive labs encourage students to hypothesize and experiment. (Life and Earth Science).

6. **Interactive Earth CD-ROM**—explore global trends, search the media library, and zoom in on a 3-D globe.

7. **Mindscape CD-ROMs**—*The Animals!™, Oceans Below,* and *How Your Body Works* bring science alive with compelling videoclips, 3-D animations, and interactive databases.

8. **A.D.A.M. The Inside Story**—take an entertaining tour of each body system, designed for middle grades students.

9. **Interactive Physics**—explore physics concepts with computer simulations that encourage what-if questions.

10. **Explorer Videotapes and Videodiscs**—explore and visualize concepts through spectacular short documentaries containing computer animations (Spanish audio track).

11. **Event-Based Science**—series of NSF-funded modules that engage students with inquiry-based projects. Includes video.

Options for Pacing *Environmental Science*

The Pacing Chart below suggests one way to schedule your instructional time. The *Science Explorer* program offers many other aids to help you plan your instructional time, whether regular class periods or **block scheduling.** Refer to the Chapter Planning Guide before each chapter to view all program resources with suggested times for Student Edition activities.

Pacing Chart

	Days	Blocks		Days	Blocks
Nature of Science: Protecting Desert Wildlife	1	$\frac{1}{2}$	**1** Conserving Land and Soil	3–4	$1\frac{1}{2}$–2
Chapter 1 Populations and Communities			**2** Solid Waste	3–4	$1\frac{1}{2}$–2
Chapter 1 Project What's a Crowd?	Ongoing	Ongoing	**3** Integrating Chemistry: Hazardous Wastes	2	1
1 Living Things and the Environment	3–4	$1\frac{1}{2}$–2	Chapter 4 Review and Assessment	1	$\frac{1}{2}$
2 Integrating Mathematics: Studying Populations	3–4	$1\frac{1}{2}$–2	**Chapter 5 Air and Water Resources**		
3 Interactions Among Living Things	3–4	$1\frac{1}{2}$–2	Chapter 5 Project Pollution vs. Purity	Ongoing	Ongoing
Chapter 1 Review and Assessment	1	$\frac{1}{2}$	**1** Air Pollution	3–4	$1\frac{1}{2}$–2
Chapter 2 Ecosystems and Biomes			**2** The Water Supply	2–3	1–$1\frac{1}{2}$
Chapter 2 Project Breaking It Down	Ongoing	Ongoing	**3** Integrating Technology: Finding Pollution Solutions	1–2	$\frac{1}{2}$–1
1 Energy Flow in Ecosystems	2–3	1–$1\frac{1}{2}$	Chapter 5 Review and Assessment	1	$\frac{1}{2}$
2 Integrating Chemistry: Cycles of Matter	2–3	1–$1\frac{1}{2}$	**Chapter 6 Energy Resources**		
3 Biogeography	1–2	$\frac{1}{2}$–1	Chapter 6 Project Energy Audit	Ongoing	Ongoing
4 Earth's Biomes	4–5	2–$2\frac{1}{2}$	**1** Fossil Fuels	2–3	1–$1\frac{1}{2}$
5 Succession	2–3	1–$1\frac{1}{2}$	**2** Renewable Sources of Energy	4–5	2–$2\frac{1}{2}$
Chapter 2 Review and Assessment	1	$\frac{1}{2}$	**3** Integrating Chemistry: Nuclear Energy	1–2	$\frac{1}{2}$–1
Chapter 3 Living Resources			**4** Energy Conservation	2–3	1–$1\frac{1}{2}$
Chapter 3 Project Variety Show	Ongoing	Ongoing	Chapter 6 Review and Assessment	1	$\frac{1}{2}$
1 Environmental Issues	3–4	$1\frac{1}{2}$–2	Interdisciplinary Exploration: African Rain Forests	2–3	1–2
2 Forests and Fisheries	3–4	$1\frac{1}{2}$–2			
3 Biodiversity	2–3	1–$1\frac{1}{2}$			
4 Integrating Health: The Search for New Medicines	1–2	$\frac{1}{2}$–1			
Chapter 3 Review and Assessment	1	$\frac{1}{2}$			
Chapter 4 Land and Soil Resources					
Chapter 4 Project What's in a Package?	Ongoing	Ongoing			

RESOURCE PRO®

The Resource Pro® CD-ROM is the ultimate scheduling and lesson planning tool. Resource Pro® allows you to preview all the resources in the *Science Explorer* program, organize your chosen materials, and print out any teaching resource. You can follow the suggested lessons or create your own, using resources from anywhere in the program.

Thematic Overview of *Environmental Science*

The chart below lists the major themes of *Environmental Science*. For each theme, the chart supplies a big idea, or concept statement, describing how a particular theme is taught in a chapter.

	Chapter 1	Chapter 2	Chapter 3	Chapter 4	Chapter 5	Chapter 6
Patterns of Change	Population size changes through births, deaths, immigration, and emigration.	Communities change over time through the process of succession.	Renewable resources such as forests and fisheries can provide sustainable yields if they are not overused.	Agriculture, development, and mining change the land.	Pollution is a change to the environment that has a negative effect on living things.	Over time, heat and pressure change dead organisms into fossil fuels.
Unity and Diversity	A population consists of one species, while a community consists of many species.	An organism's energy role may be as a producer, consumer, or decomposer.	Biodiversity is the number of species in an area. Diversity of genes helps a species adapt to change.	Wastes may be buried, burned, recycled, or composted. Hazardous and radioactive wastes need special disposal.		Energy sources can be renewable and nonrenewable. Both fission and fusion are nuclear reactions that release energy.
Systems and Interactions	The living and nonliving parts of an ecosystem interact. Types of interactions include competition, predation, and symbiosis.	Every organism has a role in the movement of energy through an ecosystem.	Environmental science is the study of the natural processes that occur in the environment and how humans can affect them.	Soil is a complex system made up of living and nonliving things.	Many important human activities result in pollution. People have developed treatment systems to clean air and water.	Electric power plants generate electricity by converting energy from one form to another.
Evolution	Over time, species develop adaptations through natural selection.	The movement of the continents has helped determine the distribution of species.	Extinction is the disappearance of all members of a species from Earth.		Over time, naturally-occurring bacteria can clean up an oil spill.	
Energy	Plants and algae use the energy of sunlight to make food on which other organisms depend.	Energy in an ecosystem moves through the food web. Some energy is lost at each level.		Burning solid waste can provide energy. Recycling some wastes can save energy.	Obtaining and using energy resources can result in pollution.	Energy can be changed from one form to another. There are renewable and nonrenewable sources of energy.
Stability	Limiting factors prevent populations from increasing in size.	Matter is recycled in ecosystems.	Forests and fisheries can be managed to provide a sustainable yield.	Many wastes take a very long time to break down in landfills.	Earth's supply of fresh water is renewed through the water cycle.	A renewable source of energy is one that is constantly supplied. Radioactive wastes can remain dangerous for a long time.
Modeling	Students observe a model ecosystem and model a method of estimating population size.	Students model different biomes and study succession in a model pond.	Students model the process of paper recycling.	Students model the structure of landfills.	Most scientists base their climate predictions on computer models.	Students model technologies to use solar energy and to conserve energy.

Inquiry Skills Chart

The Prentice Hall *Science Explorer* program provides comprehensive teaching, practice, and assessment of science skills, with an emphasis on the process skills necessary for inquiry. The chart lists the skills covered in the program and cites the page numbers where each skill is covered.

Basic Process SKILLS			
	Student Text: Projects and Labs	**Student Text: Activities**	**Student Text: Caption and Review Questions**	**Teacher's Edition: Extensions**
Observing	14–15, 22, 42–43, 60–61, 74–75, 82–83, 90, 96, 120, 154, 162–163	41, 46, 65, 76, 106, 114, 147, 149, 150, 164, 200	32, 143, 153, 163	19, 33, 34, 46, 47, 70, 77, 94, 98, 107, 116, 134, 142, 168, 188
Inferring	22, 82–83, 96, 112–113	16, 51, 67, 91, 97, 140, 181, 187, 200	25, 57, 81, 91, 101, 108, 133, 172	26, 34, 67, 70, 72, 77, 87, 107, 132, 143, 169, 173
Predicting	22, 29, 179	31, 56, 114, 121, 147, 171, 200	36, 59, 81, 87, 111, 124, 137, 147, 161, 178, 190	45, 53, 100, 176
Classifying	112–113, 162–163	37, 44, 59, 95, 97, 121, 125, 201	47, 78, 81, 115, 137, 185, 193	88, 92, 124, 131, 167
Making Models	22, 42–43, 60–61, 128–129	27, 49, 150, 182, 201		32, 49, 53, 54, 57, 64, 66, 93, 101, 103, 117, 123, 132, 145, 151, 152, 166, 175, 182, 184
Communicating	14–15, 22, 29, 42–43, 82–83, 112–113, 138–139, 162–163	20, 30, 58, 78, 87, 89, 92, 105, 111, 133, 141, 144, 175, 180, 189, 201	40, 41, 80, 81, 110, 111, 136, 137, 160, 161, 192, 193	63, 86, 99, 100, 104, 126, 133, 158, 184
Measuring	14–15, 42–43, 96, 148, 154, 186, 162–163	143, 161, 171, 202, 203		
Calculating	29, 154	24, 28, 94, 183, 203	50, 85, 161, 193	24, 25, 26, 94, 124, 169, 188
Creating Data Tables	14–15, 42–43, 60–61, 82–83, 112–113, 148, 154	18, 41, 210		
Graphing	14–15, 29	123, 156, 166, 211, 212	41, 111, 123, 137	85, 141, 150
Advanced Process SKILLS			
Posing Questions		76, 205		157
Developing Hypotheses	74–75, 120	52, 62, 155, 171, 205	41, 111, 137, 161	
Designing Experiments	14–15, 42–43, 60–61, 74–75, 90, 120, 128–129, 148, 154, 179, 186	205		
Controlling Variables	14–15, 42–43, 120, 148	205		

Advanced Process SKILLS *(continued)*

	Student Text: Projects and Labs	Student Text: Activities	Student Text: Caption and Review Questions	Teacher's Edition: Extensions
Forming Operational Definitions	179	23, 84, 130, 205		
Interpreting Data	14–15, 22, 96, 148	69, 121, 205	41, 111, 126, 161, 193	
Drawing Conclusions	14–15, 60–61, 74–75, 96, 112–113, 128–129, 162–163	18, 205	193	

Critical Thinking SKILLS

Comparing and Contrasting	74–75	206	17, 38, 41, 55, 66, 70, 73, 81, 89, 95, 127, 136, 157, 161, 176, 193	58, 71, 146
Applying Concepts	29, 60–61, 90, 128–129, 148, 179	206	21, 38, 77, 88, 98, 116, 127, 137, 146, 157, 170, 190	20, 47, 125, 152
Interpreting Diagrams, Graphs Photographs, and Maps	29	206	18, 26, 36, 45, 52, 54, 85, 92, 97, 101, 118, 141, 145, 167, 168, 183, 184	69
Relating Cause and Effect	42–43, 138–139	207	41, 68, 81, 111, 119, 151, 153, 170, 174	
Making Generalizations		207	41, 50, 64, 105, 111, 158, 161, 174	
Making Judgments	138–139, 162–163	30, 180, 207	111, 134, 137, 193	157
Problem Solving		23, 30, 127, 180, 207	28, 41, 137	172

Information Organizing SKILLS

Concept Maps		208	40, 110, 160	
Compare/ Contrast Tables		208	136, 192	
Venn Diagrams		209		
Flowcharts		209	80	
Cycle Diagrams		209	80	

The *Science Explorer* program provides additional teaching, reinforcement, and assessment of skills in the Inquiry Skills Activities Book and the Integrated Science Laboratory Manual.

Throughout the *Science Explorer* program, every effort has been made to keep the materials and equipment *affordable, reusable, and easily accessible.*

The *Science Explorer* program offers an abundance of activity options so you can pick and choose those activities that suit your needs. To help you order supplies at the beginning of the year, the Master Materials List cross-references the materials by activity. If you prefer to create your list electronically, use the electronic order forms at:
www.science–explorer.phschool.com

There are two kits available for each book of the *Science Explorer* program, a Consumable Kit and a Nonconsumable Kit. These kits are produced by **Science Kit and Boreal Laboratories,** the leader in providing science kits to schools. Prentice Hall and Science Kit collaborated throughout the development of *Science Explorer* to ensure that the equipment and supplies in the kits precisely match the requirements of the program activities.

The kits provide an economical and convenient way to get all of the materials needed to teach each book. For each book, Science Kit also offers the opportunity to buy equipment and safety items individually. For a current listing of kit offerings or additional information about materials to accompany *Science Explorer*, please, contact Science Kit at:
1-800-828-7777
or at their Internet site at:
www.sciencekit.com

Master Materials List

Consumable Materials

*	Description	Quantity per class	Textbook Section(s)	*	Description	Quantity per class	Textbook Section(s)
C	Aluminum Foil, Roll, 12" × 25'	1	6-2 (Lab)	C	Gravel, Aquarium 1 kg	2	1-1 (Lab)
C	Bag, Plastic Zip Lip, 6" × 8" (1 qt)	15	2-1 (SYS) 4-2 (Lab) 6-2 (DIS)	SS	Guppies	10	1-1 (Lab)
				C	Juice, Lemon, 15 oz	1	5-1 (TT)
C	Battery, Size D	10	5-2 (DIS)	SS	Magazine Picture	5	1-1 (DIS)
SS	Bread, Slice	5	2-1 (SYS)	SS	Marker, Black, Water Soluble	5	3-4 (DIS)
C	Brine Shrimp Eggs, 6 Dram Vial	1	1-1 (TT)	C	Marking Pencil, Black Wax	5	1-1 (TT) 2-4 (Lab) 5-1 (Lab) 5-2 (Lab)
C	Bulb, Clear, Standard Size, 60 Watt	1	1-1 (Lab) 2-3 (Lab)				
SS	Bulb, Fluorescent, 15 Watt, Pkg.	5	6-4 (DIS)	SS	Marshmallows, Bag	1	6-2 (Lab)
SS	Bulb, Incandescent, 60 Watt, Pkg.	5	6-4 (DIS)	SS	Milk	1	5-2 (DIS)
SS	Cactus, Potted	5	2-4 (TT)	SS	Milk Carton, Cardboard	5	2-3 (Lab)
C	Cards, Index, Blank, 3" × 5", Pkg/100	1	2-3 (Lab)	SS	Newspaper	5	3-1 (Lab) 4-1 (Lab) 4-2 (Lab)
C	Charcoal Pieces, 16 oz	1	5-3 (DIS)	C	Oil, Vegetable, 16 oz	1	5-1 (Lab)
C	Cheesecloth, 2 M Piece	1	4-2 (Lab)	SS	Paper, Oaktag, Sheet	15	6-2 (Lab)
C	Cup, Paper, 200 mL, with lid	10	4-1 (Lab) 6-3 (Lab)	SS	Paper, Sheet	25	1-1 (DIS) 1-1 (TT) 1-3 (DIS) 2-1 (DIS) 3-1 (DIS)
C	Cup, Plastic, Clear, 300 mL, with lid	10	5-3 (DIS) 6-3 (Lab)				
C	Cup, Plastic, Clear, 9 oz	50	1-1 (TT) 3-3 (DIS) 3-4 (DIS) 5-1 (TT) 5-2 (DIS) 5-2 (TT) 5-3 (DIS)	C	Pebbles/Gravel, 1 kg	3	4-2 (Lab)
				SS	Pencil	5	3-4 (DIS) 4-1 (DIS)
				SS	Pencils, Colored, Pkg/12	5	1-1 (DIS) 1-3 (DIS) 3-2 (Lab)
C	Cup, Plastic foam, 6 oz, with lid	5	6-3 (Lab)	SS	Perfume, Bottle	1	5-1 (DIS)
C	Detergent, Household, 14.7 oz	1	5-1 (Lab)	C	pH Test Paper-Wide Range, 100/Vial, 1/4" × 2"	5	5-1 (TT)
C	*Elodea* (16), Coupon	1	1-1 (Lab)				
C	Filter Paper, 15 cm Diam, Pkg/100	1	3-4 (DIS) 5-3 (DIS)	C	Plastic Wrap Roll, 50 sq ft	1	2-3 (Lab) 3-1 (Lab) 4-2 (Lab)
C	Food Coloring, Dark Red, 30 mL, in Dropper Bottle	2	4-2 (Lab) 5-2 (TT) 5-2 (Lab)				
				C	Plates, Paper, 9", Pkg/50	1	3-3 (DIS)
SS	Glue, School, White, 4 oz	5	1-1 (DIS) 6-2 (Lab)	C	Pond Culture, Mixed, Coupon	1	2-4 (Lab)
				SS	Pond Snails	20	1-1 (Lab)
SS	Graph Paper, Sheet	15	3-2 (DIS) 4-2 (DIS) 5-3 (SYS)	C	Rubber Band, Asst. Colors & Sizes, 1-1/2 oz Pkg	1	4-2 (Lab)

KEY: **DIS**: Discover; **SYS**: Sharpen Your Skills; **TT**: Try This; **Lab**: Lab

Quantities based on 5 lab groups per class.

* Items designated **C** are in the Consumable Kit, **NC** are in the Nonconsumable Kit, and **SS** are School Supplied.

Master Materials List

Consumable Materials (cont.)

*	Description	Quantity per class	Textbook Section(s)	*	Description	Quantity per class	Textbook Section(s)
C	Salt, Non-Iodized, 737 g	1	1-1 (TT) 5-1 (Lab)	SS	Spring Water	1	1-1 (TT)
C	Sand, Fine, 2.5 kg	1	4-1 (DIS)	C	Straws, Plastic (Wrapped), Pkg/50	1	2-3 (DIS)
C	Seeds, Corn, 30 g	1	2-3 (DIS)	C	Sugar, Granulated, 454 g	1	5-2 (TT)
C	Seeds, Grass, 30 g	1	2-3 (Lab)	C	Tape, Adding Machine Roll, 2-1/4" Width (100 ft. length)	2	2-4 (DIS)
C	Seeds, Impatiens, Pkg	1	2-3 (Lab)	SS	Tape, Masking, 3/4" × 60 yd	5	1-2 (TT) 1-3 (DIS) 2-1 (SYS) 2-3 (DIS) 2-3 (Lab) 2-4 (DIS) 3-4 (DIS) 5-1 (Lab) 6-2 (Lab)
C	Seeds, Lima Bean, 2 oz	1	2-3 (Lab)				
C	Seeds, Radish, 15 g	1	5-1 (Lab)				
C	Seeds, Sunflower, 30 g	1	4-1 (DIS)				
SS	Sod, Small Square	5	4-1 (Lab)				
C	Soil, Potting, 4 lb	2	2-3 (Lab) 5-1 (Lab)				
C	Soil, Sandy, 2.5 kg	2	2-3 (Lab) 4-1 (DIS) 4-1 (Lab) 4-2 (Lab)	SS	Tea, Herbal, 1 bag	5	5-3 (DIS)
				C	Timothy Hay, 4 oz	1	2-4 (Lab)
				SS	Trash Bag, Filled	5	4-2 (DIS)
C	Sponge, 15 × 7.5 × 1.8 cm	2	4-2 (Lab)	C	Vinegar, 500 mL	1	5-1 (Lab)
C	Spoons, Plastic, Pkg/24	1	1-1 (TT)	C	Yarn, Red, Skein	1	2-1 (TT)

Nonconsumable Materials

*	Description	Quantity per class	Textbook Section(s)	*	Description	Quantity per class	Textbook Section(s)
NC	Beaker, Pyrex, Low Form, 250 mL	5	1-2 (DIS)	NC	Cylinder, Graduated, Polypropylene, 100 mL	5	1-1 (TT) 5-1 (Lab) 5-2 (TT) 6-2 (DIS)
NC	Beaker, Pyrex, Low Form, 600 mL	5	6-3 (Lab)				
SS	Block, Wood	10	4-1 (Lab)				
SS	Book	5	3-1 (Lab)				
NC	Bowl, Opaque, 2 L	5	3-1 (Lab)	NC	Dominoes, Box of 28	3	6-3 (DIS)
SS	Box	5	1-2 (Lab)	NC	Dowel, Wood, 12" × 1/4"	15	6-2 (Lab)
SS	Clock or Watch	1	1-2 (TT) 6-2 (Lab) 6-3 (Lab)	NC	Dropper, Plastic	5	2-4 (Lab) 5-2 (DIS) 5-2 (Lab)
SS	Compass, Drawing	5	4-2 (SYS)	SS	Egg Beater	5	3-1 (Lab)
SS	Container and Lid, Glass	5	6-3 (Lab)	NC	Felt, 12" × 20"	1	2-3 (DIS)
SS	Container and Lid, Metal	5	6-3 (Lab)	NC	Flashlight, Plastic (Size D)	5	5-2 (DIS)
NC	Cup, Measuring, Polypropylene, 8 oz	5	4-2 (Lab)	NC	Forceps, Fine Tip, 115 mm	5	4-1 (DIS) 4-2 (Lab)
				NC	Funnel, Plastic, 3.25"	5	4-1 (Lab) 5-3 (DIS)

KEY: **DIS**: Discover; **SYS**: Sharpen Your Skills; **TT**: Try This; **Lab**: Lab
* Items designated **C** are in the Consumable Kit, **NC** are in the Nonconsumable Kit, and **SS** are School Supplied.

Nonconsumable Materials (cont.)

*	Description	Quantity per class	Textbook Section(s)
SS	Jar, Large, with Cover	5	1-1 (Lab)
NC	Jar, Plastic (89 mm) 8 oz	5	2-4 (Lab)
SS	Jar, Plastic, Wide-mouthed	15	1-2 (DIS) 4-2 (Lab)
SS	Labels from Hazardous Household Products, Assortment	5	4-3 (DIS)
NC	Lid, Metal, 89 mm, Screw Type	5	2-4 (Lab)
NC	Light Socket, Porcelain w/Cord	1	1-1 (Lab) 2-3 (Lab)
NC	Magnifying Glass, 3x, 6x	5	2-4 (TT) 3-2 (Lab) 6-1 (DIS)
NC	Marbles, 5/8", Pkg/20	3	6-3 (TT)
NC	Meter Stick, Half (50 cm in length)	5	1-2 (TT) 2-4 (DIS)
NC	Mirror, Plastic, 7.5 × 12.5 cm, With Beveled Edges and Ground Corners	5	2-2 (DIS)
SS	Model Paper Turtle Population	5	1-2 (Lab)
NC	Net, Dip, Fine Nylon, 3"	1	1-1 (Lab)
NC	Pan, Aluminum Foil, 31 × 22 × 3 cm	10	2-3 (DIS) 4-1 (DIS) 4-1 (Lab)
NC	Pan, Aluminum Foil, 8 × 8 × 1-1/4"	5	3-1 (Lab)
NC	Petri Dish, Disposable, Polystyrene, Sterile, 100 × 15 mm, pkg/20	1	5-1 (Lab)
SS	Plastic Products, Assortment	5	4-2 (TT)
SS	Protractor	5	4-2 (SYS)
SS	Puzzle, Jigsaw, Small	5	1-2 (TT)
NC	Rock, Coal (Bituminous) Specimen Pack (5 pieces 2-3 cm, 20 chips)	1	6-1 (DIS)
SS	Ruler, Plastic, 12"/30 cm	5	1-1 (Lab) 1-2 (DIS) 3-2 (Lab) 4-2 (Lab) 5-1 (Lab)
SS	Scissors	5	1-3 (DIS) 2-3 (Lab) 2-4 (TT) 4-2 (Lab) 6-2 (Lab)
NC	Screen, Window, 12" × 24" (Aluminum)	2	3-1 (Lab)
NC	Seeds, Bean (White) 4 oz	1	3-3 (DIS)
NC	Seeds, Bean, Kidney, lb	5	1-2 (DIS) 3-3 (DIS)
NC	Seeds, Black Bean, lb	1	3-3 (DIS)
NC	Slides, Plastic & Coverglass Set (Includes 72 plastic slides & 100 plastic coverglasses)	1	2-4 (Lab) 3-1 (Lab)
NC	Soup Mix, 15 Bean, 20 oz Pkg	1	3-3 (DIS)
NC	Spoons, Plastic, Pkg/24	1	4-1 (DIS) 5-2 (TT)
SS	Stapler	1	2-3 (Lab)
NC	Stirring Rod, Polypropylene, 10"	5	1-1 (Lab)
NC	Test Tube, 13 × 100 mm, 9 mL	45	5-2 (Lab)
NC	Test Tube Support, 80 tube	5	5-2 (Lab)
NC	Thermometer, -40°C—110°C/ -40°F—230°, High Temp, Plastic Back	15	6-2 (DIS) 6-2 (Lab) 6-3 (Lab) 6-4 (DIS)
SS	Timer	1	1-2 (DIS)
NC	Tree Cross-Sections, 3-1/2"—4-1/2" Diameter	5	3-2 (Lab)

Equipment

*	Description	Quantity per class	Textbook Section(s)
SS	Apron, Vinyl	30	3-1 (Lab) 4-1 (Lab) 4-2 (Lab) 5-2 (Lab)
SS	Calculator	5	1-2 (Lab) 3-2 (Lab)
SS	Gloves, Disposable	1	4-2 (DIS)
SS	Goggles, Chemical Splash— Class Set	1	3-1 (Lab) 4-1 (DIS) 4-1 (Lab) 4-2 (Lab) 5-1 (Lab) 5-2 (Lab) 6-2 (Lab)
SS	Microscope	5	2-4 (Lab) 3-1 (Lab)

KEY: **DIS**: Discover; **SYS**: Sharpen Your Skills; **TT**: Try This; **Lab**: Lab
* Items designated **C** are in the Consumable Kit, **NC** are in the Nonconsumable Kit, and **SS** are School Supplied.

Environmental Science

Program Resources
Student Edition
Annotated Teacher's Edition
Teaching Resources Book with Color Transparencies
Environmental Science Materials Kits

Program Components
Integrated Science Laboratory Manual
Integrated Science Laboratory Manual, Teacher's Edition
Inquiry Skills Activity Book
Student-Centered Science Activity Books
Program Planning Guide
Guided Reading English Audiotapes
Guided Reading Spanish Audiotapes and Summaries
Product Testing Activities by Consumer Reports™
Event-Based Science Series (NSF funded)
Prentice Hall Interdisciplinary Explorations
Cobblestone, Odyssey, Calliope, and *Faces* Magazines

Media/Technology
Science Explorer Interactive Student Tutorial CD-ROMs
Odyssey of Discovery CD-ROMs
Resource Pro® (Teaching Resources on CD-ROM)
Assessment Resources CD-ROM with Dial-A-Test®
Internet site at www.science-explorer.phschool.com
Life, Earth, and Physical Science Videodiscs
Life, Earth, and Physical Science Videotapes

Science Explorer Student Editions

From Bacteria to Plants

Animals

Cells and Heredity

Human Biology and Health

Environmental Science

Inside Earth

Earth's Changing Surface

Earth's Waters

Weather and Climate

Astronomy

Chemical Building Blocks

Chemical Interactions

Motion, Forces, and Energy

Electricity and Magnetism

Sound and Light

Staff Credits

The people who made up the *Science Explorer* team—representing editorial, editorial services, design services, field marketing, market research, marketing services, on-line services/multimedia development, product marketing, production services, and publishing processes—are listed below. Bold type denotes core team members.

Kristen E. Ball, **Barbara A. Bertell,** Peter W. Brooks, **Christopher R. Brown, Greg Cantone,** Jonathan Cheney, **Patrick Finbarr Connolly,** Loree Franz, Donald P. Gagnon, Jr., **Paul J. Gagnon, Joel Gendler,** Elizabeth Good, Kerri Hoar, **Linda D. Johnson,** Katherine M. Kotik, Russ Lappa, Marilyn Leitao, David Lippman, **Eve Melnechuk, Natania Mlawer,** Paul W. Murphy, **Cindy A. Noftle,** Julia F. Osborne, Caroline M. Power, Suzanne J. Schineller, **Susan W. Tafler,** Kira Thaler-Marbit, Robin L. Santel, Ronald Schachter, **Mark Tricca,** Diane Walsh, Pearl B. Weinstein, Beth Norman Winickoff

Acknowledgment for page 198: Excerpt from *The Amateur Naturalist* by Gerald Durrell. Copyright ©1982 by Dorling Kindersley Ltd., London. Reprinted by permission of Alfred A. Knopf, Inc.

ISBN 0-13-434486-3
5 6 7 8 9 10   03 02 01 00

Cover: A snail and a flower are just two examples of Earth's biodiversity.

Teacher's Edition ISBN 0-13-434567-3

Michael J. Padilla, Ph.D.
Professor
Department of Science Education
University of Georgia
Athens, Georgia

Michael Padilla is a leader in middle school science education. He has served as an editor and elected officer for the National Science Teachers Association. He has been principal investigator of several National Science Foundation and Eisenhower grants and served as a writer of the National Science Education Standards.

As lead author of *Science Explorer*, Mike has inspired the team in developing a program that meets the needs of middle grades students, promotes science inquiry, and is aligned with the National Science Education Standards.

Ioannis Miaoulis, Ph.D.
Dean of Engineering
College of Engineering
Tufts University
Medford, Massachusetts

Martha Cyr, Ph.D.
Director, Engineering
    Educational Outreach
College of Engineering
Tufts University
Medford, Massachusetts

Science Explorer was created in collaboration with the College of Engineering at Tufts University. Tufts has an extensive engineering outreach program that uses engineering design and construction to excite and motivate students and teachers in science and technology education.

Faculty from Tufts University participated in the development of *Science Explorer* chapter projects, reviewed the student books for content accuracy, and helped coordinate field testing.

CHAPTER PROJECT

Book Authors

Fred Holtzclaw
Science Instructor
Oak Ridge High School
Oak Ridge, Tennessee

Linda Cronin Jones, Ph.D.
College of Education
University of Florida
Gainesville, Florida

Steve Miller
Science Writer
State College, Pennsylvania

Contributing Writers

Thomas R. Wellnitz
Science Instructor
The Paideia School
Atlanta, Georgia

Theresa K. Holtzclaw
Former Science Instructor
Clinton, Tennessee

Reading Consultant

Bonnie B. Armbruster, Ph.D.
Department of Curriculum
    and Instruction
University of Illinois
Champaign, Illinois

Interdisciplinary Consultant

Heidi Hayes Jacobs, Ed.D.
Teacher's College
Columbia University
New York City, New York

Safety Consultants

W. H. Breazeale, Ph.D.
Department of Chemistry
College of Charleston
Charleston, South Carolina

Ruth Hathaway, Ph.D.
Hathaway Consulting
Cape Girardeau, Missouri

Tufts University Program Reviewers

Behrouz Abedian, Ph.D.
Department of Mechanical
  Engineering

Wayne Chudyk, Ph.D.
Department of Civil and
  Environmental Engineering

Eliana De Bernardez-Clark, Ph.D.
Department of Chemical Engineering

Anne Marie Desmarais, Ph.D.
Department of Civil and
  Environmental Engineering

David L. Kaplan, Ph.D.
Department of Chemical Engineering

Paul Kelley, Ph.D.
Department of Electro-Optics

George S. Mumford, Ph.D.
Professor of Astronomy, Emeritus

Jan A. Pechenik, Ph.D.
Department of Biology

Livia Racz, Ph.D.
Department of Mechanical Engineering

Robert Rifkin, M.D.
School of Medicine

Jack Ridge, Ph.D.
Department of Geology

Chris Swan, Ph.D.
Department of Civil and
  Environmental Engineering

Peter Y. Wong, Ph.D.
Department of Mechanical Engineering

Content Reviewers

Jack W. Beal, Ph.D.
Department of Physics
Fairfield University
Fairfield, Connecticut

W. Russell Blake, Ph.D.
Planetarium Director
Plymouth Community
  Intermediate School
Plymouth, Massachusetts

Howard E. Buhse, Jr., Ph.D.
Department of Biological Sciences
University of Illinois
Chicago, Illinois

Dawn Smith Burgess, Ph.D.
Department of Geophysics
Stanford University
Stanford, California

A. Malcolm Campbell, Ph.D.
Assistant Professor
Davidson College
Davidson, North Carolina

Elizabeth A. De Stasio, Ph.D.
Associate Professor of Biology
Lawrence University
Appleton, Wisconsin

John M. Fowler, Ph.D.
Former Director of Special Projects
National Science Teacher's Association
Arlington, Virginia

Jonathan Gitlin, M.D.
School of Medicine
Washington University
St. Louis, Missouri

Dawn Graff-Haight, Ph.D., CHES
Department of Health, Human
  Performance, and Athletics
Linfield College
McMinnville, Oregon

Deborah L. Gumucio, Ph.D.
Associate Professor
Department of Anatomy and Cell Biology
University of Michigan
Ann Arbor, Michigan

William S. Harwood, Ph.D.
Dean of University Division and Associate
  Professor of Education
Indiana University
Bloomington, Indiana

Cyndy Henzel, Ph.D.
Department of Geography
  and Regional Development
University of Arizona
Tucson, Arizona

Greg Hutton
Science and Health
  Curriculum Coordinator
School Board of Sarasota County
Sarasota, Florida

Susan K. Jacobson, Ph.D.
Department of Wildlife Ecology
  and Conservation
University of Florida
Gainesville, Florida

Judy Jernstedt, Ph.D.
Department of Agronomy and Range Science
University of California, Davis
Davis, California

John L. Kermond, Ph.D.
Office of Global Programs
National Oceanographic and
  Atmospheric Administration
Silver Spring, Maryland

David E. LaHart, Ph.D.
Institute of Science and Public Affairs
Florida State University
Tallahassee, Florida

Joe Leverich, Ph.D.
Department of Biology
St. Louis University
St. Louis, Missouri

Dennis K. Lieu, Ph.D.
Department of Mechanical Engineering
University of California
Berkeley, California

Cynthia J. Moore, Ph.D.
Science Outreach Coordinator
Washington University
St. Louis, Missouri

Joseph M. Moran, Ph.D.
Department of Earth Science
University of Wisconsin–Green Bay
Green Bay, Wisconsin

Joseph Stukey, Ph.D.
Department of Biology
Hope College
Holland, Michigan

Seetha Subramanian
Lexington Community College
University of Kentucky
Lexington, Kentucky

Carl L. Thurman, Ph.D.
Department of Biology
University of Northern Iowa
Cedar Falls, Iowa

Edward D. Walton, Ph.D.
Department of Chemistry
California State Polytechnic University
Pomona, California

Robert S. Young, Ph.D.
Department of Geosciences and
  Natural Resource Management
Western Carolina University
Cullowhee, North Carolina

Edward J. Zalisko, Ph.D.
Department of Biology
Blackburn College
Carlinville, Illinois

Teacher Reviewers

Stephanie Anderson
Sierra Vista Junior
    High School
Canyon Country, California

John W. Anson
Mesa Intermediate School
Palmdale, California

Pamela Arline
Lake Taylor Middle School
Norfolk, Virginia

Lynn Beason
College Station Jr. High School
College Station, Texas

Richard Bothmer
Hollis School District
Hollis, New Hampshire

Jeffrey C. Callister
Newburgh Free Academy
Newburgh, New York

Judy D'Albert
Harvard Day School
Corona Del Mar, California

Betty Scott Dean
Guilford County Schools
McLeansville, North Carolina

Sarah C. Duff
Baltimore City Public Schools
Baltimore, Maryland

Melody Law Ewey
Holmes Junior High School
Davis, California

Sherry L. Fisher
Lake Zurich Middle
    School North
Lake Zurich, Illinois

Melissa Gibbons
Fort Worth ISD
Fort Worth, Texas

Debra J. Goodding
Kraemer Middle School
Placentia, California

Jack Grande
Weber Middle School
Port Washington, New York

Steve Hills
Riverside Middle School
Grand Rapids, Michigan

Carol Ann Lionello
Kraemer Middle School
Placentia, California

Jaime A. Morales
Henry T. Gage Middle School
Huntington Park, California

Patsy Partin
Cameron Middle School
Nashville, Tennessee

Deedra H. Robinson
Newport News Public Schools
Newport News, Virginia

Bonnie Scott
Clack Middle School
Abilene, Texas

Charles M. Sears
Belzer Middle School
Indianapolis, Indiana

Barbara M. Strange
Ferndale Middle School
High Point, North Carolina

Jackie Louise Ulfig
Ford Middle School
Allen, Texas

Kathy Usina
Belzer Middle School
Indianapolis, Indiana

Heidi M. von Oetinger
L'Anse Creuse Public School
Harrison Township, Michigan

Pam Watson
Hill Country Middle School
Austin, Texas

Activity Field Testers

Nicki Bibbo
Russell Street School
Littleton, Massachusetts

Connie Boone
Fletcher Middle School
Jacksonville Beach, Florida

Rose-Marie Botting
Broward County
    School District
Fort Lauderdale, Florida

Colleen Campos
Laredo Middle School
Aurora, Colorado

Elizabeth Chait
W. L. Chenery Middle School
Belmont, Massachusetts

Holly Estes
Hale Middle School
Stow, Massachusetts

Laura Hapgood
Plymouth Community
    Intermediate School
Plymouth, Massachusetts

Sandra M. Harris
Winman Junior High School
Warwick, Rhode Island

Jason Ho
Walter Reed Middle School
Los Angeles, California

Joanne Jackson
Winman Junior High School
Warwick, Rhode Island

Mary F. Lavin
Plymouth Community
    Intermediate School
Plymouth, Massachusetts

James MacNeil, Ph.D.
Concord Public Schools
Concord, Massachusetts

Lauren Magruder
St. Michael's Country
    Day School
Newport, Rhode Island

Jeanne Maurand
Glen Urquhart School
Beverly Farms, Massachusetts

Warren Phillips
Plymouth Community
    Intermediate School
Plymouth, Massachusetts

Carol Pirtle
Hale Middle School
Stow, Massachusetts

Kathleen M. Poe
Kirby-Smith Middle School
Jacksonville, Florida

Cynthia B. Pope
Ruffner Middle School
Norfolk, Virginia

Anne Scammell
Geneva Middle School
Geneva, New York

Karen Riley Sievers
Callanan Middle School
Des Moines, Iowa

David M. Smith
Howard A. Eyer Middle School
Macungie, Pennsylvania

Derek Strohschneider
Plymouth Community
    Intermediate School
Plymouth, Massachusetts

Sallie Teames
Rosemont Middle School
Fort Worth, Texas

Gene Vitale
Parkland Middle School
McHenry, Illinois

Zenovia Young
Meyer Levin Junior
    High School (IS 285)
Brooklyn, New York

Contents

Environmental Science

Prepare your students with rich, motivating content

Science Explorer is crafted for today's middle grades student, with accessible content and in-depth coverage. **Integrated Science Sections** support every chapter and the **Interdisciplinary Exploration** provides an engaging final unit.

Check your compass— regularly assess student progress.

Self-assessment tools are built right into the student text and **on-going assessment** is woven throughout the Teacher's Edition. You'll find a wealth of **assessment technology** in the Resource Pro®, Interactive Student Tutorial, and Assessment Resources CD-ROMs.

Activities

> **Guide your students to become science explorers.**
>
> A wide range of **student-tested** activities, **from guided to open-ended**, with options for **short- and long-term** inquiry.

··
Interdisciplinary Activities

Protecting Desert Wildlife

Focus on Ecology

This four-page feature introduces the process of scientific inquiry by involving students in a high-interest, magazine-like article about a working scientist, wildlife management biologist Elroy Masters. Using Masters's efforts to protect desert wildlife and habitats as an example, the feature focuses on observing, collecting data, and problem solving as key elements of scientific inquiry.

The concept of habitat and scientific methods used to study populations are presented in Chapter 1, Section 1-1, of this book. However, students do not need to have any previous knowledge of the chapter's content to understand and appreciate this feature.

Scientific Inquiry

Before students read the feature, invite them to preview the pages and the photographs and maps. Then ask: **What kinds of animals does Elroy Masters study?** *(Fish, bighorn sheep, birds, tortoises, bats)* **Where does he work?** *(In the area around Lake Havasu in western Arizona)* **How were you able to determine these things?** *(By looking at the pictures and map and reading the captions)* Confirm this response by emphasizing that students learned these things by observing. Then point out to students that just as they were able to learn about Masters's work by observing the illustrations, scientists learn by observing the world around them.

PROTECTING DESERT WILDLIFE

Elroy Masters likes working outdoors. One day he hikes a mountain trail, looking for desert tortoises. The next morning he may be in a boat on the Colorado River, counting birds along the riverbank. Another day he may be in the Arizona hills, building a water container for thirsty bighorn sheep. Elroy is a biologist working for the federal government's Bureau of Land Management (BLM). His job is to protect wildlife habitat in the desert along the Colorado River between California and Arizona.

"People may come in wanting to run a pipeline across public land or needing to build a road," he explains. "Part of my job is to check out the biological effect of that action on different species of animals and plants. If people are going to build a road where there are a lot of tortoises, we might try to have them work from November to March. Since tortoises hibernate during those months, we reduce the chance of a tortoise getting run over."

Growing up in Arizona, Elroy lived in a farming community. "I was always out-doors. I was able to have animals that a lot of people don't have—chickens, pigeons, ducks, and a horse. I always loved animals. I always hoped for some type of career with them."

Elroy Masters studied biology at Phoenix College and Northern Arizona University. He started working for the Bureau of Land Management when he was still a college student. He now works as a Wildlife Management Biologist. In this photograph, Elroy is about to release a razorback sucker, an endangered species of fish, into the Colorado River.

Background

Ecology is the study of how living things interact with each other and with the nonliving things in their environment. Environmental science, the central topic of this book, is the study of how humans affect these interactions.

Environmental science is an applied science in which problem solving is a key element. Because environmental problems are so complex, environmental scientists must be knowledgeable in many disciplines: biology, chemistry, geology, physics, meteorology, geography, economics, mathematics, sociology, natural resource management, law, and politics. Environmental science is thus a truly interdisciplinary study.

Today, Elroy and his co-workers make surveys of desert animals. They count the animals in different areas and make maps of their habitats. They locate where the animals live, what they eat, and where they build their nests and raise their young. Elroy uses that information to protect the animals when natural events or human activities threaten them.

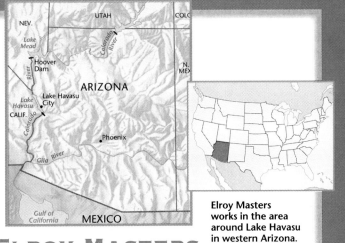

Elroy Masters works in the area around Lake Havasu in western Arizona.

TALKING WITH ELROY MASTERS

Q *What wildlife do you protect?*

A One of the neatest animals we deal with is the desert bighorn sheep. In an average summer, it can get as hot as 120 degrees here. Sometimes the heat lasts for weeks. But with the number of people living around the river, the animals are no longer able to travel to water. So we go up into the mountains to construct catchments (containers) to collect water and store it. That way the sheep can stay in the mountains without trying to cross freeways to get to water.

We fly in big storage tanks that hold about 10,000 gallons of water. We bury them in the ground or put them on a platform. We use paint to mask them into the color of the scenery. We sometimes build a dam or put out a metal sheet to catch drizzle rain.

A catchment can hold 10,000 gallons of water (right). It is buried in the ground. The drinking container provides water for desert bighorn sheep (below), mule deer, and other wildlife.

E ◆ 11

- ◆ Ask students: **What is a wildlife biologist?** *(A scientist who studies living things in their environment)* You may want to share the information in Background on the previous page.
- ◆ After students read the introductory text on pages 10–11, ask: **What is a habitat?** *(A specific place where an organism lives and that provides the things the organism needs; if students are not familiar with the term, explain it for them.)* **Is the entire desert a single habitat?** *(no)* **Why not?** *(A desert has many different kinds of "specific places" where organisms live, such as sandy flatlands, rocky hills, and riverbanks. Different types of organisms live in different specific places, or habitats.)*
- ◆ Ask: **What is the major purpose of the surveys that Elroy conducts?** *(To collect information about the desert animals' habitats and behaviors)* **Why is that information important to him?** *(Knowing where the animals live and what they need in order to survive helps him know what can threaten the animals.)* **Once Elroy knows the animals' needs and how they are being threatened, what does he have to do next?** *(Figure out a way to protect the animals from these threats)* Confirm this response by emphasizing that Elroy has to solve problems. Point out that collecting data and problem solving are two important aspects of a scientist's work.
- ◆ Have students read the first section of the interview on this page. Then ask: **What is the bighorn sheep's habitat?** *(The desert mountains)* **What threat to the sheep did Elroy identify?** *(The sheep were unable to get to the river for water because human settlements and highways blocked their route.)* **How did the scientists solve this problem?** *(They supplied water for the sheep by building catchments in the mountains where the sheep live.)* **Why do you think the catchments are camouflaged to match the scenery?** *(To make the sheep and other wild animals less afraid of the artificial structures; to make the tanks look like a natural and attractive part of the desert landscape)*

◆ After students read the first question and answer on this page, ask: **What does Elroy mean when he says that a group of sheep in his area "aren't doing as well as expected"?** *(Students should be able to infer that many of the sheep are being killed by mountain lions.)* **How would Elroy know that?** *(From counting how many sheep there are in the group from one season or year to the next, from finding carcasses of sheep killed by lions, from seeing a lion track the sheep, and other observations)*

◆ After students read the second question and answer, ask: **What is a population?** *(Confirm all answers that include the idea of a group of organisms of the same kind, or species, that live in the same area. If necessary, define the term for students.)* **Why does Elroy talk about "two different populations" of desert tortoises?** *(The two groups of desert tortoises live on opposite sides of the river, so they are considered different populations.)*

◆ After students read the third question and answer, pose the following question: **Imagine you're conducting a survey to find out how many desert tortoises live in one particular habitat, but you don't see any tortoises above ground. What could you do to estimate the size of the tortoise population?** *(Based on the text alone, students should be able to infer that they could count the number of tortoise burrows they find. Some students may also suggest counting the separate sets of tortoise tracks they see on the ground.)* Explain that these are the methods actually used by biologists who study animals in the wild.

Q *What else are you doing to protect the bighorn sheep?*

A We're going to work with the Fish and Wildlife Department to capture and transplant bighorn sheep to a mountain range in my area. There are already sheep and some mountain lions here. But the sheep aren't doing as well as we expected. We want to bring in some bighorn sheep that are used to lions. We hope these lion-savvy sheep will teach the sheep in our area how to avoid lions. To catch the sheep, we'll use a helicopter. We'll shoot a net over the sheep and a couple of guys will jump out to secure the animals and then bring them to our herd.

The Colorado River valley is home to the Southwestern willow flycatcher and the desert tortoise.

Q *What other animals are you responsible for protecting?*

A I work a lot with desert tortoises. I'm responsible for two different populations, one on either side of the river. The tortoises live in the drier, hilly areas away from the river. Any time we go out into the field, we try to collect data. We keep track of where they've been and where they feed.

Q *How do you find the tortoises?*

A We have maps that indicate their habitat. Based on the habitat, we'll go out, walk around, and look under rocks and boulders to see if we can find a burrow. The tortoises are good diggers. They find a good boulder and go underground 10 or 12 feet. That's where they'll spend the winter.

Southwestern willow flycatcher

Desert tortoise

12 ◆ E

Q *Do you also work with birds?*

A Right now we're working with the Southwestern willow flycatcher. It's a small bird that depends on thick riparian (riverbank) vegetation to build nests and breed. The flycatcher is a migratory bird. Each spring, the birds fly to Arizona from Central America and Mexico. In the early summer months, we go out to find how many are breeding. We're trying to learn what's needed to prevent flycatchers from becoming extinct. We need to survey and protect the remaining stands of habitat. The flycatchers like to nest in thick stands of willow. But they will also build nests in another tree, salt cedar. The birds don't prefer it, but sometimes salt cedar is the only vegetation remaining, so they use it.

Q *What's threatening the riverbank plants?*

A The low water level in the river—due to human use—is a big threat. So is fire. During summer months, there are large numbers of recreational boats. Careless boaters can cause fires. Some fires get pretty big along the river and destroy a lot of the habitat where the birds nest and raise their young.

Q *Can you see the benefits of your work?*

A Yes, I see it especially in riverbank zones where areas are protected so that vegetation and trees can grow back. This year we did a new bird count in one area. Species that hadn't been seen in a while, like tanagers, showed up. Some of the migratory birds are already stopping in young cottonwood trees. That's the best gauge I've had—seeing birds returning to these new trees.

There are also quick results with the water catchments in the hills. We put the water in a year ago. They're aimed at bighorn sheep and mule deer. But now we've also got a lot of different birds—doves and quails—that come into the area.

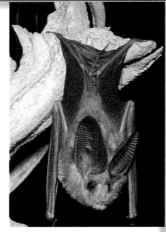

Elroy Masters also works with populations of the California leaf-nosed bat. This bat has large ears and a leaf-shaped, turned-up nose. The bats are threatened by the loss of their habitat.

In Your Journal

Elroy Masters and his co-workers "survey" the wildlife in their area in order to learn how to protect them. Think of a wild animal that lives in a park or open area near you—squirrels, frogs, birds, even insects. Work out a step-by-step plan to draw a simple map marking the places where the animal is found.

E ◆ 13

◆ After students read about the birds and riverbank plants, draw their attention to the bat photograph and its caption. Ask: **What common problem threatens the survival of willow flycatchers, riverbank plants, and leaf-nosed bats in Elroy's area?** *(Loss of habitat)* **Why do you think the flycatchers' habitat is being lost?** *(Willows are being destroyed as people build along the river; accept other reasonable answers.)* **What causes habitat loss along riverbanks?** *(Lower water levels and fires—both caused by human activities)* **What do you think could destroy the bats' habitat?** *(Accept all responses without comment, then share the information in Background below.)*

◆ After students read the last question and answer, ask: **How do you think Elroy and his co-workers feel when their work is successful?** *(Satisfied, glad, relieved)* **Why do they feel that way?** *(They were able to use their knowledge and problem-solving skills to help wild animals survive.)*

In Your Journal This activity is suitable for students to do either individually or in cooperative learning groups of three or four students each. Have students share their plans with the rest of the class. Also encourage students to carry out their plans, if feasible, and share their maps and other findings with the class. (CAUTION: *Students should visit their areas with an adult. Remind students not to try to touch wild animals.*)

Introducing Environmental Science

Have students look through the book to find the parts that relate most closely to this feature. *(Chapter 1 discusses habitats, populations, living and nonliving factors in ecosystems, the work of ecologists, interactions among organisms, and methods used to determine population size. Chapter 2, Section 4, presents information on desert biomes.)* Then ask: **What else is this book about?** *(Different kinds of resources—living resources, soil and land, air, water, and energy—and pollution)*

Background

The California leaf-nosed bat (*Macrotus californicus*) does not hibernate or migrate and cannot reduce its body temperature. To remain active year-round, the bats must have warm daytime roosts, which they find in caves, mine tunnels, and buildings.

Roosting areas are destroyed when large numbers of people visit caves, old mines, and "ghost town" buildings and when old mine entrances are sealed to prevent injury to people. New land development also reduces the bats' habitat. Bats that roost in occupied buildings are usually exterminated or kept from re-entering by blocking the entrances.

Populations and Communities

Sections	Time	Student Edition Activities	Other Activities
CHAPTER PROJECT 1 **What's a Crowd?** p. 15	Ongoing (2–3 weeks)	Check Your Progress, pp. 21, 38 Wrap Up, p. 41	
1 Living Things and the Environment pp. 16–22 ◆ Identify the needs that are met by an organism's habitat. ◆ Describe the levels of organization within an ecosystem. ◆ Identify biotic and abiotic parts of an ecosystem. ◆ Define ecology and state what ecologists do.	3–4 periods/ 1½–2 blocks	**Discover** What's in the Scene?, p. 16 **Try This** With or Without Salt?, p. 18 **Skills Lab: Making Models** A World in a Jar, p. 22	TE Building Inquiry Skills: Observing, p. 19 TE Using the Visuals: Figure 4, p. 20 IES "Where River Meets Sea," pp. 18–21
2 INTEGRATING MATHEMATICS **Studying Populations** pp. 23–30 ◆ Describe how ecologists determine the size of a population. ◆ Explain what causes populations to change in size. ◆ Identify factors that limit population growth.	3–4 periods/ 1½–2 blocks	**Discover** What's the Population of Beans in a Jar?, p. 23 **Sharpen Your Skills** Calculating, p. 24 **Try This** Elbow Room, p. 27 **Science at Home**, p. 28 **Real-World Lab: Careers in Science** Counting Turtles, p. 29	TE Inquiry Challenge, p. 24 TE Building Inquiry Skills: Calculating, p. 26 ISLM E–1 "Weather and Whooping Cranes"
3 Interactions Among Living Things pp. 31–38 ◆ Explain how an organism's adaptations help it to survive. ◆ Describe the major types of interactions among organisms. ◆ Identify the three forms of symbiotic relationships.	3–4 periods/ 1½–2 blocks	**Discover** How Well Can You Hide a Butterfly?, p. 31 **Sharpen Your Skills** Classifying, p. 37	TE Inquiry Challenge, p. 32 TE Building Inquiry Skills: Observing, p. 33 TE Building Inquiry Skills: Observing, p. 34
Study Guide/Chapter Review pp. 39–41	1 period/ ½ block		ISAB Provides teaching and review of all inquiry skills

 For Standard or Block Schedule The Resource Pro® CD-ROM gives you maximum flexibility for planning your instruction for any type of schedule. Resource Pro® contains Planning Express®, an advanced scheduling program, as well as the entire contents of the Teaching Resources and the Computer Test Bank.

CHAPTER PLANNING GUIDE

Program Resources	Assessment Strategies	Media and Technology
TR Chapter 1 Project Teacher Notes, pp. 8–9 TR Chapter 1 Project Overview and Worksheets, pp. 10–13 TR Chapter 1 Project Scoring Rubric, p. 14	SE Performance Assessment: Chapter 1 Project Wrap Up, p. 41 TE Performance Assessment: Chapter 1 Project Wrap Up, p. 41 TE Check Your Progress, pp. 21, 38 TR Chapter 1 Project Scoring Rubric, p. 14	Science Explorer Internet Site
TR 1-1 Lesson Plan, p. 15 TR 1-1 Section Summary, p. 16 TR 1-1 Review and Reinforce, p. 17 TR 1-1 Enrich, p. 18 TR Chapter 1 Skills Lab, pp. 27–28 SES Book H, *Earth's Waters,* Chapters 2 and 5	SE Section 1 Review, p. 21 SE Analyze and Conclude, p. 22 TE Ongoing Assessment, pp. 17, 19 TE Performance Assessment, p. 21 TR 1-1 Review and Reinforce, p. 17	Exploring Earth Science Videodisc, Unit 6 Side 2, "Touch the Earth Gently" Audiotapes: English-Spanish Summary 1-1 Transparency 1, "Levels of Organization in an Ecosystem" Interactive Student Tutorial CD-ROM, E-1
TR 1-2 Lesson Plan, p. 19 TR 1-2 Section Summary, p. 20 TR 1-2 Review and Reinforce, p. 21 TR 1-2 Enrich, p. 22 TR Chapter 1 Real-World Lab, pp. 29–31	SE Section 2 Review, p. 28 SE Analyze and Conclude, p. 29 TE Ongoing Assessment, pp. 25, 27 TE Performance Assessment, p. 28 TR 1-2 Review and Reinforce, p. 21	Audiotapes: English-Spanish Summary 1-2 Interactive Student Tutorial CD-ROM, E-1
TR 1-3 Lesson Plan, p. 23 TR 1-3 Section Summary, p. 24 TR 1-3 Review and Reinforce, p. 25 TR 1-3 Enrich, p. 26 SES Book C, *Cells and Heredity,* Chapter 5	SE Section 3 Review, p. 38 TE Ongoing Assessment, pp. 33, 35, 37 TE Performance Assessment, p. 38 TR 1-3 Review and Reinforce, p. 25	Exploring Life Science Videodisc, Unit 3 Side 2, "How Does Everything Fit?" Audiotapes: English-Spanish Summary 1-3 Interactive Student Tutorial CD-ROM, E-1
	SE Chapter 1 Review, pp. 39–41 TR Chapter 1 Performance Assessment, pp. 180–182 TR Chapter 1 Test, pp. 183–186 CTB Test E-1	Interactive Student Tutorial CD-ROM, E-1 Computer Test Bank, Test E-1

Key: **SE** Student Edition   **TE** Teacher's Edition   **TR** Teaching Resources
      CTB Computer Test Bank   **SES** Science Explorer Series Text   **ISLM** Integrated Science Laboratory Manual
      ISAB Inquiry Skills Activity Book   **PTA** Product Testing Activities by *Consumer Reports*   **IES** Interdisciplinary Explorations Series

Meeting the National Science Education Standards and AAAS Benchmarks

National Science Education Standards	Benchmarks for Science Literacy	Unifying Themes
Science As Inquiry (Content Standard A) ◆ **Design and conduct a scientific investigation** Students design an experiment to determine the effect of crowding on plant growth. *(Chapter Project)* ◆ **Use appropriate tools and techniques to gather, analyze, and interpret data** Students model using the mark-and-recapture method to estimate the size of a population. *(Real-World Lab)* ◆ **Develop descriptions, explanations, predictions, and models using evidence** Students study the interactions between biotic and abiotic factors in a model ecosystem. *(Skills Lab)* ◆ **Communicate scientific procedures and explanations** Students present a report and graph of their project results. *(Chapter Project)* **Life Science** (Content Standard C) ◆ **Populations and ecosystems** The levels of organization in the environment include organism, population, community, and ecosystem. Populations can change in size when new members enter the population or when members leave the population. The three major types of interactions among organisms are competition, predation, and symbiosis. *(Sections 1, 2, 3)* **Science in Personal and Social Perspectives** (Content Standard F) ◆ **Science and technology in society** Students analyze the issue of animal overpopulation. *(Science and Society)*	**1B Scientific Inquiry** Students design and conduct an experiment to determine the effect of crowding on plant growth. Students study the interactions between biotic and abiotic factors in a model ecosystem. *(Chapter Project; Skills Lab)* **2B Mathematics, Science, and Technology** Students model using the mark-and-recapture method to estimate the size of a population. *(Real-World Lab)* **5D Interdependence of Life** An organism obtains food, water, shelter, and other things it needs to live, grow, and reproduce from its surroundings. Some limiting factors for populations are food, space, and weather conditions. The three major types of interactions among organisms are competition, predation, and symbiosis. *(Sections 1, 2, 3)* **7D Social Trade-Offs** Students analyze the issue of animal overpopulation. *(Science and Society)*	◆ **Energy** Sunlight is necessary for photosynthesis, a process plants and algae use to make food that supplies energy to most living things. *(Section 1; Skills Lab)* ◆ **Evolution** Changes that make organisms better suited to their environment develop through natural selection. *(Section 3)* ◆ **Modeling** Students use a model ecosystem to study biotic and abiotic factors. Students model using the mark-and-recapture method to estimate the size of a population. *(Skills Lab; Real-World Lab)* ◆ **Patterns of Change** Populations can change in size when new members enter the population or when members leave the population. Over time, species develop adaptations through natural selection. *(Sections 2, 3)* ◆ **Stability** Organisms can live in a closed ecosystem. A limiting factor is an environmental factor that prevents a population from increasing. *(Skills Lab; Section 2)* ◆ **Systems and Interactions** Students observe the effect of crowding on plant growth. An organism obtains food, water, shelter, and other things it needs to live, grow, and reproduce from its surroundings. Some limiting factors for populations are food, space, and weather conditions. Overpopulation of white-tailed deer affects the environment, humans, and the deer themselves. The three major types of interactions among organisms are competition, predation, and symbiosis. *(Chapter Project; Sections 1, 2, 3; Science and Society)*

Media and Technology

Exploring Earth Science Videodisc

◆ **Section 1** "Touch the Earth Gently" features Chief Seattle as he explains the web of life and cautions humans to not disturb the delicate balance.

Exploring Life Science Videodisc

◆ **Section 3** "How Does Everything Fit?" demonstrates the important interactions among all types of animals and the humans on Earth.

Student Edition Connection Strategies

◆ **Section 1** Language Arts Connection, p. 20

◆ **Section 2** Integrating Mathematics, pp. 23–29
Science and Society, p. 30

◆ **Section 3** Integrating Chemistry, p. 33
Integrating Health, p. 37

USING THE INTERNET

www.science-explorer.phschool.com

Visit the Science Explorer Internet site to find an up-to-date activity for Chapter 1 of *Environmental Science.*

ACTIVITY	Time (minutes)	Materials Quantities for one work group	Skills
Section 1			
Discover, p. 16	10–15	**Consumable** old magazines, paste or glue, sheet of white paper **Nonconsumable** scissors, three pencils of different colors	Inferring
Try This, p. 18	10–15; 5 × 3 days	**Consumable** masking tape, 2 L spring water, 25 g noniodized salt, 4 paper squares, brine shrimp eggs **Nonconsumable** 4 600-mL beakers, pen, stirrers, hand lens (optional)	Drawing Conclusions
Skills Lab, p. 22	40; 5 × 10 days	**Consumable** 2-day-old tap water, 2 guppies, 4 aquatic plants, 4 small pond snails **Nonconsumable** aquarium gravel, plastic stirring rod, large jar with cover (about 2 L), lamp with 60-watt bulb, metric ruler, dip net	Making Models, Predicting, Inferring
Section 2			
Discover, p. 23	5–10	**Nonconsumable** 2 large plastic jars, ruler, small beaker, timer, dried beans	Forming Operational Definitions
Sharpen Your Skills, p. 24	5	No special materials are required.	Calculating
Try This, p. 27	10–15	**Consumable** masking tape **Nonconsumable** meter stick, small jigsaw puzzle, watch or clock	Making Models
Science at Home, p. 28	15	**Nonconsumable** dictionary or other book	Calculating
Real-World Lab, p. 29	40	**Consumable** model paper turtle population, graph paper **Nonconsumable** calculator	Calculating, Graphing, Predicting
Section 3			
Discover, p. 31	10–15	**Consumable** sheet of white paper, tape **Nonconsumable** colored pencils or markers	Predicting
Sharpen Your Skills, p. 37	5–10	No special materials are required.	Classifying

A list of all materials required for the Student Edition activities can be found on pages T14–T15. You can order Materials Kits by calling 1-800-828-7777 or by accessing the Science Explorer Internet site at **www.science-explorer.phschool.com.**

What's a Crowd?

Limiting factors affect the distribution, health, and size of populations. In this project, students will design their own experiments to test the effect of one limiting factor—crowding—on sample populations of plants.

Purpose In addition to giving students an opportunity to observe the effect of crowding on plant growth, this project will enhance understanding of the procedures involved in scientific experimentation. To complete the project successfully, students must develop a testable hypothesis about crowding and plant growth; design an experiment that involves identifying and controlling variables, measuring plant growth, and recording data; infer the effects of the limiting factor; and communicate results to the rest of the class. If students have had limited experience designing and carrying out experiments, use the Skills Handbook in the back of this text to support development of these skills.

Skills Focus After completing the Chapter 1 Project, students will be able to
◆ design an experiment to test the effect of crowding on plant growth;
◆ identify and control variables;
◆ measure plant growth, record data, and analyze results;
◆ communicate experimental procedures and results in a written report and graph.

Project Time Line The project requires two to three weeks to complete, depending on the type of plants students use. (See Possible Materials below.) During the first phase, each group should plan an experiment and submit the plan for your review, culminating with planting the seeds before the conclusion of Section 1. While students study sections 2 and 3, each group should conduct its experiment and record data. At the conclusion of Section 3, groups should prepare their written reports and their presentations to the class.

Possible Materials
◆ Wisconsin Fast Plants™ (*Brassica rapa*), a strain of radishlike plants specifically developed for their short

WHAT'S AHEAD

life cycle, are the preferred choice for this project. They germinate within 24 hours, develop leaves within one week and flowers in about two weeks, and can be grown easily in a small space. Fast Plant seeds are available from biological supply houses. Alternatively, students could use radish seeds. (More information about Wisconsin Fast Plants™ can be obtained by accessing the Internet site at **www.fastplants.cals.wisc.edu.**)
◆ Each group will need several identical planting containers. Possibilities include

large margarine tubs, plastic shoeboxes or similar-size storage containers, or half-gallon milk cartons with one of the larger sides removed.
◆ Provide potting soil, trowels or large spoons, watering cans or spray bottles, and metric rulers.
◆ Set aside a location in the classroom where the plant containers will receive direct sunlight or strong indirect light for several hours each day. If sunlight is limited, set up lamps on tables.

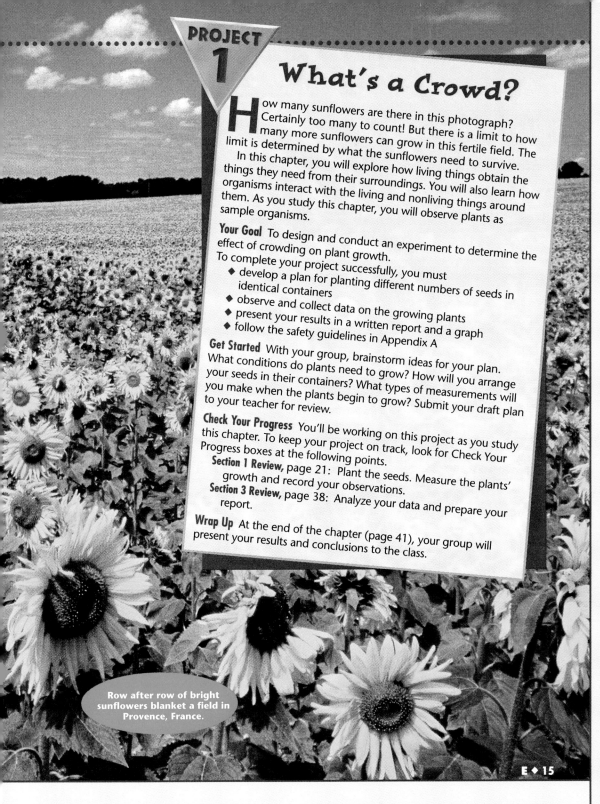

What's a Crowd?

How many sunflowers are there in this photograph? Certainly too many to count! But there is a limit to how many more sunflowers can grow in this fertile field. The limit is determined by what the sunflowers need to survive.

In this chapter, you will explore how living things obtain the things they need from their surroundings. You will also learn how organisms interact with the living and nonliving things around them. As you study this chapter, you will observe plants as sample organisms.

Your Goal To design and conduct an experiment to determine the effect of crowding on plant growth.

To complete your project successfully, you must
♦ develop a plan for planting different numbers of seeds in identical containers
♦ observe and collect data on the growing plants
♦ present your results in a written report and a graph
♦ follow the safety guidelines in Appendix A

Get Started With your group, brainstorm ideas for your plan. What conditions do plants need to grow? How will you arrange your seeds in their containers? What types of measurements will you make when the plants begin to grow? Submit your draft plan to your teacher for review.

Check Your Progress You'll be working on this project as you study this chapter. To keep your project on track, look for Check Your Progress boxes at the following points.

Section 1 Review, page 21: Plant the seeds. Measure the plants' growth and record your observations.

Section 3 Review, page 38: Analyze your data and prepare your report.

Wrap Up At the end of the chapter (page 41), your group will present your results and conclusions to the class.

Row after row of bright sunflowers blanket a field in Provence, France.

E ♦ 15

Launching the Project To introduce the project, have students examine the photograph and read the first paragraph on page 15. Then ask: **What do sunflowers need to grow well?** *(Students may mention sunlight, water, and soil or the nutrients in soil.)* If students do not mention space, ask: **Do you think every sunflower seed in this field grew into a mature plant? Why or why not?** *(Students should realize that due to overcrowding, some sprouting plants probably died.)*

Allow time for students to read the project

description on page 15. Distribute Chapter 1 Project Student Overview on pages 10–11 in Teaching Resources, and let students review the project rules and procedures. Encourage questions and comments.

Program Resources

♦ **Teaching Resources** Chapter 1 Project Teacher Notes, pp. 8–9; Chapter 1 Project Overview and Worksheets, pp. 10–13; Chapter 1 Project Scoring Rubric, p. 14

Divide the class into groups of two to four students each. Give each student a copy of Chapter 1 Project Worksheet 1 on page 12 in Teaching Resources. This worksheet provides structured support for planning an experiment. Allow time for the groups to meet and begin brainstorming ideas. Tell students to use the worksheet to take notes as they brainstorm. Also explain that when their group decides on a final experiment, they should prepare a written plan based on the worksheet steps. Emphasize that you will review the plans before groups begin their experiments.

Tell students that each group's members may divide the project responsibilities among themselves in any way they wish. However, emphasize that *every* group member should help plan the experiment, make observations, analyze results, and develop the class presentation and should be prepared to answer questions about the experiment.

In Check Your Progress at the conclusion of Section 3, distribute Chapter 1 Project Worksheet 2 on page 13 in Teaching Resources. This worksheet is designed to help students prepare their written reports and graphs.

Performance Assessment

The Chapter 1 Project Scoring Rubric on page 14 in Teaching Resources will help you evaluate how well students complete the Chapter 1 Project. Students will be assessed on
♦ their ability to design an experiment to test the effect of crowding on plant growth;
♦ how carefully they have identified and controlled variables in the experiment and their completeness and accuracy in making observations and recording data;
♦ how well they have communicated their procedures, results, and conclusion to the rest of the class;
♦ their participation in their groups.
You may want to share the scoring rubric with students so they are clear about what will be expected of them.

Living Things and the Environment

Objectives

After completing the lesson, students will be able to
◆ identify the needs that are met by an organism's habitat;
◆ describe the levels of organization within an ecosystem;
◆ identify biotic and abiotic parts of an ecosystem;
◆ define ecology and state what ecologists do.

Key Terms ecosystem, habitat, biotic factor, abiotic factor, photosynthesis, species, population, community, ecology

1 Engage/Explore

Activating Prior Knowledge

Ask: **What is an ecosystem?** (*Students may say it is a particular type of place with different kinds of plants, animals, and other living things living in it. Accept all responses without comment at this time.*)
What kinds of ecosystems do you know of? (*Students may mention a swamp, desert, seashore, forest, and so forth.*)

········ DISCOVER ········

Skills Focus inferring
Materials *old magazines, scissors, paste or glue, sheet of white paper, three pencils of different colors*
Time 10–15 minutes
Tips Encourage students to look for pictures with close-enough views to allow them to distinguish various living and nonliving things. Also emphasize that the scenes do not have to be "beautiful" so long as each shows a variety of living and nonliving things.
Expected Outcome The specific living things shown will vary. Students should identify water, soil, sunlight, and air among the nonliving things.
Think It Over Students should indicate that living things need water, air, and sunlight and that plants also need soil.

DISCOVER

What's in the Scene?

1. Choose a magazine picture of a nature scene. Paste the picture onto a sheet of paper, leaving space all around the picture.

2. Identify all the things in the picture that are alive. Use a colored pencil to draw a line from each living thing, or organism. Label the organism if you know its name.

3. Use a different colored pencil to draw a line from each nonliving thing and label it.

Think It Over

Inferring How do the organisms in the picture depend on the nonliving things? Using a third color, draw lines connecting organisms to the nonliving things they need.

GUIDE FOR READING

◆ What needs are met by an organism's surroundings?

◆ What are the levels of organization within an ecosystem?

Reading Tip Write the section headings in your notebook. As you read, make a list of main ideas and supporting details under each heading.

Black-tailed prairie dogs ▼

A s the sun rises on a warm summer morning, the Nebraska town is already bustling with activity. Some residents are hard at work building homes for their families. They are building underground, where it is dark and cool. Other inhabitants are collecting seeds for breakfast. Some of the town's younger residents are at play, chasing each other through the grass.

Suddenly, an adult spots a threatening shadow approaching—an enemy has appeared in the sky! The adult cries out several times, warning the others. Within moments, the town's residents disappear into their underground homes. The town is silent and still, except for a single hawk circling overhead.

Have you guessed what kind of town this is? It is a prairie dog town on the Nebraska plains. As these prairie dogs dug their burrows, searched for food, and hid from the hawk, they interacted with their environment, or surroundings. The prairie dogs interacted with living things, such as the grass and the hawk, and with nonliving things, such as the soil. All the living and nonliving things that interact in a particular area make up an **ecosystem**.

READING STRATEGIES

Outlining Students should create an outline of the section, with the main headings *Habitats, Biotic Factors, Abiotic Factors, Populations, Communities,* and *What Is Ecology?* labeled I through VI. Students can then label the main ideas for each heading A, B, C, and so forth and the supporting details 1, 2, 3, and so forth.

(The subheadings *Water, Sunlight, Oxygen, Temperature,* and *Soil* on pages 18–19 can be labeled A through E below the main heading *Abiotic Factors.*) If any students had difficulty identifying main ideas and supporting details or differentiating between them, work with those students individually or in small groups to provide guidance.

A prairie is just one of the many different ecosystems found on Earth. Other ecosystems in which living things make their homes include mountain streams, deep oceans, and dense forests.

Habitats

A prairie dog is one type of organism, or living thing. Organisms live in a specific place within an ecosystem. **An organism obtains food, water, shelter, and other things it needs to live, grow, and reproduce from its surroundings.** The place where an organism lives and that provides the things the organism needs is called its **habitat.**

A single ecosystem may contain many habitats. For example, in a forest ecosystem, mushrooms grow in the damp soil, rabbits live on the forest floor, termites live under the bark of tree trunks, and flickers build nests in the trunks.

Organisms live in different habitats because they have different requirements for survival. A prairie dog obtains the food and shelter it needs from its habitat. It could not survive in a tropical rain forest or on the rocky ocean shore. Likewise, the prairie would not meet the needs of a gorilla, a penguin, or a hermit crab.

Biotic Factors

An organism interacts with both the living and nonliving things in its environment. The living parts of an ecosystem are called **biotic factors** (by AHT ik factors). Biotic factors in the prairie dogs' ecosystem include the grass and plants that provide seeds and berries. The hawks, ferrets, badgers, and eagles that hunt the prairie dogs are also biotic factors. In addition, worms, fungi, and bacteria are biotic factors that live in the soil underneath the prairie grass. These organisms keep the soil rich in nutrients as they break down the remains of other living things.

☑ *Checkpoint* *Name a biotic factor in your environment.*

Figure 1 A stream tumbles over mossy rocks in a lush Tennessee forest. This ecosystem contains many different habitats. *Comparing and Contrasting How is the mushrooms' habitat in the forest different from the flicker's habitat?*

Program Resources

◆ **Teaching Resources** 1-1 Lesson Plan, p. 15; 1-1 Section Summary, p. 16
   Science Explorer Series *Earth's Waters*, Chapter 2, covers fresh water habitats. Chapter 5 covers marine habitats.

Media and Technology

🎧 **Audiotapes** English-Spanish Summary 1-1

Answers to Self-Assessment

Caption Question

Figure 1 Mushrooms grow in damp soil on the forest floor, whereas the flicker builds nests in tree trunks.

☑ *Checkpoint*

Students may name living organisms such as other people, trees, dogs, or birds.

2 Facilitate

Habitats

Addressing Naive Conceptions

Students may not have a clear understanding of the difference between the terms *ecosystem* and *habitat*, since both refer to places where organisms live. Emphasize that the *type* of place where an organism lives—a prairie or a forest, for example—is an ecosystem. The specific *part* of the ecosystem that meets the organism's needs and in which it lives is its habitat. To clarify this difference, first have students name the four specific habitats identified in the text as being part of a forest ecosystem. Create a concept map on the board with *Forest* in one circle and the four habitats in circles below it. Invite students to identify another ecosystem and several habitats within it, and let them come to the board to create another concept map. Continue with other ecosystems and habitats. **learning modality: visual**

Biotic Factors

Including All Students

Invite students who need extra help to identify examples of biotic factors found in other ecosystems, such as the forest ecosystem described on this page and the ecosystems that the class has discussed. (*In the forest ecosystem, biotic factors include mushrooms, rabbits, termites, trees, and flickers.*) **learning modality: verbal**

Ongoing Assessment

Concept Mapping Have each student choose one ecosystem and create a concept map about it. The ecosystem should be identified in the top circle and at least three specific habitats in circles below it.

Portfolio Students can save their concept maps in their portfolios.

Abiotic Factors

Including All Students

Write *abiotic* on the board and underline the prefix *a-*. Ask: **What does *a-* at the beginning of the word mean?** (*"Not" or "opposite of"; if students do not know, have them compare the terms* biotic *and* abiotic *and infer the meaning of* a-.) Emphasize that the English language uses several different prefixes to change the meanings of words. Ask: **What are some other prefixes in English that mean "not"?** (*ab-, un-, non-, dis-*) List the prefixes on the board as students identify them, and ask them to give examples of words with those prefixes, such as *unhappy, nontoxic,* and *disagree.* **limited English proficiency**

Skills Focus drawing conclusions
Materials *4 600-mL beakers, masking tape, pen, 2 L spring water, 25 g noniodized salt, stirrers, brine shrimp eggs, 4 paper squares large enough to cover cups, hand lens (optional)*
Time 10–15 minutes for initial setup, 5 minutes per day for follow-up observations
Tips Let the spring water sit overnight to reach room temperature. Put a small sample of brine shrimp eggs in a paper cup for each group. You may add $\frac{1}{2}$ teaspoon of dry yeast to each beaker to feed the shrimp when they hatch. NOTE: Newly hatched brine shrimp are very tiny and orange in color.
Expected Outcome Eggs will not hatch in beaker A. Eggs will likely hatch best in beaker B, less well in beaker C, and not well or not at all in beaker D. The brine shrimp's habitat must contain salt, but cannot be too salty.
Extend Have each group prepare a larger jar with the saltwater solution that they think is best for brine shrimp, add $\frac{1}{4}$ teaspoon of eggs, and set the covered jar aside. Encourage students to examine the jar every day or two to observe changes in the population's size.
learning modality: kinesthetic

Figure 2 This eastern banjo frog is burrowing in the sand to stay cool in the hot Australian desert. *Interpreting Photographs With which abiotic factors is the frog interacting in this scene?*

With or Without Salt?

In this activity you will explore salt as an abiotic factor.

1. Label four 600-mL beakers A, B, C, and D. Fill each with 500 mL of room-temperature spring water.
2. Set beaker A aside. It will contain fresh water. To beaker B, add 2.5 grams of noniodized salt. Add 7.5 grams of salt to beaker C and 15 grams of salt to beaker D. Stir beakers B, C, and D.
3. Add $\frac{1}{8}$ teaspoon of brine shrimp eggs to each beaker.
4. Cover each beaker with a square of paper. Keep them away from direct light or heat. Wash your hands.
5. Observe the beakers daily for three days.

Drawing Conclusions In which beakers did the eggs hatch? What can you conclude about the amount of salt in the shrimps' natural habitat?

Abiotic Factors

The nonliving parts of an ecosystem are called **abiotic factors** (ay by AHT ik factors). Abiotic factors that affect living things in the prairie are similar to those found in most ecosystems. They include water, sunlight, oxygen, temperature, and soil.

Water All living things require water to carry out their life processes. Water also makes up a large part of the bodies of most organisms. Your body, for example, is about 65 percent water. A watermelon consists of more than 95 percent water! Water is particularly important to plants and algae. These organisms use water, along with sunlight and carbon dioxide, to make food in a process called **photosynthesis** (foh toh SIN thuh sis). Other living things eat the plants and algae to obtain energy.

Sunlight Because sunlight is necessary for photosynthesis, it is an important abiotic factor for plants, algae, and other living things. In places that do not receive sunlight, such as dark caves, plants cannot grow. Without plants or algae to provide a source of food, few other organisms can live.

Oxygen Most living things require oxygen to carry out their life processes. Oxygen is so important to the functioning of the human body that you can live only a few minutes without it. Organisms that live on land obtain oxygen from the air, which is about 20 percent oxygen. Fish and other water organisms obtain dissolved oxygen from the water around them.

Temperature The temperatures that are typical of an area determine the types of organisms that can live there. For example, if you took a trip to a warm tropical island, you would see palm trees, bright hibiscus flowers, and tiny lizards. These organisms could not survive on the frozen plains of Siberia. But the thick, warm fur of wolves and short, strong branches of dwarf willows are suited to the blustery winters there.

Background

Integrating Science Students may already know that plants and algae require carbon dioxide to carry on photosynthesis. Chlorophyll, the green pigment in plants and some algae, absorbs energy in sunlight. The organism uses this energy to combine carbon dioxide (CO_2) and water (H_2O) in a reaction that produces sugars, including glucose ($C_6H_{12}O_2$), with water and oxygen (O_2) as byproducts. The sugars provide energy for sustaining the organism's life processes. Other organisms can obtain and use this energy by eating plants or algae. Cellular respiration breaks down glucose into carbon dioxide and water, releasing energy.

Some animals alter their environments to overcome very hot or very cold temperatures. For example, prairie dogs dig underground dens to find shelter from the blazing summer sun. They line the dens with grass. The grass keeps the prairie dogs warm during the cold and windy winters.

Soil Soil is a mixture of rock fragments, nutrients, air, water, and the decaying remains of living things. Soil in different areas consists of varying amounts of these materials. The type of soil in an area influences the kinds of plants that can grow there. Many animals, such as the prairie dogs, use the soil itself as a home. Billions of microscopic organisms such as bacteria also live in the soil. These tiny organisms play an important role in the ecosystem by breaking down the remains of other living things.

☑ *Checkpoint* *How do biotic factors differ from abiotic factors?*

Populations

In 1900, travelers saw a prairie dog town in Texas covering an area twice the size of the city of Dallas. The sprawling town contained more than 400 million prairie dogs! These prairie dogs were all members of one species, or single kind, of organism. A **species** (SPEE sheez) is a group of organisms that are physically similar and can reproduce with each other to produce fertile offspring.

All the members of one species in a particular area are referred to as a **population.** The 400 million prairie dogs in the Texas town are one example of a population. All the pigeons in New York City make up a population, as do all the daisies in a field. In contrast, all the trees in a forest do not make up a population, because they do not all belong to the same species. There may be pines, maples, birches, and many other tree species in the forest.

The area in which a population lives can be as small as a single blade of grass or as large as the whole planet. Scientists studying a type of organism usually limit their study to a population in a defined area. For example, they might study the population of bluegill fish in a pond, or the population of alligators in the Florida Everglades.

Some populations, however, do not stay in a contained area. For example, to study the population of finback whales, a scientist might need to use the entire ocean.

Figure 3 This milkweed plant is home to a small population of ladybug beetles.

E ◆ 19

Answers to Self-Assessment

Caption Question

Figure 2 Soil (sand), oxygen (air), sunlight, temperature

☑ *Checkpoint*
Biotic factors are living; abiotic factors are nonliving.

E ◆ 19

Communities

Using the Visuals: Figure 4

Materials *pencil and paper*

Time 10–15 minutes

Challenge students to think of a way to show an ecosystem's levels of organization in a diagram. Have each student create a diagram for an ecosystem of his or her own choice. Let students share their diagrams in a class discussion. *(Possible diagram: Concentric circles with the individual organism in the center circle, a population in the second circle, a community with that population and other species in the third circle, and the entire ecosystem with abiotic factors in the outer circle.)* **learning modality: visual**

What Is Ecology?

Language Arts
CONNECTION

Challenge students to think of other words that end in *-ology. (biology, geology)* Then have them use a dictionary to learn what the first root word in each means. (Bio- *means life*, geo- *means earth.)*

In Your Journal Students' answers may vary slightly depending on the dictionaries they used.

Habitat: from Latin *habitare,* "to inhabit, live in"; *inhabit, habitation, habitual*

Biotic: from Greek *bios,* "life"; *biology, biography, biome*

Community: from Latin *communis,* "common"; *communicate, communication, communal*

Population: from Latin *populus,* "people"; *popular, popularity, populous*

learning modality: verbal

Organism **Population**

Language Arts
CONNECTION

The word *ecology* comes from two Greek root words: *oikos,* which means house or place to live, and *logos,* which means *study.* Put together, these root words create a term for studying organisms in the place where they live. Many science terms are derived from Greek and Latin root words.

In Your Journal

Use a dictionary to find root words for the following terms from this section: *habitat, biotic, community,* and *population.* For each root word, list its meaning, original language, and other English words containing the root.

Communities

Of course, most ecosystems contain more than one type of organism. The prairie, for instance, includes prairie dogs, hawks, grasses, badgers, and snakes, along with many other organisms. All the different populations that live together in an area make up a **community.**

Figure 4 shows the levels of organization in the prairie ecosystem. **The smallest unit of organization is a single organism, which belongs to a population of other members of its species. The population belongs to a community of different species. The community and abiotic factors together form an ecosystem.**

To be considered a community, the different populations must live close enough together to interact. One way the populations in a community may interact is by using the same resources, such as food and shelter. For example, the tunnels dug by the prairie dogs also serve as homes for burrowing owls and black-footed ferrets. The prairie dogs share the grass with other animals. Meanwhile, prairie dogs themselves serve as food for many species.

What Is Ecology?

Because the populations in the prairie ecosystem interact with one another, any changes in a community affect all the different populations that live there. The study of how living things interact with each other and with their environment is called **ecology.** Ecologists, scientists who study ecology, look at how all the biotic and abiotic factors in an ecosystem are related.

Background

Integrating Science All of Earth's communities are part of a higher level of organization, the *biosphere.* The organisms that make up the biosphere interact with each other. But they also interact in various ways with Earth's other "spheres": the atmosphere (the gases that envelop Earth); the hydrosphere (Earth's water); and the lithosphere (Earth's rocky outer covering and soils). While ecologists study the relationships among the organisms of the biosphere, they also consider the biosphere in relation to the other spheres of the physical environment.

Community

Ecosystem

Figure 4 The smallest level of ecological organization is an individual organism. The largest is the entire ecosystem.

As part of their work, ecologists study how organisms react to changes in their environment. Living things constantly interact with their surroundings, responding to changes in the conditions around them. Some responses are very quick. When a prairie dog sees a hawk overhead, it gives a warning bark. The other prairie dogs hear the bark and respond by returning to their burrows to hide. Other responses to change in the environment occur more slowly. For example, after a fire on the prairie, it takes some time for the grass to reach its former height and for all the animals to return to the area.

 Section 1 Review

1. What basic needs are provided by an organism's habitat?
2. List these terms in order from the smallest unit to the largest: population, organism, ecosystem, community.
3. Explain how water and sunlight are two abiotic factors that are important to all organisms.
4. Why do ecologists study both biotic and abiotic factors in an ecosystem?
5. **Thinking Critically Applying Concepts** Would all the insects in a forest be considered a population? Why or why not?

Check Your Progress   CHAPTER PROJECT 1

After your teacher has reviewed your plan, prepare the containers and plant the seeds. Design a data table to record the information you will use to compare the growth in the different containers. When the plants begin to grow, examine them daily and record your observations. Be sure to continue caring for your plants according to your plan. *(Hint:* Use a metric ruler to measure your growing plants. Besides size, look for differences in leaf color and the number of buds among the plants.)

Section 1 Review Answers
1. Food, water, shelter, air, and other things it needs to grow and reproduce
2. Organism, population, community, ecosystem
3. All organisms need water to survive and carry out their life processes. Plants and algae need water and sunlight to make their own food in photosynthesis. All other organisms depend, directly or indirectly, on plants and algae for food.
4. Accept all reasonable answers. *Sample answer:* The biotic and abiotic factors in an ecosystem are all related to one another.
5. No; the insects would be of many different species. Only organisms of the same species form a population.

Check Your Progress   CHAPTER PROJECT 1

Evaluate each group's plan to make sure students have identified and will control the major variables that will affect plant growth in the containers. These include the size of the containers, the amount of soil in each, how densely and how deep the seeds will be planted, the amount and frequency of watering, and the location in which the containers will be placed. Also review students' data tables to make sure they will be recording all relevant data, including plant heights and other observations such as the number and color of leaves and the number of buds on the developing plants.

Media and Technology

 Transparencies "Levels of Organization in an Ecosystem," Transparency 1

 Interactive Student Tutorial CD-ROM E-1

Program Resources

◆ **Teaching Resources** 1-1 Review and Reinforce, p. 17; 1-1 Enrich, p. 18

Performance Assessment

Concept Mapping Have each student choose any organism and draw a concept map to identify several biotic and abiotic factors in the organism's habitat.

 Students can save their concept maps in their portfolios.

E ◆ 21

A World in a Jar

Preparing for Inquiry

Key Concept Organisms can survive in a closed ecosystem so long as their biotic and abiotic needs are met.

Skills Objectives Students will be able to
◆ build a model of an aquatic ecosystem;
◆ predict whether the habitat will meet the organisms' needs;
◆ make inferences about how the model ecosystem operates.

Time 40 minutes for set-up; 5 minutes per day for observation

Advance Planning Collect materials. Let water stand uncovered for two days.

Guiding Inquiry

Troubleshooting the Experiment

◆ Students should position the lamp so it shines into the jar from one side. Students may need to adjust the lamp to keep the water pale green.
◆ Do not let the water temperature exceed 23°C.
◆ If algae are slow to grow, have students feed the guppies small amounts of food. Once algae are plentiful, the guppies will not require feeding.

Expected Outcome

Algae should be clearly visible within five days. The guppies and snails should easily survive ten days in the closed jars.

Analyze and Conclude

1. *Biotic:* guppies, snails, plants, algae; *abiotic:* gravel, water, light, jar
2. Yes, light (an abiotic factor)
3. Some algae must have been present (perhaps on the plants) when they assembled the models. Over time, the algae became visible because they reproduced.
4. Students' diagrams should show the fish and snails breathing oxygen in the water and feeding on the algae and plants, the plants and algae using light to make food, and so forth.
5. The guppies and snails would not be able to live for long in separate jars. The plants and algae could survive for a while because they can make their own food.

A World in a Jar

In this lab, you will study the interactions that take place between biotic and abiotic factors in a model ecosystem.

Problem

How can organisms live in a closed ecosystem?

Materials

aquarium gravel	metric ruler
plastic stirring rod	dip net
2-day-old tap water	4 aquatic plants
2 guppies	4 small pond snails
large jar with cover (about 2 liters)	
UL-listed lamp with a 60-watt bulb	

Procedure

1. In this lab, you will put guppies, snails, and plants together in a sealed jar of water. Record your prediction about whether this habitat will meet the needs of these organisms.
2. Find a safe location for the jar away from windows and other areas where light and temperature are likely to change often. There should be an electrical outlet nearby for the lamp.
3. Add aquarium gravel to the jar to a depth of 3 cm. Add water to about 6 cm from the top.
4. Place the plants in the jar one at a time. Use a stirring rod to gently brush aside a little gravel. Position the roots of each plant against the bottom of the jar. Move gravel back over the roots to hold the plant in place.

5. Using a dip net, carefully place the guppies in the water. Gently place the snails in the jar. Put the lid on the jar, and close it tightly.
6. Position the lamp so that the light shines into the jar. The light bulb should be 15 to 20 cm from the jar. **CAUTION:** *Lighted bulbs get very hot. Do not allow the bulb to touch any objects.*
7. Observe the jar every day. Record your observations in your notebook.
8. Within 5 days, the water in the jar should turn slightly green. The green color indicates the presence of algae. If the water is bright green, move the light away from the jar. If the water is not green after 5 days, move the light closer to the jar. Record in your notebook any changes to the setup.
9. Observe the jar for at least one more week.

Analyze and Conclude

1. What biotic and abiotic factors are part of the ecosystem in the jar?
2. Are any biotic or abiotic factors able to enter the sealed jar? If so, which one(s)?
3. Where did the green algae come from?
4. Draw a diagram of the interactions between the biotic and abiotic factors in the jar.
5. Would the guppies, snails, and plants be able to live alone in separate jars? Why or why not?
6. **Think About It** Explain how your jar and its contents model an ecosystem. How is your model different from an ecosystem on Earth?

More to Explore

Make a plan to model a saltwater or land ecosystem. How would this model be different from the freshwater ecosystem? Obtain your teacher's approval before carrying out your plan.

---

6. The model shows that organisms interact with each other and with nonliving things in their environment. The model differs from a natural ecosystem in that it is closed, not as complex, and contains fewer organisms.

Extending the Inquiry

More to Explore Review students' plans for feasibility in the classroom and for proper handling of living organisms.

Safety

Make sure students handle the jars, electrical plug, and living organisms carefully. Review the safety guidelines in Appendix A. After the lab, use the organisms in a classroom aquarium.

Program Resources

◆ **Teaching Resources** Chapter 1 Skills Lab, pp. 27–28

SECTION 2 Studying Populations

DISCOVER ········· ACTIVITY····

What's the Population of Beans in a Jar?

1. Fill a plastic jar with dried beans. This is your model population.

2. Your goal is to determine the number of beans in the jar, but you will not have time to count every bean. You may use any of the following to help you determine the size of the bean population: a ruler, a small beaker, another large jar. Set a timer for two minutes when you are ready to begin.

3. After two minutes, record your answer. Then count the actual number of beans. How close was your answer?

Think It Over
Forming Operational Definitions
In this activity, you came up with an estimate of the size of the bean population. Write a definition of the term *estimate* based on what you did.

How would you like to change jobs for the day? Instead of being a student, today you are an ecologist. You are working on a project to study the bald eagle population in your area. One question you might ask is how the population has changed over time. Is the number of bald eagles more, less, or the same as it was 50 years ago? To answer these questions, you must first determine the present size of the bald eagle population.

Population Density

One way to state the size of a population is in terms of **population density** — the number of individuals in a specific area. Population density can be written as an equation:

$$\text{Population density} = \frac{\text{Number of individuals}}{\text{Unit area}}$$

For instance, suppose you counted 50 monarch butterflies in a garden measuring 10 square meters. The population density would be 50 butterflies per 10 square meters, or 5 butterflies per square meter.

GUIDE FOR READING

◆ How do ecologists determine the size of a population?

◆ What causes populations to change in size?

◆ What factors limit population growth?

Reading Tip Before you read, predict some factors that might cause a population to increase or decrease.

 Bald eagles in Alaska ▶

E ◆ 23

SECTION 2 Studying Populations

Objectives

After completing the lesson, students will be able to

◆ describe how ecologists determine the size of a population;

◆ explain what causes populations to change in size;

◆ identify factors that limit population growth.

Key Terms population density, estimate, birth rate, death rate, immigration, emigration, limiting factor, carrying capacity

1 Engage/Explore

Activating Prior Knowledge

Ask: **What does *density* mean?** (*Answers will vary but should include the idea of "how tightly packed something is."*) **What are some examples of dense populations of organisms?** (*Grass in a lawn, bees in a hive, a school of fish*)

········ DISCOVER ········

Skills Focus forming operational definitions

Materials *2 large plastic jars, dried beans, ruler, small beaker, timer*

Time 5–10 minutes

Tips If you do not have enough timers, set one timer yourself for the entire class.

Expected Outcome Students could use various ways of estimating, including the following: (1) Fill the small beaker with beans, count those beans, estimate how many small beakers would fit in the large jar, and multiply the first bean count by that number. (2) Put a 1-cm-deep layer of beans in the second large jar, count those beans, measure the height of the jar, and multiply the height by the number of beans in one layer.

Think It Over Students' definitions may vary but should focus on the idea of making a "rough guess" or "close guess."

2 Facilitate

Population Density

Including All Students

For students who need extra help, provide additional examples so they can practice the calculations—for example, 144 dandelion plants in a lawn 12 m long by 6 m wide (2 plants per square meter). You may want to let students use calculators to solve the problems. Also invite students to make up problems for the class to solve. **learning modality: logical/mathematical**

Determining Population Size

Sharpen your Skills

Calculating

Time 5 minutes
Expected Outcome The total population is 100,000 oysters (100 m × 50 m = 5000 square meters × 20 oysters per square meter).
Extend Ask: **Why is your answer only an estimate of the total population?** *(Maybe not every square meter has exactly 20 oysters.)* **learning modality: logical/mathematical**

Inquiry Challenge

Materials *500 wooden toothpicks*
Time 10–15 minutes

Scatter 500 toothpicks over a rectangular area large enough to provide a 1-square-meter section for each student, or use a floor with 1-square-foot tiles, allowing one tile per student. Tell students the total area, but not how many toothpicks you used. Let each student count the number of toothpicks in his or her section (the sample) and then calculate the total "population" of toothpicks. In a follow-up discussion, ask: **Why did different students get different estimates?** *(Different sections—samples—contained different numbers of toothpicks.)* **learning modality: logical/ mathematical**

Figure 5 These cone-shaped structures are nests built by cliff swallows in Dinosaur National Monument, Utah. Counting the nests is one way to estimate the cliff swallow population.

Sharpen your Skills

Calculating

A bed of oysters measures 100 meters long and 50 meters wide. In a one-square-meter area you count 20 oysters. Estimate the population of oysters in the bed. *(Hint: Drawing a diagram may help you set up your calculation.)*

24 ◆ E

Determining Population Size

In your work as an ecologist, how can you determine the size of the population you are studying? **Some methods of determining the size of a population are direct and indirect observations, sampling, and mark-and-recapture studies.**

Direct Observation The most obvious way to determine the size of a population is to count, one by one, all of its members. You could count all the bald eagles that live along a river, all the red maple trees in a forest, or all the elephants in a valley in Kenya.

Indirect Observation The members of a population may be small or hard to find. It may then be easier to observe their tracks or other signs rather than the organisms themselves. Look at the mud nests built by cliff swallows in Figure 5. Each nest has one entrance hole. By counting the entrance holes, you can determine the number of swallow families nesting in this area. Suppose that the average number of swallows per nest is four: two parents and two offspring. If there are 120 nests in an area, you can find the number of swallows by multiplying 120 by 4, or 480 swallows.

Sampling In most cases, it is not possible to count every member of a population. The population may be very large, or it may be spread over a wide area. It may be hard to find every individual or to remember which ones have already been counted. Instead, ecologists usually make an estimate. An **estimate** is an approximation of a number, based on reasonable assumptions.

One type of estimating involves counting the number of organisms in a small area (a sample), and then multiplying to find the number in a larger area. To get an accurate estimate, the sample should have the same population density as the larger area. For example, suppose you count 8 red maples in a 10 meter-by-10 meter area of the forest. If the entire forest were 100 times that size, you would multiply your count by 100 to estimate the total population, or 800 red maples.

Mark-and-Recapture Studies Another estimating method is a technique called "mark and recapture." This technique gets its name because some animals are first captured, marked, and released into the environment. Then another group of animals is captured. The

---

Background

Facts and Figures For a species to survive, there must be enough males and females present in a range to mate and reproduce successfully. If the population density and size fall below a critical minimum level, the population declines and may become extinct. This very nearly occurred with the California condor, a scavenger that requires a large range in which to feed.

Development has greatly reduced the California condor's wilderness habitat. In the late 1980s, there were no condors living in the wild. A program to reintroduce zoo-bred condors into the wild began in 1992. Two colonies, one in California and one in Arizona, appear to be succeeding.

24 ◆ E

number of marked animals in this second group indicates the population size. For example, if half the animals in the second group are marked, it means that the first sample represented about half the total population.

Here's an example showing how mark and recapture works. First, deer mice in a field are caught in a trap that does not harm the mice. Ecologists count the mice and mark each mouse's belly with a dot of hair dye before releasing it again. Two weeks later, the researchers return and capture mice again. They count how many mice have marks, showing that they were captured the first time, and how many are unmarked. Using a mathematical formula, the scientists can estimate the total population of mice in the field. You can try this technique for yourself in the Real-World Lab at the end of this section.

☑ *Checkpoint* When is sampling used to estimate a population?

Changes in Population Size

By returning to a location often and using one of the methods described above, ecologists can monitor the size of a population over time. **Populations can change in size when new members enter the population or when members leave the population.**

Births and Deaths The major way in which new individuals are added to a population is through the birth of offspring. The **birth rate** of a population is the number of births in a population in a certain amount of time. For example, suppose a population of 1,000 snow geese produces 1,400 goslings in a year. The birth rate in this population would be 1,400 goslings per year.

Similarly, the major way that individuals leave a population is by dying. The **death rate** is the number of deaths in a population in a certain amount of time. Suppose that in the same population, 100 geese die in a year. The death rate would be 100 geese per year.

Figure 6 This young hawk is part of a mark-and-recapture study in a Virginia marsh. *Inferring What is the purpose of the silver band on the hawk's leg?*

Figure 7 The birth of new individuals can increase the size of a population. This cheetah mother added five offspring to the population in her area.

Chapter 1 **E ◆ 25**

Changes in Population Size, continued

Building Inquiry Skills: Calculating

Continuing with the example on the previous page, ask: **Suppose 1,600 snow geese died in same year that 1,400 were born. What would the growth rate be for that year?** *(1,400 − 1,600 = a growth rate of − 200 geese per year)* **What does a negative growth rate mean?** *(The population is declining.)* **What might account for a death rate that is higher than the birth rate?** *(Disease; not enough food; eggs, young geese, or adults being eaten by other animals; poisons in the environment; and so on)* **learning modality: logical/mathematical**

ACTIVITY

Using the Visuals: Figure 8

Review the population changes described in the caption and shown on the graph. Then ask: **Why is it helpful to show population changes in a graph?** *(The lines make the changes easier to see and understand than reading a list of numbers.)* **learning modality: visual**

Limiting Factors

Building Inquiry Skills: Inferring

Ask students: **Is food a limiting factor for plants?** *(no)* **Why not?** *(Plants make their own food.)* **What factors do limit the size of plant populations?** *(The amount of available sunlight, carbon dioxide in the air, water, and nutrients in the soil)* **Why do these factors limit plant populations?** *(Plants need light, carbon dioxide, and water to conduct photosynthesis, and they need nutrients for their other life processes.)* **learning modality: logical/mathematical**

The Population Equation When the birth rate in a population is greater than the death rate, the population will generally increase in size. This statement can be written as a mathematical statement using the "is greater than" sign:

If birth rate > death rate, population size increases.

For example, in the snow goose population, the birth rate of 1,400 goslings per year was greater than the death rate of 100 geese per year, and the population would increase in size.

However, if the death rate in a population is greater than the birth rate, the population size will generally decrease. This can also be written as a mathematical statement:

If death rate > birth rate, population size decreases.

Immigration and Emigration The size of a population also can change when individuals move into or out of the population, just as the population of your town changes when families move into town or move away. **Immigration** (im ih GRAY shun) means moving into a population. **Emigration** (em ih GRAY shun) means leaving a population. Emigration can occur when part of a population gets cut off from the rest of the population. For instance, if food is scarce, some members of an antelope herd may wander off in search of better grassland. If they become permanently separated from the original herd, they will no longer be part of that population.

Graphing Changes in Population You can see an example of changes in a population of rabbits in Figure 8. The vertical axis shows the numbers of rabbits in the population, while the horizontal axis shows time. The graph shows the size of the population over a 10-year period.

☑ *Checkpoint* Name two ways individuals can join a population.

Figure 8 From Year 0 to Year 4, more rabbits joined the population than left it, so the population increased. From Year 4 to Year 8, more rabbits left the population than joined it, so the population decreased. From Year 8 to Year 10, the rates of rabbits leaving and joining the population were about equal, so the population remained steady. *Interpreting Graphs In what year did the rabbit population reach its highest point? What was the size of the population in that year?*

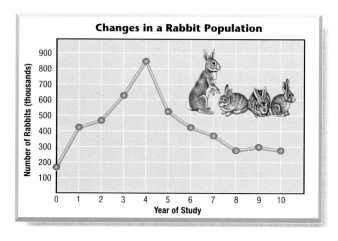

Changes in a Rabbit Population

Background

Facts and Figures When the size of a population grows beyond the carrying capacity of its habitat, a *population crash* may occur. Food shortages, insufficient space for successful reproduction, disease, and other limiting factors result in a death rate much higher than the birth rate, and the population declines sharply.

One example of such a crash occurred with the moose population on Isle Royale (see page 36) before wolves arrived in 1949. Moose came to Isle Royale around 1900 by walking across the frozen lake in winter. Over the next 35 years, the moose population increased to about 3,000. This exhausted their food supply, leading to starvation for 90 percent of the moose. The population increased again until 1948, then declined sharply once more because of lack of food.

Figure 9 These gannets seem to have heard the saying "Birds of a feather flock together." When there are more birds than the space can support, the population will have exceeded the carrying capacity of the shore.

Limiting Factors

When conditions are good, a population will generally increase. But a population does not keep growing forever. Eventually, some factor in its environment causes the population to stop growing. A **limiting factor** is an environmental factor that prevents a population from increasing. **Some limiting factors for populations are food, space, and weather conditions.**

Food Organisms require food to survive. In an area where food is scarce, this becomes a limiting factor. Suppose a giraffe needs to eat 10 kilograms of leaves each day to survive. The trees in an area can provide 100 kilograms of leaves a day while remaining healthy. Five giraffes could live easily in this area, since they would only require a total of 50 kilograms of food. But 15 giraffes could not all survive—there would not be enough food for all of them. No matter how much shelter, water, and other resources there might be, the population will not grow much higher than 10 giraffes. The largest population that an environment can support is called its **carrying capacity.** The carrying capacity of this environment is 10 giraffes.

Space The birds in Figure 9 are rarely seen on land. These birds, called gannets, spend most of their lives flying over the ocean. They only land on this rocky shore to nest. But as you can see, the shore is very crowded. If a pair of gannets does not have room to build a nest, that pair will not be able to produce any offspring.

Elbow Room

Using masking tape, mark off several one-meter squares on the floor of your classroom. Your teacher will form groups of 2, 4, and 6 students. Each group's task is to put together a small jigsaw puzzle in one of the squares. All the group members must keep their feet within the square. Time how long it takes your group to finish the puzzle.

Making Models How long did it take each group to complete the task? How does this activity show that space can be a limiting factor? What is the carrying capacity of puzzle-solvers in a square meter?

3 Assess

Section 2 Review Answers

1. Direct observation, indirect observation, sampling, mark and recapture

2. If the birth rate is higher than the death rate, the population increases. If the birth rate is lower than the death rate, the population decreases. If the rates are the same, the population stays the same size.

3. Food, space, weather; *food:* The population cannot grow beyond the number that can be supported by the amount of food available (carrying capacity); *space:* If organisms are crowded, some will not be able to reproduce or even survive; *weather:* Severe weather conditions can kill many members of the population.

4. The population may be very large or spread over a wide area, or individual members may be hard to find, or it may be difficult to determine which members have already been counted.

5. 13,500 mice; the sampling method

Science at Home

Tips Let students try the activity in class before they present it to their family members. Possible methods include: (1) Count the number of words in one line, then multiply by the number of lines on the page. (2) Count the number of words in each of three or four lines, calculate the average number of words per line, and multiply by the number of lines on the page. The second method should produce a more accurate estimate.

Performance Assessment

Oral Presentation Call on various students to identify a factor that affects the size of a population (birth/death rates and immigration/emigration numbers as well as limiting factors).

Figure 10 A snowstorm can limit the size of the orange crop.

Those gannets will not contribute to an increase in the gannet population. This means that space for nesting is a limiting factor for these gannets. If the shore were bigger, more gannets would be able to nest there, and the population would increase.

Space is often a limiting factor for plants. The amount of space in which a plant grows can determine how much sunlight, water, and other necessities the plant can obtain. For example, many pine seedlings sprout each year in a forest. But as the trees get bigger, those that are too close together do not have room to spread their roots underground. Other tree branches block out the sunlight they need to live. Some of the seedlings die, limiting the size of the pine population.

Weather Weather conditions such as temperature and amount of rainfall can also limit population growth. Many insect species breed in the warm spring weather. As winter begins, the first frost kills many of the insects. This sudden rise in the death rate causes the insect population to decrease.

A single severe weather event can dramatically change the size of a population by killing many organisms. For instance, a flood or hurricane can wash away nests and burrows just as it damages the homes of humans. If you live in a northern state, you may have seen an early frost limit the population of tomatoes in a vegetable garden.

Section 2 Review

1. List four ways of determining population size.
2. How is birth rate related to population size?
3. List three limiting factors for populations. Choose one and explain how this factor can limit population growth.
4. Explain why it is often necessary for ecologists to estimate the size of a population.
5. **Thinking Critically** **Problem Solving** A field measures 50 meters by 90 meters. In one square meter, you count 3 mice. Estimate the total population of mice in the field. What method did you use to make your estimate?

Science at Home

Choose a page of a dictionary or other book that has a lot of type on it. Challenge your family members to estimate the number of words on the page. After everyone has come up with an estimate, have each person explain the method he or she used. Now count the actual number of words on the page. Whose estimate was closest?

Program Resources

◆ **Teaching Resources** 1-2 Review and Reinforce, p. 21; 1-2 Enrich, p. 22
◆ **Integrated Science Laboratory Manual** E-1 "Weather and Whooping Cranes"

Media and Technology

Interactive Student Tutorial CD-ROM E-1

Counting Turtles

For three years, ecologists have been using the mark-and-recapture method to monitor the population of turtles in a pond. In this lab, you will model recapturing the turtles to complete the study. Then you will analyze the results.

Problem

How can the mark-and-recapture method help ecologists monitor the size of a population?

Skills Focus

calculating, graphing, predicting

Materials

model paper turtle population
calculator   graph paper

Procedure

1. The data table shows the results from the first three years of the study. Copy it into your notebook, leaving spaces for your data as shown.
2. Your teacher will give you a box representing the pond. Fifteen of the paper turtles have been marked, as shown in the data table.
3. Capture a member of the population by randomly selecting one turtle. Set it aside.
4. Repeat Step 3 nine times. Record the total number of turtles you captured.
5. Examine each turtle to see whether it has a mark. Count the number of recaptured (marked) turtles. Record this number in your data table.

Analyze and Conclude

1. Use the equation below to estimate the turtle population for each year. The first year is done for you as a sample. If your answer is a decimal, round it to the nearest whole number so that your estimate is in "whole turtles." Record the population for each year in the last column of the data table.

$$\text{Total population} = \frac{\text{Number marked} \times \text{Total number captured}}{\text{Number recaptured (with marks)}}$$

Sample (Year 1):
$$\frac{32 \times 28}{15} = 59.7 \text{ or } 60 \text{ turtles}$$

2. Graph the estimated total populations for the four years. Mark years on the horizontal axis. Mark population size on the vertical axis.
3. Describe how the turtle population has changed over the four years of the study. Suggest three possible causes for the changes.
4. **Apply** Use your graph to predict the turtle population in Year 5. Explain your prediction.

Getting Involved

Find out whether any wildlife populations in your area are being monitored by national, state, or local agencies. Make a poster or write an article for the school paper about the population and the method being used to study it.

DATA TABLE

Year	Number Marked	Total Number Captured	Number Recaptured (with Marks)	Estimated Total Population
1	32	28	15	
2	25	21	11	
3	23	19	11	
4	15			

Graph for Question 2

Extending the Inquiry

Getting Involved

To find information, students can contact their state department of natural resources and wildlife.

Program Resources

◆ **Teaching Resources** Chapter 1 Real-World Lab, pp. 29–31

Careers in Science

Counting Turtles

Preparing for Inquiry

Key Concept The mark-and-recapture method can be used to estimate the size of a population over time.
Skills Objectives Students will be able to
◆ calculate to estimate a population using the mark-and-recapture method;
◆ graph population estimates;
◆ predict the future population.
Time 40 minutes
Advance Planning Prepare a model turtle population for each group. Use 30 small squares cut from paper or index cards to represent turtles. Mark a dot on one side of 15 turtles. Spread all 30 turtles in a box, marked sides down.

Guiding Inquiry

Troubleshooting the Experiment

◆ In Step 2, clarify that the 15 marked turtles refers to the bottom box in the second column of the table, the number marked in Year 4.
◆ Work through the sample calculation in Question 1 with the class.

Expected Outcome

The number of marked turtles recaptured will vary. Thus, students' estimates of the total population for Year 4 will also vary.

Analyze and Conclude

1. The estimated total populations for Years 1–3 are 60, 48, and 40. The total number captured for Year 4 is 10. The number recaptured and the total population for Year 4 will vary. If 0 recaptured, total population = 0; if 1, 150; if 2, 75; if 3, 50; if 4, 38; if 5, 30; if 6, 25; if 7, 21; if 8, 19; if 9, 17; and if 10, 15.
2. See sample graph. Year 4 will vary.
3. The turtle population has declined steadily. Possible causes include limited food, overcrowding, disease, predation, and use of insecticides or herbicides in the pond.
4. Most students will probably predict a continuing decline in the population. Accept other responses so long as students defend their predictions.

Animal Overpopulation: How Can People Help?

Purpose

Identify problems caused by deer overpopulation, evaluate possible solutions, and recommend one way for a community to deal with the problem.

Panel Discussion

Time 40 minutes

◆ Allow time for students to read the introductory text and the three sections under The Issues. Then ask: **What solution would you support if our area had a deer overpopulation problem? Why would you choose that solution?** As students identify possible solutions, list them on the board. Let students discuss the issues freely until different viewpoints are clear.

◆ Divide the class into as many groups as there are solutions listed. Provide time for each group to discuss the pros and cons of each possibility.

◆ Ask each group to select one student to take part in a panel discussion of people who are trying to solve the deer problem in the community.

Extend If your community has had an actual problem with animal overpopulation—with deer, starlings, gypsy moths, or pigeons, for example— suggest that students discuss the issue with family members and, if possible, consult with community and state agencies to find out how people have dealt with the problem.

You Decide

Students' responses to Identify the Problem and Analyze the Options should be based on the concepts and issues presented in the text. In response to Find a Solution, however, students may suggest their own ideas or solutions based on their small-group discussions.

Animal Overpopulation: How Can People Help?

Populations of white-tailed deer are growing rapidly in many parts of the United States. As populations soar, food becomes a limiting factor. Many deer die of starvation. Others grow up small and unhealthy. In search of food, hungry deer move closer to where humans live. There they eat farm crops, garden vegetables, shrubs, and even trees. This affects birds and small animals that depend on the plants for shelter or food. In addition, increased numbers of deer near roads can cause more automobile accidents.

People admire the grace, beauty, and swiftness of deer. Most people don't want these animals to suffer from starvation or illness. Should people take action to limit growing deer populations?

The Issues

Should People Take Direct Action?
Many people argue that hunting is the simplest way to reduce animal populations. Wildlife managers look at the supply of resources in an area and determine its carrying capacity. Then hunters are issued licenses to help reduce the number of deer to the level that can be supported.

Other people favor nonhunting approaches to control deer populations. One plan is to trap the deer and relocate them. But this method is expensive and requires finding another location that can accept the deer without unbalancing its own system. Few such locations are available.

Scientists are also working to develop chemicals to reduce the birth rate in deer populations. This plan will help control overpopulation, but it is effective for only one year at a time.

Should People Take Indirect Action?
Some suggest bringing in natural enemies of deer, such as wolves, mountain lions, and bears, to areas with too many deer. But these animals could also attack cattle, dogs, cats, and even humans. Other communities have built tall fences around areas they don't want deer to invade. Although this solution can work for people with small yards, it is impractical for farmers or ranchers.

Should People Do Nothing? Some people oppose any kind of action. They support leaving the deer alone and allowing nature to take its course. Animal populations in an area naturally cycle up and down over time. Doing nothing means that some deer will die of starvation or disease. But eventually, the population will be reduced to a size within the carrying capacity of the environment.

You Decide

1. Identify the Problem
In your own words, explain the problem created by the over-population of white-tailed deer.

2. Analyze the Options
List the ways that people can deal with overpopulation of white-tailed deer. State the negative and positive points of each method.

3. Find a Solution
Suppose you are an ecologist in an area that has twice as many deer as it can support. Propose a way for the community to deal with the problem.

Background

Facts and Figures Deer overpopulation can also be hazardous to human health, as shown by the increasing occurrence of Lyme disease in the United States. White-tailed deer may carry tiny ticks that are smaller than the head of a pin. The ticks in turn carry a bacterium, *Borrelia burgdorferi,* which causes Lyme disease. The ticks attach themselves to people walking through infested areas. The tick's bite transfers the bacteria to humans.

A reddish rash shaped like a bull's-eye usually appears within days of the tick's bite. Other early symptoms of Lyme disease may include fatigue, fever, chills, and headache. Left untreated, the disease can inflame the heart muscle and nerves, or cause painful arthritis in the joints. Antibiotics, if taken soon after symptoms appear, are an effective treatment for Lyme disease. In 1998, the U.S. FDA approved a vaccine for Lyme disease.

SECTION
3 **Interactions Among Living Things**

DISCOVER ······················· ACTIVITY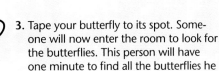

How Well Can You Hide a Butterfly?

1. Using the outline at the right, trace a butterfly on a piece of paper.

2. Look around the classroom and pick a spot where you will place your butterfly. The butterfly must be placed completely in the open. Color your butterfly so it will blend in with the spot you choose.

3. Tape your butterfly to its spot. Someone will now enter the room to look for the butterflies. This person will have one minute to find all the butterflies he or she can. Will your butterfly be found?

Think It Over

Predicting Over time, how do you think the population size would change for butterflies that blend in with their surroundings?

I magine giving a big hug to the plant in the photo. Ouch! The sharp spines on its trunk would make you think twice before hugging—or even touching—the saguaro (suh GWAHR oh) cactus. But if you could spend a day hidden inside a saguaro, you would see that many species do interact with this spiky plant.

As the day breaks, you hear a twittering noise coming from a nest tucked in one of the sagauro's arms. Two young red-tailed hawks are preparing to fly for the first time. Farther down the trunk, a tiny elf owl peeks out of its nest in a small hole. The elf owl is so small it could fit in your palm! A rattlesnake slithers around the base of the saguaro, looking for lunch. Spying a nearby shrew, the snake moves in for the kill. With a sudden movement, it strikes the shrew with its sharp fangs.

The activity around the saguaro doesn't stop after the sun goes down. At night, long-nosed bats feed on the nectar from the saguaro's blossoms. They stick their faces into the flowers to feed, covering their long snouts with a dusting of white pollen in the process. As the bats move from plant to plant, they carry the pollen along. This enables the cactuses to reproduce.

GUIDE FOR READING

◆ How do an organism's adaptations help it to survive?

◆ What are the major types of interactions among organisms?

◆ What are the three forms of symbiotic relationships?

Reading Tip As you read, use the section headings to make an outline. Fill in details under each heading.

◀ Saguaro cactus in the Arizona desert

 E ◆ 31

READING STRATEGIES

Reading Tip Students should use the headings *Adapting to the Environment, Competition, Predation,* and *Symbiosis* as the main headings in their outlines. They can use the purple subheads in the text as their secondary headings. They should use main points from the text to complete their outlines. Students can use their outlines as study aids.

Program Resources

◆ **Teaching Resources** 1-3 Lesson Plan, p. 23; 1-3 Section Summary, p. 24

Media and Technology

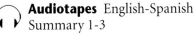 **Audiotapes** English-Spanish Summary 1-3

Objectives

After completing the lesson, students will be able to

◆ explain how an organism's adaptations help it to survive;

◆ describe the major types of interactions among organisms;

◆ identify the three forms of symbiotic relationships.

Key Terms natural selection, adaptation, niche, competition, predation, predator, prey, symbiosis, mutalism, commensalism, parasitism, parasite, host

1 Engage/Explore

Activating Prior Knowledge

Ask students: **What features enable fish to survive in an underwater habitat?** *(Fins and a tail for moving through the water, gills for breathing oxygen dissolved in the water)* Encourage students to think of other examples of how organisms are adapted to their environments.

········· **DISCOVER** ·········

Skills Focus predicting
Materials *sheet of white paper, colored pencils or markers, tape*
Time 10–15 minutes
Tips Tell students that the butterflies do not have to be colored realistically. Arrange to have another staff member or a student from another class look for the butterflies.
Expected Outcome Butterflies whose colors and patterns closely match their background will be most difficult to see.
Think It Over Butterflies that blend well with their surroundings will escape predators and survive to reproduce, thus increasing the population.

2 Facilitate

Adapting to the Environment

Addressing Naive Conceptions

When students have read about species changing over time, emphasize that the changes are not deliberate or conscious on the organisms' part. That is, organisms do not "decide" to develop characteristics that will enable them to survive more successfully. Also explain that individual organisms do not develop new physical adaptations within their own lifespans. Rather, the species changes over time as organisms are born with new, favorable adaptations (caused by mutations) that are then passed on to their offspring. To illustrate this point, share the example described in Background below, then present the following Inquiry Challenge. **learning modality: verbal**

Inquiry Challenge

Materials *construction paper in shades of gray; black and gray markers*

Time 10–15 minutes
Challenge small groups of students to make a model illustrating the changes in the peppered moth populations described in Background below. Let each group present its model to the rest of the class and describe the changes. **cooperative learning**

Including All Students

If students did the lab "A World in a Jar," help reinforce the concept of *niche* by asking: **What was the guppies' niche in the aquarium you made earlier?** *(The guppies lived in water, ate the algae, breathed oxygen in the water, released carbon dioxide that the plants used, hid among the leaves, and so on.)* **What was the snails' niche? The plants' niche?** Continue by asking volunteers to name other familiar organisms and letting the rest of the class describe each organism's niche. **limited English proficiency**

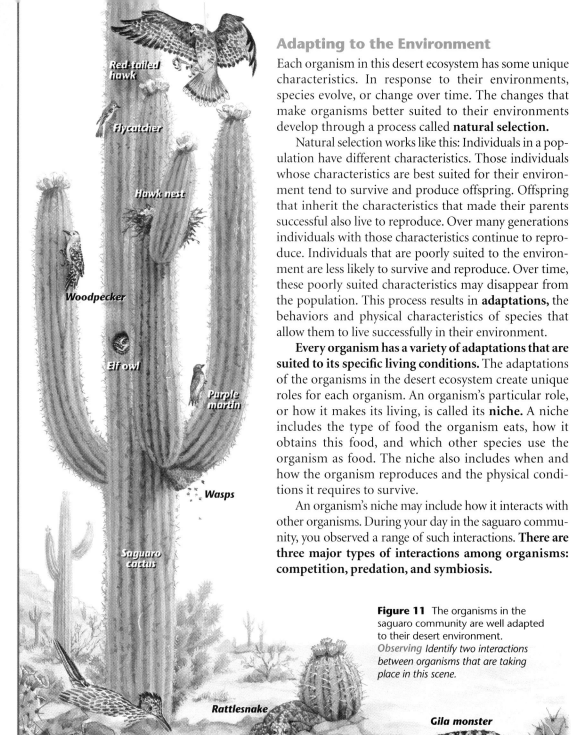

Red-tailed hawk

Flycatcher

Hawk nest

Woodpecker

Elf owl

Purple martin

Wasps

Saguaro cactus

Rattlesnake

Gila monster

Scorpion

Roadrunner

32 ◆ E

Adapting to the Environment

Each organism in this desert ecosystem has some unique characteristics. In response to their environments, species evolve, or change over time. The changes that make organisms better suited to their environments develop through a process called **natural selection.**

Natural selection works like this: Individuals in a population have different characteristics. Those individuals whose characteristics are best suited for their environment tend to survive and produce offspring. Offspring that inherit the characteristics that made their parents successful also live to reproduce. Over many generations individuals with those characteristics continue to reproduce. Individuals that are poorly suited to the environment are less likely to survive and reproduce. Over time, these poorly suited characteristics may disappear from the population. This process results in **adaptations,** the behaviors and physical characteristics of species that allow them to live successfully in their environment.

Every organism has a variety of adaptations that are suited to its specific living conditions. The adaptations of the organisms in the desert ecosystem create unique roles for each organism. An organism's particular role, or how it makes its living, is called its **niche.** A niche includes the type of food the organism eats, how it obtains this food, and which other species use the organism as food. The niche also includes when and how the organism reproduces and the physical conditions it requires to survive.

An organism's niche may include how it interacts with other organisms. During your day in the saguaro community, you observed a range of such interactions. **There are three major types of interactions among organisms: competition, predation, and symbiosis.**

Figure 11 The organisms in the saguaro community are well adapted to their desert environment.
Observing Identify two interactions between organisms that are taking place in this scene.

Background

History of Science Although we tend to think of natural selection as occurring over vast periods of time, species can and do change relatively quickly when subjected to environmental pressures. The case of the English peppered moth is a famous example. The peppered moth occurs in both a speckled light-gray form and a dark-gray form.

During the day, the moths rest on tree trunks covered with light-colored lichens.

Before the Industrial Revolution, the dark form was more obvious to predators and thus very rare. Then soot and other pollutants from factories killed the lichens and darkened the tree trunks. Within a 50-year period, the dark moths became more abundant. Environmental conditions changed again in the early 1950s when anti-pollution laws were enacted. Lichens grew again on soot-free tree trunks, and the frequency of dark moths declined.

The bay-breasted warbler *feeds in the middle part of the tree.*

The Cape May warbler *feeds at the tips of branches near the top of the tree.*

The yellow-rumped warbler *feeds in the lower part of the tree and at the bases of the middle branches.*

Competition

Different species can share the same habitat, such as the many animals that live in and around the saguaro. Different species can also share similar food requirements. For example, the red-tailed hawk and the elf owl both live on the saguaro and eat similar food. However, these two species do not occupy exactly the same niche. The hawk is active during the day, while the owl is active mostly at night. If two species occupy the same niche, one of the species will eventually die off. The reason for this is **competition,** the struggle between organisms to survive in a habitat with limited resources.

An ecosystem cannot satisfy the needs of all the living things in a particular habitat. There is a limited amount of food, water, and shelter. Organisms that survive have adaptations that enable them to reduce competition. For example, the three species of warblers in Figure 12 live in the same spruce forest habitat. They all eat insects that live in the spruce trees. How do these birds avoid competing for the limited insect supply? Each warbler "specializes" in feeding in a certain part of a spruce tree. By finding their own places to feed, the three species can coexist.

 INTEGRATING CHEMISTRY Many plants use chemicals to ward off their competition. Plants often compete with one another for growing space and water. Some shrubs release toxic, or poisonous, chemicals into the ground around them. These chemicals keep grass and weeds from growing around the shrubs, sometimes forming a ring of bare ground a meter or two wide.

☑ *Checkpoint* Why can't two species occupy the same niche?

Figure 12 Each of these warblers occupies a different niche in its spruce tree habitat. By feeding in different areas of the tree, the birds avoid competing with each other for food.

Competition

Building Inquiry Skills: Observing

Materials *several male crickets, terrarium, soil, materials to provide hiding places, paint of different colors*
Time 15 minutes for initial setup

ACTIVITY

Obtain several male crickets from a pet shop. Tell students that male crickets in the wild compete for territory. Let volunteers set up a cricket habitat in a terrarium, with soil on the bottom and several items under which the crickets can hide, such as rocks, dead leaves, pieces of tree bark, or small branches. Before students put the crickets in the terrarium, have them mark each one's back with a different color dot of paint so they can tell the crickets apart. (Remind students to handle the crickets gently and to wash their hands afterward.) When the crickets are first introduced into the habitat, they will fight each other. In time, however, each cricket will establish its own territory, remain in it most of the time, and defend it against the other males. (After the activity, you can release the crickets or return them to the pet store.) **learning modality: visual**

Integrating Chemistry

Point out that some plants produce bad-tasting or toxic chemicals that discourage animals from eating them. The leaves of the milkweed plant, for example, contain chemicals that are toxic to most animals except monarch butterfly caterpillars. Poison ivy, poison oak, and poison sumac produce chemicals that are extremely irritating to humans' skin. Animals also have chemical defenses, as shown by the frog pictured and described on page 35. **learning modality: verbal**

Answers to Self-Assessment

Caption Question

Figure 11 *Sample answers:* The owl is nesting in a hole in the cactus. The woodpecker is eating insects on the cactus.

☑ *Checkpoint*

If two species try to occupy the same niche, they will compete directly against each other, and one species eventually will die off.

Ongoing Assessment

Writing Have students explain how natural selection causes changes in a species over time.

Predation

Building Inquiry Skills: Inferring

Ask students: **Suppose you set up a cricket habitat in a terrarium. What do you think would happen if you added a toad to the habitat?** *(It would eat the crickets.)* **What would happen if you then added a snake to the habitat?** *(It would eat the toad.)* **Which of these animals would be the prey?** *(The crickets and the toad, when it is eaten by the snake.)* **Which would be a predator?** *(The toad, when it eats crickets, and the snake.)* Challenge students to identify other feeding relationships in which one organism is a predator at some times and the prey at other times. **learning modality: logical/mathematical**

Building Inquiry Skills: Observing

ACTIVITY

Materials *sundew or Venus flytrap, cooked hamburger, tweezers*
Time periodic observation

Students are often intrigued by insect-eating plants. Obtain a sundew or Venus flytrap from a plant shop, the plant section of a large supermarket, or a biological supply house. Let students take turns feeding the plant small pieces of cooked hamburger from time to time. (Remind students to wash their hands afterward.) Encourage interested students to find out why the plant catches and digests insects. *(Carnivorous plants are capable of making their own food through photosynthesis, but the boggy, acidic soil in which they grow does not provide sufficient nitrogen for the plants' needs. The plants obtain nitrogen from the insects they catch.)* **learning modality: kinesthetic**

Predation

A tiger shark lurks beneath the surface of the clear blue water, looking for shadows of young albatross floating above it. The shark sees a chick and silently swims closer. Suddenly, the shark bursts through the water and seizes the albatross with one snap of its powerful jaw. This interaction between two organisms has an unfortunate ending for the albatross.

An interaction in which one organism kills and eats another is called **predation.** The organism that does the killing, in this case the tiger shark, is the **predator.** The organism that is killed, the albatross, is the **prey.**

Predator Adaptations Predators have adaptations that help them catch and kill their prey. For example, a cheetah can run very fast for a short time, enabling it to catch its prey. A jellyfish's tentacles contain a poisonous substance that paralyzes tiny water

EXPLORING *Defense Strategies*

Organisms display a wide array of adaptations that help them avoid becoming prey.

Camouflage ▲
These delicate spiny bugs are a perfect match for their branch habitat. The more an organism resembles its surroundings, the less likely it is that a predator will notice it. Some animals, such as flounder, can even change their colors to match a variety of settings.

Protective Coverings
This sea urchin sends a clear message to predators: "Don't touch!" Porcupines, hedgehogs, and cactuses all use the same spiny strategy. After a few painful encounters, a predator will look for less prickly prey. ▼

Background

History of Science In nature, predator species rarely kill and eat all their prey species, which would reduce community diversity. In fact, studies have shown that predation can actually help *maintain* diversity.

One example of this process involves the gray wolf, a top predator in its ecosystem. Where wolves were hunted to extinction, such as in many parts of North America, populations of deer and other herbivores increased dramatically. As these populations overgrazed the vegetation, many plant species that could not tolerate such grazing pressure disappeared from the ecosystem. In turn, many insects and other small animals that depended on the plants for food also disappeared. The elimination of wolves thus produced an ecosystem with considerably less species diversity.

animals. You can probably think of many predators that have claws, sharp teeth, or stingers. Some plants, too, have adaptations for catching prey. The sundew is covered with sticky bulbs on stalks—when a fly lands on the plant, it remains snared in the sticky goo while the plant digests it.

Some predators have adaptations that enable them to hunt at night. For example, the big eyes of an owl let in as much light as possible to help it see in the dark. Bats can hunt without seeing at all. Instead, they locate their prey by producing pulses of sound and listening for the echoes. This precise method enables a bat to catch a flying moth in complete darkness.

Prey Adaptations How do prey organisms manage to avoid being killed by such effective predators? In *Exploring Defense Strategies,* below, you can see some examples of how an organism's physical characteristics can help protect it.

Mimicry
If you've ever been stung by a bee, you'd probably keep your distance from this insect. But actually this "bee" is a harmless fly. The fly's resemblance to a stinging bee protects it from birds and other predators, who are fooled into staying away. ▼

Warning Coloring ▲
A frog this bright certainly can't hide. How could such a color be an advantage? The bright red and blue of this poison arrow frog warn predators not to eat it— glands on the frog's back that release toxic chemicals make it a bad choice for a meal.

◄ **False Coloring**
Which way is this butterfly fish swimming? The black dot on its tail is a false eye. A predator may bite this end of the fish, allowing it to escape with only part of its tail missing.

Chapter 1 **E ◆ 35**

Media and Technology

🔘 **Exploring Life Science Videodisc**
Unit 3, Side 2,
"How Does
Everything Fit?"

[barcode] Chapter 4

EXPLORING
Defense Strategies

Review each of the defense strategies with the class, then list the five strategies on the board. Ask: **What kind of defense strategy does a poison ivy plant have?** (*Chemical defense; add this defense to the list on the board.*) Ask: **Can you think of an example of an animal using a chemical defense?** (*Students might mention a skunk spraying.*) **How does this defense help a skunk survive?** (*The foul odor repels predators that try to attack it; any predator who has been sprayed by a skunk will avoid skunks in the future.*) Tell students that some animals use another defense strategy called a threat display. When attacked by a predator, the prey animal does something to startle or intimidate the predator. For example, a baboon being chased by a leopard may suddenly turn to face the leopard, bare its teeth, and scream loudly, startling the leopard long enough for the baboon to escape. Add *threat display* to the list. Then divide the class into seven groups, and secretly assign one of the listed defenses to each group. Have each group act out its defense strategy and challenge the rest of the students to guess what it is. **cooperative learning**

Ongoing Assessment

Oral Presentation Call on various students to each identify and describe a defense strategy used by prey organisms.

Predation, continued

Using the Visuals: Figure 13

To help students focus on specific phases of the cycles, ask questions such as the following: **What happened to the wolf population from 1965 to 1969?** *(It declined—from 29 wolves in 1965 to 19 wolves in 1969.)* **What happened to the moose population during that same period?** *(It increased—from about 700 moose in 1965 to about 1,200 moose in 1969.)* **Why do you think the moose population increased so much during those years?** *(The wolf population was declining, so fewer moose were killed by wolves.)* **After 1969, in what year did the moose population first reach a peak? What was the size of the population?** *(1974; about 1,400 moose)* **What was the size of the wolf population that year?** *(22 or 23 wolves)* **When did the wolf population reach its peak? How many wolves were there?** *(In 1980; 50 wolves)* **How many wolves were there two years later?** *(About 25)* **Why did the wolf population decline so much during that period?** *(The moose population continued to decline and reached one of its lowest points, so there was less food for the wolves.)* **What do you think accounts for the two dramatic increases in the moose population between 1986 and 1995?** *(The wolf population was small during those years.)* **What might have accounted for the sharp dip in the moose population between 1990 and 1991?** *(Since the number of wolves did not increase significantly in that year, students should suggest other limiting factors, possibly disease or insufficient food.)* **What do you think caused the sharp dip in the moose population between 1995 and 1996?** *(The wolf population increased again during that period.)* **learning modality: logical/mathematical**

Figure 13 The populations of wolves and moose on Isle Royale are related. The predator wolf population depends on the size of the prey moose population, and vice versa.
Predicting How might a disease in the wolf population one year affect the moose population the next year?

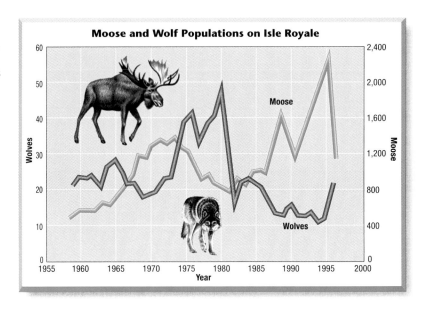

The Effect of Predation on Population Size Predation can have a major effect on the size of a population. As you learned in Section 2, when the death rate exceeds the birth rate in a population, the size of the population usually decreases. If predators are very effective at hunting their prey, the result is often a decrease in the size of the prey population. But a decrease in the prey population in turn affects the predator population.

To see how predator and prey populations can affect each other, look at the graph above. The graph shows the number of moose and wolves living on Isle Royale, an island in Lake Superior. From 1965 to 1975, the number of prey moose increased. The wolves now had enough to eat, so more of them survived. Within a few years, the wolf population began to increase. The growing number of wolves killed more and more moose. The moose population decreased. By 1980, the lack of moose had greatly affected the wolves. Some wolves starved, and others could not raise as many young. Soon the moose population began to climb again. This cycle for the two species has continued.

Of course, other factors also affect the populations on Isle Royale. For instance, cold winters and disease can also reduce the size of one or both of the populations.

☑ *Checkpoint* *If predation removes more members of a population than are born, how will the population change?*

Background

Facts and Figures Although the moose and wolf populations on Isle Royale have cycled up and down for decades, a new phase may have begun in the early 1980s when the wolf population declined sharply. Biologists hypothesize that the extreme genetic uniformity of the wolf population is one of the reasons for this decline. Populations that lack genetic variability often have low reproductive success. For example, in 1994 only two wolf pups were born on the island. Genetic uniformity also makes a population more susceptible to disease. Analysis of the wolves' blood has revealed antibodies to canine parvovirus, indicating that the wolves had been exposed to this lethal disease. The population may continue to have such poor reproductive success that it will disappear completely from Isle Royale.

Symbiosis

Many of the interactions in the saguaro community you read about earlier are examples of symbiosis. **Symbiosis** (sim bee OH sis) is a close relationship between two species that benefits at least one of the species. **The three types of symbiotic relationships are mutualism, commensalism, and parasitism.**

Mutualism A relationship in which both species benefit is called **mutualism** (MYOO choo uh liz um). The relationship between the saguaro and the long-eared bats is an example of mutualism. The bat benefits because the cactus flowers provide it with food. The saguaro benefits as its pollen is carried to another plant on the bat's nose.

INTEGRATING HEALTH At this very moment, you are participating in a mutualistic relationship with a population of bacteria in your large intestine. These bacteria, called *Escherichia coli*, live in the intestines of most mammals. They break down some foods that the mammal cannot digest. The bacteria benefit by receiving food and a place to live. You also benefit from the relationship because the bacteria help you digest your food. Your *Escherichia coli* also provide you with vitamin K, a nutrient that is needed to make your blood clot.

Commensalism A relationship in which one species benefits and the other species is neither helped nor harmed is called **commensalism** (kuh MEN suh liz um). The red-tailed hawks' interaction with the saguaro is an example of commensalism. The hawks are helped by having a place to build their nest, while the cactus is not affected by the birds.

Commensalism is not very common in nature because two species are usually either helped or harmed a little by any interaction. For example, by creating a small hole for its nest in the cactus trunk, the elf owl slightly damages the cactus.

Sharpen your Skills

Classifying

Classify each interaction as an example of mutualism, commensalism, or parasitism. Explain your answers.

- a remora fish attaches itself to the underside of a shark without harming the shark, and eats leftover bits of food from the shark's meals
- a vampire bat drinks the blood of horses
- bacteria living in cows' stomachs help them break down the cellulose in grass

Figure 14 Three yellow-billed oxpeckers get a cruise and a snack aboard an obliging hippopotamus. The oxpeckers eat ticks living on the hippo's skin. Since both the birds and the hippo benefit from this interaction, it is an example of mutualism.

Answers to Self-Assessment

Caption Question

Figure 13 The moose population would probably increase, since there would be fewer predators.

☑ **Checkpoint**

The size of the population will decrease.

Symbiosis

Including All Students

Give students dictionaries and have them find the word derivations for *symbiosis, mutualism, commensalism,* and *parasitism.* Then students can use index cards to make vocabulary review cards that have the term on the front and the term's derivation, definition, and an example on the back. **limited English proficiency**

Integrating Health

Students are probably unaware that their bodies are normally inhabited by other types of living things. For example, microscopic mites *(Demodex folliculorum)* live at the base of eyelashes, feeding on tiny bits of dead skin and other detritus. The mites benefit, and humans are neither harmed nor helped—an example of commensalism. Obtain a video about the human body's invisible inhabitants so students can observe them. **learning modality: visual**

Sharpen your Skills

Classifying

Time 5–10 minutes

Tips Have students do this activity after they have read about parasitism on the next page.

Expected Outcome *Remora/shark:* Commensalism; the remora benefits, and the shark is neither helped nor harmed. *Vampire bat/horses:* Parasitism; the bat benefits, and the horses are harmed. *Bacteria/cows:* Mutualism; the bacteria receive food and a place to live, and the cows benefit because the bacteria help them digest their food.

Extend Challenge students to find and classify symbiotic relationships shown in Figure 11 on page 32. **learning modality: logical/mathematical**

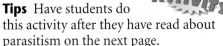

Ongoing Assessment

Writing Have each student name and briefly describe the three types of symbiotic relationships and give an example of each.

3 Assess

Section 3 Review Answers

1. An organism's adaptations enable it to fill a unique role in its ecosystem—eating particular types of food, obtaining its food in unique ways, and using other abiotic and biotic factors to meet its needs.
2. *Competition*: the struggle between organisms to survive in a habitat with limited resources; *predation*: an interaction between organisms in which one kills and eats the other; *symbiosis*: a close relationship between two species that benefits at least one of the species
3. *Mutualism*: a relationship in which both species benefit; *commensalism*: a relationship in which one species benefits and the other species is neither helped nor harmed; *parasitism*: a relationship in which one organism lives on or inside another organism and harms it
4. By staying motionless among a plant's branches, the walking stick is camouflaged and cannot easily be seen by predators.
5. *Similarity:* One organism (the parasite or the predator) benefits, while the other organism (the host or the prey) is harmed. *Difference:* In parasitism, the parasite usually does not kill the host, whereas in predation, the predator kills the prey.

·· **CHAPTER PROJECT 1**

Check Your Progress

Distribute Chapter 1 Project Worksheet 2, which is designed to help students prepare their written reports and graphs. All groups should graph the data they collected on plant height; some groups may want to create additional graphs for the numbers of leaves and buds. (See Chapter 1 Project Teacher Notes, Teaching Resources page 9, for information on graphing possibilities.)

Performance Assessment

Writing Have each student explain how each of the types of interactions among species described in this section affects organisms' survival.

Figure 15 The white objects on this sphinx moth larva are wasp cocoons. When the wasps emerge, they will feed on the larva. *Applying Concepts Which organism in this interaction is the parasite? Which organism is the host?*

Parasitism The third type of symbiosis is called parasitism. **Parasitism** (PA ruh sit iz um) involves one organism living on or inside another organism and harming it. The organism that benefits is called a **parasite,** and the organism it lives on or in is called a **host.** The parasite is usually smaller than the host. In a parasitic relationship, the parasite benefits from the interaction while the host is harmed.

Some common parasites you may be familiar with are fleas, ticks, and leeches. These parasites have adaptations that enable them to attach to their host and feed on its blood. Other parasites live inside the host's body, such as tapeworms that live inside the digestive systems of dogs and wolves.

Unlike a predator, a parasite does not usually kill the organism it feeds on. If the host dies, the parasite loses its source of food. An interesting example of this rule is shown by a species of mite that lives in the ears of moths. The mites almost always live in just one of the moth's ears. If they live in both ears, the moth's hearing is so badly affected that it is likely to be quickly caught and eaten by its predator, a bat.

 ## Section 3 Review

1. How do an organism's adaptations help it to survive?
2. Name and define the three major types of interactions among organisms.
3. List the three types of symbiosis. For each one, explain how the two organisms are affected.
4. A walking stick is an insect that resembles a small twig. How do you think this insect avoids predators?
5. **Thinking Critically Comparing and Contrasting** How are parasitism and predation similar? How are they different?

·· **CHAPTER PROJECT 1**

Check Your Progress

By now you should be making your final observations of your plants and planning your report. How can you present your data in a graph? Think about what you should put on each axis of your graph. *(Hint: Draft the written portion of your report early enough to look it over and make any necessary changes.)*

Program Resources

◆ **Teaching Resources** 1-3 Review and Reinforce, p. 25; 1-3 Enrich, p. 26

Media and Technology

 Interactive Student Tutorial CD-ROM E-1

Answers to Self-Assessment

Caption Question

Figure 15 The wasp is the parasite, and the sphinx moth larva is the host.

 Living Things and the Environment

Key Ideas

◆ An organism's habitat provides food, water, shelter, and other things the organism needs to live, grow, and reproduce.

◆ An ecosystem includes both biotic and abiotic factors. Abiotic factors found in many environments include water, sunlight, oxygen, temperature, and soil.

◆ A population consists of a single species. The different populations living together in one area make up a community. The community plus abiotic factors form an ecosystem.

◆ Ecologists study how the biotic and abiotic factors interact within an ecosystem.

Key Terms

ecosystem	species
habitat	population
biotic factor	community
abiotic factor	ecology
photosynthesis	

 Studying Populations

 *INTEGRATING MATHEMATICS*

Key Ideas

◆ Ecologists can estimate population size by direct and indirect observations, sampling, and mark-and-recapture studies.

◆ A population changes in size as a result of changes in the birth rate or death rate, or when organisms move into or out of the population.

◆ Population size is controlled by limiting factors such as food, space, and weather conditions.

Key Terms

population density	immigration
estimate	emigration
birth rate	limiting factor
death rate	carrying capacity

③ Interactions Among Living Things

Key Ideas

◆ Over time, species of organisms develop specialized adaptations and behaviors that help them succeed in their environments.

◆ The major types of interactions among organisms are competition, predation, and symbiosis.

◆ Predators have many adaptations that enable them to catch their prey, while prey organisms have adaptations to protect themselves from predators.

◆ Symbiosis is a close relationship between two species. The three types of symbiotic relationships are mutualism, commensalism, and parasitism.

Key Terms

natural selection	predator	commensalism
adaptation	prey	parasitism
niche	symbiosis	parasite
competition	mutualism	host
predation		

  USING THE INTERNET *ACTIVITY*

www.science-explorer.phschool.com

Chapter 1 **E ◆ 39**

Reviewing Content:
Multiple Choice

1. b **2.** a **3.** c **4.** c **5.** b

True or False

6. biotic **7.** true **8.** competition **9.** host
10. true

Checking Concepts

11. Sample answer: *Biotic:* trees, birds
Abiotic: sunlight, soil
12. Plants and algae use the energy of
sunlight to combine water and carbon
dioxide to make their own food in
photosynthesis. All living things feed
directly or indirectly on plants and algae.
13. Ecologists count the number of
organisms in a small area, then multiply
by the number of units in the entire area
to estimate the total population.
14. Limited space may make it
impossible for all members of the
population to find places to breed or
make nests.
15. Any two: *Camouflage:* The organism
blends in with its surroundings, making
it difficult for predators to see. *Protective
covering:* The organism's spines, shell, or
other outer covering makes it painful or
difficult for predators to eat it. *Warning
coloring:* An organism that is poisonous
has bright colors to warn predators not
to eat it. *Mimicry:* A harmless organism
looks like another organism that
predators have learned not to eat. *False
coloring:* False "eyes" or other structures
fool predators into attacking the wrong
part of an organism.
16. Students' descriptions will vary.
Make sure they describe several biotic
and abiotic factors on which they depend
for survival—plants and animals they
use for food, for example—and
interactions with other species, such as
pets, insects carrying diseases that can
infect humans, and the like.

Thinking Visually

17. a. Predation **b.** Symbiosis
c. Parasitism **d.** Commensalism **e.** Prey
f. Host. Sample title: Types of
Interactions Among Organisms

Reviewing Content

 *For more review of key concepts, see the
Interactive Student Tutorial CD-ROM.*

Multiple Choice
Choose the letter of the best answer.

1. A prairie dog, a hawk, and a badger all are
members of the same
   a. habitat.   **b.** community.
   c. species.   **d.** population.
2. Which of the following is *not* an example
of a population?
   a. the pets in your neighborhood
   b. the people in a city
   c. the rainbow trout in a stream
   d. the ants in an anthill
3. All of the following are examples of
limiting factors for populations *except*
   a. space   **b.** food
   c. time   **d.** weather
4. Which of these relationships is an
example of parasitism?
   a. a bird building a nest on a tree branch
   b. a bat pollinating a saguaro cactus
   c. a flea living on a cat's blood
   d. *Escherichia coli* bacteria making
     vitamin K in your intestine
5. In which type of interaction do both
species benefit?
   a. predation   **b.** mutualism
   c. commensalism   **d.** parasitism

True or False
*If the statement is true, write true. If it is
false, change the underlined word or words
to make the statement true.*

6. Grass is an example of a(n) <u>abiotic</u>
factor in a habitat.
7. A rise in birth rate while the death
rate remains steady will cause a
population to <u>increase</u> in size.
8. The struggle between organisms for
limited resources is called <u>mutualism</u>.
9. A parasite lives on or inside its
<u>predator</u>.
10. An organism's specific role in its
habitat is called its <u>niche</u>.

Checking Concepts

11. Name two biotic and two abiotic factors
you might find in a forest ecosystem.
12. Explain how sunlight is used by plants
and algae. How is this process important
to other living things in an ecosystem?
13. Describe how ecologists use the technique
of sampling to estimate population size.
14. Give an example showing how space can
be a limiting factor for a population.
15. What are two adaptations that prey
organisms have developed to protect
themselves? Describe how each adaptation
protects the organism.
16. Writing to Learn Write a description
of your niche in the environment. Include
details about your habitat, including both
biotic and abiotic factors around you. Be
sure to describe your feeding habits as
well as any interactions you have with
members of other species.

Thinking Visually

17. Concept Map Copy the concept map
about interactions among organisms onto
a separate sheet of paper. Complete the
concept map and add a title. (For more on
concept maps, see the Skills Handbook.)

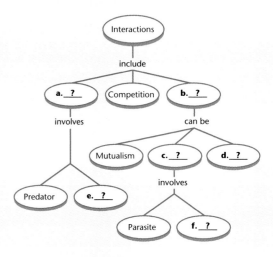

Applying Skills

18.

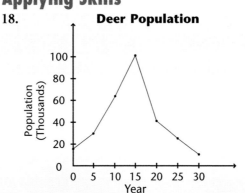

Deer Population

19. *Highest:* Year 15; *lowest:* Year 30
20. *Example:* Beginning with 15,000 deer at the
beginning of the study, the population increased
steadily through Year 15. From Year 15 through
the end of the study, the deer population
declined steadily, reaching the population's
lowest point, 10,000 deer, in Year 30.
21. The severe winter may have killed weak or
injured deer. Food shortages during this winter
also may have weakened deer or caused them
to starve.

Applying Skills

Ecologists monitoring a deer population collected data during a 30-year study. Use the data to answer Questions 18–21.

🐾 **18. Graphing** Make a line graph using the data in the table. Plot years on the horizontal axis and population on the vertical axis.

Year	0	5	10	15	20	25	30
Population (thousands)	15	30	65	100	40	25	10

🐾 **19. Interpreting Data** In which year did the deer population reach its highest point? Its lowest point?

🐾 **20. Communicating** Write a few sentences describing how the deer population changed during the study.

🐾 **21. Developing Hypotheses** In Year 16 of the study, this region experienced a very severe winter. How might this have affected the deer population?

Thinking Critically

22. Making Generalizations Explain why ecologists usually study a specific population of organisms rather than studying the entire species.

🐾 **23. Problem Solving** As a summer job working for an ecologist, you have been assigned to estimate the population of grasshoppers in a field. Propose a method to get an estimate and explain how you would carry it out.

24. Comparing and Contrasting Explain how parasitism and mutualism are similar and how they are different.

25. Relating Cause and Effect Competition for resources in an area is usually more intense within a single species than between two different species. Can you suggest an explanation for this observation? *(Hint:* Consider how niches help organisms avoid competition.)

24. In both parasitism and mutualism, one of the organisms benefits from the interaction. However, in mutualism the other organism also benefits, whereas in parasitism the other organism is harmed.

25. Within a single species, there is a smaller range of adaptation than between species. Organisms within a species share the same niche. Because individuals within a species are more similar, they will share many of the same advantages and disadvantages in surviving in a certain environment, which intensifies competition for the limited resources.

Performance Assessment

Wrap Up

CHAPTER PROJECT 1

Present Your Project
Review each group's written report, and let groups present their results to the rest of the class in a poster, display, or oral report. As indicated in the Scoring Rubric, base your evaluation of each group's report on both the written report and the class presentation.

Reflect and Record After all groups have made their class presentations, allow time for students to compare their results and discuss the factors that may have accounted for any differences.

Performance Assessment

Wrap Up
CHAPTER PROJECT 1

Present Your Project Review your report and graph to be sure that they clearly state your conclusion about the effects of crowding on plant growth. With your group, decide how you will present your results. Do a practice run-through to make sure all group members feel comfortable with their part.

Reflect and Record Compare your group's results with those of your classmates. Suggest possible explanations for any differences. How could you have improved your plan for your experiment? Record these thoughts in your project notebook.

Getting Involved

In Your School Get permission to set up a bird observation center outside your school. Work with other students to make a bird feeder from a plastic jug. Use a birdwatching guide or contact a local wildlife organization to determine what type of feed to put in your container. Hang the feeder in a location that is safe from neighborhood cats. Nearby, place a shallow pan of water for the birds to drink and bathe in. Refill the food and water regularly. Keep a log of the species that visit your center, what type of food they prefer, and how they interact.

Chapter 1 **E ◆ 41**

Thinking Critically

22. It is usually not possible to study the entire population of the species because it is too spread out. In addition, because the organism's interaction with other organisms and the environment is specific to that environment, studying a population produces more accurate results than studying an entire species.

23. Answers may include indirect observation (counting egg clusters), sampling (counting the number in a small area, then multiplying by the number of units in the entire area), or mark and recapture.

Program Resources

◆ **Inquiry Skills Activity Book** Provides teaching and review of all inquiry skills

Getting Involved

In Your School Ask volunteers to draft a letter to the principal requesting permission for the class to set up a bird feeding station. Many science activity books available in libraries contain instructions for making simple bird feeders. A local chapter of the Audubon Society may be able to supply you with such instructions as well as pamphlets on the types of seed preferred by different bird species. Encourage students to set up and maintain a class chart showing the types of foods offered in the station and the bird species that visit. If possible, provide two or three sets of binoculars so students can observe the birds closely without frightening them.

Ecosystems and Biomes

Sections	Time	Student Edition Activities	Other Activities	
CHAPTER PROJECT 2 **Breaking It Down** p. 43	Ongoing (4 weeks minimum)	Check Your Progress, pp. 50, 55, 73 Wrap Up, p. 81		
1 Energy Flow in Ecosystems pp. 44–50 ◆ Describe the energy roles of organisms in an ecosystem. ◆ Describe how much energy is available at each level of an energy pyramid. ◆ Explain food chains and food webs.	2–3 periods/ 1–1½ blocks	**Discover** Where Did Your Dinner Come From?, p. 44 **Sharpen Your Skills** Observing, p. 46 **Try This** Weaving a Food Web, p. 49	TE TE TE TE ISLM	Building Inquiry Skills: Predicting, p. 45; Observing, p. 47 Real-Life Learning, p. 46 Using the Visuals: Figure 5, p. 47 Including All Students, p. 49 E-2, "Ecosystem Food Chains"
2 *INTEGRATING CHEMISTRY* **Cycles of Matter** pp. 51–55 ◆ Describe the three processes that make up the water cycle. ◆ Describe the nitrogen cycle and the carbon-oxygen cycle.	2–3 periods/ 1–1½ blocks	**Discover** Are You Part of a Cycle?, p. 51 **Sharpen Your Skills** Developing Hypotheses, p. 52	TE TE IES	Inquiry Challenge, p. 53 Using the Visuals: Figure 10, p. 54 "Where River Meets Sea," pp. 15–16
3 Biogeography pp. 56–59 ◆ Describe means by which organisms disperse. ◆ Identify the factors that limit the distribution of a species.	1–2 periods/ ½–1 block	**Discover** How Can You Move a Seed?, p. 56 **Science at Home,** p. 59	TE IES	Integrating Earth Science, p. 57 "Where River Meets Sea," pp. 28–29
4 Earth's Biomes pp. 60–73 ◆ List and describe Earth's major land biomes. ◆ List and describe Earth's major freshwater and ocean biomes.	4–5 periods/ 2–2½ blocks	**Real-World Lab: How It Works** Biomes in Miniature, pp. 60–61 **Discover** How Much Rain Is That?, p. 62 **Try This** Desert Survival, p. 65 **Sharpen Your Skills** Inferring, p. 67 **Sharpen Your Skills** Interpreting Data, p. 69	TE TE TE	Building Inquiry Skills: Communicating, p. 63; Making Models, pp. 64, 66; Inferring, p. 67, 72 Inquiry Challenge, p. 69 Real-Life Learning, p. 70
5 Succession pp. 74–78 ◆ Describe the differences between primary and secondary succession.	2–3 periods/ 1–1½ blocks	**Skills Lab: Observing** Change in a Tiny Community, pp. 74–75 **Discover** What Happened Here?, p. 76 **Science at Home,** p. 78	TE	Building Inquiry Skills: Observing, p. 77
Study Guide/Chapter Review pp. 79–81	1 period/ ½ block		ISAB	Provides teaching and review of all inquiry skills

For Standard or Block Schedule The Resource Pro® CD-ROM gives you maximum flexibility for planning your instruction for any type of schedule. Resource Pro® contains Planning Express®, an advanced scheduling program, as well as the entire contents of the Teaching Resources and the Computer Test Bank.

CHAPTER PLANNING GUIDE

Program Resources	Assessment Strategies	Media and Technology
TR Chapter 2 Project Teacher Notes, pp. 32–33 **TR** Chapter 2 Project Overview and Worksheets, pp. 34–37 **TR** Chapter 2 Project Scoring Rubric, p. 38	**SE** Performance Assessment: Chapter 2 Project Wrap Up, p. 81 **TE** Check Your Progress, pp. 50, 55, 73 **TR** Chapter 2 Project Scoring Rubric, p. 38	🌐 Science Explorer Internet Site
TR 2-1 Lesson Plan, p. 39 **TR** 2-1 Section Summary, p. 40 **TR** 2-1 Review and Reinforce, p. 41 **TR** 2-1 Enrich, p. 42 **SES** Book A, *From Bacteria to Plants*, Chapter 4 **SES** Book H, *Earth's Waters*, Chapter 5	**SE** Section 1 Review, p. 50 **TE** Ongoing Assessment, pp. 45, 47, 49 **TE** Performance Assessment, p. 50 **TR** 2-1 Review and Reinforce, p. 41	📀 Exploring Life Science Videodisc, Unit 6 Side 2, "The Wonder of Ngorongoro" 🎧 Audiotapes, English-Spanish Summary 2-1 📽 Transparencies 2, "Exploring a Food Web"; 3, "An Energy Pyramid" 💽 Interactive Student Tutorial CD-ROM, E-2
TR 2-2 Lesson Plan, p. 43 **TR** 2-2 Section Summary, p. 44 **TR** 2-2 Review and Reinforce, p. 45 **TR** 2-2 Enrich, p. 46	**SE** Section 2 Review, p. 55 **TE** Ongoing Assessment, p. 53 **TE** Performance Assessment, p. 55 **TR** 2-2 Review and Reinforce, p. 45	📀 Exploring Life Science Videodisc, Unit 6 Side 2, "Cycles in Nature" 🎧 Audiotapes, English-Spanish Summary 2-2 📽 Transparencies 4, "Water Cycle"; 5, "Carbon and Oxygen Cycles"; 6, "Nitrogen Cycle" 💽 Interactive Student Tutorial CD-ROM, E-2
TR 2-3 Lesson Plan, p. 47 **TR** 2-3 Section Summary, p. 48 **TR** 2-3 Review and Reinforce, p. 49 **TR** 2-3 Enrich, p. 50 **SES** Book F, *Inside Earth*, Chapter 1	**SE** Section 3 Review, p. 59 **TE** Ongoing Assessment, p. 57 **TE** Performance Assessment, p. 59 **TR** 2-3 Review and Reinforce, p. 49	📀 Exploring Life Science Videodisc, Unit 5 Side 2, "Extinction" 🎧 Audiotapes, English-Spanish Summary 2-3 💽 Interactive Student Tutorial CD-ROM, E-2
TR 2-4 Lesson Plan, p. 51 **TR** 2-4 Section Summary, p. 52 **TR** 2-4 Review and Reinforce, p. 53 **TR** 2-4 Enrich, p. 54 **TR** Chapter 2 Real-World Lab, pp. 59–61 **SES** Book H, *Earth's Waters*, Chapters 2 and 5	**SE** Analyze and Conclude, p. 61 **SE** Section 4 Review, p. 73 **TE** Ongoing Assessment, pp. 63, 65, 67, 69, 71 **TE** Performance Assessment, p. 73 **TR** 2-4 Review and Reinforce, p. 53	📀 Exploring Life Science Videodisc, Unit 6 Side 2, "Earth's Many Biomes" 🎧 Audiotapes, English-Spanish Summary 2-4 💽 Interactive Student Tutorial CD-ROM, E-2
TR 2-5 Lesson Plan, p. 55 **TR** 2-5 Section Summary, p. 56 **TR** 2-5 Review and Reinforce, p. 57 **TR** 2-5 Enrich, p. 58 **TR** Chapter 2 Skills Lab, pp. 62–63	**SE** Analyze and Conclude, p. 75 **SE** Section 5 Review, p. 78 **TE** Ongoing Assessment, p. 77 **TE** Performance Assessment, p. 78 **TR** 2-5 Review and Reinforce, p. 57	🎧 Audiotapes, English-Spanish Summary 2-5 📽 Transparency 7, "Primary and Secondary Succession" 💽 Interactive Student Tutorial CD-ROM, E-2
TR Chapter 2 Performance Assessment, pp. 187–189 **TR** Chapter 2 Test, pp. 190–193	**SE** Chapter 2 Review, pp. 79–81 **TR** Chapter 2 Performance Assessment, pp. 187–189 **TR** Chapter 2 Test, pp. 190–193 **CTB** Test E-2	💽 Interactive Student Tutorial CD-ROM, E-2 💾 Computer Test Bank, Test E-2

Key: **SE** Student Edition   **TE** Teacher's Edition   **TR** Teaching Resources
      CTB Computer Test Bank   **SES** Science Explorer Series Text   **ISLM** Integrated Science Laboratory Manual
      ISAB Inquiry Skills Activity Book   **PTA** Product Testing Activities by *Consumer Reports*   **IES** Interdisciplinary Explorations Series

Meeting the National Science Education Standards and AAAS Benchmarks

National Science Education Standards	Benchmarks for Science Literacy	Unifying Themes
Science As Inquiry (Content Standard A) ◆ **Design and conduct a scientific experiment** Students investigate the effects of variables on decomposition. (*Chapter Project*) ◆ **Develop descriptions, explanations, predictions, and models using evidence** Students investigate how abiotic factors create different biomes. Students observe how a community changes over time. (*Real-World Lab; Skills Lab*) **Life Science** (Content Standard C) ◆ **Populations and ecosystems** Students observe the role of soil organisms on decomposition. An organism's energy role in an ecosystem may be that of producer, consumer, or decomposer. Producers use carbon from carbon dioxide to produce other carbon-containing molecules. Biogeography is the study of where organisms live. Students observe how climate affects biomes. A biome is a group of ecosystems with similar climates and organisms. Students observe succession in a pond community. Succession is the series of predictable changes that occur in a community over time. (*Chapter Project; Sections 1, 2, 3, 4, 5; Real-World Lab; Skills Lab*) **Earth and Space Science** (Content Standard D) ◆ **Structure of the Earth system** The water cycle is the continuous process by which water moves from Earth's surface to the atmosphere and back. Primary succession is the series of changes that occur in an area where no ecosystem previously existed. (*Sections 2, 5*)	**1B Scientific Inquiry** Students investigate the effects of different variables on decomposition. Students investigate how abiotic factors create different biomes. Students observe how a community changes over time. (*Chapter Project; Real-World Lab; Skills Lab*) **4B The Earth** The water cycle is the continuous process by which water moves from Earth's surface to the atmosphere and back. (*Section 2*) **4C Processes That Shape the Earth** Primary succession is the series of changes that occur in an area where no ecosystem previously existed. (*Section 5*) **5A Diversity of Life** A food web consists of many overlapping food chains in an ecosystem. (*Section 1*) **5D Interdependence of Life** Students observe the role of soil organisms on decomposition. An organism's energy role in an ecosystem may be that of producer, consumer, or decomposer. Biogeography is the study of where organisms live. Students observe how climate affects biomes. A biome is a group of ecosystems with similar climates and organisms. Succession is the series of predictable changes that occur in a community over time. (*Chapter Project; Sections 1, 3, 4, 5; Real-World Lab*) **5E Flow of Matter and Energy** The most energy is available at the producer level. Producers use carbon from carbon dioxide to produce other carbon-containing molecules. Students observe succession in a pond community. (*Sections 1, 2; Skills Lab*)	◆ **Energy** Energy first enters most ecosystems as sunlight. Unlike matter, energy is not recycled in an ecosystem. (*Sections 1, 2*) ◆ **Evolution** The movement of the continents has had a great impact on the distribution and development of species. (*Section 3*) ◆ **Modeling** Students build model compost chambers to investigate decomposition. Students model abiotic factors to study different biomes. Students use a model pond community to observe succession. (*Chapter Project; Real-World Lab; Skills Lab*) ◆ **Patterns of Change** Water, oxygen, carbon, and nitrogen cycle continuously through an ecosystem. Succession is the series of predictable changes that occur in a community over time. (*Sections 2, 5; Skills Lab*) ◆ **Stability** Matter is recycled in ecosystems. Biomes are areas with similar climates and organisms. (*Sections 2, 4*) ◆ **Systems and Interactions** Students investigate decomposition. Each organism has a role in the movement of energy. One factor that can limit dispersal of a species is competition. The types of plants determine the kinds of animals that live in an area. (*Chapter Project; Sections 1, 3, 4*) ◆ **Unity and Diversity** An organism's energy role may be that of a producer, consumer, or decomposer. Ecologists classify ecosystems into land and water biomes. The two kinds of succession are primary succession and secondary succession. (*Sections 1, 4, 5*)

Media and Technology

Exploring Life Science Videodiscs
◆ **Section 1** "The Wonder of Ngorongoro" provides a tour of the natural world of Ngorongoro, Africa.
◆ **Section 2** "Cycles in Nature" follows the water, oxygen-carbon dioxide, and nitrogen cycles.
◆ **Section 3** "Extinction" examines causes of extinction and evolution of new species.
◆ **Section 4** "Earth's Many Biomes" explores Earth's biomes.

Interactive Student Tutorial CD-ROM
◆ **Chapter Review** Interactive questions help students to self-assess their mastery of key chapter concepts.

Student Edition Connection Strategies

◆ **Section 2** Integrating Chemistry, pp. 51–55
Integrating Technology, p. 55

◆ **Section 3** Integrating Earth Science, p. 56
Social Studies Connection, p. 58
Integrating Earth Science, p. 59

USING THE INTERNET

www.science-explorer.phschool.com

Visit the Science Explorer Internet site to find an up-to-date activity for Chapter 2 of *Environmental Science*.

ACTIVITY	Time (minutes)	Materials Quantities for one work group	Skills
Section 1			
Discover, p. 44	10	No special materials are required.	Classifying
Sharpen Your Skills, p. 46	5	**Consumable** slice of bread, water, sealable plastic bag, tape	Observing
Try This, p. 49	10–15	**Consumable** long pieces of yarn	Making Models
Section 2			
Discover, p. 51	5	**Nonconsumable** small mirror	Inferring
Sharpen Your Skills, p. 52	5	No special materials are required.	Developing Hypotheses
Section 3			
Discover, p. 56	10–15	**Consumable** corn kernels, water, straw, tape **Nonconsumable** shallow pan	Predicting
Science at Home, p. 59	home	**Consumable** small plastic bags, sheet of heavy paper **Nonconsumable** stapler, hand lens (optional)	Classifying
Section 4			
Real-World Lab, pp. 60–61	30; 5–10 × 5 days	**Consumable** tape; index card; 10 impatiens seeds; 5 lima bean seeds; 30 rye grass seeds; empty, clean cardboard milk carton; sandy soil or potting soil; clear plastic wrap **Nonconsumable** scissors, lamp, stapler	Making Models, Observing, Drawing Conclusions
Discover, p. 62	20	**Consumable** adding-machine paper, masking tape **Nonconsumable** meter stick, scissors	Developing Hypotheses
Try This, p. 65	10	**Nonconsumable** small potted cactus, hand lens, scissors	Observing
Sharpen Your Skills, p. 67	5	No special materials are required.	Inferring
Sharpen Your Skills, p. 69	10	No special materials are required.	Interpreting Data
Section 5			
Skills Lab, pp. 74–75	15; 20 × 3 days	**Consumable** hay solution, pond water **Nonconsumable** small baby-food jar, wax pencil, plastic dropper, microscope slide, coverslip, microscope	Observing, Comparing and Contrasting, Drawing Conclusions
Discover, p. 76	10	No special materials are required.	Posing Questions
Science at Home, p. 78	home	**Nonconsumable** tape recorder (optional)	Communicating

A list of all materials required for the Student Edition activities can be found on pages T14–T15. You can order Materials Kits by calling 1-800-828-7777 or by accessing the Science Explorer Internet site at **www.science-explorer.phschool.com.**

CHAPTER PROJECT 2 — Breaking It Down

In Chapter 2, students study organisms' energy roles in ecosystems. The Chapter 2 Project focuses on decomposition, the process in which organic matter is broken down into simpler molecules, returning raw materials to the environment.

Purpose Each student or student group will construct two compost chambers and investigate how one variable affects decomposition. This project gives students an opportunity to apply the procedures involved in scientific experimentation. This project is challenging in that students must choose which variable to investigate and then design an experiment on their own. To complete the project successfully, students will identify and control variables, monitor changes in the compost chambers, record observations, analyze data, draw conclusions, and communicate their results to the class.

Skills Focus After completing the Chapter 2 Project, students will be able to

♦ make a model compost chamber;
♦ design an experiment to test the effect of one variable on decomposition;
♦ observe, measure, and record changes in the composted material;
♦ communicate experimental procedures and results in a report, poster, or other product.

Project Time Line This project requires at least four weeks to complete. During the first phase, each student or group will choose one variable to investigate (moisture, oxygen, temperature, or activity of soil organisms), design the experiment, and construct the compost chambers. At the end of Section 2, students will add organic material to the chambers and begin the experiment. While students study Sections 3 and 4, they will observe the decomposition process occurring in the two chambers and record data daily. At the end of Section 4, students will analyze the data collected and prepare their reports.

CHAPTER 2 — Ecosystems and Biomes

WHAT'S AHEAD

Integrating Chemistry

SECTION 1 — Energy Flow in Ecosystems
Discover Where Did Your Dinner Come From?
Sharpen Your Skills Observing
Try This Weaving a Food Web

SECTION 2 — Cycles of Matter
Discover Are You Part of a Cycle?
Sharpen Your Skills Developing Hypotheses

SECTION 3 — Biogeography
Discover How Can You Move a Seed?

Possible Materials

♦ Each student or group will need to build two compost chambers—one as the control and the other as the test chamber in which the chosen variable is changed. Instructions for building the chambers are provided on the Chapter 2 Project Student Worksheet, pages 36–37 in Teaching Resources.
♦ Provide chopped leaves as the base material to be composted. You may wish to add other types of organic waste, such as eggshells, paper, grass clippings, and orange peels, or nonorganic waste such as bottle caps or plastic foam pieces. This will allow students to make predictions about decomposition.
♦ Provide garden soil (not commercial potting soil) and earthworms for groups that choose to investigate the effect of soil organisms.
♦ Set aside suitable locations in the classroom where students can leave their compost chambers during the experiments.

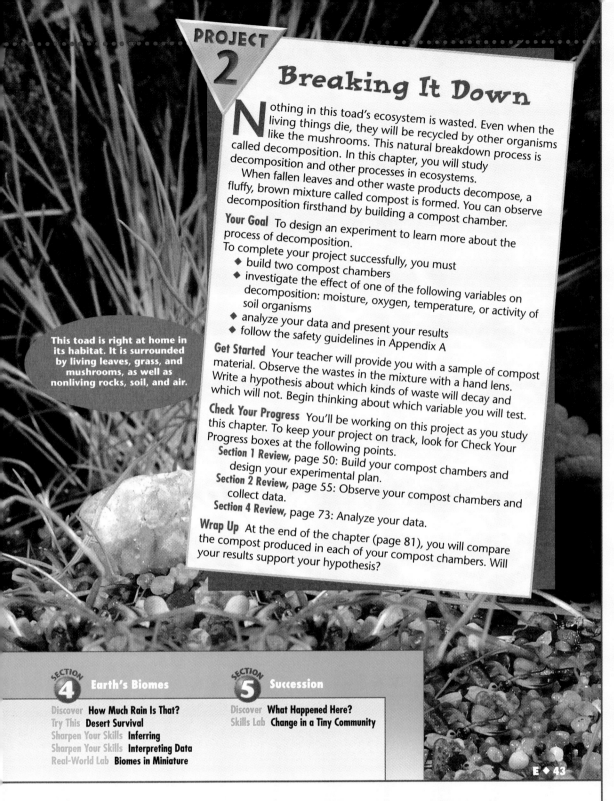

Breaking It Down

Nothing in this toad's ecosystem is wasted. Even when the living things die, they will be recycled by other organisms like the mushrooms. This natural breakdown process is called decomposition. In this chapter, you will study decomposition and other processes in ecosystems.

When fallen leaves and other waste products decompose, a fluffy, brown mixture called compost is formed. You can observe decomposition firsthand by building a compost chamber.

Your Goal To design an experiment to learn more about the process of decomposition.

To complete your project successfully, you must

◆ build two compost chambers

◆ investigate the effect of one of the following variables on decomposition: moisture, oxygen, temperature, or activity of soil organisms

◆ analyze your data and present your results

◆ follow the safety guidelines in Appendix A

Get Started Your teacher will provide you with a sample of compost material. Observe the wastes in the mixture with a hand lens. Write a hypothesis about which kinds of waste will decay and which will not. Begin thinking about which variable you will test.

Check Your Progress You'll be working on this project as you study this chapter. To keep your project on track, look for Check Your Progress boxes at the following points.

Section 1 Review, page 50: Build your compost chambers and design your experimental plan.
Section 2 Review, page 55: Observe your compost chambers and collect data.
Section 4 Review, page 73: Analyze your data.

Wrap Up At the end of the chapter (page 81), you will compare the compost produced in each of your compost chambers. Will your results support your hypothesis?

This toad is right at home in its habitat. It is surrounded by living leaves, grass, and mushrooms, as well as nonliving rocks, soil, and air.

E ◆ 43

Launching the Project Invite students to read the first paragraph on page 43. To determine what students already know about the decomposition process, ask, **What happens during decomposition? What kinds of organisms break down the remains of living things?**

Have students read the rest of the project description on page 43. Then show and describe the compost chamber you made. Explain that each student or group will need to make two such chambers—a control chamber and a test chamber.

Distribute Chapter 2 Project Overview on pages 34–35 in Teaching Resources, and let students review the project rules and procedures. Encourage questions and comments. Also distribute Chapter 2 Project Student Worksheet, which provides instructions for constructing the compost chambers.

If you divide the class into groups, tell students that every group member should help plan the experiment, make observations, analyze results, and develop the report.

Additional information on guiding the project is provided in Chapter 2 Project Teacher Notes on pages 32–33 in Teaching Resources.

Performance Assessment

The Chapter 2 Project Scoring Rubric on page 38 in Teaching Resources will help you evaluate how well students complete the Chapter 2 Project. You may want to share the scoring rubric with students so they are clear about what will be expected of them. Students will be assessed on

◆ their ability to design an experiment to test the effect of one variable— moisture, oxygen, temperature, or the presence of soil organisms—on decomposition;

◆ their completeness and accuracy in doing the experiment, making observations, and recording data;

◆ their ability to draw reasonable conclusions based on experimental results and communicate their procedures, results, and conclusions;

◆ their group participation, if they worked in groups.

Advance Preparation Before introducing the project, construct a compost chamber yourself as a prototype, following the instructions on the Chapter 2 Project Worksheet. Fill the chamber with the compost material, but do not add water. Set your chamber aside until the end of the project so students can compare their composted material with the original material.

Program Resources

◆ **Teaching Resources** Chapter 2 Project Teacher Notes, pp. 32–33; Chapter 2 Project Overview and Worksheets, pp. 34–37; Chapter 2 Project Scoring Rubric, p. 38

Objectives

After completing the lesson, students will be able to
◆ describe the energy roles of organisms in an ecosystem;
◆ describe how much energy is available at each level of an energy pyramid;
◆ explain food chains and food webs.

Key Terms producer, consumer, herbivore, carnivore, omnivore, scavenger, decomposer, food chain, food web, energy pyramid

1 Engage/Explore

Activating Prior Knowledge

Help students recall what they learned in the previous chapter by asking: **What is an ecosystem?** *(All the living and nonliving things that interact in a particular area)* **What are some things you learned about ecosystems in the last chapter?** *(Major concepts include habitat, biotic and abiotic factors, levels of organization, methods of determining population size, the causes of changes in population size, limiting factors, adaptations, and types of interactions among organisms.)*

• • • • • • • • DISCOVER • • • • • • • •

Skills Focus classifying
Time 10 minutes
Tips Circulate among students as they work to answer questions about the sources or ingredients of some foods.
Expected Outcome As a class, students will undoubtedly cite a wide variety of foods and sources.
Think It Over Answers will vary depending on the foods eaten. Except for students whose families are strict vegetarians and eat no animal products of any kind, most students will probably cite both plant and animal sources and possibly fungi, protists, or monerans.

DISCOVER • ACTIVITY

Where Did Your Dinner Come From?

1. Across the top of a page, list the different types of foods you ate for dinner last night.
2. Under each item, write the name of the plant, animal, or other organism that is the source of that food. Some foods have more than one source. For example, bread is made from flour (which is made from a plant such as wheat) and yeast (which is a fungus).

Think It Over
Classifying Count the different organisms that contributed to your dinner. How many of your food sources were plants? How many were animals?

GUIDE FOR READING

◆ What energy roles do organisms play in an ecosystem?
◆ How much energy is available at each level of an energy pyramid?

Reading Tip As you read, create a flowchart showing one possible path of energy through an ecosystem.

Pushing off from its perch on an oak tree limb, the kestrel glides over a field dotted with yellow flowers. In the middle of the field, the bird pauses. It hovers above the ground like a giant hummingbird. Despite strong gusts of wind, the bird's head remains steady as it looks for prey. It takes a lot of energy for the kestrel to hover in this way, but from this position it can search the field below for food.

Soon the kestrel spots a mouse munching the ripening seedhead of a blade of grass. Seconds later the kestrel swoops down and grasps the mouse in its talons. The bird carries the mouse back to the tree to feed.

Meanwhile, a lynx spider hides among the petals of a nearby flower. An unsuspecting bee lands on the flower for a sip of nectar. The spider grabs the bee and injects its venom into the bee's body. The venom kills the bee before it can respond with its own deadly sting.

This sunny field is an ecosystem, made up of living and nonliving things that interact with one another. You can see that many interactions in this ecosystem involve eating. The spider eats a bee that eats nectar, while the kestrel eats a mouse that eats grass. Ecologists study such feeding patterns to learn how energy flows within an ecosystem.

Figure 1 Cradled in a gumweed flower, a green lynx spider attacks an unsuspecting bee. These organisms are involved in feeding interactions.

READING STRATEGIES

Reading Tip Point out that energy flow in an ecosystem is usually indicated by drawing an arrow *from* the organism being eaten *to* the organism doing the eating, as shown in Figure 5 on page 47. Let students complete their flowcharts without any further assistance.

Study and Comprehension After students have read about food chains and food webs, have each student write a paragraph describing the food chain shown in Figure 5. They should incorporate the terms *producer, herbivore, carnivore, first-level consumer,* and *second-level consumer.* In a follow-up discussion, ask students to share their paragraphs.

Energy Roles

Do you play an instrument in your school band? If so, you know that each instrument has a role in a piece of music. For instance, the flute may provide the melody, while the drum provides the beat. Although the two instruments are quite different, they both play important roles in creating the band's music. In the same way, each organism has a role in the movement of energy through its ecosystem. This role is part of the organism's niche in the ecosystem. The kestrel's role is different from that of the giant oak tree where it was perched. But all parts of the ecosystem, like all parts of the band, are necessary for the ecosystem to work.

An organism's energy role is determined by how it obtains energy and how it interacts with the other living things in its ecosystem. **An organism's energy role in an ecosystem may be that of a producer, consumer, or decomposer.**

Producers Energy first enters most ecosystems as sunlight. Some organisms, such as plants, algae, and certain microorganisms, are able to capture the energy of sunlight and store it as food energy. As Figure 2 shows, these organisms use the sun's energy to turn water and carbon dioxide into molecules such as sugars and starches. As you recall from Chapter 1, this process is called photosynthesis.

An organism that can make its own food is a **producer.** Producers are the source of all the food in an ecosystem. For example, the grass and oak tree are the producers for the field ecosystem you read about at the beginning of the section.

In a few ecosystems the producers obtain energy from a source other than sunlight. One such ecosystem is found in rocks deep beneath the ground. Since the rocks are never exposed to sunlight, how is energy brought into this ecosystem? Certain bacteria in this ecosystem produce their own food using the energy in a gas, hydrogen sulfide, that is found in their environment.

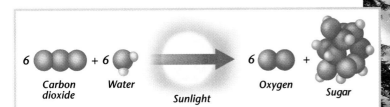

6	+ 6	→	6	+	
Carbon dioxide	Water	Sunlight	Oxygen		Sugar

Figure 2 The sunlight streaming through this redwood forest is the source of energy for the ecosystem. Plants convert the sun's energy to stored food energy through the process of photosynthesis.
Interpreting Diagrams What substances are needed for photosynthesis? What substances are produced?

E ◆ 45

Program Resources

- **Science Explorer Series** *From Bacteria to Plants,* Chapter 4, also discusses photosynthesis.
- ◆ **Teaching Resources** 2-1 Lesson Plan, p. 39; 2-1 Section Summary, p. 40

Media and Technology

 Audiotapes English-Spanish Summary 2-1

Answers to Self-Assessment

Caption Question

Figure 2 The substances needed for photosynthesis are water and carbon dioxide. The substances produced are sugar and oxygen.

2 Facilitate

Energy Roles

Using the Visuals: Figure 2

Focus students' attention on the chemical formula and ask: **What happens during photosynthesis?** *(The plant uses the energy in sunlight to combine carbon dioxide and water to make its own food. Oxygen is also produced.)* **What happens when photosynthetic organisms do not get sunlight?** *(They die because they cannot make food.)* **learning modality: verbal**

Building Inquiry Skills: Predicting

Materials *sheet of cardboard about 30 cm by 40 cm, rock or other heavy object*
Time 10–15 minutes for set-up; 5 minutes for later observation

Give each small group a sheet of cardboard, and take the class outdoors to a grassy area. Have each group select a spot to put the cardboard on the ground, weighting it down with a rock or other heavy object. Ask: **What do you predict will happen to the plants under the cardboard?** *(Accept all responses without comment.)* Let students check under the cardboard each day for a week. Ask: **What happened to the plants?** *(They turned yellow as photosynthesis stopped.)* **What do you predict will happen if you remove the cardboard and allow the plants to receive light again?** *(Accept all responses, then let students test their ideas. The grass will turn green again after a few days.)* **learning modality: visual**

Ongoing Assessment

Drawing Have each student draw a simple diagram to show what happens during photosynthesis and write a brief caption summarizing the process. Students can save their diagrams in their portfolios.

E ◆ 45

Energy Roles, continued

Addressing Naive Conceptions

Many students might think that all ecosystems are dependent on photosynthesis. Ask: **Do you know of any ecosystems in which producers do not depend on sunlight?** Students may be aware of the ecosystem that exists around deep-ocean hydrothermal vents known as "black smokers." If so, ask them to describe this ecosystem. *(Bacteria use chemicals spewed out of the vents to make their own food; the bacteria in turn are food for other organisms such as shrimp and giant clams.)* **learning modality: verbal**

Sharpen your Skills

Observing

Materials *slice of bread, water, sealable plastic bag, tape*

Time 5 minutes for setup

Tips Students will be able to observe changes most easily if they use white sandwich bread.

Expected Outcome After a few days, students should observe mold growing on the bread. Gradually, the mold will cover the bread and cause it to break down.

Extend Have students classify what energy role the mold plays. *(decomposer)* **learning modality: visual**

Real-Life Learning

Ask students: **What examples of herbivores, carnivores, and scavengers have you seen in your own environment?** *(Answers will depend on where students live.)* Suggest that students visit an outdoor area near their homes and sit quietly for a time to observe interactions among organisms. The area can be as simple as a vacant lot or small patch of weeds. Have students list the types of organisms they see, note any feeding behaviors they observe, and classify each organism as an herbivore, carnivore, omnivore, or scavenger. Let students share their lists and classifications in a class discussion. **learning modality: visual**

Figure 3 Consumers are classified by what they eat. **A.** An agile gerenuk stands on its hind legs to reach these leaves. Consumers that eat plants are called herbivores. **B.** Carnivores like this collared lizard eat only animals. **C.** A black vulture is a scavenger, a carnivore that feeds on the remains of dead organisms.

Consumers Other members of the ecosystem cannot make their own food. These organisms depend on the producers for food and energy. An organism that obtains energy by feeding on other organisms is a **consumer.**

Consumers are classified by what they eat. Consumers that eat only plants are called **herbivores.** This term comes from the Latin words *herba,* which means grass or herb, and *vorare,* which means to eat. Some familiar herbivores are caterpillars, cattle, and deer. Consumers that eat only animals are called **carnivores.** This term comes from the same root word *vorare,* plus the Latin word for flesh, *carnis.* Lions, spiders, and snakes are some examples of carnivores. A consumer that eats both plants and animals is called an **omnivore.** The Latin word *omni* means all. Crows, goats, and most humans are examples of omnivores.

Some carnivores are scavengers. A **scavenger** is a carnivore that feeds on the bodies of dead organisms. Scavengers include catfish and vultures.

Decomposers What would happen if there were only producers and consumers in an ecosystem? As the organisms in the ecosystem continued to take water, minerals, and other raw materials from their surroundings, these materials would begin to run low. If these materials were not replaced, new organisms would not be able to grow.

All the organisms in an ecosystem produce waste and eventually die. If these wastes and dead organisms were not somehow removed from the ecosystem, they would pile up until they overwhelmed the living things. Organisms that break down wastes and

Background

Facts and Figures Other important consumers in ecosystems are detritus feeders, or *detritivores.* These organisms, which are sometimes classified as decomposers, are similar to scavengers in that they feed on the remains of dead animals. Like decomposers, they also consume dead plants, leaf litter, animal wastes, and other organic matter.

Detritus feeders such as snails, crabs, and clams are plentiful in aquatic ecosystems. Detritus feeders on land include land snails, beetles, millipedes, and earthworms. Along with microbial decomposers (fungi and bacteria), detritus feeders break down dead organisms and animal wastes.

dead organisms and return the raw materials to the environment are called **decomposers.** Two major groups of decomposers are bacteria and fungi, such as molds and mushrooms. While obtaining energy for their own needs, decomposers return simple molecules to the environment. These molecules can be used again by other organisms.

Checkpoint *What do herbivores and carnivores have in common?*

Food Chains and Food Webs

As you have read, energy enters most ecosystems as sunlight, and is converted into sugar and starch molecules by producers. This energy is transferred to each organism that eats a producer, and then to other organisms that feed on these consumers. The movement of energy through an ecosystem can be shown in diagrams called food chains and food webs.

A **food chain** is a series of events in which one organism eats another and obtains energy. You can follow one food chain from the field ecosystem below. The first organism in a food chain is always a producer, such as the grass in the field. The second organism is a consumer that eats the producer, and is called a first-level consumer. The mouse is a first-level consumer. Next, a second-level consumer eats the first-level consumer. The second-level consumer in this example is the kestrel.

A food chain shows one possible path along which energy can move through an ecosystem. But just as you do not eat the same thing every day, neither do most other organisms. Most producers and consumers are part of many food chains. A more realistic way to show the flow of energy through an ecosystem is a food web. A **food web** consists of the many overlapping food chains in an ecosystem.

Figure 4 A cluster of honey mushrooms grows among dead leaves. Mushrooms are familiar decomposers.

Figure 5 These organisms make up one food chain in a field ecosystem.
Classifying Which organism shown is acting as an herbivore? Which is a carnivore?

Kestrel
(Second-level consumer)

Grass
(Producer)

Mouse
(First-level consumer)

Chapter 2 **E ◆ 47**

Answers to Self-Assessment

Caption Question

Figure 5 The mouse is acting as an herbivore, and the kestrel is a carnivore.

Checkpoint

Herbivores and carnivores are similar in that both are consumers; they cannot make their own food but must obtain food by eating other organisms.

E ◆ 47

Food Chains and Food Webs, continued

EXPLORING

a Food Web

Call on different students in turn to name the organisms in each food chain shown in the food web, starting with a producer and ending with the top consumer, the fox. As students identify each chain, make a tally mark on the board. When students have identified all the chains, ask: **With just this one top consumer, the fox, how many food chains are in the web?** *(at least 6)* **What are the producers in this food web?** *(grasses, trees, and other plants)* **What are the first- level consumers?** *(rabbit, mouse, grasshopper, and termite)* **What are the second-level consumers?** *(mouse, garter snake, shrew, fox, and woodpecker)* **What are the third-level consumers?** *(garter snake and fox)* **How can the mouse be both a first- and second-level consumer?** *(It's an omnivore that eats both plants and insects.)* **How do the decomposers fit into this food web?** *(Their energy needs are met by consuming the wastes and remains of the other organisms in this food web, and, in turn, they supply raw materials needed by the producers.)* **learning modality: visual**

Including All Students

To help students who are having difficulty understanding the concept of a food web, challenge them to make two or three food-chain diagrams for any ecosystem. Then have students combine their food chains to create a food web. Encourage students to use the same color coding as in *Exploring a Food Web* to indicate the various levels of consumers. Have students identify where the individual food chains overlap in the food web. **learning modality: visual**

48 ◆ E

EXPLORING *a Food Web*

A food web consists of many inter-connected food chains. Trace the path of energy through the producers, consumers, and decomposers.

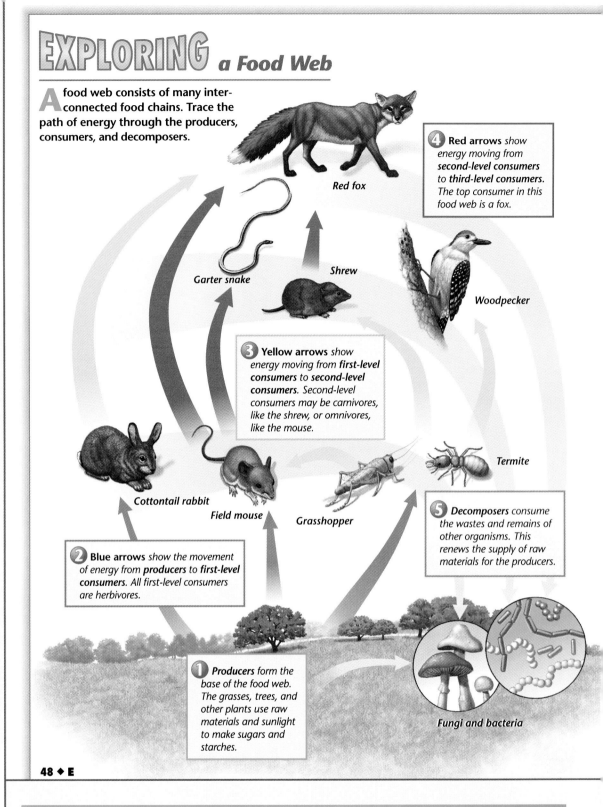

4 **Red arrows** *show energy moving from* ***second-level consumers*** *to* ***third-level consumers.*** *The top consumer in this food web is a fox.*

Red fox

Garter snake

Shrew

Woodpecker

3 **Yellow arrows** *show energy moving from* ***first-level consumers*** *to* ***second-level consumers***. *Second-level consumers may be carnivores, like the shrew, or omnivores, like the mouse.*

Cottontail rabbit

Field mouse

Grasshopper

Termite

5 **Decomposers** *consume the wastes and remains of other organisms. This renews the supply of raw materials for the producers.*

2 **Blue arrows** *show the movement of energy from* ***producers*** *to* ***first-level consumers***. *All first-level consumers are herbivores.*

1 **Producers** *form the base of the food web. The grasses, trees, and other plants use raw materials and sunlight to make sugars and starches.*

Fungi and bacteria

48 ◆ E

History of Science Unlike energy, toxic substances become more concentrated as they move through a food web. This process, called *biological magnification,* can have dire results. A famous example occurred in Borneo when the World Health Organization sprayed DDT to control malaria-carrying mosquitoes. The DDT also killed wasps that preyed on caterpillars. The caterpillars increased rapidly and devoured the thatched roofs of homes, causing them to collapse.

When more DDT was sprayed indoors to kill house flies, gecko lizards that ate flies were poisoned. The dying lizards in turn were eaten by house cats, who also died. The rat population then increased dramatically, attacking human food supplies and threatening an outbreak of bubonic plague. The government had to parachute healthy cats into villages to control the rats.

In *Exploring a Food Web* on the facing page, you can trace the many food chains in a woodland ecosystem. Note that an organism may play more than one role in an ecosystem. For example, an omnivore such as the mouse is a first-level consumer when it eats grass. But when the mouse eats a grasshopper, it is a second-level consumer.

☑ *Checkpoint* *What are the organisms in one food chain shown in the food web on the facing page?*

Energy Pyramids

When an organism in an ecosystem eats, it obtains energy. The organism uses some of this energy to move, grow, reproduce, and carry out other life activities. This means that only some of the energy will be available to the next organism in the food web.

A diagram called an **energy pyramid** shows the amount of energy that moves from one feeding level to another in a food web. The organisms at each level use some of the energy to carry out their life processes. **The most energy is available at the producer level. At each level in the pyramid, there is less available energy than at the level below.** An energy pyramid gets its name from the shape of the diagram—wider at the base and narrower at the top, resembling a pyramid.

In general, only about 10 percent of the energy at one level of a food web is transferred to the next, higher, level. The other

Figure 6 Organisms use energy to carry out their life activities. A lioness uses energy to chase her zebra prey. The zebras use energy to flee.

3 Assess

Section 1 Review Answers

1. *Producers* use energy, usually in the form of sunlight, to make their own food. *Consumers* obtain energy by eating other living organisms. *Decomposers* obtain energy by breaking down wastes and the remains of dead organisms.
2. Each organism uses 90 percent of the energy for its own life processes. Only 10 percent is available to the next-level consumer.
3. *Herbivores* eat only plants. *Carnivores* eat only animals. *Omnivores* eat both plants and animals. *Scavengers* eat the remains of dead organisms.
4. Sunlight is the energy source for most ecosystems. It is used by organisms to carry out photosynthesis.
5. Most producers and consumers are part of many overlapping food chains.

Check Your Progress   CHAPTER PROJECT 2

When students prepare their written plans, instruct them to use this format: a statement of the hypothesis, a list of materials, a step-by-step procedure, and a data table for recording results. Review students' plans to make sure they will keep all variables the same for both chambers except for the variable being tested with the second chamber. Also review students' planned data tables.

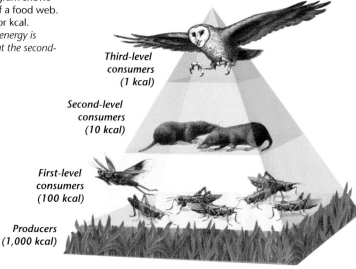

Figure 7 This energy pyramid diagram shows the energy available at each level of a food web. Energy is measured in kilocalories, or kcal. *Calculating* How many times more energy is available at the producer level than at the second-level consumer level?

Third-level consumers (1 kcal)

Second-level consumers (10 kcal)

First-level consumers (100 kcal)

Producers (1,000 kcal)

90 percent of the energy is used for the organism's life processes or is lost as heat to the environment. Because of this, most food webs only have three or four feeding levels. Since 90 percent of the energy is lost at each step, there is not enough energy to support many feeding levels.

But the organisms at higher feeding levels of an energy pyramid do not necessarily require less energy to live than organisms at lower levels. Since so much energy is lost at each level, the amount of energy in the producer level limits the number of consumers the ecosystem can support. As a result, there usually are few organisms at the highest level in a food web.

Section 1 Review

1. Name the three energy roles of organisms in an ecosystem. How does each type of organism obtain energy?
2. How does the amount of available energy change from one level of an energy pyramid to the next level up?
3. Name and define the four types of consumers.
4. What is the source of energy for most ecosystems?
5. **Thinking Critically Making Generalizations** Why are food webs a more realistic way of portraying ecosystems than food chains?

Check Your Progress   CHAPTER PROJECT 2

By now you should have constructed your compost chambers and chosen a variable to investigate. Design your plan for observing the effect of this variable on the decomposition process. Submit your plan to your teacher for approval. (*Hint:* As part of your plan, include how you will collect data to measure decomposition in your compost chambers.)

Performance Assessment

Drawing Have each student draw a food chain of his or her own choice and label each organism to show *(1)* its energy role, *(2)* whether each consumer is an herbivore, carnivore, omnivore, or scavenger, and *(3)* the percentage of energy available at each level in the food chain.

Program Resources

◆ **Teaching Resources** 2-1 Review and Reinforce, p. 41; 2-1 Enrich, p. 42
◆ **Integrated Science Laboratory Manual** E-2 "Ecosystem Food Chains"

Media and Technology

Interactive Student Tutorial CD-ROM E-2

Answers to Self-Assessment

Caption Question
Figure 7 There is 100 times as much energy available at the producer level as at the second-level consumer level.

SECTION 2 Cycles of Matter

DISCOVER

Are You Part of a Cycle?

1. Hold a small mirror a few centimeters from your mouth.
2. Exhale onto the mirror.
3. Observe the surface of the mirror.

Think It Over

Inferring What is the substance that forms on the mirror? Where did this substance come from?

A pile of crumpled cars is ready for loading into a giant compactor. Junkyard workers have already removed many of the cars' parts. The aluminum and copper pieces were removed so that they could be recycled, or used again. Now a recycling plant will reclaim the steel in the bodies of the cars. Earth has a limited supply of aluminum, copper, and the iron needed to make steel. Recycling old cars is one way to provide a new supply of these materials.

Recycling Matter

The way matter is recycled in ecosystems is similar to the way the metal in old cars is recycled. Like the supply of metal for building cars, the supply of matter in an ecosystem is limited. If matter could not be recycled, ecosystems would quickly run out of the raw materials necessary for life.

Energy, on the other hand, is not recycled. You must constantly supply a car with energy in the form of gasoline. Ecosystems must also be constantly supplied with energy, usually in the form of sunlight. Gasoline and the sun's energy cannot be recycled—they must be constantly supplied.

As you read in Section 1, energy enters an ecosystem and moves from the producers to the consumers to the decomposers. In contrast, matter cycles through an ecosystem over and over. Matter in an ecosystem includes water, oxygen, carbon, nitrogen, and many other substances. To understand how these substances cycle through an ecosystem, you need to know a few basic terms that describe the structure of matter. Matter is made

GUIDE FOR READING

◆ What three major processes make up the water cycle?

◆ How is carbon dioxide used by producers?

Reading Tip As you read, use the section headings to make an outline of the section.

Cars awaiting recycling at a Utah plant ▼

E ◆ 51

INTEGRATING CHEMISTRY

SECTION 2 Cycles of Matter

Objectives

After completing the lesson, students will be able to
◆ describe the three major processes that make up the water cycle;
◆ describe the nitrogen cycle and the carbon and oxygen cycles.

Key Terms water cycle, evaporation, condensation, precipitation, nitrogen fixation, nodules

1 Engage/Explore

Activating Prior Knowledge

Ask students: **What is a cycle?** *(A series of things that repeat over and over again)* **What are some examples of cycles?** *(Seasons of the year, days of the week, life cycles of plants and animals, and so forth)*

DISCOVER

Skills Focus inferring
Materials *small mirror*
Time 5 minutes
Tips If the weather is very warm and humid when students do this activity, moisture may not condense on the mirror. In this case, you can cool the mirrors in a refrigerator for a short time beforehand.
Expected Outcome As water vapor from the students' breath cools, tiny droplets of liquid water will condense on the mirrors.
Think It Over Water; it came from water vapor in the students' exhaled breath.

READING STRATEGIES

Reading Tip Students' outlines should include the heads *Recycling Matter, The Water Cycle, The Carbon and Oxygen Cycles* and *The Nitrogen Cycle.* They may use the purple subheadings under *The Water Cycle* and *The Nitrogen Cycle* as subheads in their outlines.

Program Resources

◆ **Teaching Resources** 2-2 Lesson Plan, p. 43; 2-2 Section Summary, p. 44
◆ **Interdisciplinary Exploration Series** "Where River Meets Sea," pp. 15–16

Media and Technology

 Audiotapes English-Spanish Summary 2-2

2 Facilitate

Recycling Matter

Including All Students

To reinforce the role of decomposers for students who need more help, ask: **What role do decomposers play in recycling matter?** *(They break down living organisms' wastes and dead organisms' remains into simple molecules and return the molecules to the environment so they can be used again.)* **learning modality: verbal**

The Water Cycle

Sharpen your Skills

Developing Hypotheses

Time 5 minutes

Tips Have students do **ACTIVITY** this activity after they have read the section about the water cycle.

Expected Outcome The water droplets on the cold window condensed from the water vapor that evaporated from the boiling water.

Extend Have students draw and label a simple diagram, similar to Figure 8, showing the water cycle operating in this example. For precipitation, students could show tiny water droplets joining to form larger drops that trickle down the window. **learning modality: logical/mathematical**

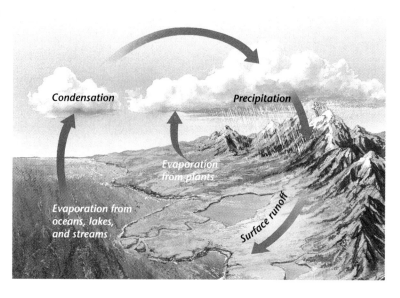

Figure 8 In the water cycle, water moves continuously from Earth's surface to the atmosphere and back. *Interpreting Diagrams In which step of the water cycle does water return to Earth's surface?*

Condensation · Precipitation · Evaporation from plants · Evaporation from oceans, lakes, and streams · Surface runoff

Sharpen your Skills

Developing Hypotheses

You're having cocoa at a **ACTIVITY** friend's house on a cold, rainy day. As your friend boils some water, you notice that a window next to the stove is covered with water droplets. Your friend thinks the window is leaking. Using what you know about the water cycle, can you propose another explanation for the water droplets on the window?

up of tiny particles called atoms. Combinations of two or more atoms chemically bonded together are called molecules. For example, a molecule of water consists of two hydrogen atoms bonded to one oxygen atom. In this section, you will learn about some of the most important cycles of matter: the water cycle, the carbon and oxygen cycles, and the nitrogen cycle.

The Water Cycle

How could you determine whether life has ever existed on another planet in the solar system? One piece of evidence scientists look for is the presence of water. This is because water is the most common compound in all living cells on Earth. Water is necessary for life as we know it.

Water is recycled through the water cycle. The **water cycle** is the continuous process by which water moves from Earth's surface to the atmosphere and back. **The processes of evaporation, condensation, and precipitation make up the water cycle.** As you read about these processes, follow the cycle in Figure 8.

Evaporation The process by which molecules of liquid water absorb energy and change to the gas state is called **evaporation.** In the water cycle liquid water evaporates from Earth's surface and forms water vapor, a gas, in the atmosphere. Most water evaporates from the surfaces of oceans and lakes. The energy for evaporation comes from the sun.

Background

Integrating Science In 1998, new photographs of Jupiter's moon Europa revealed shapes and contours that many scientists believe could only be created by liquid water. Pictures taken by the *Voyager* and *Galileo* spacecraft have suggested that a giant ocean lies beneath Europa's permanent layer of ice. Further evidence of water on Europa may come from a NASA mission scheduled for launch in 2003.

Also in 1998, space scientists studying photographs taken by the *Mars Global Surveyor* reported finding a possible ice-covered lake on Mars. Scientists hypothesize that the lake may be similar to lakes in Antarctica where algae and other organisms thrive under a thick layer of ice.

Some water is also given off by living things. For example, plants take in water through their roots and release water vapor from their leaves. You take in water when you drink and eat. You release liquid water in your wastes and water vapor when you exhale.

Condensation What happens next to the water vapor in the atmosphere? As the water vapor rises higher in the atmosphere, it cools down. When it cools to a certain temperature the vapor turns back into tiny drops of liquid water. The process by which a gas changes to a liquid is called **condensation.** The water droplets collect around particles of dust in the air, eventually forming clouds like those in Figure 8.

Precipitation As more water vapor condenses, the drops of water in the cloud grow larger and heavier. Eventually the heavy drops fall back to Earth as a form of **precipitation**—rain, snow, sleet, or hail. Most precipitation falls back into oceans or lakes. The precipitation that falls on land may soak into the soil and become groundwater. Or the precipitation may run off the land, ultimately flowing into a river or ocean once again.

✓ Checkpoint *What change of state occurs when water from the surface of the ocean enters the atmosphere as water vapor?*

The Carbon and Oxygen Cycles

Two other chemicals necessary for life are carbon and oxygen. The processes by which they are recycled are linked together, as shown in Figure 9. Carbon is the building block for the matter that makes up the bodies of living things. It is present in the atmosphere in the gas carbon dioxide. Producers take in carbon dioxide from

Figure 9 This scene shows how the carbon and oxygen cycles are linked together. Producers use carbon dioxide to carry out photosynthesis. In this process, carbon is used to create sugar molecules such as those found in apples. The producers release oxygen, which is then used by other organisms. These organisms take in carbon in food and release it in the form of carbon dioxide again.

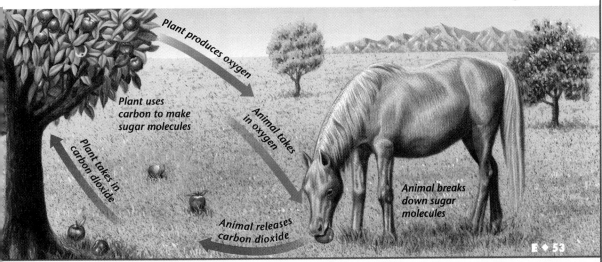

Plant produces oxygen

Plant uses carbon to make sugar molecules

Plant takes in carbon dioxide

Animal takes in oxygen

Animal breaks down sugar molecules

Animal releases carbon dioxide

E ◆ 53

Answers to Self-Assessment

Caption Question

Figure 8 Precipitation

✓ Checkpoint

Evaporation (a liquid changes into a gas)

The Nitrogen Cycle

Including All Students

Since students normally think of the word *fixed* as meaning "repaired," they may be confused by the word's other usage in the text. Suggest that they consult dictionaries to find other definitions of *fix* and *fixed*. Then have students suggest a sample sentence illustrating each other meaning—for example, "He looked at me with a fixed stare," "I'll fix lunch now," "I think the game was fixed," and "I'm in a fix!"
limited English proficiency

Using the Visuals: Figure 10

Materials *white and blue index cards, tape*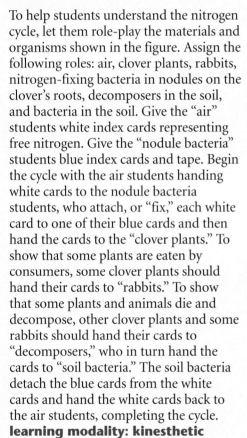
Time 10–15 minutes

To help students understand the nitrogen cycle, let them role-play the materials and organisms shown in the figure. Assign the following roles: air, clover plants, rabbits, nitrogen-fixing bacteria in nodules on the clover's roots, decomposers in the soil, and bacteria in the soil. Give the "air" students white index cards representing free nitrogen. Give the "nodule bacteria" students blue index cards and tape. Begin the cycle with the air students handing white cards to the nodule bacteria students, who attach, or "fix," each white card to one of their blue cards and then hand the cards to the "clover plants." To show that some plants are eaten by consumers, some clover plants should hand their cards to "rabbits." To show that some plants and animals die and decompose, other clover plants and some rabbits should hand their cards to "decomposers," who in turn hand the cards to "soil bacteria." The soil bacteria detach the blue cards from the white cards and hand the white cards back to the air students, completing the cycle.
learning modality: kinesthetic

the atmosphere during photosynthesis. **In this process, the producers use carbon from the carbon dioxide to produce other carbon-containing molecules.** These molecules include sugars and starches. To obtain energy from these molecules, consumers break them down into simpler molecules. Consumers release water and carbon dioxide as waste products.

At the same time, oxygen is also cycling through the ecosystem. Producers release oxygen as a result of photosynthesis. Other organisms take in oxygen from the atmosphere and use it in their life processes.

☑ *Checkpoint* How is oxygen returned to the environment?

The Nitrogen Cycle

Like carbon, nitrogen is a necessary building block in the matter that makes up living things. Since the air around you is about 78 percent nitrogen gas, you might think that it would be easy for living things to obtain nitrogen. However, most organisms cannot use the nitrogen gas in the air. Nitrogen gas is called "free" nitrogen, meaning it is not combined with other kinds of atoms. Most organisms can use nitrogen only once it has been "fixed," or combined with other elements to form nitrogen-containing compounds. You can follow this process in Figure 10 below.

Figure 10 In the nitrogen cycle, nitrogen moves from the air to the soil, into living things, and back into the air.
Interpreting Diagrams How do consumers obtain nitrogen?

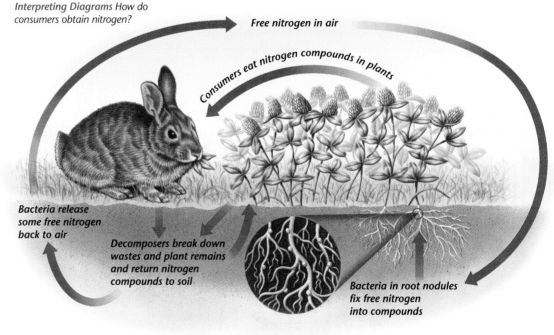

Free nitrogen in air

Consumers eat nitrogen compounds in plants

Bacteria release some free nitrogen back to air

Decomposers break down wastes and plant remains and return nitrogen compounds to soil

Bacteria in root nodules fix free nitrogen into compounds

Nitrogen Fixation The process of changing free nitrogen gas into a usable form of nitrogen is called **nitrogen fixation.** Most nitrogen fixation is performed by certain kinds of bacteria. Some of these bacteria live in bumps called **nodules** (NAHJ oolz) on the roots of certain plants. These plants, known as legumes, include clover, beans, peas, alfalfa, and peanuts.

The relationship between the bacteria and the legumes is an example of mutualism. As you recall from Chapter 1, a symbiotic relationship in which both species benefit is called mutualism. Both the bacteria and the plant benefit from this relationship: The bacteria have a place to live, and the plant is supplied with nitrogen in a usable form.

 INTEGRATING TECHNOLOGY Many farmers make use of the nitrogen-fixing bacteria in legumes to enrich their fields. Every few years, a farmer may plant a legume such as alfalfa in a field. The bacteria in the alfalfa roots build up a new supply of nitrogen compounds in the soil. The following year, the new crops planted in the field benefit from the improved soil.

Return of Nitrogen to the Environment Once the nitrogen has been fixed into chemical compounds, it can be used by organisms to build proteins and other complex substances. Decomposers break down these complex compounds in animal wastes and in the bodies of dead organisms. This returns simple nitrogen compounds to the soil. Nitrogen can cycle from the soil to producers and consumers many times. At some point, however, bacteria break down the nitrogen compounds completely. These bacteria release free nitrogen back into the air. Then the cycle starts again.

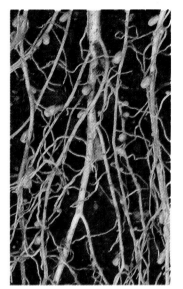

Figure 11 Lumpy nodules are clearly visible on the roots of this clover plant. Bacteria inside the nodules carry out nitrogen fixation.

Section 2 Review

1. Name and define the three major processes that occur during the water cycle.
2. Explain the role of plants in the carbon cycle.
3. How is nitrogen fixation a necessary part of the nitrogen cycle?
4. Where do nitrogen-fixing bacteria live?
5. **Thinking Critically Comparing and Contrasting** Explain how the movement of matter through an ecosystem is different than the movement of energy through an ecosystem.

Check Your Progress CHAPTER PROJECT 2
Once your teacher has approved your plan, place the waste into your compost chambers. Record your hypothesis about the effect of the variable you are investigating. Observe the two containers daily. (*Hint:* If there are no signs of decomposition after several days, you may wish to stir the contents of each chamber. Stirring allows more oxygen to enter the mixture.)

Program Resources

◆ **Teaching Resources** 2-2 Review and Reinforce, p. 45; 2-2 Enrich, p. 46

Media and Technology

Interactive Student Tutorial CD-ROM E-2

Transparencies "The Nitrogen Cycle," Transparency 6

Answers to Self-Assessment

☑ **Checkpoint**
Plants and other producers release oxygen as a byproduct of photosynthesis.

Caption Question
Figure 10 They eat nitrogen compounds in plants.

 Integrating Technology

Ask students: **What happens to nitrogen that is fixed in plant roots?** (*The plants take it in and use it for their life processes.*) **How do consumers get the nitrogen?** (*By eating the plants*) **If the plants aren't eaten, what happens to the nitrogen?** (*It enters the soil when the plants die and decompose.*) **learning modality: logical/mathematical**

3 Assess

Section 2 Review Answers
1. *Evaporation:* Liquid water changes into water vapor. *Condensation:* Water vapor cools and changes into liquid water. *Precipitation:* Drops of water fall as rain, snow, sleet, or hail.
2. Plants take in carbon dioxide and produce carbon-containing molecules through photosynthesis.
3. Most organisms cannot use free nitrogen in the atmosphere. Nitrogen fixation combines free nitrogen with other elements to form compounds that organisms can use.
4. They live in the nodules on the roots of legumes.
5. Matter can be recycled over and over again. In contrast, once energy has moved from the producers to the consumers and then to the decomposers, it cannot be recycled. A new supply must be "captured" by the producers.

Check Your Progress CHAPTER PROJECT 2
Provide compost materials. Remind students to put the same amount of waste in both chambers. CAUTION: *As students do their daily observations, make sure those who are allergic to molds do not sniff or handle the chambers' contents. Remind students to wash their hands after each observation.*

Performance Assessment

Skills Check Have students explain various phrases that you point out in each cycle diagram in this section.

Objectives

After completing the lesson, students will be able to
◆ describe means by which organisms disperse;
◆ identify the factors that limit the distribution of a species.

Key Terms biogeography, continental drift, dispersal, native species, exotic species, climate

1 Engage/Explore

Activating Prior Knowledge

Ask students: **What are some reasons that animals move from one place to another?** (*Seasonal migration, overpopulation or too much competition in the original area, need for food or water, and so forth*)

········ DISCOVER ········

Skills Focus predicting
Materials *shallow pan,* ACTIVITY
corn kernels, possible materials to move corn, such as water, straw, and tape
Time 10–15 minutes
Tips Students may have their own ideas about materials to use besides those you have provided.
Expected Outcome Students will find various ways to move the kernels—by pouring water next to them, blowing at them through a straw, picking them up with a piece of tape, and so forth.
Think It Over Based on the results of this activity, students might suggest that seeds are moved by wind, by moving water, and by being caught on an animal's fur or a person's clothing.

SECTION 3 Biogeography

DISCOVER ···················· ACTIVITY ···

How Can You Move a Seed?

1. Place a few corn kernels at one end of a shallow pan.
2. Make a list of ways you could move the kernels to the other side of the pan. You may use any of the simple materials your teacher has provided.
3. Now try each method. Record whether or not each was successful in moving the kernels across the pan.

Think It Over
Predicting How might seeds be moved from place to place on Earth?

GUIDE FOR READING

◆ How does dispersal of organisms occur?
◆ What factors can limit the distribution of a species?

Reading Tip As you read, look for reasons why organisms live in certain places in the world. Make a list of these reasons.

◀ Australian wallaby

Imagine how European explorers must have felt when they saw the continent of Australia for the first time. Instead of familiar grazing animals such as horses and deer, they saw what looked like giant rabbits with long tails. Peering into the branches of eucalyptus trees, these explorers saw bearlike koalas. And who could have dreamed up an egg-laying animal with a beaver's tail, a duck's bill, and a thick coat of fur? You can see why people who heard the first descriptions of the platypus accused the explorers of lying!

Ecologists had many questions about the plants and animals of Australia. Why had no one ever seen a kangaroo, a eucalyptus tree, or a koala in Europe? Why were there no reindeer, camels, or gorillas in Australia?

Different species live in different parts of the world. The study of where organisms live is called **biogeography.** The word *biogeography* is made up of three Greek word roots: *bio,* meaning "life"; *geo,* meaning "Earth"; and *graph,* meaning "description." Together, these root words tell what biogeographers do—they describe where living things are found on Earth.

Continental Drift

INTEGRATING EARTH SCIENCE In addition to studying where species live today, biogeographers also study how these species spread into different parts of the world. One factor that has affected how species are distributed is the motion of Earth's continents. The continents are huge blocks of solid rock floating on a layer of hot, dense liquid. The very slow motion of the continents is called **continental drift.**

56 ◆ E

READING STRATEGIES

Reading Tip Students' lists should include reasons such as the movement of Earth's continents, dispersal by wind, water, and other organisms, and barriers that prevent them from moving into certain other areas.

Concept Mapping After students read this section, have each draw a concept map of the section content. The term *Dispersal* should be labeled in the top circle, *Means of Dispersal* and *Limits to Dispersal* in the two circles below it, the specific methods and limits in the third row of circles, and examples of each method and limit in the bottom row.

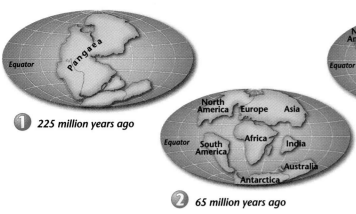

1 225 million years ago

2 65 million years ago

3 Present day

Figure 12 The continents have drifted far from their positions 225 million years ago. Their movement is one factor affecting the distribution of organisms.

Figure 12 shows how much the continents have moved. About 225 million years ago, all the continents were touching each other. But after millions of years of slow drifting, they have moved apart. Looking at the globe today, it is hard to believe that at one time India was next to Antarctica, or that Europe and North America once were connected.

The movement of the continents has had a great impact on the distribution of species. Consider Australia, for example. Millions of years ago Australia drifted apart from the other land masses. Organisms from other parts of the world could not reach the isolated island. Kangaroos, koalas, and other unique species developed in this isolation.

Means of Dispersal

The movement of organisms from one place to another is called **dispersal.** Organisms may be dispersed in several different ways. **Dispersal can be caused by wind, water, or living things, including humans.**

Wind and Water Many animals move into new areas by simply walking, swimming, or flying. But plants and small organisms need assistance to move from place to place. Wind provides a means of dispersal for seeds, the spores of fungi, tiny spiders, and many other small, light organisms. Similarly, water transports objects that float, such as coconuts and leaves. Insects and small animals may get a free ride to a new home on top of these floating rafts.

Other Living Things Organisms may also be dispersed by other living things. For example, a goldfinch may eat seeds in one area and deposit them elsewhere in its wastes. A duck may carry algae or fish eggs on its feet from pond to pond. And if your dog or cat has ever come home covered with sticky plant burs, you know another way seeds can get around.

Figure 13 The stiff brown pods of the milkweed plant contain seeds fringed with silky threads.
Inferring By what means of dispersal are milkweed seeds spread?

Chapter 2 **E ◆ 57**

Answers to Self-Assessment

Caption Question

Figure 13 By wind

Program Resources

◆ **Science Explorer Series** *Inside Earth*, Chapter 1, describes continental drift.
◆ **Teaching Resources** 2-3 Lesson Plan, p. 47; 2-3 Section Summary, p. 48

2 Facilitate

Continental Drift

Integrating Earth Science

Materials *world outline map, scissors*
Time 15 minutes

Give each student a copy of a world outline map. Invite students to cut out the continents and arrange them in the positions shown in the first map in Figure 12. Then have students move the continents apart until they are in the locations shown in the second map. Ask: **Where would organisms still be able to move freely from one continent to another?** *(Between North America and Europe/Asia and between Antarctica and Australia)* **Which continents became separated from the others?** *(South America, Africa, India, and Australia/ Antarctica)* Have students move the continents to their present locations in the third map. **What happened to India as continental drift continued?** *(It joined Europe/Asia.)* **What do you think happened to organisms on the continents that remained separated?** *(They evolved into unique species found nowhere else in the world.)* **learning modality: kinesthetic**

Means of Dispersal

Including All Students

If students did the Discover activity at the beginning of this section, connect the activity to the section's content for students who need extra help by asking: **Which of these dispersal methods did you model when you moved the corn kernels?** *(Answers will vary, though most will have modeled all of the methods of dispersal mentioned in the text.)* **learning modality: logical/ mathematical**

Ongoing Assessment

Oral Presentation Call on students at random to describe how wind, water, and living things help disperse organisms.

Means of Dispersal, continued

Social Studies CONNECTION

Have students brainstorm a list of other crops to investigate, so a wide variety of crops are reported on. Provide almanacs and other sources for students' research.

In Your Journal Encourage students to share their findings with the class in brief oral reports or posters. **learning modality: verbal**

Limits to Dispersal

Building Inquiry Skills: Comparing and Contrasting

Ask students: **Do any of the factors that limit dispersal also limit a population's size? Which ones?** (*Students can compare these factors with those described in Chapter 1, on pages 27–28. Competition limits both dispersal and population size. Physical barriers are also a common factor, since barriers can limit the amount of space available to a population. Seasonal changes, an aspect of climate, also limit some populations' sizes, but students should not equate weather conditions and climate.*) **learning modality: logical/mathematical**

Integrating Earth Science

For students who are having difficulty with the difference between weather and climate, give examples of climate and weather conditions, and ask students to identify each as an example of climate or weather. For example: **It's very cold out today.** (*weather*) **Our part of the country usually has cold winters.** (*climate*) **We don't get much rain in the summer.** (*climate*) **The meteorologist predicts rain tonight.** (*weather*) **learning modality: verbal**

Figure 14 Clumps of purple loosestrife line the banks of a Massachusetts river. Loosestrife is an exotic species that has thrived in its new home, often crowding out native species.

Humans are important to the dispersal of other species. As people move around the globe, they take plants, animals, and other organisms with them. Sometimes this is intentional, such as when people bring horses to a new settlement. Sometimes it is unintentional, such as when someone carries a parasite into a country.

Species that have naturally evolved in an area are referred to as **native species.** When an organism is carried into a new location by people, it is referred to as an **exotic species.** Some exotic species are so common in their new environment that people think of them as native. For example, you probably know the dandelion, one of the most common flowering plants in North America. But the dandelion is not a native species. It was brought by colonists who valued its leaves for eating and for tea for the sick.

✓ Checkpoint *How can humans disperse a species?*

Limits to Dispersal

With all these means of dispersal, you might expect to find the same organisms everywhere in the world. Of course, that's not so. Why not? What determines the limits of a species' distribution? **Three factors that limit dispersal of a species are physical barriers, competition, and climate.**

Physical Barriers Barriers such as water, mountains, and deserts are hard to cross. These features can limit the movement of organisms. For example, once Australia became separated from the other continents, the ocean acted as a barrier to dispersal. Organisms could not easily move to or from Australia.

Competition When an organism enters a new area, it must compete for resources with the species already there. To survive, the organism must find a unique niche. If the existing species are thriving, they may outcompete the new species. In this case competition is a barrier to dispersal. Sometimes, however, the new species is more successful than the existing species. The native species may be displaced.

Social Studies CONNECTION

Many important crops are actually exotic species. When settlers in new lands brought crops with them from their old homes, they caused the dispersal of these species. Some examples of crops dispersed by people are peanuts, potatoes, cotton, corn, and rice.

In Your Journal

Choose a crop to investigate. Research your crop to learn where it is a native species and how it spread to different parts of the world. In what conditions does it grow well? (*Hint*: Almanacs and encyclopedias are good sources of this information.)

Background

Facts and Figures Ecologists estimate that there are 6,000 exotic species in the United States. While most are harmless, some of these exotic species pose a significant threat to native species. Ecologists search for ways to control harmful invaders without causing other environmental problems. As one example, Eurasian watermilfoil, a freshwater weed, entered the United States as an aquarium decoration, then escaped and spread through waterways nationwide. Lakes in Michigan and Massachusetts that were being overgrown with watermilfoil have been stocked with thousands of water weevils, one of the few organisms that attack the plant. Within months the weevils had appeared to noticeably damage the watermilfoil.

Climate The typical weather pattern in an

 INTEGRATING EARTH SCIENCE area over a long period of time is the area's **climate.** Climate is different from weather, which is the day-to-day conditions in an area. Climate is largely determined by temperature and precipitation.

Differences in climate can be a barrier to dispersal. For example, conditions at the top of the mountain shown in Figure 15 are very different from those at the base. The base is warm and dry. Low shrubs and cactuses grow there. Just up the mountain, mostly grasses grow. Higher up the mountain, the climate becomes cooler and wetter. Larger trees such as pines, oaks, and firs can grow. The squirrel in the closeup lives in this region. Climate differences act as a barrier that keeps the squirrel species from dispersing down or up the mountain. Near the top of the mountain, it is very cold and windy. Small alpine wildflowers and mosses grow best in this region.

Places with similar climates tend to have similar niches for species to occupy. For example, most continents have a large area of flat, grassy plains. The organisms that occupy the niche of "large, grazing mammal" on each continent have some similarities. In North America, the large, grazing mammals of the grasslands are bison; in Africa, they are wildebeests and antelopes; in Australia, they are kangaroos.

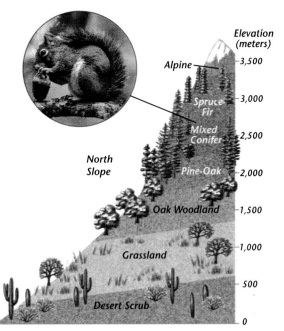

Figure 15 Climate conditions change at different elevations on this mountainside. These conditions determine the distribution of species on the mountain. Each zone begins at a lower elevation on the north slope of the mountain, which is cooler than the south slope.

Section 3 Review

1. List three ways that species can disperse.
2. Explain how mountain ranges and climate can each limit a species' distribution.
3. What is biogeography?
4. Give an example of a physical barrier. How might it affect where species are found?
5. **Thinking Critically Predicting** If an exotic insect species were introduced to your area, do you think it would be easy or difficult to eliminate the species? Give reasons to support your answer.

Science at Home

Take an adult family member on a seed hunt. When you spot a new seed, place a plastic bag over your hand. Pick up the seed with the bag and then turn the bag inside out to hold the seed. When you get home, observe the seeds and compare them to one another. Based on your observations, classify the seeds by their methods of dispersal. Staple the bags to a sheet of heavy paper in the groups in which you have classified them.

Program Resources

- **Teaching Resources** 2-3 Review and Reinforce, p. 49; 2-3 Enrich, p. 50
- **Interdisciplinary Exploration Series** "Where River Meets Sea," pp. 28–29

Media and Technology

Interactive Student Tutorial CD-ROM E-2

Answers to Self-Assessment

☑ *Checkpoint*

They take plants, animals, and other organisms with them as they move, sometimes intentionally and sometimes unintentionally.

3 Assess

Section 3 Review Answers

1. Wind, water, other organisms
2. Mountains ranges may be impossible or difficult for a species to cross. A species that is adapted for life in one climate could not survive in a climate with different temperatures and precipitation amounts.
3. The study of where organisms live
4. Physical barriers include water, mountains, deserts, and canyons. *Sample answer:* A species that requires a constant supply of water would not be able to disperse by crossing a large desert.
5. Accept divergent responses so long as students support their answers with well-reasoned explanations. Some students may say that the exotic species might be difficult to eliminate if there are few or no natural competitors, predators, or parasites in the new environment. Others may say exotic species that are not well adapted to the new environment might be eliminated easily.

Science at Home

Materials *small plastic bags, stapler, sheet of heavy paper, hand lens (optional)* **ACTIVITY**

Tips Before students do the activity at home, discuss seed characteristics that would allow them to identify each seed's method of dispersal—fluffy structures for dispersal by wind, for example, and sharp stickers for dispersal by other organisms. Encourage students to bring the classified seeds to class for discussion and display.

Performance Assessment

Writing Have each student define climate in his or her own words, then explain how climate conditions limit a species' habitat.

Biomes in Miniature

NOTE: *Biomes are presented in detail in the next section, Section 4. However, this lab has been placed immediately before that section because it is appropriate as an introduction to the section's concepts and also to allow sufficient time for plant growth while students study biomes.*

Preparing for Inquiry

Key Concept Differences in soil, light, and precipitation create different biomes.
Skills Objectives Students will be able to
◆ make models of given biomes by varying abiotic factors;
◆ observe and compare the growth of different plants in the model biomes;
◆ conclude that each plant is adapted to conditions in a specific biome.
Time 30 minutes for set-up; 5–10 minutes each day for at least one week for follow-up observations and recording data

Advance Planning

◆ Ask students to bring in large milk or juice cartons that have been thoroughly washed.
◆ Obtain sufficient quantities of potting soil and sandy (cactus) soil from a nursery or gardening store.
◆ Allocate enough table space and lamps for students to expose each model biome to the amount of light required.

Guiding Inquiry

Invitation Ask students: **Why don't we see [name a non-native plant] growing in our area?** (*Students should describe climate conditions needed by the plant that would not be met in your area.*)

Introducing the Procedure

◆ Invite students to read the entire lab procedure. Then ask: **What is the purpose of this lab?** (*To determine how well three kinds of plants grow in different biomes*)
◆ Direct students' attention to the Growing Conditions chart and ask: **What variables will you change to create models of four different**

BIOMES IN MINIATURE

Climate is one factor that affects where organisms live. A group of ecosystems with similar climates and organisms is called a biome. In this lab, you will investigate some key factors that make biomes different from each other.

Problem

What biotic and abiotic factors create different biomes around the world?

Skills Focus

making models, observing, drawing conclusions

Materials

scissors
index card
10 impatiens seeds
5 lima bean seeds
about 30 rye grass seeds
empty, clean cardboard milk carton
sandy soil or potting soil

clear plastic wrap
lamp
tape
stapler

Procedure

1. Your teacher will assign your group a biome. You will also observe the other groups' biomes. Based on the chart below, predict how well you think each of the three kinds of seeds will grow in each set of conditions. Record these predictions in your notebook. Then copy the data table on the facing page four times, once for each biome.
2. Staple the spout of the milk carton closed. Completely cut away one of the four sides of the carton. Poke a few holes in the opposite side for drainage, then place that side down.
3. Fill the carton to 3 centimeters from the top with the type of soil given in the table. Divide the surface of the soil into three sections by making two lines in it with a pencil.
4. In the section near the spout, plant the impatiens seeds. In the middle section, plant the lima bean seeds. In the third section, scatter the rye grass seeds on the surface.

GROWING CONDITIONS			
Biome	**Soil Type**	**Hours of Light Per Day**	**Watering Instructions**
Forest	Potting soil	1–2 hours direct light	Let the surface dry, then add water.
Desert	Sandy soil	5–6 hours direct light	Let the soil dry to a depth of 2.5 cm below the surface.
Grassland	Potting soil	5–6 hours direct light	Let the surface dry, then add water.
Rain forest	Potting soil	No direct light; indirect light for 5–6 hours	Keep the surface of the soil moist.

biomes? (*Soil type, amount of light, and amount of water*)

Troubleshooting the Experiment

◆ In Step 1, do not comment on the accuracy of students' predictions. Rather, have them review their predictions at the end of the investigation and write a conclusion based on their actual results.
◆ Step 8 does not specify the kinds of observations to be made and recorded. You may want to discuss possibilities with

students beforehand and agree on one or more criteria for all groups to use. Criteria could include the number of seeds that germinate successfully, plant height, the number and color of leaves, and yellowing (a sign of too much water) or wilting (a sign of not enough water). Alternatively, you could allow each group to choose the criteria it will use.

DATA TABLE

Name of biome: _____

Day	Impatiens	Lima Beans	Rye Grass
1			
2			
3			

5. Water all the seeds well. Then cover the open part of the carton with plastic wrap.

6. On an index card, write the name of your biome, the names of the three types of seeds in the order you planted them, and the names of your group members. Tape the card to the carton. Put it in a warm place where it will not be disturbed.

7. Once the seeds sprout, provide your biome with light and water as specified in the chart. Keep the carton covered with plastic wrap except when you add water.

8. Observe all the biomes daily for at least one week. Record your observations.

Analyze and Conclude

1. In which biome did each type of seed grow best? In which biome did each type of seed grow least well?

2. How was each type of seed affected by the soil type, amount of light, and availability of water? How do your results relate to biomes in nature?

3. Ecologists studying land biomes often begin a description of the biome by describing key abiotic factors and the typical plants. Why do you think they do this?

4. **Apply** Describe the rainfall pattern and other abiotic factors that make up the climate where you live. How do those factors affect the kinds of plants and animals that live there?

Design an Experiment

After reading Section 4, write a plan for setting up a model rain forest or desert terrarium. Include typical plants found in that biome. Obtain your teacher's approval before trying this activity.

2. In general, the seeds will sprout most rapidly when water is plentiful. Every type of plant is adapted to survive in a specific set of soil, light, and water conditions, so each of the three plant types in this lab thrived in only one or two biomes. In nature, the same abiotic factors limit the types of plants that can survive in a specific biome.

3. The abiotic factors limit the types of plants that can grow in a particular biome, and the types of plants in turn determine the types of animals and other consumers that can survive in that biome.

4. Answers will depend on the climate conditions in your region.

Extending the Inquiry

Design an Experiment Provide field guides and other resources for students to use in selecting typical plants. Discourage students from trying to start plants from seed; provide small but mature plants that will do well in a model rain forest or desert. To simulate the damp conditions found in a rain forest, students will need to put a cover on the rain forest container to prevent evaporation.

Data Table

Students' data tables will vary depending on the criteria they used for assessing the health of the plants. For general guidelines, see Analyze and Conclude Question 1 answer.

Analyze and Conclude

1. In general, the rye and beans will grow best in the grassland biome, and the impatiens will grow best in the deciduous forest biome. The seeds will all likely grow most poorly in the dry conditions of the desert biome.

Program Resources

◆ **Teaching Resources** Chapter 2 Real-World Lab, pp. 59–61

Safety

Make sure students wash their hands after they handle the soil and seeds. Review the safety guidelines in Appendix A.

Objectives

After completing the lesson, students will be able to
- list and describe Earth's major land biomes;
- list and describe Earth's major freshwater and ocean biomes.

Key Terms biome, canopy, understory, desert, grassland, savanna, deciduous trees, hibernation, coniferous trees, tundra, permafrost, estuary, intertidal zone, neritic zone

1 Engage/Explore

Activating Prior Knowledge

Ask: **What is the climate like in our area?** *(Students should describe conditions of temperature, precipitation, amount of sunlight during the seasons, and so forth.)* **How do you think our climate affects which organisms live here?** *(Answers will vary depending on the climate of the area. For example, students may say that a warm, humid climate allows a great variety of organisms to live in the area.)*

DISCOVER

Skills Focus developing hypotheses
Materials *meter stick, adding-machine paper, scissors, marker, tape*
Time 20 minutes

CAUTION: *Hanging the Costa Rican rain forest strip will require the use of a ladder. Choose three reliable students for this task, one to climb the ladder and two to hold the ladder securely. If you are not certain that students can do this task safely, have them hang the strips horizontally.*
Expected Outcome Students should sequence the strips from least to most rainfall, as indicated in the table.
Think It Over The Costa Rican rain forest receives the most precipitation, and the Mojave Desert the least. The amount of rainfall affects what plant species can survive in a particular biome, and the plants in turn determine the consumer species found there.

DISCOVER ····· ACTIVITY

How Much Rain Is That?

The table shows the average amount of precipitation that falls each year in four different regions. With your classmates, you will create a full-size bar graph on a wall to help you visualize these amounts of rain.

Biome	Rainfall (cm)
Mojave Desert	15
Illinois prairie	70
Smoky Mountains	180
Costa Rican rain forest	350

1. Using a meter stick, measure a strip of adding-machine paper 15 centimeters long. Label this piece of paper "Mojave Desert."

2. Repeat Step 1 for the other three locations. If necessary, tape strips of paper together to make the correct length. Label each strip.

3. Now find a place where you can display the four strips vertically. If the wall of your classroom is not tall enough, you may need to use another wall in your school building. Follow your teacher's instructions to hang your precipitation strips.

Think It Over
Developing Hypotheses Which ecosystem receives the most precipitation? Which receives the least? What effect do you think the amount of rainfall might have on the types of species that live in these ecosystems?

GUIDE FOR READING

- What determines the type of biome found in an area?
- Where can photosynthesis occur in water biomes?

Reading Tip As you read, make a list of the biomes described in this section. Under each biome name, take notes on the characteristics of that biome.

Congratulations! You and your classmates have been selected as the student members of an around-the-world scientific expedition. Your mission is to study the major types of ecosystems on Earth. You will be collecting data on the climate conditions and typical organisms found in each of these ecosystems. The result of this expedition will be a database of information on the biomes you visit. A **biome** is a group of ecosystems with similar climates and organisms.

Classifying ecosystems into biomes helps ecologists describe the world. As you might expect, not all ecologists agree on the exact number and kinds of biomes. The scientists guiding your expedition have chosen to focus on six major land biomes and two major water biomes.

Be sure to pack a variety of clothing for your journey. During your trip, you will visit places ranging from frozen, windy Arctic plains to steamy tropical jungles. **In fact, it is mostly the climate conditions—temperature and rainfall—in an area that determine its biome.** This is because climate limits the distribution of plants in the area. In turn, the types of plants determine the kinds of animals that live there.

READING STRATEGIES

Reading Tip Invite students to preview the headings in this section and name the eight major biomes described (rain forest, desert, grassland, deciduous forest, boreal forest, tundra, freshwater, and marine) and the "sub-biomes" or ecosystems within those biomes (tropical rain forests, temperate rain forests, freshwater ponds and lakes, freshwater streams and rivers, estuaries, and the ocean's intertidal, neritic, surface, and deep zones). To organize their notes, students can construct a table with the names of the biomes listed in the first column and the characteristics that differentiate biomes labeled across the top of the table—*Temperature, Rainfall, Variety of Species,* and *Typical Organisms,* for example. Students can use their completed biome summaries as a study guide.

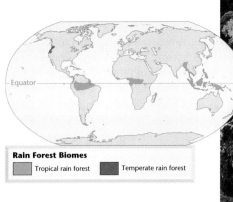

Rain Forest Biomes
- Tropical rain forest
- Temperate rain forest

Rain Forest Biomes

The first stop on your expedition is a tropical rain forest close to the equator. The rain forest is warm and humid—in fact, it's pouring rain! Fortunately, you remembered to pack a poncho. After just a short shower, the sun reappears. But even though the sun is shining, very little light penetrates the thick vegetation.

Plants are everywhere in the rain forest. Some, such as the ferns, orchids, and vines you observe hanging from tree limbs, even grow on other plants. Among the plants are many species of birds as bright as the numerous flowers all around you.

Tropical Rain Forests Tropical rain forests are found in warm regions close to the equator. Tropical rain forests typically receive a lot of rain. The warm temperatures do not vary much throughout the year, and the sunlight is fairly constant all year.

Tropical rain forests contain an astounding variety of species. For example, scientists studying a 100-square-meter area of one rain forest identified 300 different kinds of trees! These trees form several distinct layers. The tall trees form a leafy roof called the **canopy.** A few giant trees poke out above the canopy. Below the canopy, a second layer of shorter trees and vines form an **understory.** Understory plants grow well in the shade formed by the canopy. Finally, some plants thrive in the near-darkness of the forest floor.

Figure 16 Tropical rain forests contain an amazing variety of plants and other organisms. In the large photo, a river winds through the lush Indonesian rain forest. The top closeup shows a young orangutan swinging from tree limbs. In the bottom closeup, a tarantula climbs over a brightly colored bracket fungus on the forest floor.

---

2 Facilitate

Rain Forest Biomes

Building Inquiry Skills: Communicating

As an ongoing activity throughout this section, encourage students to research additional information about the biomes described in the text. Divide the class into eight groups, and assign one biome to each group. (You may want to use 12 groups and divide the 5 marine habitats among different groups.) Explain that each group should look for additional photographs of the biome and of organisms typically found in it. Students can photocopy (or print out) the pictures and incorporate them into a large poster labeled with the name of the biome. As students read about each biome in the text, call on the group who researched that biome to present its poster to the class. Display the posters in the classroom. **cooperative learning**

Using the Visuals: Figure 16

Display a world map or globe, and have students locate Indonesia. Then have them locate Indonesia on the biome map. Ask: **What do you notice about the locations of the world's tropical rain forests?** *(All are located at or close to the equator.)* **learning modality: visual**

Program Resources

◆ **Teaching Resources** 2-4 Lesson Plan, p. 51; 2-4 Section Summary, p. 52

Media and Technology

Audiotapes English-Spanish Summary 2-4

Exploring Life Science Videodisc Unit 6, Side 2, "Earth's Many Biomes"

Chapter 5

Ongoing Assessment

Writing Have each student explain how temperature and rainfall determine the types of organisms that live in a particular biome.

Rain Forest Biomes,
continued

Cultural Diversity

Have students examine a map of northwestern United States and locate temperate rain forests. They will undoubtedly notice the unusual names of several forests—for example, Tillamook State Forest, Siuslaw National Forest, Siskiyou National Forest (all in Oregon), and Klamath National Forest (California). Ask: **Where do you think those names came from?** *(They are the names of Native American tribes living in those areas.)* Encourage interested students to find out about the history and cultures of indigenous peoples of the American northwest. **learning modality: verbal**

Desert Biomes

Building Inquiry Skills: Making Models

Materials *terrarium with cover; sandy soil; water; desert organisms such as cactus plants, insects, small lizard*

Time 20 minutes

Ask students: **If you wanted to build a model of a desert biome in a terrarium, what abiotic materials would you need?** *(Sandy soil; perhaps some gravel and rocks; a source of strong, direct sunlight or artificial light; some water for infrequent watering)* **What organisms would you place in the model biome?** *(Cactus plants, desert insects, a small lizard or other organism)* Encourage a group of volunteers to gather the materials and construct a model desert biome. **learning modality: kinesthetic**

The abundant plant life provides many habitats for animals. The number of insect species in tropical rain forests is not known, but has been estimated to be in the millions. These in turn feed many bird species, which feed other animals. Although tropical rain forests cover only a small part of the planet, they probably contain more species of plants and animals than all the other land biomes combined.

Temperate Rain Forests The land along the northwestern coast of the United States resembles a tropical rain forest in some ways. This region receives more than 300 centimeters of rain a year. Huge trees grow there, including cedars, redwoods, and Douglas firs. However, it is difficult to classify this region. It is too far north and too cool to be a tropical rain forest. Instead many ecologists refer to this ecosystem as a temperate rain forest. The term *temperate* means having moderate temperatures.

Desert Biomes

The next stop on your expedition is a desert. It couldn't be more different from the tropical rain forest you just left. You step off the bus into the searing summer heat. At midday, you cannot even walk into the desert—the sand feels as hot as the hot water that comes from your bathroom faucet at home.

A **desert** is an area that receives less than 25 centimeters of rain per year. The amount of evaporation in a desert is greater than the amount of precipitation. Some of the driest deserts may not receive any rain at all in a year! Deserts often also undergo large shifts in temperature during the course of a day. A scorching hot desert like the

Figure 17 Desert organisms have adaptations that enable them to live in the harsh conditions of their biome. For example, this shovel-snouted lizard "dances" to avoid burning its feet on the hot sand dunes of the Namib Desert in Africa. *Making Generalizations Describe the climate conditions of a typical desert.*

Desert and Grassland Biomes
Desert Grassland

Background

Facts and Figures The continuing destruction of tropical rain forests around the world may be a factor in climate change. Each year, thousands of square kilometers of rain forest are cut and burned to clear land and access mineral resources. Burning the forests not only kills the unique organisms of the rain forest ecosystem but also releases large quantities of carbon dioxide, contributing to global warming.

Between 1978 and 1996, more than 12.5 percent of the Amazon rain forest was destroyed. In 1998, after analysis of satellite photographs, the Brazilian government reported that rain forest destruction reached a record level of 30,000 square kilometers in 1995. Brazil planned to increase its monitoring and control of the area and implement new measures to protect the rain forest.

Namib Desert cools rapidly each night when the sun goes down. Other deserts, such as the Gobi in central Asia, are cooler, even experiencing freezing temperatures in the winter.

The organisms that live in the desert are adapted to the lack of rain and to the extreme temperatures. For example, the trunk of a saguaro cactus has folds that work like the pleats in an accordion. The trunk of the cactus expands to hold more water when it is raining. Many desert animals are most active at night when the temperatures are cooler. A gila monster, for instance, spends much of its time in a cool underground burrow. It may go for weeks without coming up to the surface of the desert.

☑ *Checkpoint* *What are some adaptations that help an organism to live in the desert?*

Grassland Biomes

The next stop on the expedition is a grassland called a prairie. The temperature here is much more comfortable than that in the desert. The breeze carries the scent of soil warmed by the sun. This rich soil supports grass as tall as you and your classmates. Sparrows flit among the grass stems, looking for their next meal. Startled by your approach, a rabbit quickly bounds away.

Like other grasslands located in the middle latitudes, this prairie receives more rain than deserts, but not enough for many trees to grow. A **grassland** receives between 25 and 75 centimeters of rain each year, and is typically populated by grasses and other non-woody plants. Grasslands that are located closer to the equator than prairies, called **savannas,** receive as much as 120 centimeters of

TRY THIS

Desert Survival

✂ Use a hand lens **ACTIVITY** to carefully observe a small potted cactus. Be careful of the spines! With a pair of scissors, carefully snip a small piece from the tip of the cactus. Observe the inside of the plant. Note any characteristics that seem different from those of other plants.

Observing How is the inside of the cactus different from the outside? Suggest how the features you observe might be related to its desert habitat.

Figure 18 Migrating wildebeest make their way across a vast Kenyan savanna.

Chapter 2 **E ◆ 65**

TRY THIS

Skills Focus observing
Materials *small potted cactus, hand lens, scissors*
Time 10 minutes
Tips Divide the class into small groups and provide a separate cactus plant for each group. Use cactus varieties with narrow tube-shaped or flat segments that will be easy for students to snip through with scissors.
Expected Outcome Students should observe that unlike most other plants, cactuses have sharp spines or other projections, not flat, wide leaves, and they also have a waxy outer covering. The inside of a cactus is fleshy and moist. The lack of wide, flat leaves and the waxy outer covering help conserve water in the hot, dry desert; the fleshy inner core stores moisture for the plant.
Extend Provide books on raising cactuses as houseplants so students can see the wide range of cactus types.
learning modality: visual

Grassland Biomes

Using the Visuals: Figure 18

Begin by having students locate Kenya on a world map or globe. Also have them locate prairie areas in the midwestern United States. **What typical features of grassland biomes are visible in the photograph?** *(tall grass, large herbivores)*
learning modality: visual

Answers to Self-Assessment

Caption Question

Figure 17 Deserts are typically hot during the day and very dry, receiving less than 25 cm of rain per year.

☑ *Checkpoint*

Sample answer: The saguaro cactus has folds that allow the trunk to expand and hold more water when it rains.

Ongoing Assessment

Skills Check Have each student create a compare/contrast table showing the temperature and rainfall differences among the three biomes described so far in the text—rain forest, desert, grassland.

Deciduous Forest Biomes

Building Inquiry Skills: Making Models

Ask students: **Could you build a model** ACTIVITY **of a deciduous forest in a terrarium?** *(No, not of the entire forest, but specific habitats could be modeled in a terrarium.)* **Suppose you want to model a rotting-log habitat on the forest floor. What abiotic materials would you need?** *(Soil, a source of filtered light, water, a rotting log, dead leaves or other plant material)* **What organisms would you place in the model habitat?** *(Mosses, ferns, fungi, earthworms, sowbugs, crickets, toad or salamander)* Encourage volunteers to gather materials and construct a model rotting-log habitat. **learning modality: kinesthetic**

Addressing Naive Conceptions

After students have read about hibernation on the next page, ask: **What animals hibernate during the winter?** *(Students will probably mention bears, among other animals. List responses on the board without commenting on their accuracy.)* Encourage students to find out whether the animals they named do indeed hibernate and what other animals should be added to the list. *(Animals that undergo true hibernation include bats, ground squirrels, chipmunks, groundhogs, frogs, toads, lizards, snakes, and turtles. Students will also discover that some of the animals they named—bears, for example—do not undergo true hibernation, which involves extreme metabolic changes. These animals go through prolonged periods of deep sleep over the winter months but wake up from time to time.)* **learning modality: verbal**

Forest Biomes
■ Deciduous forest ■ Boreal forest

Figure 19 This Michigan forest in autumn is a beautiful example of a deciduous forest. The closeup shows a red fox, a common resident of North American deciduous forests. *Comparing and Contrasting How do deciduous forests differ from rain forests?*

rain each year. Scattered shrubs and small trees grow on savannas along with the grass.

Grasslands are home to many of the largest animals on Earth—herbivores such as bison, antelopes, zebras, rhinoceros, giraffes, and kangaroos. Grazing by these large herbivores helps to maintain the grasslands. They keep young trees and bushes from sprouting and competing with the grass for water and sunlight.

Deciduous Forest Biomes

Your trip to the next biome takes you to another forest. It is now late summer. Cool mornings here give way to warm days. Several members of the expedition are busy recording the numerous plant species. Others are looking through their binoculars, trying to identify the songbirds in the trees. You step carefully to avoid a small salamander on the forest floor. Chipmunks chatter at all the disturbance.

You are now visiting the deciduous forest biome. The trees found in this forest, called **deciduous trees** (dee SIJ oo us), shed their leaves and grow new ones each year. Oaks and maples are examples of deciduous trees. Deciduous forests receive enough rain to support the growth of trees and other plants, at least 50 centimeters per year. Temperatures vary during the year. The growing season usually lasts five to six months. As in the rain forest, different plants grow to different heights, ranging from a canopy of tall trees to small ferns and mosses on the forest floor.

66 ◆ E

The variety of plants in the forest creates many different habitats. You and your classmates note that different species of birds live at each level, eating the insects and fruits that live and grow there. You observe opossums, mice, and a skunk looking for food in the thick layer of damp leaves on the ground. Other common North American deciduous forest species include wood thrushes, white-tailed deer, and black bears.

If you were to return to this biome in the winter, you would not see much of the wildlife you are now observing. One reason is that many of the bird species migrate to warmer areas. Some of the mammals enter a low-energy state similar to sleep called **hibernation.** During hibernation an animal relies on fat it has stored in its body.

☑ *Checkpoint* *What are deciduous trees?*

Boreal Forest Biomes

Now the expedition heads north into a colder climate. The expedition leaders claim they can identify the next biome, a boreal forest, by its smell. When you arrive, you catch a whiff of the spruce and fir trees that blanket the hillsides. Feeling the chilly early fall air, you pull a jacket and hat out of your bag.

This forest contains **coniferous trees** (koh NIF ur us), that produce their seeds in cones and have leaves shaped like needles. The boreal forest is sometimes referred to by its Russian name, the *taiga* (TY guh). Winters in these forests are very cold. The yearly

Figure 20 Common organisms of the boreal forest include moose like this one in Alaska's Denali National Park, and porcupines.

E ◆ 67

Answers to Self-Assessment

Caption Question

Figure 19 Rain forests get a lot of rain, and the warm temperatures and amount of sunlight are fairly constant year-round. Deciduous forests receive less rainfall, and temperatures vary during the year.

☑ *Checkpoint*
Deciduous trees are trees that shed their leaves and grow new ones each year.

Boreal Forest Biomes

Sharpen your Skills

Inferring

Time 5 minutes
Expected Outcome

Boreal forests grow in climates that are too cold for deciduous forests. Such climates typically occur in a band at latitudes far from the equator. There are no such areas in the Southern Hemisphere because that hemisphere does not have large continental land areas at the appropriate latitudes.
learning modality: logical/ mathematical

Building Inquiry Skills: Inferring

Materials *globe, flashlight, masking tape*
Time 10–15 minutes

Have pairs of students mark the locations of deciduous and boreal forests on a globe with strips of masking tape labeled *D* and *B*. With the room darkened, one student should shine a flashlight at the globe's equator as the other student slowly turns the globe on its axis. Ask: **Which biome, the deciduous forest or the boreal forest, gets stronger [more direct] light?** (*The deciduous forest*) **What do you think this has to do with the climate differences between the deciduous forest and the boreal forest?** (*"Stronger" [more-direct] sunlight during the year makes the deciduous forests warmer than the boreal forests.*)
learning modality: kinesthetic

Ongoing Assessment

Writing Have students describe the differences between deciduous forest and boreal forest biomes.

Tundra Biomes

snowfall can reach heights well over your head—or even two or three times your height! Even so, the summers are rainy and warm enough to melt all the snow.

A limited number of trees have adapted to the cold climate of boreal forests. Fir, spruce, and hemlock are the most common species because their thick, waxy needles keep water from evaporating. Since water is frozen for much of the year in these areas, prevention of water loss is a necessary adaptation for trees in the boreal forest.

Many of the animals of the boreal forest eat the seeds produced by the conifers. These animals include red squirrels, insects, and birds such as finches and chickadees. Some of the larger herbivores, such as porcupines, deer, elk, moose, and beavers, eat tree bark and new shoots. This variety of herbivores in the boreal forest supports a variety of large predators, including wolves, bears, wolverines, and lynxes.

Tundra Biomes

The driving wind brings tears to the eyes of the members of the expedition as you arrive at your next stop. It is now fall. The slicing wind gives everyone an immediate feel for this biome, the tundra. The **tundra** is an extremely cold, dry, land biome. Expecting deep snow, many are surprised that the tundra may receive no more precipitation than a desert. Most of the soil in the tundra is frozen all year. This frozen soil is called **permafrost**.

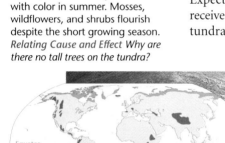

Figure 21 Far from being a barren terrain, the tundra explodes with color in summer. Mosses, wildflowers, and shrubs flourish despite the short growing season. *Relating Cause and Effect Why are there no tall trees on the tundra?*

Tundra Biomes, Mountains, and Ice
☐ Tundra ☐ Mountains ☐ Ice

Equator

During the short summer the top layer of soil on the tundra thaws, but the underlying soil remains frozen.

Plants on the tundra include mosses, grasses, shrubs, and dwarf forms of a few trees, such as willows. Looking across the tundra, you observe that the landscape is already brown and gold. The short growing season is over. Most of the plant growth takes place during the long summer days when many hours of sunshine combine with the warmest temperatures of the year. North of the Arctic Circle the sun does not set during midsummer.

If you had visited the tundra during the summer, the animals you might remember most are insects. Swarms of black flies and mosquitos provide food for many birds. The birds take advantage of the plentiful food and long days by eating as much as they can. Then, when winter approaches again, many birds migrate south to warmer climates.

Mammals of the tundra include caribou, foxes, wolves, and hares. The animals that remain in the tundra during the winter grow thick fur coats. What can these animals find to eat on the tundra in winter? The caribou scrape snow away to find lichens, which are fungi and algae that grow together on rocks. Wolves follow the caribou and look for weak members of the herd to prey upon.

☑ *Checkpoint* *What is the climate of the tundra?*

Mountains and Ice

Some areas of land on Earth do not fall into one of the major land biomes. These areas include mountain ranges and land that is covered with thick sheets of ice.

You read in Section 3 that the climate conditions of a mountain change from its base to its summit. As a result, different species of plants and other organisms inhabit different parts of the mountain. If you hiked to the top of a tall mountain, you would pass through a series of biomes. At the base of the mountain, you might find a grassland. As you climbed, you might pass through a deciduous forest, and then a boreal forest. Finally, as you neared the top, the trees would disappear. Your surroundings would resemble the rugged tundra.

Some land on Earth is covered year-round with thick ice sheets. Most of the island of Greenland and the continent of Antarctica fall into this category. Some organisms are adapted to life on the ice, including penguins, polar bears, and seals.

Figure 22 Many waterfowl spend summers on the tundra. This black brant is tending her nest.

Sharpen your Skills

Interpreting Data
ACTIVITY

An ecologist has collected climate data from two locations. The total yearly precipitation is 250 cm in Location A and 14 cm in Location B. The graph below shows the average monthly temperature in the two locations. Based on this information, of which biome is each location a part? Explain.

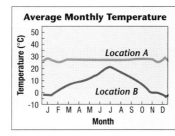

Average Monthly Temperature

Location A

Location B

Month

Chapter 2 **E ◆ 69**

Answers to Self-Assessment

Caption Question

Figure 21 The short, cool growing season does not allow tall trees to grow.

☑ *Checkpoint*

The tundra is extremely cold during the winter. It receives very little precipitation. Most of the soil is frozen all year long. Days are long in the summer, but the growing season is very short.

Sharpen your Skills

Interpreting Data

Time 10 minutes
Tips If students have
ACTIVITY
difficulty determining whether Location B is a desert or tundra, focus their attention on the biome's average monthly temperatures, which are too high for the tundra.
Expected Outcome Location A is a rain forest; it receives a lot of rain, and its warm temperatures are steady throughout the year. Location B is a desert; it receives little rainfall, and its temperatures are cold—but not extremely so—in winter and warm in summer.
Extend Invite students to describe the shape of the line that would be shown on the graph if they plotted the average monthly temperatures for the biome in which they live. **learning modality: logical/mathematical**

Mountains and Ice

Inquiry Challenge

Time 10 minutes

Have each small group
ACTIVITY
draw a side-view diagram of a mountain and label it with the biome names given in the text: grassland at the base, deciduous forest next, then boreal forest, and finally tundra at the top. Challenge students to use the diagram, with any additions they choose, to answer the following question: **Why do the biomes vary at different locations on a mountain?** *(By adding information on temperature to the labels, students will be able to see that the climate becomes colder from the base of a mountain to its top. They should then be able to conclude that the altitude of a location on a mountain determines its climate conditions and thus its biome.)* **cooperative learning**

Ongoing Assessment

Skills Check Have students add the tundra biome to the compare/contrast table they created in Ongoing Assessment on page 65.

Freshwater Biomes

Building Inquiry Skills: Classifying

As students read about freshwater biomes on these two pages, have them identify each specific habitat described in the text and in the caption for Figure 23 and name some organisms typically found in each habitat. In a lake, for example, specific habitats include the shoreline, the shallow water near shore, the deep water away from shore, the bottom of the lake, and the water surface.
learning modality: verbal

Real-Life Learning

Time 45 minutes

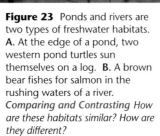

Take the class to visit a nearby freshwater biome—a pond, lake, stream, or river. Tell students to observe the area very quietly for a time to allow any organisms initially disturbed by the class's presence to settle down again. Encourage students to look for different habitats within the biome and try to identify some of the specific organisms found in each habitat. You may want to let students collect water and some of the smaller organisms to take back to the classroom to use in constructing a model freshwater habitat. (If necessary, obtain permission from local authorities first.)
learning modality: visual

Building Inquiry Skills: Inferring

Remind students that organisms are adapted to live in specific habitats. Then ask: **What adaptations does a fish have that allow it to live in a lake's water? How does each adaptation enable it to survive?** (*Gills for breathing oxygen dissolved in the water; fins, a tail, and a streamlined body shape for moving through the water; scales for insulation and for protection against water loss; and so forth*) Continue this line of questioning with other organisms found in freshwater biomes. **learning modality: logical/mathematical**

Figure 23 Ponds and rivers are two types of freshwater habitats. **A.** At the edge of a pond, two western pond turtles sun themselves on a log. **B.** A brown bear fishes for salmon in the rushing waters of a river. *Comparing and Contrasting How are these habitats similar? How are they different?*

Freshwater Biomes

The next stops for the expedition are located in water biomes. Since almost three quarters of Earth's surface is covered with water, it is not surprising that many living things make their homes in the water. Water biomes include both freshwater and saltwater (also called marine) biomes. All of these are affected by the same abiotic factors: temperature, sunlight, oxygen, and salt content.

An especially important factor in water biomes is sunlight. Sunlight is necessary for photosynthesis in the water just as it is on land. **However, because water absorbs sunlight, there is only enough light for photosynthesis near the surface or in shallow water.** The most common producers in most water biomes are algae rather than plants.

Ponds and Lakes First stop among the freshwater biomes is a calm pond. Ponds and lakes are bodies of standing, or still, fresh water. Lakes are generally larger and deeper than ponds. Ponds are often shallow enough that sunlight can reach the bottom even in the center of the pond, allowing plants to grow there. Plants that grow along the shore have their roots in the soil, while their leaves stretch to the sunlit water at the surface. In the center of a lake, algae floating at the surface are the major producers.

Many animals are adapted for life in the still water. Along the shore of the pond you observe insects, snails, frogs, and salamanders. Sunfish live in the open water, feeding on insects and algae from the surface. Scavengers such as catfish live near the pond bottom. Bacteria and other decomposers also feed on the remains of other organisms.

Streams and Rivers When you arrive at a mountain stream, you immediately notice how different it is from the still waters of a lake. Where the stream begins, called the headwaters, the cold, clear water flows rapidly. Animals that live in this part must be adapted to the strong current. Trout, for instance, have stream-lined bodies that allow them to swim despite the pull of the rushing water. Insects and other small animals may have hooks or suckers to help them cling to rocks. Few plants or algae can grow in this fast-moving water. Instead, first-level consumers rely on leaves and seeds that fall into the stream.

As the river flows along, it is joined by other streams. The current slows. The water becomes cloudy with soil. With fewer rapids, the slower-moving, warmer water contains less oxygen. Different organisms are adapted to live in this lower part of the river. More plants take root among the pebbles on the river bottom, providing homes for insects and frogs. As is true in every biome, organisms are adapted to live in this specific habitat.

☑ *Checkpoint* *What are two abiotic factors that affect organisms in a river?*

Marine Biomes

Next the members of the expedition head down the coast to explore some marine biomes. The oceans contain many different habitats. These habitats differ in sunlight amount, water temperature, wave action, and water pressure. Different organisms are adapted to life in each type of habitat. The first habitat, called an **estuary** (ES choo ehr ee), is found where the fresh water of a river meets the salt water of the ocean.

Estuaries The shallow, sunlit water, plus a large supply of nutrients carried in by the river, makes an estuary a very rich habitat for living things. The major producers in estuaries are plants, such as marsh grasses, as well as algae.

Figure 24 Fresh river water and salty ocean water meet in an estuary. Estuaries such as this Georgia salt marsh provide a rich habitat for many organisms, including a wading tricolored heron.

Chapter 2 **E ◆ 71**

Program Resources

🔵 **Science Explorer Series** *Earth's Waters,* Chapter 2 and Chapter 5, provide detailed information on freshwater and marine habitats.

Answers to Self-Assessment

Caption Question

Figure 23 *Similarities:* Both have fresh water. *Differences:* The pond has warm, calm water, whereas the river has cold, fast-moving water.

☑ *Checkpoint*

Any two: temperature, speed of current, rocks and pebbles, soil in water, oxygen level

---

Marine Biomes

Using the Visuals: Figure 24

After students have examined the photos and read the caption, ask: **What abiotic factor makes an estuary so different from the river flowing into it and the ocean beyond it?** *(Fresh water and salt water mix together in the estuary.)* **How do you think this affects the types of organisms that can live there?** *(They must be able to tolerate changes in the water's salt content throughout the day.)* **learning modality: verbal**

Building Inquiry Skills: Comparing and Contrasting

After students have read about the intertidal zone on the next page, ask: **How are an estuary and the intertidal zone different?** *(Different organisms live there; the water in the intertidal zone is saltier than the water in an estuary; the estuary is calmer because it is not subjected to heavy waves.)* **How are an estuary and the intertidal zone alike?** *(In both, the land is sometimes covered with water and at other times exposed to the air and sunlight.)* To identify this similarity, students must infer that estuaries are affected by the ocean's tides so mudflats are exposed during low tide and completely covered with water during high tide. If students have difficulty making this inference, guide them by asking: **Do you think estuaries are affected by ocean tides?** **learning modality: logical/mathematical**

Ongoing Assessment

Oral Presentation Call on various students to each choose one freshwater biome, identify one specific habitat in that biome, and name at least three organisms found in that habitat.

Marine Biomes, continued

Real-Life Learning

If students live in or have visited a coastal area, encourage them to describe what an estuary and an ocean beach (the intertidal zone) look like and to name some of the organisms they have seen there. **learning modality: verbal**

Building Inquiry Skills: Inferring

Materials *coral*
Time 10 minutes

Provide samples of different types of coral for students to examine. Visually impaired students can closely examine the coral by feeling it. Emphasize that these pieces of coral are not the coral animals, which are soft, but the hard structures they produced and left behind when they died. Ask: **Where do you think the coral animals lived?** (*Inside the tiny holes*) **How do you think this hard structure helps coral animals survive?** (*It provides protection for the animals' soft bodies and also anchors them to the ocean floor.*) **learning modality: visual**

Including All Students

Encourage students who need extra challenges to consult field guides, encyclopedias, nonfiction library books, nature magazines, and other sources to find additional photographs of organisms that live in the intertidal, neritic, surface, and deep zones. Suggest that students photocopy or hand copy the pictures they find and arrange the pictures in a bulletin-board display of the four ocean zones with each organism placed in its correct zone. **learning modality: visual**

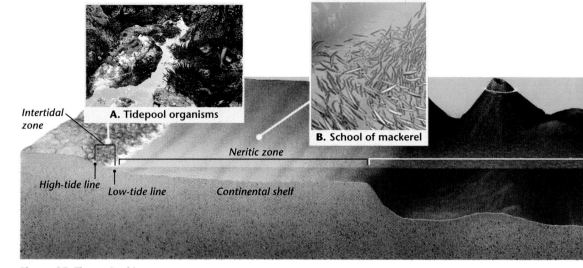

A. Tidepool organisms

B. School of mackerel

Intertidal zone

High-tide line   Low-tide line   Continental shelf   Neritic zone

Figure 25 The marine biome is divided into several zones. **A.** Tidepools are common in the intertidal zone. This zone lies between the highest high-tide line and lowest low-tide line. **B.** Many fish, such as these silvery mackerel, inhabit the shallow waters over the continental shelf, called the neritic zone. **C.** A humpback whale feeds on algae at the surface of the open-ocean zone. **D.** This eerie deep-sea gulper is a predator in the deepest part of the ocean.

These organisms provide food and shelter for a variety of animals, including crabs, worms, clams, oysters, and fish. Many of these organisms use the calm waters of estuaries for breeding grounds.

Intertidal Zone Next, you take a walk along the rocky shoreline. The part of the shore between the highest high-tide line and the lowest low-tide line is called the **intertidal zone.** Organisms here must be able to withstand the pounding action of waves, sudden changes in temperature, and being both covered with water and then exposed to the air. It is a difficult place to live! You observe many animals, such as barnacles and sea stars, clinging to the rocks. Others, such as clams and crabs, burrow in the sand.

Neritic Zone Now it's time to set out to sea to explore the waters near shore. From your research vessel, your group will explore the next type of marine habitat. The edge of a continent extends into the ocean for a short distance, like a shelf. Below the low-tide line is a region of shallow water, called the **neritic zone** (nuh RIT ik), that extends over the continental shelf. Just as in freshwater biomes, the shallow water in this zone allows photosynthesis to occur. As a result, this zone is particularly rich in living things. Many large schools of fish such as sardines and anchovies feed on the algae in the neritic zone. In the warm ocean waters of the tropics, coral reefs may form in the neritic zone. Though a coral reef may look like stone, it is actually a living home to a wide variety of other organisms.

Surface Zone Out in the open ocean, light penetrates through the water only to a depth of a few hundred meters. Algae floating in these surface waters carry out photosynthesis. These algae

---

Background

Facts and Figures The deep zone includes over 90 percent of the ocean. Because food is extremely scarce in the deep ocean, predators there have developed some unusual adaptations. The bodies of many fish consist almost entirely of their mouths—for

example, the viper fish has huge curved teeth and gaping jaws that enable it to catch and swallow prey even larger than itself. Other fish, such as the gulper eel, have baglike stomachs that expand to hold prey of any size they are fortunate enough to catch.

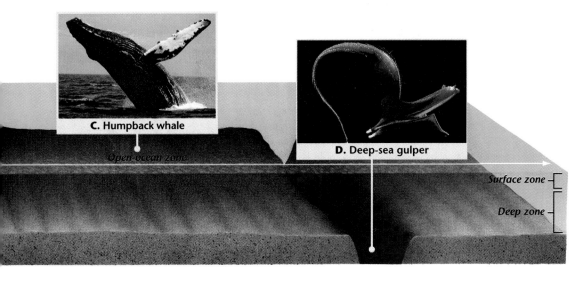

C. Humpback whale

Open-ocean zone

D. Deep-sea gulper

Surface zone

Deep zone

are the producers that form the base of almost all open-ocean food webs. Other marine animals, such as tuna, swordfish, and whales, depend directly or indirectly on the algae for food.

Deep Zone The deep zone is located in the open ocean below the surface zone. Throughout most of the deep ocean, the water is completely dark. Your expedition will need to use a submarine with bright headlights to explore this region. How can anything live in a place with no sunlight? Most animals in this zone feed on remains of organisms that sink down from the surface zone. The deepest parts of the deep zone are home to bizarre-looking animals, such as giant squid that glow in the dark and fish with rows and rows of sharp teeth.

After you have recorded your deep-zone observations, your long expedition is over at last. You can finally return home.

Section 4 Review

1. How does climate determine a biome's characteristics?
2. Where in water biomes can photosynthesis occur?
3. Which land biome receives the most precipitation? Which two receive the least?
4. In which biome would you find large herbivores such as antelope and elephants? Explain your answer.
5. **Thinking Critically Comparing and Contrasting** How are the three forest biomes (rain forests, deciduous forests, and boreal forests) alike? How are they different?

Check Your Progress

CHAPTER PROJECT 2

By now you should be ready to start analyzing the data you have collected about your compost chambers. Do your observations of the two chambers support your hypothesis? Begin to prepare your report.

Chapter 2 **E ◆ 73**

Program Resources

◆ **Teaching Resources** 2-4 Review and Reinforce, p. 53; 2-4 Enrich, p. 54

Media and Technology

 Interactive Student Tutorial CD-ROM E-2

3 Assess

Section 4 Review Answers

1. Climate limits the types of plants that can survive in the biome, and the types of plants in turn determine the kinds of animals that live there.
2. In shallow water and at the surface
3. *Most:* the tropical rain forest (accept also simply rain forest); *least:* the desert and tundra biomes
4. Grassland or savanna; grasslands are home to many large herbivores, which help to maintain the grasslands by keeping young trees and bushes from sprouting.
5. All have tall trees and many habitats for organisms. Students should cite differences in location (latitude), temperature, amount of sunlight, amount of precipitation, and specific types of plants and other organisms.

Check Your Progress

CHAPTER PROJECT 2

Monitor students as they analyze the data they have collected, compare results in the two chambers, and draw a conclusion about the effect of the variable they investigated. Remind students that the report can be in the form of a written summary, a poster, or some other product they can share with the class.

Performance Assessment

Drawing Have each student draw a diagram showing the ocean's four zones and label each zone with its name without referring to Figure 25.
 Portfolio Students can save their drawings in their portfolios.

Observing

Change in a Tiny Community

NOTE: This lab has been placed immediately before its related section to allow sufficient time for succession to occur as students study Section 5.

Preparing for Inquiry

Key Concept The types of organisms that predominate in a community change over time.

Skills Objectives Students will be able to
◆ make and observe a model of a microscopic pond community;
◆ compare and contrast the types of organisms and the sizes of the populations present in the community at intervals;
◆ conclude that the predominance of various populations changed during the observation period.

Time *Day 1, set up community: 15 minutes; Days 3, 6, and 9, examine community: 20 minutes each day*

Advance Planning

◆ The day before students will begin the lab, prepare a hay solution by adding a small amount of hay (preferably timothy hay) for each liter of hot water. Let the hay soak overnight, then use a strainer to remove the hay from the solution.
◆ Collect a sample of pond water.
◆ Ask students to help you collect enough clean baby-food jars to provide one for each student or group.
◆ Collect field guides and other sources showing the types of microscopic organisms found in ponds.

Alternative Materials Instead of pond water, use water from a freshwater aquarium or add a commercially prepared culture of microorganisms.

Guiding Inquiry

Invitation Focus students' attention on the illustrations of microorganisms and ask: **Have you ever seen organisms like these before? Where? What were they like?** (*Answers will depend on students'*

CHANGE IN A TINY COMMUNITY

The types of organisms in an ecosystem may change gradually over time. You will learn more about this process, called succession, in the next section. In this lab you will observe succession in a pond community.

Problem

How does a pond community change over time?

Materials

hay solution	pond water
small baby-food jar	wax pencil
plastic dropper	microscope slide
coverslip	microscope

Procedure

1. Use a wax pencil to label a small jar with your name.
2. Fill the jar about three-fourths full with hay solution. Add pond water until the jar is nearly full. Examine the mixture, and record your observations in your notebook.
3. Place the jar in a safe location out of direct sunlight where it will remain undisturbed. Always wash your hands thoroughly with soap after handling the jar or its contents.
4. After two days, examine the contents of the jar, and record your observations.
5. Use a plastic dropper to collect a few drops from the surface of the solution in the jar. Make a slide following the procedures in the box at the right. **CAUTION:** *Slides and coverslips are fragile, and their edges are sharp. Handle them carefully.*
6. Examine the slide under a microscope using both low and high power following the procedures in the box at the right. Draw each type of organism you observe. Estimate the number of each type in your sample. The illustration below shows some of the organisms you might see.
7. Repeat Steps 5 and 6 with a drop of solution taken from the side of the jar beneath the surface.
8. Repeat Steps 5 and 6 with a drop of solution taken from the bottom of the jar. When you are finished, follow your teacher's directions about cleaning up.
9. After 3 days, repeat Steps 5 through 8.
10. After 3 more days, repeat Steps 5 through 8 again. Then follow your teacher's directions for returning the solution.

Daphnia

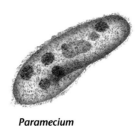

Paramecium

Spirogyra

---

prior experience. If they have not observed living microorganisms, they may have at least seen photographs or drawings.)

Introducing the Procedure

◆ Review all procedures related to the correct and safe handling of slides, coverslips, and microscopes. If students have not prepared slides or used a microscope before, demonstrate these processes for them.
◆ Introduce or review guidelines for making scientific drawings: the drawings should be

as realistic and accurate as possible, labeled appropriately, and drawn to scale in proportion to each other.

Troubleshooting the Experiment

◆ Make sure students store their jars where they will not be exposed to bright sunlight.
◆ Caution students not to tip or shake the jars when handling them.
◆ In Steps 5–10, circulate among students as they work to provide assistance in preparing the slides and using the microscope. You may

Making and Viewing a Slide

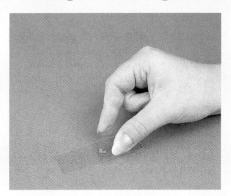

A. Place one drop of the solution to be examined in the middle of a microscope slide. Place one edge of a coverslip at the edge of the drop, as shown above. Gently lower the coverslip over the drop. Try not to trap any air bubbles.

B. Place the slide on the stage of a microscope so the drop is over the opening in the stage. Adjust the stage clips to hold the slide.

C. Look from the side of the microscope, and use the coarse adjustment knob to move the low-power objective close to, but not touching, the coverslip.

D. Look through the eyepiece, and use the coarse adjustment knob to raise the body tube and bring the slide into view. Use the fine adjustment knob to bring the slide into focus.

E. To view the slide under high power, look from the side of the microscope, and revolve the nosepiece until the high-power objective clicks into place just over, but not touching, the slide.

F. While you are looking through the eyepiece, use the fine adjustment knob to bring the slide into focus.

Analyze and Conclude

1. Identify as many of the organisms you observed as possible. Use the diagrams on the facing page and any other resources your teacher provides.
2. How did the community change over the time that you made your observations?
3. What factors may have influenced the changes in this community?
4. Where did the organisms you observed in the jar come from?
5. **Think About It** Do you think your observations gave you a complete picture of the changes in this community? Explain your answer.

Design an Experiment

Write a hypothesis about what would happen if you changed one biotic or abiotic factor in this activity. Design a plan to test your hypothesis. Obtain your teacher's permission before carrying out your experiment.

need to show students how to regulate the light, adjust the mirror, or make other adjustments for clear viewing.
◆ Emphasize to students that they should always view each slide under low power first, then switch to high power. Remind them to take care in switching lenses so they do not break the slide.

Program Resources

◆ **Teaching Resources** Chapter 2 Skills Lab, pp. 62–63

Safety

Make sure students handle the slide and coverslip carefully and wash their hands each time they handle the jar and solution. Review the safety guidelines in Appendix A. Follow the guidelines in Appendix A Teacher's Edition for the recommended safe disposal of bacteria cultures.

Expected Outcome

In general, large populations of smaller organisms such as bacteria and tiny protists will be present early in the succession, whereas populations of larger protists and tiny animals will increase toward the end of the succession.

Analyze and Conclude

1. Answers will vary. Students can usually expect to see a variety of microorganisms, including the three pictured.
2. After one or two days, the solution may become cloudy as bacteria and other microorganisms multiply. Small protists may appear early, followed by larger protists such as green algae, paramecia, and amoebas. Tiny animals such as water fleas and rotifers may be visible toward the end of the sequence.
3. Abiotic factors include the amount of light received, the temperature of the water, and the space available for the populations. Biotic factors include predation of some organisms by other organisms. As smaller organisms multiplied, they provided a growing food supply for larger organisms, which could in turn increase in numbers as well.
4. The organisms were already in the hay solution or pond water, are offspring of those original organisms, or developed from fertilized eggs in the hay solution or pond water.
5. Answers may vary. Some students may say the picture of the model community was complete because they used a valid method of taking samples and made logical inferences and generalizations. Other students may say the picture was incomplete because only three small samples were taken on just three occasions, revealing only a small percentage of the organisms living in the community.

Extending the Inquiry

Design an Experiment Possible changes in abiotic factors include keeping the jar in a slightly warmer or cooler place or exposing it to more or less light. Changes in biotic factors include varying the amounts of hay solution and pond water (the sources of organisms) or adding a specific population of producers or consumers to the community.

Objective

After completing the lesson, students will be able to
◆ Describe the differences between primary and secondary succession.

Key Terms succession, primary succession, pioneer species, secondary succession

1 Engage/Explore

Activating Prior Knowledge

Ask students: **Have you ever observed a vacant lot or an untended garden over time? What changes did you see?** *(Answers will depend on students' experience. They will probably say that first small, grassy weeds grew, then larger weeds and some shrubs, and finally small trees.)*

DISCOVER

Skills Focus posing questions
Time 10 minutes
Expected Outcome *A:* Soil is bare and scorched; trees in background have been damaged. *B:* Soil is covered with small plants; damaged trees are leafy.
Think It Over Small plants began to grow again; the existing trees recovered. Students' questions will vary. *Sample questions:* What kinds of plants come back first? Will the area ever look like it did before the fire? How long will that take?

DISCOVER .... **ACTIVITY**

What Happened Here?

1. The two photographs at the right show the same area in Yellowstone National Park in Wyoming. Photograph A was taken soon after a major fire. Photograph B was taken a few years later. Observe the photographs carefully.

2. Make a list of all the differences you notice between the two scenes.

Think It Over
Posing Questions How would you describe what happened during the time between the two photographs? What questions do you have about this process?

GUIDE FOR READING

◆ How are primary and secondary succession different?

Reading Tip Before you read, write a definition of what you think the term *succession* might mean. As you read, revise your definition.

In 1988, a huge fire raged through Yellowstone National Park. The fire was so hot that it jumped from tree to tree without burning along the ground between them. In an instant, huge trees burst into flame from the intense heat. It took weeks for the fires to burn themselves out. All that remained of that part of the forest were thousands of blackened tree trunks sticking out of the ground like charred toothpicks.

You might think it unlikely that Yellowstone could recover from such a disastrous fire. But within just a few months, signs of life had returned. First tiny green shoots of new grass appeared in the black ground. Then small tree seedlings began to grow again. The forest was coming back!

Fires, floods, volcanoes, hurricanes, and other natural disasters can change communities in a very short period of time. But even without a disaster, communities change. The series of predictable changes that occur in a community over time is called **succession.** This section describes two types of succession: primary succession and secondary succession.

READING STRATEGIES

Vocabulary When students encounter the definition of *succession* on this page, write the term on the board and underline the root success. Explain that the word *success* comes from the word *succeed*. Have students define *succeed* in their own words. *(They will most likely focus on the idea of "doing something you were trying to do.")*

Invite students to look in dictionaries to find definitions of *succeed* and read them aloud. *(1. to come next in time; 2. to accomplish something desired or intended)*
Which meaning fits the word *succession*? *(To come next in time)*

Primary Succession

Primary succession is the series of changes that occur in an area where no ecosystem previously existed. Such an area might be a new island formed by the eruption of an undersea volcano, or an area of rock uncovered by a melting sheet of ice.

You can follow the series of changes an area might undergo in Figure 26 below. These scenes show an area after a violent volcanic eruption. At first there is no soil, just ash and rock. The first species to populate the area are called **pioneer species.** Pioneer species are often lichens and mosses carried to the area by wind or water. These species can grow on bare rocks with little or no soil. As these organisms grow, they help break up the rocks. When they die, they provide nutrients that enrich the thin layer of soil that is forming on the rocks.

Over time, plant seeds land in the new soil and begin to grow. The specific plants that grow depend on the biome of the area. For example, in a cool, northern area, early seedlings might include alder and cottonwood trees. As the soil grows older and richer, these trees might be replaced by spruce and hemlock. Eventually, succession may lead to a community of organisms that does not change unless the ecosystem is disturbed. Reaching this stable community can take centuries.

☑ *Checkpoint* *What are some pioneer species?*

Figure 26 Primary succession occurs in an area where no ecosystem previously existed. **A.** After a volcanic eruption, the ground surface consists of ash and rock. **B.** The first organisms to appear are lichens and moss. **C.** Weeds and grasses take root in the thin layer of soil. **D.** Eventually, tree seedlings and shrubs sprout. *Applying Concepts What determines the particular species that appear during succession?*

Program Resources

◆ **Teaching Resources** 2-5 Lesson Plan, p. 55; 2-5 Section Summary, p. 56

Media and Technology

 Audiotapes English-Spanish Summary 2-5

Answers to Self-Assessment

Caption Question

Figure 26 The particular species depend on the biome of the area.

☑ *Checkpoint*
Lichens and mosses

2 *Facilitate*

Primary Succession

Building Inquiry Skills: Inferring

Read aloud the definition of *succession* on the previous page, stressing the word "predictable." Then ask: **Why are the changes predictable? How can ecologists tell what will happen in a particular community after a natural disaster?** *(Students should infer that the types of plants that will grow in the area and the types of animals that will live there are determined by climate conditions, which are usually not changed over the long term by a disaster. Certain organisms appear first because they can survive in those conditions. Other organisms appear later when conditions become suitable for them.)* **learning modality: logical/ mathematical**

Building Inquiry Skills: Observing

Materials *lichens, mosses, hand lens*
Time 10–15 minutes

Encourage students to bring in lichens and mosses they have found growing on small rocks and loose tree bark. Let them examine the samples and draw what they see, first without and then with a hand lens. Ask: **What are lichens?** *(Fungi and algae that grow together; if students cannot recall this information, let them look back at page 69.)* **How are mosses different from other plants you've seen?** *(They are smaller and do not have true leaves or roots. Students may know of other differences from previous science classes.)* Have students return the lichens and mosses to the area where they were collected. **learning modality: visual**

Ongoing Assessment

Drawing Have each student draw a flowchart showing the stages of primary succession.

 Students could save their flow charts in their portfolios.

E ◆ 77

Secondary Succession

Real-Life Learning

Provide students with a variety of resources that show examples of secondary succession after human disturbances to natural ecosystems—for example, the regrowth of a forest after logging or the natural renewal of a prairie ecosystem when cattle or sheep are no longer grazed there (nature magazines often feature such articles). After reviewing several resources, encourage discussion about each disturbance's benefits to people and the environmental costs. **learning modality: visual**

3 Assess

Section 5 Review Answers

1. Primary succession occurs in an area where no ecosystem existed before, whereas secondary succession occurs after a disturbance in an existing ecosystem. Secondary succession generally occurs more rapidly than primary succession.
2. The first species to populate an area
3. *Natural disturbances:* fires, hurricanes, volcanoes, tornadoes; *human disturbances:* farming, logging, mining
4. Secondary succession; before the sidewalk was built, an ecosystem existed there.

Science at Home

Tips Suggest to students **ACTIVITY** that they use a tape recorder during the interview. If not, they should take notes so they do not forget what the person said. Let students present their summaries in a class discussion, focusing on any examples of succession they identified.

Performance Assessment

Writing Have students explain the difference between primary and secondary succession and give an example of each.

Figure 27 Secondary succession occurs following a disturbance to an ecosystem, such as clearing a forest for farmland. When the farm is abandoned, the forest gradually returns. **A.** After two years, weeds and wildflowers fill the field. **B.** After five years, pine seedlings and other plants populate the field. **C.** After 30 years, a pine forest has grown up. **D.** After 100 years, a mixed forest of pine, oak, and hickory is developing in the field.

Secondary Succession

The changes following the Yellowstone fire were an example of secondary succession. **Secondary succession** is the series of changes that occur after a disturbance in an existing ecosystem. Natural disturbances that have this effect include fires, hurricanes, and tornadoes. Human activities, such as farming, logging, or mining, may also disturb an ecosystem. **Unlike primary succession, secondary succession occurs in a place where an ecosystem has previously existed.**

Secondary succession occurs somewhat more rapidly than primary succession. Consider, for example, an abandoned field in the southeastern United States. Follow the process of succession in such a field in Figure 27. After a century, a hardwood forest is developing. This forest is very stable and will remain for a long time. Of course, the particular species that come and go in the process of succession depend on the biome.

 ## Section 5 Review

 ### Science at Home

1. How are primary and secondary succession different?
2. What is a pioneer species?
3. Give two examples of natural disturbances and two examples of human disturbances that can result in secondary succession.
4. **Thinking Critically Classifying** Grass poking through the cracks in a sidewalk is an example of succession. Is this primary or secondary succession? Explain.

Interview an older family member or neighbor who has lived in your neighborhood for a long time. Ask the person to describe how the neighborhood has changed over time. Have areas that were formerly grassy been paved or developed? Have any farms, parks, or lots returned to a wild state? Write a summary of your interview. Can you classify any of the changes as examples of succession?

Program Resources

◆ **Teaching Resources** 2-5 Review and Reinforce, p. 57; 2-5 Enrich, p. 58

Media and Technology

Transparencies "Primary and Secondary Succession," Transparency 7

Interactive Student Tutorial CD-ROM E-2

SECTION 1 Energy Flow in Ecosystems

Key Ideas

◆ The energy role of an organism is that of a producer, consumer, or decomposer.
◆ Producers are the source of all the food in an ecosystem. Most producers use sunlight to make food molecules through photosynthesis.
◆ Consumers include herbivores, carnivores, omnivores, and scavengers.
◆ Decomposers return nutrients to the environment where they can be used again.
◆ A food web shows the feeding relationships that exist in an ecosystem.
◆ At each level in an energy pyramid, there is less available energy than at the level below.

Key Terms

producer	omnivore	food chain
consumer	scavenger	food web
herbivore	decomposer	energy pyramid
carnivore		

 SECTION 2 Cycles of Matter

INTEGRATING CHEMISTRY

Key Ideas

◆ Matter, such as water, carbon dioxide, oxygen, and nitrogen, cycles through an ecosystem. Energy must be supplied constantly.
◆ The processes of evaporation, condensation, and precipitation form the water cycle.
◆ Producers use carbon dioxide to produce other carbon-containing molecules.
◆ Free nitrogen in the atmosphere cannot be used by most living things. Nitrogen must be fixed by certain types of bacteria.

Key Terms

| water cycle | condensation | nitrogen fixation |
| evaporation | precipitation | nodules |

 SECTION 3 Biogeography

Key Ideas

◆ Means of dispersal of organisms include continental drift, wind, water, and living things.
◆ Three factors that limit dipersal are physical barriers, competition, and climate.

Key Terms

biogeography	native species
continental drift	exotic species
dispersal	climate

 SECTION 4 Earth's Biomes

Key Ideas

◆ Temperature and precipitation mostly determine the type of ecosystem found in an area.
◆ Land biomes include rain forests, deserts, grasslands, deciduous forests, boreal forests, and tundras.
◆ There is only enough sunlight for photosynthesis to occur near the surface or in shallow areas of water biomes.

Key Terms

biome	savanna	permafrost
canopy	deciduous trees	estuary
understory	hibernation	intertidal zone
desert	coniferous trees	neritic zone
grassland	tundra	

SECTION 5 Succession

Key Idea

◆ Primary succession occurs where no previous ecosystem exists. Secondary succession occurs after a disturbance.

Key Terms

| succession | pioneer species |
| primary succession | secondary succession |

USING THE INTERNET

www.science-explorer.phschool.com

Chapter 2 **E ◆ 79**

Program Resources

◆ **Teaching Resources** Chapter 2 Project Scoring Rubric, p. 38; Chapter 2 Performance Assessment, pp. 187–189; Chapter 2 Test, pp. 190–193

Media and Technology

Interactive Student Tutorial CD-ROM E-2

Computer Test Bank Test E-2

Reviewing Content:
Multiple Choice

1. d 2. b 3. d 4. c 5. b

True or False

6. scavenger 7. true 8. biogeography
9. true 10. rain forest

Checking Concepts

11. *Producers* capture the energy of sunlight to make their own food. *Consumers* obtain energy by feeding on other organisms. *Decomposers* obtain energy by breaking down wastes and dead organisms.
12. A food chain is a single path of events in which one organism eats another. A food web is a combination of interconnected and overlapping food chains.
13. The sun or sunlight
14. Nitrogen-fixing bacteria convert free nitrogen gas in the atmosphere into nitrogen-containing molecules that other organisms can use.
15. A native species is one that naturally evolved in an area. An exotic species is one that was introduced to the area.
16. When the continents were touching one another in one land mass, organisms could move freely between them. When the continents moved apart, organisms were separated and evolved independently.
17. Algae
18. Students should describe the temperature and precipitation conditions, the plants, and the other organisms typically found in the chosen biome.

Thinking Visually

19. **a.** Plant uses carbon to make sugar molecules. **b.** Animal releases carbon dioxide into the air.

Applying Skills

20. Grass: producer; mouse, rabbit, and deer: first-level consumers; snake and mountain lion: second-level consumers
21. The producers (grass)
22. The snake and mountain lion populations would decrease because there would be fewer prey organisms for them to eat. The deer population would probably decrease at first as hungry lions

---

Reviewing Content

 For more review of key concepts, see the Interactive Student Tutorial CD-ROM.

Multiple Choice
Choose the letter of the best answer.

1. A diagram that shows how much energy is available at each feeding level in an ecosystem is a(n)
   a. food chain.   b. food web.
   c. succession.   d. energy pyramid.
2. Which of the following organisms are typical decomposers?
   a. grasses and ferns
   b. bacteria and mushrooms
   c. mice and deer
   d. lions and snakes
3. Which of the following is *not* recycled in an ecosystem?
   a. carbon   b. nitrogen
   c. water   d. energy
4. Organisms may be dispersed in all the following ways *except* by
   a. wind.   b. water.
   c. temperature.   d. other organisms.
5. Much of Canada is covered in pine and spruce forests. The winter is cold and long. What is this biome?
   a. tundra   b. boreal forest
   c. deciduous forest   d. grassland

True or False
If the statement is true, write true. If it is false, change the underlined word or words to make the statement true.

6. An organism that eats the remains of dead organisms is called a(n) <u>herbivore</u>.
7. The step of the water cycle is which liquid water changes to water vapor is <u>evaporation</u>.
8. The study of the past and present distribution of species on Earth is called <u>succession</u>.
9. <u>Precipitation</u> and temperature are the two major abiotic factors that determine what types of plants can grow in an area.
10. The land biome that gets the highest average amount of precipitation is the tropical <u>grassland</u> biome.

Checking Concepts

11. Name and briefly define each of the three energy roles organisms can play in an ecosystem.
12. How are food chains and food webs different?
13. What is the source of energy for most ecosystems?
14. Describe the role of nitrogen-fixing bacteria in the nitrogen cycle.
15. Explain the difference between a native species and an exotic species.
16. How has continental drift affected the distribution of species on Earth?
17. What organisms are the producers in most marine ecosystems?
18. **Writing to Learn** Choose any of the biomes described in this chapter. Imagine that you are a typical animal found in that biome. Write a paragraph describing the conditions and other organisms in your animal's biome.

Thinking Visually

19. **Flowchart** Copy the flowchart below on a separate sheet of paper. Complete the flowchart to show how carbon cycles through an ecosystem. (For more on flowcharts, see the Skills Handbook.)

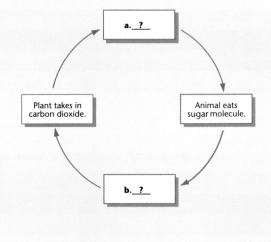

---

preyed on deer. Later as the lion population decreased, the deer population would increase. Also, the deer would have less competition for grass.

Thinking Critically

23. Clover plants are legumes that have nitrogen-fixing bacteria in nodules on their roots. Planting clover enriches the field by returning nitrogen-containing molecules to the soil.
24. Both the desert and the tundra are very dry and have extreme living conditions. The desert

may be very hot during the day in summer, with large shifts in temperature between day and night; the tundra is cool in summer and bitterly cold in winter. Desert soil is sandy; most of the soil in the tundra is frozen all year long.
25. Climate; polar bears' thick, insulating fur would make it difficult for them to live in a warmer environment; the white fur would make them stand out against land that was not covered with ice and snow.
26. First, lichens and mosses would grow on the bare volcanic rock and begin to break it up to

Applying Skills

Use the diagram of a food web below to answer Questions 20–22.

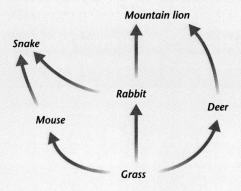

20. Classifying Identify the energy role of each organism in this food web. For consumers, specify whether they are first-level, second-level, or third-level.

21. Inferring Which level of the food web contains the greatest amount of available energy?

22. Predicting If a disease were to kill most of the rabbits in this area, predict how the snakes, deer, and mountain lions would be affected.

Thinking Critically

23. Relating Cause and Effect Every few years, a farmer plants clover in a wheat-field. Explain this practice.

24. Comparing and Contrasting How are the desert biome and the tundra biome similar? How are they different?

25. Inferring Polar bears are very well adapted to life around the Arctic Ocean. Their white fur camouflages them in the snow. They can swim and hunt in very cold water. Is the distribution of polar bears limited by physical barriers, competition, or climate? Explain your answer.

26. Predicting A volcano has just erupted in the ocean near Hawaii, forming a new island. How might succession change this island over time?

Performance Assessment

Wrap Up

Present Your Project Check over your report, poster, or other product. It should clearly present your data and conclusions about the effect of your variable on the decomposition process.

Reflect and Record In your notebook, compare your results to your predictions about the different waste materials in the compost mixture. Were you surprised by any of your results? Based on what you have learned from your project and those of your classmates, make a list of the ideal conditions for decomposition.

Getting Involved

In Your School With your classmates, take a group of younger students on a "sock walk" to learn about seed dispersal. Give the students thick white socks to wear over their shoes. Lead the students on a short walk through a field, woods, or park near your school. Back at school, the students can remove the socks and observe how many seeds they collected. Help them plant the socks in pans of soil. Place the pans in a sunny spot and water them regularly. How many species did the students successfully disperse?

---

form soil. Next, seeds would float or be blown onto the island or be carried and deposited there by birds; the seeds would grow in the thin layer of soil created by the lichens and mosses. As more plants grew and died, more soil would form, supporting larger plants and trees. In time, a mature biome would develop.

Program Resources

◆ **Inquiry Skills Activity Book** Provides teaching and review of all inquiry skills

---

Performance Assessment

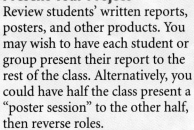

Wrap Up
Present Your Project
Review students' written reports, posters, and other products. You may wish to have each student or group present their report to the rest of the class. Alternatively, you could have half the class present a "poster session" to the other half, then reverse roles.

Reflect and Record Allow time for all students to compare their results so they can compile a list of "ideal" conditions. In general, compost will form most quickly when the compost is kept moist (molds grow better), well-aerated (many decomposers are aerobic), and warm (metabolic activity is higher) and when soil organisms are added.

Getting Involved

In Your School Coordinate the "sock walk" with a lower-grade teacher and supervise students during the activity. Fuzzy terry cloth or wool athletic socks will work best. You can purchase these at a discount store or ask students to donate old socks from home. After the seeds germinate, provide field guides for students to use in identifying the plants.

3 Living Resources

Sections	Time	Student Edition Activities	Other Activities	
CHAPTER PROJECT 3 **Variety Show** p. 83	Ongoing (2–3 weeks)	Check Your Progress, pp. 89, 108 Wrap Up, p. 111		
1 Environmental Issues pp. 84–90 ◆ Identify the main types of environmental issues. ◆ Define environmental science. ◆ Describe how decision makers balance different needs and concerns related to environmental issues.	3–4 periods/ $1\frac{1}{2}$–2 blocks	**Discover** How Do You Decide?, p. 84 **Sharpen Your Skills** Communicating, p. 89 **Real-World Lab: You and Your Environment** Is Paper a Renewable Resource?, p. 90	TE TE TE IES	Building Inquiry Skills: Graphing, p. 85 Including All Students, p. 86 Science and History, p. 87 "Fate of the Rain Forest," pp. 32–35; "Where River Meets Sea," pp. 39–40
2 Forests and Fisheries pp. 91–96 ◆ Describe different ways that forests can be managed to provide resources. ◆ Describe ways that fisheries can be managed to provide resources.	3–4 periods/ $1\frac{1}{2}$–2 blocks	**Discover** What Happened to the Tuna?, p. 91 **Sharpen Your Skills** Calculating, p. 94 **Science at Home,** p. 95 **Skills Lab: Interpreting Data** Tree Cookie Tales, p. 96	TE TE ISLM	Inquiry Challenge, p. 93 Real-Life Learning, p. 94 E–3, "Managing Fisheries"
3 Biodiversity pp. 97–105 ◆ Identify factors that affect biodiversity. ◆ Name some human activities that threaten biodiversity. ◆ List some ways that biodiversity can be protected. ◆ Explain the value of biodiversity.	2–3 periods/ 1–$1\frac{1}{2}$ blocks	**Discover** How Much Variety Is There?, p. 97 **Science at Home,** p. 105	TE TE TE TE TE TE IES	Building Inquiry Skills: Observing, pp. 98, 107; Communicating, pp. 99, 104; Making Models, p. 101 Demonstration, p. 99 Addressing Naive Conceptions, p. 100 Inquiry Challenge, p. 103 Demonstration, p. 104 Real-Life Learning, p. 107 "Fate of the Rain Forest," pp. 10–11, 22–23
4 **INTEGRATING HEALTH** **The Search for New Medicines** pp. 106–108 ◆ Explain why many rain forest plants are sources of medicines.	1–2 periods/ $\frac{1}{2}$–1 block	**Discover** How Are Plant Chemicals Separated?, p. 106	TE IES	Building Inquiry Skills: Observing, p. 107 "Fate of the Rain Forest," pp. 12–13
Study Guide/Chapter Review pp. 109–111	1 period/ $\frac{1}{2}$ block		ISAB	Provides teaching and review of all inquiry skills

For Standard or Block Schedule The Resource Pro® CD-ROM gives you maximum flexibility for planning your instruction for any type of schedule. Resource Pro® contains Planning Express®, an advanced scheduling program, as well as the entire contents of the Teaching Resources and the Computer Test Bank.

CHAPTER PLANNING GUIDE

Program Resources	Assessment Strategies	Media and Technology
TR Chapter 3 Project Teacher Notes, pp. 64–65 **TR** Chapter 3 Project Overview and Worksheets, pp. 66–69 **TR** Chapter 3 Project Scoring Rubric, p. 70	**SE** Performance Assessment: Chapter 3 Project Wrap Up, p. 111 **TE** Check Your Progress, pp. 89, 108 **TE** Performance Assessment: Chapter 3 Project Wrap Up, p. 111 **TR** Chapter 3 Project Scoring Rubric, p. 70	Science Explorer Internet Site
TR 3-1 Lesson Plan, p. 71 **TR** 3-1 Section Summary, p. 72 **TR** 3-1 Review and Reinforce, p. 73 **TR** 3-1 Enrich, p. 74 **TR** Chapter 3 Real-World Lab, pp. 87–89	**SE** Section 1 Review, p. 89 **SE** Analyze and Conclude, p. 90 **TE** Ongoing Assessment, pp. 85, 87 **TE** Performance Assessment, p. 89 **TR** 3-1 Review and Reinforce, p. 73	Exploring Life Science Videodisc, Unit 1 Side 2, "Can We Still Get What We Need?" Audiotapes, English-Spanish Summary 3-1 Interactive Student Tutorial CD-ROM, E-3
TR 3-2 Lesson Plan, p. 75 **TR** 3-2 Section Summary, p. 76 **TR** 3-2 Review and Reinforce, p. 77 **TR** 3-2 Enrich, p. 78 **TR** Chapter 3 Skills Lab, pp. 90–91 **SES** Book H, *Earth's Waters,* Chapter 5	**SE** Section 2 Review, p. 95 **SE** Analyze and Conclude, p. 96 **TE** Ongoing Assessment, p. 93 **TE** Performance Assessment, p. 95 **TR** 3-2 Review and Reinforce, p. 77	Audiotapes, English-Spanish Summary 3-2 Transparency 8, "Logging Methods" Interactive Student Tutorial CD-ROM, E-3
TR 3-3 Lesson Plan, p. 79 **TR** 3-3 Section Summary, p. 80 **TR** 3-3 Review and Reinforce, p. 81 **TR** 3-3 Enrich, p. 82 **SES** Book H, *Earth's Waters,* Chapter 5 **SES** Book C, *Cells and Heredity,* Chapter 3	**SE** Section 3 Review, p. 105 **TE** Ongoing Assessment, pp. 99, 101, 103 **TE** Performance Assessment, p. 105 **TR** 3-3 Review and Reinforce, p. 81	Exploring Life Science Videodisc, Unit 6, Side 2, "Can We Save the Tigers?"; "It's All Happening at the Zoo" Audiotapes, English-Spanish Summary 3-3 Interactive Student Tutorial CD-ROM, E-3
TR 3-4 Lesson Plan, p. 83 **TR** 3-4 Section Summary, p. 84 **TR** 3-4 Review and Reinforce, p. 85 **TR** 3-4 Enrich, p. 86	**SE** Section 4 Review, p. 108 **TE** Ongoing Assessment, p. 107 **TE** Performance Assessment, p. 109 **TR** 3-4 Review and Reinforce, p. 85	Exploring Life Science Videodisc, Unit 6 Side 2, "A Question of Balance" Audiotapes, English-Spanish Summary 3-4 Interactive Student Tutorial CD-ROM, E-3
TR Chapter 3 Performance Assessment, pp. 194–196 **TR** Chapter 3 Test, pp. 197–200	**SE** Chapter 3 Review, pp. 110–111 **TR** Chapter 3 Performance Assessment, pp. 194–196 **TR** Chapter 3 Test, pp. 197–200 **CTB** Test E-3	Interactive Student Tutorial CD-ROM, E-3 Computer Test Bank, Test E-3

Key: **SE** Student Edition   **TE** Teacher's Edition   **TR** Teaching Resources
     CTB Computer Test Bank   **SES** Science Explorer Series Text   **ISLM** Integrated Science Laboratory Manual
     ISAB Inquiry Skills Activity Book   **PTA** Product Testing Activities by *Consumer Reports*   **IES** Interdisciplinary Explorations Series

Meeting the National Science Education Standards and AAAS Benchmarks

National Science Education Standards	Benchmarks for Science Literacy	Unifying Themes
Science As Inquiry (Content Standard A) ◆ **Design and conduct an investigation** Students observe diversity of organisms. *(Chapter Project)* ◆ **Develop descriptions, explanations, predictions, and models using evidence** Students model paper recycling. Students observe a tree cross section to draw conclusions about how the tree grew. *(Real-World Lab; Skills Lab)* **Life Science** (Content Standard C) ◆ **Diversity and adaptions of organisms** The number of different species in an area is called biodiversity. Plants in many ecosystems produce chemicals that protect them. *(Chapter Project; Sections 3, 4)* **Science in Personal and Social Perspectives** (Content Standard F) ◆ **Populations, resources, and environments** Environmental science is the study of natural processes and how humans affect them. Forests and fisheries are renewable resources. Human activities can threaten biodiversity. *(Sections 1, 2, 3)* ◆ **Science and technology in society** Environmental issues include resource management, population growth, and pollution. Some chemicals from rain forest plants can be used to fight diseases. *(Sections 1, 4)* **History and Nature of Science** (Content Standard G) ◆ **History of science** Certain individuals have influenced the viewpoints of others toward the environment. *(Science & History)*	**1B Scientific Inquiry** Students survey a plot of land to observe the diversity of organisms, model paper recycling, and observe a tree cross section to draw conclusions about the conditions in which the tree grew. *(Chapter Project; Real-World Lab; Skills Lab)* **1C The Scientific Enterprise** Certain individuals have influenced the viewpoints of many others toward environmental issues. *(Science & History)* **3A Technology and Society** Students model the process of recycling paper. Some chemicals rainforest plants produce to protect their leaves and bark can also be used to fight human diseases. *(Real-World Lab; Section 4)* **3C Issues in Technology** The three main types of environmental issues are resource management, population growth, and pollution. Some methods of logging and fishing are harmful to the environment. Human activities can threaten biodiversity. *(Sections 1, 2, 3)* **4B The Earth** Forests and fisheries are renewable resources if managed properly. *(Section 2)* **5A Diversity of Life** The number of different species in an area is called biodiversity. Many plants produce chemicals that protect them from predators, parasites, and disease. *(Chapter Project; Sections 3, 4)*	◆ **Evolution** Extinction is the disappearance of all members of a species from Earth. *(Section 3)* ◆ **Modeling** Students model paper recycling. *(Real-World Lab)* ◆ **Patterns of Change** Any change to the environment that has a negative effect on the environment is called pollution. If fish are caught at a faster rate than they can breed, the population of a fishery decreases. Human activities have reduced biodiversity. *(Sections 1, 2, 3)* ◆ **Scale and Structure** Each pair of light and dark rings in a tree cross section represents one year's growth. *(Skills Lab)* ◆ **Stability** Managing forests and fisheries helps conserve these living resources for the future. Many people are working to preserve the world's biodiversity. *(Sections 2, 3)* ◆ **Systems and Interactions** Environmental science is the study of the natural processes that occur in the environment and how humans can affect them. Factors that affect biodiversity in an ecosystem include area, climate, and diversity of niches. Some plants produce chemicals that protect them from predators, parasites, and diseases. *(Sections 1, 3, 4)* ◆ **Unity and Diversity** The three main types of environmental issues are resource management, population growth, and pollution. The number of different species in an area is called biodiversity. *(Sections 1, 3; Chapter Project)*

Media and Technology

Exploring Life Science Videodiscs

◆ **Section 1** "Can We Still Get What We Need?" examines how increasing global population affects Earth's resources.

◆ **Section 3** "Can We Save the Tigers?" features a program to save tigers from extinction. "It's All Happening at the Zoo" examines a zoo's education, research, preservation, and breeding efforts.

◆ **Section 4** "A Question of Balance" considers rain forest resources and exploitation.

Interactive Student Tutorial CD-ROM

◆ **Chapter Review** Interactive questions help students to self-assess their mastery of key chapter concepts.

Student Edition Connection Strategies

◆ **Section 1** Science & History, pp. 86–87

◆ **Section 2** Social Studies Connection, p. 92

◆ **Section 3** Integrating Health, pp. 106–108

USING THE INTERNET ACTIVITY

www.science-explorer.phschool.com

Visit the Science Explorer Internet site to find an up-to-date activity for Chapter 3 of *Environmental Science*.

Student Edition Activities Planner

Activity	Time (minutes)	Materials *Quantities for one work group*	Skills
Section 1			
Discover, p. 84	15	No special materials are required.	Forming Operational Definitions
Sharpen Your Skills, p. 89	20	No special materials are required.	Communicating
Real-World Lab, p. 90	15; 40; 10	**Consumable** newspaper, water, plastic wrap **Nonconsumable** microscope, microscope slide, eggbeater, square pan, screen, heavy book, mixing bowl	Observing, Designing Experiments
Section 2			
Discover, p. 91	15	**Consumable** graph paper **Nonconsumable** ruler, pencil	Inferring
Sharpen Your Skills, p. 94	15	**Nonconsumable** calculator	Calculating
Science at Home, p. 95	home	No special materials are required.	Classifying
Skills Lab, p. 96	40	**Nonconsumable** tree cookie (tree cross section), metric ruler, hand lens, colored pencils, calculator (optional)	Observing, Measuring, Drawing Conclusions
Section 3			
Discover, p. 97	20	**Nonconsumable** two different birdseed or dried bean mixtures, two cups, paper plate	Inferring
Science at Home, p. 105	home	**Nonconsumable** map of community or state	Communicating
Section 4			
Discover, p. 106	15	**Consumable** strip of filter paper, water, tape **Nonconsumable** black marking pen, clear plastic cup, pencil	Observing

A list of all materials required for the Student Edition activities can be found on pages T14–T15. You can order Materials Kits by calling 1-800-828-7777 or by accessing the Science Explorer Internet site at **www.science-explorer.phschool.com.**

The Chapter 3 Project is designed to develop students' appreciation for the rich diversity of living things that can be found in even a very small plot of land. The project also provides an opportunity for students to apply methods and skills that are used by field biologists.

Purpose After marking study plots of land, students will observe their plots regularly and record observations and data in a notebook. To conclude the project, students will communicate their findings in a class presentation.

Skills Focus After completing the Chapter 3 Project, students will be able to
◆ observe, compare and contrast, and classify organisms;
◆ infer relationships among organisms and between organisms and the abiotic factors in their environment;
◆ create a data table for recording observations;
◆ communicate observations and conclusions to others.

Project Time Line The Chapter 3 Project requires two to three weeks to complete. Each small group of students will begin by staking out a 1.5-by-1.5 meter plot of land and preparing a notebook for recording observations, including notes and drawings of the organisms observed, and the date, time, air temperature, and weather conditions during each observation. The major portion of the project involves making regular observations and recording data. During this time, students can use field guides to identify organisms. At the conclusion of the observation period, each group will prepare a class presentation that may include support materials such as photographs, drawings, videos, or computer displays.

Possible Materials
◆ To mark the plot, each group will need a meter stick or metric tape measure, four small stakes, a hammer, surveyor's tape or sturdy string, and a directional compass.
◆ When students observe their plots, each group will need a thermometer, hand lenses, rulers, and trowels.

WHAT'S AHEAD

◆ Provide a variety of field guides so students can research the names and classification of any unfamiliar organisms they observe. A field guide to animal tracks will also be helpful for students who find trace evidence of organisms that have visited the plot.
◆ When students are ready to prepare their class presentations, provide art supplies and audiovisual equipment such as cameras and videocassette recorders, if available.

Advance Preparation Before introducing the Chapter 3 Project, survey the grounds around your school so that you can guide students to areas where they are likely to find a good variety of organisms. If the school grounds are not appropriate, locate a nearby field, park, vacant lot, or other natural area to which you can take the class during school hours. Obtain permission to use the land, if necessary.

Launching the Project Invite students to read the project description on page 83. Then guide a class brainstorming session about nearby areas that might be good for setting up the study plots. Share what you know about

Variety Show

The colors in this meadow show that many different types of organisms live here. In other places, life's variety is less obvious. In this chapter's project, you will become an ecologist as you study the diversity of life in a small plot of land. Keep in mind that the area you will study has just a small sample of the huge variety of organisms that live on Earth.

Your Goal To observe the diversity of organisms in a plot of land.

To complete this project you must
- ◆ stake out a 1.5 meter-by-1.5 meter plot of ground
- ◆ keep a record of your observations of the abiotic conditions
- ◆ identify the species of organisms you observe
- ◆ follow the safety guidelines in Appendix A

Get Started Read over the project and prepare a notebook in which to record your observations. Include places to record the date, time, air temperature, and other weather conditions during each observation. Leave space for drawings or photographs of the organisms in your plot.

Check Your Progress You'll be working on this project as you study this chapter. To keep your project on track, look for Check Your Progress boxes at the following points.

Section 1 Review, page 89: Stake out your plot, and begin to observe it.

Section 4 Review, page 108: Identify the organisms in your plot. Begin to prepare your presentation.

Wrap Up At the end of the chapter (page 111), you will present your findings to the class. You will describe your observations and share the diversity of life in your plot.

A woodchuck feasts on wildflowers in a meadow exploding with color. Black-eyed Susans, Queen Anne's lace, and butterflyweed are part of the meadow's diversity.

SECTION 4
Integrating Health
The Search for New Medicines

Discover **How Are Plant Chemicals Separated?**

possible areas. Help students agree on appropriate areas. Suggest that students may select an area near their homes where they can carry out observations.

Distribute Chapter 3 Project Overview on pages 66–67 in Teaching Resources. Have students review the project rules and procedures. Encourage students' questions. Clarify whether students will be given class time for observing the plots or they must carry out the observations on their own time.

Divide the class into groups of four to six students each. Explain that each group's members may divide the project responsibilities among themselves in any way they wish. However, every group member should help plan the notebook, stake out the plot, make and record observations, and develop the group's presentation and should be prepared to answer questions. You may wish to also offer the option for students to work alone surveying plots near their homes if space in the schoolyard is an issue.

To get students started, allow time for groups to meet and begin planning the project notebook. Distribute Worksheet 1, which provides instructions and a grid for making a scale drawing of the study plot. At the end of Section 1, distribute Worksheet 2, which provides guidance for recording information about the organisms that students observe.

Additional information on guiding the project is provided in Chapter 3 Project Teacher Notes on pages 32–33 in Teaching Resources.

Program Resources

- ◆ **Teaching Resources** Chapter 3 Project Teacher Notes, pp. 64–65; Chapter 3 Project Overview and Worksheets, pp. 66–69; Chapter 3 Project Scoring Rubric, p. 70

Performance Assessment

The Chapter 3 Project Scoring Rubric on page 70 in Teaching Resources will help you evaluate how well students complete the Chapter 3 Project. You may want to share the scoring rubric with students so they are clear about what will be expected of them. Students will be assessed on
- ◆ their completeness and accuracy in making observations and recording data;
- ◆ their ability to use previous knowledge and reference sources to identify and classify organisms;
- ◆ how well they have communicated their findings to the rest of the class;
- ◆ participation in their groups.

Objectives

After completing the lesson, students will be able to

◆ identify the main types of environmental issues;

◆ define environmental science;

◆ describe how decision makers balance different needs and concerns related to environmental issues.

Key Terms renewable resources, nonrenewable resources, pollution, development viewpoint, preservation viewpoint, conservation viewpoint

1 Engage/Explore

Activating Prior Knowledge

Ask students: **What is an "issue"?** (*Students' responses should include the idea of a problem or question on which people have different viewpoints.*) **What are some examples of issues that you've heard about?** (*Sample answers: Should a run-down historic building in town be restored or demolished? Should owners of beachfront property be allowed to restrict public access to beaches? Should the federal government fund daycare facilities?*)

•••••••• **DISCOVER** ••••••••

Skills Focus forming operational definitions
Time 15 minutes
Tips As students identify general issues such as "air pollution," encourage them to think of specific, *debatable* questions such as "Should car manufacturers be forced to build more efficient engines so our air is cleaner?"
Expected Outcome Decisions regarding the most important issue will vary.
Think It Over Students' definitions will vary but should include the idea of environment-related questions or problems on which people have different viewpoints.

DISCOVER •••••••••••••••••••••••••••••••••••••**ACTIVITY**•••

How Do You Decide?

1. On a sheet of paper, list the three environmental issues you think are most important.

2. Form a group with three other classmates. Share your lists. As a group decide which one of the issues is the most important.

Think It Over
Forming Operational Definitions
Based on your group's discussion, how would you define the term *environmental issue*?

GUIDE FOR READING

◆ What are the main types of environmental issues?

◆ What is environmental science?

◆ How do decision makers balance different needs and concerns?

Reading Tip Before you read, make a list of ways that humans depend on the environment. As you read, add examples from the text.

Figure 1 This leopard seal's habitat could be affected if oil drilling is allowed in Antarctica. This tradeoff is an example of an environmental issue.

ere's a puzzle for you: What is bigger than the United States and Mexico combined; is covered with two kilometers of ice; is a source of oil, coal, and iron; and is a unique habitat for many animals? The answer is Antarctica. People once thought of Antarctica as a useless, icy wasteland. But when explorers told of its huge populations of seals and whales, hunters began going to Antarctica. Then scientists set up research stations to study the unique conditions there. They soon discovered valuable minerals beneath the thick ice.

Now the puzzle is what to do with Antarctica. Many people want its rich deposits of minerals and oil. Others worry that mining will harm the delicate ecosystems there. Some people propose building hotels, parks, and ski resorts. But others feel that Antarctica should remain undisturbed. It is not even obvious who should decide Antarctica's fate.

In 1998, 26 nations agreed to ban mining and oil exploration in Antarctica for at least 50 years. As resources become more scarce elsewhere in the world, the debate will surely continue. What is the best use of Antarctica?

Types of Environmental Issues

People have always used Earth's resources. But as the human population has grown, so has its effect on the environment. People compete with each other and with other living things for Earth's limited resources. Disposing of wastes created by people can change ecosystems. And while people are continuing to take resources from the environment, many resources cannot be replaced. These resources could eventually run out.

READING STRATEGIES

Reading Tip Prompt students' thinking by guiding them to recall what they learned about biotic and abiotic factors in Chapter 1 and about cycles of matter and relationships among organisms in Chapter 2.

Paraphrasing This section includes many abstract concepts that some students may find difficult to comprehend or to relate

directly to their own experience. To ensure understanding as students read the section, have different volunteers summarize the text under each heading and subheading in their own words. Encourage the rest of the class to suggest additions and improvements to the volunteers' summaries and to offer specific examples of the concepts based on their own experience.

Figure 2 Cherries are a renewable resource. After they are harvested, new cherries will grow in their place. In contrast, the aluminum and iron used to make these kitchen tools are nonrenewable resources.

The three main types of environmental issues are resource use, population growth, and pollution. These issues are all connected, making them very difficult to solve.

Resource Use Anything in the environment that is used by people is a natural resource. Some natural resources, called **renewable resources,** are naturally replaced in a relatively short time. Renewable resources include sunlight, wind, and trees. But it is possible to use up some renewable resources. For example, if people cut down trees faster than they can grow back, the supply of this resource will decrease.

Natural resources that are not replaced as they are used are called **nonrenewable resources.** Most nonrenewable resources, such as coal and oil, exist in a limited supply. As nonrenewable resources are used, the supply may eventually be depleted.

Population Growth Figure 3 shows how the human population has changed in the last 3,000 years. You can see that the population grew very slowly until about A.D. 1650. Around that time, improvements in medicine, agriculture, and sanitation enabled people to live longer. The death rate decreased. But as the population has continued to grow, the demand for resources has also grown.

Pollution Any change to the environment that has a negative effect on living things is called **pollution.** Pollution is an issue because it is often the result of an activity that benefits humans. For example, generating electricity by burning coal can result in air pollution. Some pesticides used to kill insects that eat crops are harmful to other animals.

✓ *Checkpoint* What is a natural resource?

Figure 3 If two's company, six billion is certainly a crowd! The human population has grown rapidly in the last few centuries. *Calculating How much has the population grown since 1650?*

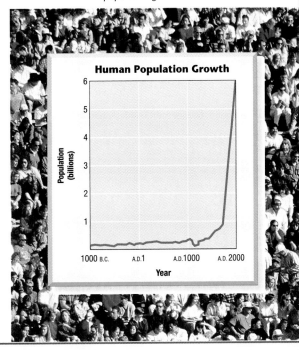

Human Population Growth

Population (billions) vs *Year* (1000 B.C., A.D.1, A.D.1000, A.D.2000)

Program Resources

♦ **Teaching Resources** 3-1 Lesson Plan, p. 71; 3-1 Section Summary, p. 72
♦ **Interdisciplinary Exploration Series** "Fate of the Rain Forest," pp. 32–35; "Where River Meets Sea," pp. 39–40

Media and Technology

 Audiotapes English-Spanish Summary 3-1

Answers to Self-Assessment

Caption Question

Figure 3 By more than 5 million people (from about 750 thousand to about 6 million)

✓ *Checkpoint*

A natural resource is anything in the environment that is used by people.

Types of Environmental Issues

Building Inquiry Skills: Graphing

Materials *graph paper, ruler, pencil, world map* **ACTIVITY**
Time 15 minutes

Point out that Figure 3 shows the entire world population and that growth rates and population sizes vary among different regions and countries of the world. Give students the current populations of several countries listed below, and have each student make a bar graph to compare the population sizes. Then have students use their graphs to answer the following questions: **Which country has the largest population?** *(China)* **The next largest?** *(India)* **How many times larger than Japan's population is the U.S. population?** *(About twice as large)* Have students compare the United States' and Japan's land areas on a world map, and ask: **Which country has a higher population density?** *(Japan; if needed, help students recall the term* population density *from Chapter 1.)* **learning modality: logical/mathematical**

1998 Population of Selected Countries	
Brazil	165,200,000
China	1,255,100,000
Great Britain	58,200,000
India	975,800,000
Indonesia	207,400,000
Japan	125,900,000
Mexico	95,800,000
Nigeria	121,800,000
Russia	147,200,000
United States	270,000,000

Ongoing Assessment

Writing Have each student explain why the world's human population has grown so dramatically in the past 350 years.

Approaches to Environmental Issues

Real-Life Learning

Ask students: **What things that you do now or could start doing would help protect the environment if a lot of other people did them, too?** *(Accept all reasonable responses, such as recycling soft drink cans instead of throwing them in the trash or putting on a sweater instead of turning up the heat at home.)* As students suggest actions, list each one on the board and ask: **How does this help solve environmental problems?** *(Sample answers: Recycling cans reduces our need to mine more aluminum, which is a nonrenewable resource. Putting on a sweater instead of turning up the heat reduces our use of heating fuel, another nonrenewable resource, and the air pollution that is released when fuels are burned.)* **learning modality: logical/mathematical**

Including All Students

Materials *current newspapers and magazines, scissors, large sheet of construction paper, tape or glue, markers*
Time 20–40 minutes

For students who need additional challenges, provide a variety of magazines and local and national newspapers. Let students work in groups of two or three to look through the sources and find articles about environmental issues in their community, state, or region. Suggest that each group choose one issue to use as the subject of a poster that summarizes the problem in the students' own words, briefly describes different viewpoints on or proposed solutions to the problem, and includes a photograph, graph, or other visual related to the issue. Display the completed posters in the classroom. Allow time for students to review one another's posters and discuss their ideas and views about the issues. **learning modality: verbal**

Approaches to Environmental Issues

Dealing with environmental issues means making choices. These choices can be made at personal, local, national, or global levels. Whether to ride in a car, take a bus, or ride your bicycle to the mall is an example of a personal choice. Whether to build a landfill or an incinerator for disposing of a town's wastes is a local choice. Whether the United States should allow oil drilling in a wildlife refuge is a national choice. How to protect Earth's atmosphere is a global choice.

Choices that seem personal are often part of much larger issues. Choices of what you eat, what you wear, and how you travel all affect the environment in a small way. When the choices made by millions of people are added together, each person's actions can make a difference.

SCIENCE & History

Making a Difference

Can one individual change the way people think? The leaders featured in this time line have influenced the way that many people think about environmental issues.

1892
California writer John Muir founds the Sierra Club. The group promotes the setting aside of wild areas as national parks. Muir's actions lead to the establishment of Yosemite National Park.

1905
Forestry scientist Gifford Pinchot is appointed the first director of the United States Forest Service. His goal is to manage forests scientifically to meet current and future lumber needs.

| 1875 | 1900 | 1925 |

1903
President Theodore Roosevelt establishes the first National Wildlife Refuge on Pelican Island, Florida, to protect the brown pelican.

Theodore Roosevelt (left) and John Muir (right)

Background

History of Science Students could also research these people for *In Your Journal*.

◆ **Jacques Cousteau** Through his many TV films, marine explorer Cousteau educated millions about ocean life and environmental damage caused by humans.

◆ **Dian Fossey** A zoologist known for her field studies of the rare mountain gorilla in east-central Africa, Fossey urged the preservation of this endangered species.

◆ **Jane Goodall** This animal behaviorist's multigenerational studies discovered meat eating and tool use among wild chimpanzees and increased our knowledge of the ecology of nonhuman primates.

◆ **Chico Mendes** Brazilian rubber tapper Mendes fought to prevent the destruction of rain forests and to establish extractive reserves where products could be harvested without causing ecological damage.

The first step in making environmental decisions is to understand how humans interact with the environment. **Environmental science is the study of the natural processes that occur in the environment and how humans can affect them.**

When people make decisions about environmental issues, the information provided by environmental scientists is a starting point. The next step is to decide what to do with the information. But environmental decisions also involve discussions of values, not just facts and figures. Environmental decisions usually require considering many different points of view. Most of these viewpoints fall into one of these three categories: development, preservation, or conservation.

☑ *Checkpoint* *What is an example of a local choice about an environmental issue?*

In Your Journal

Find out more about one of the people featured in this time line. Write a short biography of the person's life explaining how he or she became involved in environmental issues. What obstacles did the person overcome to accomplish his or her goal?

1949

Naturalist Aldo Leopold publishes *A Sand County Almanac*. This classic book links wildlife management to the science of ecology.

1969

At the age of 79, journalist Marjory Stoneman Douglas founds Friends of the Everglades. This grassroots organization is dedicated to preserving the unique Florida ecosystem. She continues to work for the Everglades until her death in 1998.

1950	1975	2000

1962

Biologist Rachel Carson writes *Silent Spring*, which describes the harmful effects of pesticides on the environment. The book raises awareness of how human activities can affect the environment.

1977

Biologist Wangari Maathai founds the Green Belt Movement. This organization encourages restoring forests in Kenya and other African nations.

Chapter 3   **E ◆ 87**

Answers to Self-Assessment

☑ *Checkpoint*

Answers will vary. *Sample answer:* Whether to build a landfill or an incinerator for disposing of a town's wastes

---

Building Inquiry Skills: Inferring

Point out the text statement that making decisions about environmental issues involves values, and ask: **What is a value?** *(An idea or standard that people think is important or worthwhile)* **What are some examples of values?** *(People should be honest, fair, reliable, and so forth.)* Draw students' attention to an environmental issue discussed in the text, and ask: **How would people's values affect their opinions and decisions about this issue?** *(Sample answer: Government decision makers might decide that wildlife refuges are too important to the survival of certain species to risk damaging them by oil drilling.)* **learning modality: verbal**

SCIENCE & History

Call on volunteers to read **ACTIVITY** the entries on the time line. Provide a U.S. and world map and ask other volunteers to locate the places mentioned in the entries. Ask students to share any experiences or information that they have about the featured people or places. Ask students to consider which of these people they would like to learn more about.

In Your Journal Provide a variety of source materials for students' research. After students have written their biographical sketches, encourage them work in small groups to create short skits based on their research, with one member of each group playing the role of the historical person. Encourage students to make their skits fun and interesting by using costumes and props in their portrayal of the person. Also suggest that they incorporate quotations taken from the person's writings, speeches, or interviews. **learning modality: verbal**

Ongoing Assessment

Writing Have each student explain how the actions of individuals can have a large effect on environmental issues.
 Students can save their explanations in their portfolios.

Approaches to Environmental Issues, continued

Building Inquiry Skills: Classifying

After students have read about development, preservation, and conservation viewpoints, direct their attention to an environmental issue in the text or from your local area, and ask: **What would be the development viewpoint on this issue?** *(Wildlife refuge example: We need to use all possible new sources of oil in the United States.)* **The preservation viewpoint?** *(Wildlife refuges must be kept natural and unspoiled by human activity.)* **The conservation viewpoint?** *(We need to find ways to use less oil in this country so we don't have to risk damaging natural areas to get it.)* Continue the same procedure using several other issues as examples.
learning modality: logical/mathematical

Weighing Costs and Benefits

Sharpen your Skills

Communicating

Time 20 minutes
Tips The three students in each group should represent the development, preservation, and conservation viewpoints.
Expected Outcome *Similarities:* All three viewpoints recognize that Antarctica has valuable resources and unique conditions. *Differences:* The development viewpoint gives priority to people's need for Antarctica's rich supply of oil and mineral resources; the preservation viewpoint gives priority to the needs of the organisms that live in Antarctica; the conservation viewpoint tries to strike a balance between the other two viewpoints.
Extend Let each group choose a local issue and create a compare/contrast table from the same three viewpoints.
learning modality: verbal

Economic value
The hills are a source of resources such as lumber and minerals.

Recreational value
The river is a good place to canoe and raft. Hikers can enjoy the surrounding hills.

Scenic value
The river valley is a beautiful and peaceful area.

Ecological value
The river valley is home to many plants, animals, and other organisms.

Health value
The river is a source of clean drinking water.

Figure 4 The environment is valued for many different reasons. *Applying Concepts In what other ways might this area be valuable?*

Development The belief that humans should be able to freely use and benefit from all of Earth's resources is referred to as the **development viewpoint.** This viewpoint considers the environment in terms of economics. Economics involves business, money, and jobs. According to the development viewpoint, the most valuable parts of the environment are those resources that are most useful to human beings.

Preservation The belief that all parts of the environment are equally important, no matter how useful they are to humans, is the **preservation viewpoint.** This viewpoint considers humans to be the caretakers of nature. Preservationists feel that Earth and its resources should be a source of beauty, comfort, and recreation. The preservation viewpoint is that living things and ecosystems should not be disturbed for the benefit of people.

Conservation The **conservation viewpoint** is the belief that people should use resources from the environment as long as they do not destroy those resources. Conservationists feel that people must balance development and preservation. The conservation viewpoint is that people should manage Earth's resources for the future, not just for today.

✓ *Checkpoint* *What are three viewpoints about how humans should interact with the environment?*

Background

History of Science Should oil exploration be allowed in the Arctic National Wildlife Refuge? Visitors to this vast preserve of boreal forest and tundra in northeastern Alaska can see wildlife ranging from polar bears and musk oxen to arctic foxes and caribou. Opponents of exploration worry that oil exploration and production could damage the refuge's fragile ecosystems. Proponents argue that the United States needs to produce more oil domestically, rather than import it from other countries, to meet the nation's energy needs. In 1995, the Department of the Interior issued a study concluding that oil drilling would adversely affect the refuge's ecosystems. Nonetheless, Congress passed a bill to permit oil exploration there. President Clinton vetoed that measure, but the controversy over the refuge continues.

Weighing Costs and Benefits

Lawmakers work with many different government agencies to make environmental decisions. Together they must consider the needs and concerns of people with many different viewpoints. **To help balance these different opinions, decision makers weigh the costs and benefits of a proposal.**

Costs and benefits are often economic. Will a proposal provide jobs? Will it cost too much money? But costs and benefits are not only measured in terms of money. For example, building an incinerator might reduce the beauty of a natural landscape (a scenic cost). But the incinerator might be safer than an existing open dump site (a health benefit). It is also important to consider short-term and long-term effects. A proposal's short-term costs might be outweighed by its long-term benefits.

Consider the costs and benefits of drilling for oil in Antarctica. Drilling for oil would have many costs. It would be very expensive to set up a drilling operation in such a cold and distant place. Transporting the oil would be difficult and costly. An oil spill in the seas around Antarctica could harm the fish, penguins, and seals there.

On the other hand, there would be many benefits to drilling in Antarctica. A new supply of oil would provide fuel for heat, electricity, and transportation. The plan would create many new jobs. There would be a greater opportunity to study Antarctica's ecosystems. Do the benefits of drilling outweigh the costs? This is the kind of question lawmakers ask when they make environmental decisions.

Sharpen your Skills

Communicating ACTIVITY

Form a group with two other students. Each person will be assigned a different viewpoint toward the environment. Hold a panel discussion in which each person proposes how the continent of Antarctica should be used. What similarities and differences are there among your responses?

Section 1 Review

1. List the three main types of environmental issues.
2. Define environmental science.
3. What is one way to balance different viewpoints on an environmental issue?
4. How has the growth of the human population affected the environment?
5. List three costs and three benefits of drilling for oil on Antarctica.
6. **Thinking Critically Comparing and Contrasting** Compare renewable and nonrenewable resources. Give an example of each type of resource.

Check Your Progress
CHAPTER PROJECT 3

Stake out a square plot measuring 1.5 meters on each side. Record the date, time, temperature, and weather. Observe the organisms in your plot, and record them with notes and drawings. Include enough detail so that you can identify any unfamiliar organisms later. (*Hint:* Also note evidence such as feathers or footprints that shows that other organisms may have visited the plot.)

Answers to Self-Assessment

Caption Question

Figure 4 Accept all reasonable responses. *Sample answer:* The valley might be the source of fish or other animals used for food.

☑ *Checkpoint*

The three viewpoints are development, preservation, and conservation.

---

3 Assess

Section 1 Review Answers

1. Resource management, population growth, pollution
2. The study of natural processes that occur in the environment and how humans can affect those processes
3. Weigh the costs and benefits of a proposal
4. As the population grew, people used more and more of Earth's resources. They also produced more wastes.
5. *Costs:* Setting up drilling operations and transporting the oil would be difficult and expensive. Oil spills could damage ecosystems. *Benefits:* New oil supplies would provide fuel for heating, generating electricity, and transportation. Drilling for and transporting the oil would provide new jobs. Setting up oil operations in Antarctica would allow people to study its ecosystems and plan ways to protect its wildlife.
6. Renewable resources are those that are replaced naturally within a fairly short time as they are used, such as trees, sunlight, and wind. Nonrenewable resources are those that are not replaced within a short time as they are used, such as coal and oil.

Check Your Progress
CHAPTER PROJECT 3

If students' plots are grouped in the same area, make sure they leave enough space between the plots so they can move around without walking on another group's plot. In this and subsequent observation sessions, encourage students to note any animal behaviors they see, such as feeding, fighting, or cooperating in some way—for example, ants collecting food.

Performance Assessment

Skills Check Have each student choose one action related to an environmental issue and create a table with the costs of the action listed in one column and its benefits in a second column.

You and Your Community

Is Paper a Renewable Resource?

Preparing for Inquiry

Key Concept Paper is a renewable resource because it can be recycled.

Skills Objectives Students will be able to
- observe and compare dry newspaper and recycled paper made from newspaper pulp;
- design an experiment to recycle other types of paper.

Time *Day 1:* 15 minutes; *Day 2:* 40 minutes; *Day 3:* 10 minutes

Advance Planning Gather an ample supply of old newspapers.

Guiding Inquiry

Introducing the Procedure
- Have students read the entire procedure. Clarify that they will do the lab on three different days: Steps 1–2 on Day 1, Steps 3–6 on Day 2, and Step 7 on Day 3.

Troubleshooting the Experiment
- *Day 1:* Draw students' attention to the fibers in Step 1 by asking: What do you see in the paper?
- *Day 2:* Have students reread Steps 3–6. Remind them to replace the newspaper under the screen each day if it is wet.
- *Day 3:* Tell students to make sure the pulp is completely dry before handling it.

Expected Outcome
The dried pulp will be rough, stiff, and grayish—like cardboard egg cartons. Cellulose fibers will be visible.

Analyze and Conclude
1. Fibers; they are made of plant material and come from the plants used to make the paper.
2. When the paper is soaked in water and mashed into a pulp, the fibers are broken up and separated. When the pulp is flattened and dried, the fibers intertwine again.

You and Your Community

Is Paper a Renewable Resource?

Recycling is a common local environmental issue. In this lab, you will explore how well paper can be recycled.

Problem
What happens when paper is recycled?

Skills Focus
observing, designing experiments

Materials

newspaper	microscope	water
eggbeater	square pan	screen
plastic wrap	mixing bowl	heavy book
microscope slide		

Procedure

1. Tear off a small piece of newspaper. Place the paper on a microscope slide and examine it under a microscope. Record your observations.
2. Tear a sheet of newspaper into pieces about the size of postage stamps. Place the pieces in the mixing bowl. Add enough water to cover the newspaper. Cover the bowl and let the mixture stand overnight.
3. The next day, add more water to cover the paper if necessary. Use the eggbeater to mix the wet paper until it is smooth. This thick liquid is called paper pulp.
4. Place the screen in the bottom of the pan. Pour the pulp onto the screen, spreading it out evenly. Then lift the screen above the pan, allowing most of the water to drip into the pan.
5. Place the screen and pulp on several layers of newspaper to absorb the rest of the water. Lay a sheet of plastic wrap over the pulp. Place a heavy book on top of the plastic wrap to press more water out of the pulp.
6. After 30 minutes, remove the book. Carefully turn over the screen, plastic wrap, and pulp. Remove the screen and plastic wrap. Let the pulp sit on the newspaper for one or two more days to dry. Replace the newspaper layers if necessary.
7. When the pulp is dry, observe it closely. Record your observations.

Analyze and Conclude
1. What kind of structures did you observe when you examined torn newspaper under a microscope? What are these structures made of? Where do they come from?
2. What do you think happens to the structures you observed when paper is recycled?
3. Based on your results, predict how many times a sheet of newspaper can be recycled.
4. **Apply** Should paper be classified as a renewable or nonrenewable resource? Explain.

Design an Experiment
Using procedures like those in this lab, design an experiment to recycle three different types of paper, such as shiny magazine paper, paper towels, and cardboard. Find out how the resulting papers differ. Obtain your teacher's approval for your plans before you try your experiment.

---

3. Eventually (after two or three recyclings), the fibers would become too short or too fragile to intertwine again.
4. Renewable; paper can be recycled, and new trees can be planted. However, students should note that paper cannot be recycled endlessly.

Extending the Inquiry
Design an Experiment Students' plans should be similar to the lab procedure.

Program Resources
- **Teaching Resources** Chapter 3 Real-World Lab, pp. 87–89

Safety
Students should handle the microscope slide carefully to avoid breakage. Review the safety guidelines in Appendix A.

SECTION 2 Forests and Fisheries

DISCOVER · ACTIVITY

What Happened to the Tuna?

1. Use the data in the table to make a line graph. Label the axes of the graph and add a title. (To review graphing, see the Skills Handbook.)

2. Mark the high and low points on the graph.

Think It Over

Inferring How did the tuna population change during this period? Can you suggest a possible reason for this change?

Year	Western Atlantic Bluefin Tuna Population
1970	240,000
1975	190,000
1980	90,000
1985	60,000
1990	45,000
1994	60,000

At first glance, a bluefin tuna and a pine tree may not seem to have much in common. One is an animal and the other is a plant. One lives in the ocean and the other lives on land. However, tuna and pine trees are both living resources. Tuna are a source of food for people. People don't eat pine trees, but they do use them to make lumber, paper, and turpentine. People also use pine needles as mulch in gardens.

Every day you use many different products that are made from living organisms. In this section, you will read about two major types of living resources: forests and fisheries. As you read, think about how they are similar and how they are different.

Forest Resources

Forests are a resource because they contain valuable materials. Many products are made from the flowers, fruits, seeds, and other parts of forest plants. Some of these products, such as maple syrup, rubber, and nuts, come from living trees. Other products, such as lumber and pulp for paper, require cutting trees down. Conifers, including pine and spruce, are used for construction and for making paper. Hardwoods, such as oak, cherry, and maple, are used for furniture because of their strength and beauty.

Trees and other plants produce oxygen that other organisms need to survive. They also absorb carbon dioxide and many pollutants from the air. Trees also help prevent flooding and control soil erosion. Their roots absorb rainwater and hold the soil together.

GUIDE FOR READING

◆ How can forests and fisheries be managed?

Reading Tip As you read, make a list of ways to conserve forests and fisheries.

Figure 5 One important use of forest resources is for building housing.

Objectives

After completing the lesson, students will be able to
◆ describe different ways that forests can be managed to provide resources;
◆ describe ways that fisheries can be managed to provide resources.

Key Terms clear-cutting, selective cutting, sustainable yield, fishery, aquaculture

1 Engage/Explore

Activating Prior Knowledge

Invite students to look around the classroom and identify as many products as they can that are derived from trees. (*Examples include writing paper, cardboard, posterboard, paper towels, wood furniture, pencils, rulers, and plywood.*)

· · · · · · · · DISCOVER · · · · · · · ·

Skills Focus inferring
Materials graph paper, ruler, pencil
Time 15 minutes
Expected Outcome Increments used for the vertical axis may vary.
Sample Graph

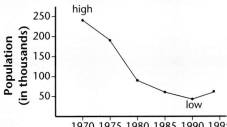

Changes in Western Atlantic Bluefin Tuna Population

Think It Over The tuna population declined steadily from 1970 to 1990, then increased from 1990 to 1994. The decline was probably due to overfishing of tuna; the rebound may have resulted from limits on tuna fishing.

Figure 6 Clear-cutting has left large portions of these hillsides bare. *Interpreting Photographs What problems might clear-cutting cause?*

2 Facilitate

Forest Resources

Including All Students

Review for students who need more help the amount of land area on Earth suitable for forests. Have students look back at the following biome maps in Chapter 2: page 63, tropical and temperate rain forests; page 66, deciduous and boreal forests; and page 68, mountains. Trace each map onto an overhead transparency. Overlay the maps while projecting them so students can see the total land area where forests can grow. **learning modality: visual**

Managing Forests

Social Studies
CONNECTION

Provide a picture of a small village with a commons, such as ones found in England or New England. To help students understand how this problem could arise, ask them to put themselves in the place of the local people. Would they stop bringing their cattle to the commons for the greater good, or would they expect others to stop?

In Your Journal Volunteers can share their ideas in a class discussion. Encourage students to comment on each idea's feasibility. **learning modality: verbal**

Building Inquiry Skills: Classifying

After students have read about the two logging methods, ask: **Is clear-cutting an example of the development, preservation, or conservation viewpoint toward the environment?** *(development)* **Which viewpoint does selective cutting represent?** *(conservation)* **What would represent the preservation viewpoint?** *(Not cutting the forest at all)* **learning modality: logical/mathematical**

Social Studies
CONNECTION

Many of the world's living resources are owned by no one—they are shared by everyone. A word that is sometimes used to describe such a shared resource is a "commons." This word comes from a time when villages were built around common areas of open land. All the town's residents grazed their cattle on the commons. This worked well as long as there weren't too many people. But as more and more people brought their cattle to the commons, the area would become overgrazed. There would not be enough pasture to feed even one cow—the "tragedy of the commons."

In Your Journal

Suppose you live in a farming community with a central commons. Propose a solution that will allow residents to use the commons while protecting it from overuse.

Managing Forests

There are about 300 million hectares of forests in the United States. That's nearly a third of the nation's area! Many forests are located on publicly owned land. Others are owned by private timber and paper companies or by individuals. Forest industries provide jobs for 1.5 million people.

Because new trees can be planted to replace trees that are cut down, forests can be renewable resources. The United States Forest Service and environmental organizations work with forestry companies to conserve forest resources. They try to develop logging methods that maintain forests as renewable resources.

Logging Methods There are two major methods of logging: clear-cutting and selective cutting. **Clear-cutting** is the process of cutting down all the trees in an area at once. Cutting down only some trees in a forest and leaving a mix of tree sizes and species behind is called **selective cutting.**

Each logging method has advantages and disadvantages. Clear-cutting is usually quicker and cheaper than selective cutting. It may also be safer for the loggers. In selective cutting, the loggers must move the heavy equipment and logs around the remaining trees in the forest. But selective cutting is usually less damaging to the forest environment than clear-cutting. When an area of forest is clear-cut, the habitat changes. Clear-cutting exposes the soil to wind and rain. Without the protection of the tree roots, the soil is more easily blown or washed away. Soil washed into streams may harm the fish and other organisms that live there.

Sustainable Forestry Forests can be managed to provide a sustained yield. A **sustainable yield** is a regular amount of a renewable resource such as trees that can be harvested without

Background

Integrating Science Forests can have a profound effect on climate. Scientists think that deforestation contributes to changes in climate at regional and global scales. Through transpiration, trees add huge amounts of water vapor to the atmosphere. In fact, a tree returns to the air about 97 percent of the water that the tree's roots absorb from the ground. This water eventually falls back to Earth through the water cycle. Removal of a forest may cause the rainfall in a region to decline and increase the frequency of droughts.

The deforestation of tropical rain forests, so prevalent in recent years, may contribute to an increase in global temperatures. Burning the felled trees adds carbon dioxide to the atmosphere. The higher the concentration of CO_2 in the atmosphere, the more heat the atmosphere holds in and does not radiate back into space.

reducing the future supply. This works sort of like a book swap: as long as you donate a book each time you borrow one, the total supply of books will not be affected. Planting a tree to replace one being cut down is like donating a book to replace a borrowed one.

Part of forest management is planning how frequently the trees must be replanted to keep a constant supply. Different species grow at different rates. Trees with softer woods, such as pines, usually mature faster than trees with harder woods, such as hickory, oak, and cherry. Forests containing faster-growing trees can be harvested and replanted more often. For example, pine forests may be harvested every 20 to 30 years. On the other hand, some hardwood forests may be harvested only every 40 to 100 years. One sustainable approach is to log small patches of forest. This way, different sections of forest can be harvested every year.

Certified Wood Forests that are managed in a sustainable way can be certified by the Forest Stewardship Council. Once a forest is certified, all wood logged from that forest may carry a "well-managed" label. This label allows businesses and individuals to select wood from forests that are managed for sustainable yields.

☑ *Checkpoint* *What is a sustainable yield?*

Figure 7 Two logging methods are clear-cutting and selective cutting. **A.** After clear-cutting, the new trees are usually all the same age and species. **B.** Selective cutting results in a more diverse forest.

Original forest *Clear-cutting* *Replanted growth*

Original forest *Selective cutting* *Diverse regrowth*

Chapter 3 **E ◆ 93**

Media and Technology

 Transparencies "Logging Methods," Transparency 8

Answers to Self-Assessment

Caption Question

Figure 6 The soil on the hill may erode, and silt may clog streams. Without tree roots to absorb water, areas may flood. Many organisms would lose their habitat.

☑ *Checkpoint*

A regular amount of a renewable resource that can be harvested without reducing the future supply

---

Inquiry Challenge

Materials *colored plastic chips, construction paper squares, or similar objects*
Time 15 minutes

Tell students that another sustainable forestry practice is to harvest all the mature trees in an area at intervals—a practice known as shelterwood cutting. In the first harvest, all the unwanted tree species and dead or diseased trees are cut down. The forest is then left alone so the remaining trees can continue to grow and new seedlings can become established. After a period of time, many of the mature trees are removed in a second harvest, and the forest is again left alone to grow. In a third harvest, the remaining mature trees are cut down. By this time, though, the seedlings have grown into young trees, and more new seedlings are growing. Challenge small groups of students to devise a simple model of shelterwood cutting. Team students who have difficulty seeing or whose movements are limited with students who do not have these disabilities. (*Sample model: Use green paper squares to represent mature trees and brown squares to represent unwanted trees. For the "first harvest," remove all brown squares. Add red squares to represent seedlings. In the "second harvest," remove some of the green squares. Replace the red squares with yellow squares to represent the growth of the seedlings into young trees, and add more red squares. In the "third harvest," remove the remaining green squares, replace the yellow squares with green squares and the red squares with yellow squares, and add more red squares.*) Have each group describe their model in writing. Ask: **How does shelterwood cutting provide a sustainable yield?** (*The forest constantly replenishes itself.*) **learning modality: kinesthetic**

Ongoing Assessment

Skills Check Have each student construct a table comparing the advantages and disadvantages of clear-cutting and selective cutting.

 Students could save their tables in their portfolios.

Fisheries

Sharpen your Skills

Calculating

Materials *calculator*
Time 15 minutes
Expected Outcome China–21.6%, Japan–6.0%, United States–5.0%, Peru–7.9%
Extend Have students devise a way of visually comparing these amounts (such as a circle graph or bar graph).
learning modality: logical/ mathematical

Real-Life Learning

Suggest that students visit a fish market or the seafood and canned-fish sections of a supermarket and list the names of all the fish and seafoods they see on display. Encourage students to interview store personnel and examine labels to determine each food's country of origin. Which foods are obtained locally? Which are shipped in from other parts of the country? Which are imported from other countries? Have students report and compare their findings in class. (As an alternative, you could bring supermarket flyers and cookbooks to class and have students make a list of all the fish and seafood they find.) **learning modality: visual**

Sharpen your Skills

Calculating

In a recent year, the total catch of fish in the world was 112.9 million metric tons. Based on the data below, calculate the percent of this total each country caught.

Country	Catch (millions of metric tons)
China	24.4
Japan	6.8
United States	5.6
Peru	8.9

Figure 8 A fishing boat returns to harbor at the end of a long day. Overfishing has forced the crews of many boats to find other work until the fisheries recover.

Fisheries

Until recently, the oceans seemed like an unlimited resource. The waters held such huge schools of fish, it seemed impossible that they could ever disappear. And fish reproduce in incredible numbers. A single codfish can lay as many as nine million eggs in a single year! But people have discovered that this resource has limits. After many years of big catches, the number of sardines off the California coast suddenly declined. The same thing happened to the huge schools of cod off the New England coast. What caused these changes?

An area with a large population of valuable ocean organisms is called a **fishery.** Some major fisheries include the Grand Banks off Newfoundland, Georges Bank off New England, and Monterey Canyon off California. Fisheries like these are valuable renewable resources. But if fish are caught at a faster rate than they can breed, the population decreases. This situation is known as overfishing.

Scientists estimate that 70 percent of the world's major fisheries have been overfished. But if those fish populations are allowed to recover, a sustainable yield of fish can once again be harvested. **Managing fisheries for a sustainable yield includes setting fishing limits, changing fishing methods, developing aquaculture techniques, and finding new resources.**

Fishing Limits Laws can help protect individual fish species. Laws may also limit the amount that can be caught or require that fish be at least a certain size. This ensures that young fish

---

Background

History of Science In 1994, a section of the Georges Bank fishery was closed because of overfishing. A 1998 study of the area found that there were more than three times the number of scallops there than in areas where fishing had continued. Based on these findings, scallopers wanted regulators to let them back into the closed area. However, scallopers can catch 70 to 80 percent of the scallops in areas that are open to fishing.

Taking this many scallops could swiftly decimate the scallop population on Georges Bank again. Scallopers' dredges also catch groundfish, endangering those populations.

Some scallop researchers advocate another approach: closing selected scallop beds from time to time to let the scallop populations regenerate, much as areas of forest are allowed to regrow after being cut.

survive long enough to reproduce. Also, setting an upper limit on the size of fish caught ensures that breeding fish remain in the population. But if a fishery has been severely overfished, the government may need to completely ban fishing until the populations can recover.

Fishing Methods Today fishing practices are regulated by laws. Some fishing crews now use nets with a larger mesh size to allow small, young fish to escape. Some methods have been outlawed. These methods include poisoning fish with cyanide and stunning them by exploding dynamite underwater. These techniques kill all the fish in an area rather than selecting certain fish.

Aquaculture The practice of raising fish and other water-dwelling organisms for food is called **aquaculture.** The fish may be raised in artificial ponds or bays. Salmon, catfish, and shrimp are farmed in this way in the United States.

However, aquaculture is not a perfect solution. The artificial ponds and bays often replace natural habitats such as salt marshes. Maintaining the farms can cause pollution and spread diseases into wild fish populations.

New Resources Today about 9,000 different fish species are harvested for food. More than half the animal protein eaten by people throughout the world comes from fish. One way to help feed a growing human population is to fish for new species. Scientists and chefs are working together to introduce people to deep-water species such as monkfish and tile fish, as well as easy-to-farm freshwater fish such as tilapia.

Figure 9 As fishing limits become stricter, aquaculture is playing a larger role in meeting the worldwide demand for fish. This fish farm in Hawaii raises tilapia.

Section 2 Review

1. Describe one example of a sustainable forestry practice.
2. What are three ways fisheries can be managed so that they will continue to provide fish for the future?
3. Why are forests considered renewable resources?
4. **Thinking Critically Comparing and Contrasting** Describe the advantages and disadvantages of clear-cutting and selective cutting.

Science at Home

With a family member, conduct a "Forest and Fishery" survey of your home. Make a list of all the things that are made from either forest or fishery products. Then ask other family members to predict how many items are on the list. Are they surprised by the answer?

Program Resources

◆ **Teaching Resources** 3-2 Review and Reinforce, p. 77; 3-2 Enrich, p. 78

  Science Explorer Series *Earth's Waters*, Chapter 5, discusses marine fisheries in detail and includes a map showing the locations of the world's major fisheries.

◆ **Integrated Science Laboratory Manual** E–3, "Managing Fisheries"

Media and Technology

Interactive Student Tutorial CD-ROM E-3

---

3 Assess

Section 2 Review Answers

1. *Any one:* replant trees, plan frequency of cutting, log small patches of forest in stages
2. *Any three:* Fishing limits can be imposed; nets with a larger mesh size can be used; dynamiting, poisoning, and other fishing methods that kill all the fish in an area can be outlawed; aquaculture can replace fishing in natural areas.
3. New trees can be planted to replace trees that are cut down.
4. Clear-cutting is quicker, cheaper, and may be safer for loggers, but selective cutting is less damaging to the environment.

Science at Home

Encourage students to look beyond the most obvious products, such as wood and paper from forests, and salt and seafood from oceans, and check labels closely to see if they can find the names of other items. Examples include nuts, spices, tree bark and salt hay for mulch, seaweeds (used both as food and in shampoos and other products), and cuttlebone for pet birds.

Performance Assessment

Oral Presentation Call on students at random to name a way to conserve forests or fisheries.

E ◆ 95

Interpreting Data

Tree Cookie Tales

Preparing for Inquiry

Key Concept Growth rings provide information about a tree's age and the growing conditions during its life.

Skills Objectives Students will be able to
♦ observe growth rings in a tree cookie to determine a tree's age;
♦ draw conclusions from their observations about conditions that affected the tree's growth.

Time 40 minutes

Advance Planning Purchase or prepare a tree cookie for each group. Inexpensive classroom sets of tree cookies are available from biological supply houses. The tree cookies should come from trees that were more than 10 years old. You can also make tree cookies by sawing a tree trunk into cross sections 1.5–2.5 cm thick. To preserve homemade tree cookies, spray or paint all surfaces with clear polyurethane or other clear sealant.

Guiding Inquiry

Troubleshooting the Experiment
♦ Clarify that each year's growth is shown by a pair of rings—a light ring for spring and a dark ring for summer.

Expected Outcome
Results will vary depending on the particular tree cookies used.

Analyze and Conclude
1. Ages will vary. The tree's age is equal to the number of annual rings.
2. Answers will vary. The largest proportion of tree growth usually occurs during a tree's early years.
3. Observations may vary. Spring rings are usually wider, as trees undergo a burst of new growth in the spring when it is usually wetter followed by slower growth in the summer when it is usually drier.
4. Growth rings reflect weather conditions. Generally, rings are wider during years when temperatures are warmer and rainfall is plentiful.
5. Answers will vary. In addition to the tree's age and weather-related growth

---

Skills Lab

Interpreting Data

Tree Cookie Tales

Tree cookies aren't snacks! They're slices of a tree trunk that contain clues about the tree's age, past weather conditions, and fires that occurred during its life. In this lab, you'll interpret the data hidden in a tree cookie.

Problem

What can tree cookies reveal about the past?

Materials

tree cookie   metric ruler   hand lens
colored pencils   calculator (optional)

Procedure

1. Use a hand lens to examine your tree cookie. Draw a simple diagram of your tree cookie. Label the bark, tree rings, and center, or pith.
2. Notice the light-colored and dark-colored rings. The light ring results from fast springtime growth. The dark ring, where the cells are smaller, results from slower summertime growth. Each pair of light and dark rings represents one year's growth, so the pair is called an annual ring. Observe and count the annual rings.
3. Compare the spring and summer portions of the annual rings. Identify the thinnest and thickest rings.
4. Measure the distance from the center to the outermost edge of the last summer growth ring. This is the radius of your tree cookie. Record your measurement.
5. Measure the distance from the center to the outermost edge of the 10th summer growth ring. Record your measurement.
6. Examine your tree cookie for any other evidence of its history, such as damaged bark or burn marks. Record your observations.

Analyze and Conclude

1. How old was your tree? How do you know?
2. What percent of the tree's growth took place during the first 10 years of its life? (*Hint:* Divide the distance from the center to the 10th growth ring by the radius. Then multiply by 100. This gives you the percent of growth that occurred during the tree's first 10 years.)
3. How did the spring rings compare to the summer rings for the same year? Suggest a reason.
4. Why might the annual rings be narrower for some years than for others?
5. Using evidence from your tree cookie, summarize the history of the tree.
6. **Think About It** Suppose you had cookies from two other trees of the same species that grew near your tree. How could you verify the interpretations you made in this lab?

More to Explore

Examine and compare several tree cookies. Record any similarities and differences you observe. Do you think any of the tree cookies came from trees growing in the same area? Support your answer with specific evidence.

---

patterns, students may note holes made by insects or birds, blackening due to fire or lightning, a hollow pith due to disease, or cracks or gashes from tools.
6. You could look for annual growth patterns indicating the weather conditions and additional evidence of fire, disease, or other environmental conditions.

Extending the Inquiry

More to Explore Answers will depend on the specific tree cookies used.

Program Resources

♦ **Teaching Resources** Chapter 3 Skills Lab, pp. 90–91

DISCOVER ····· ACTIVITY

How Much Variety Is There?

1. You will be given two cups of seeds and a paper plate. The seeds in Cup A represent the trees in a section of tropical rain forest. The seeds in Cup B represent the trees in a section of deciduous forest.

2. Pour the seeds from Cup A onto the plate. Sort the seeds by type. Count the different types of seeds. This number represents the number of different kinds of trees in that type of forest.

3. Pour the seeds back into Cup A.

4. Repeat Steps 2 and 3 with the seeds in Cup B.

5. Share your results with your class. Use the class results to calculate the average number of different kinds of seeds in each type of forest.

Think It Over

Inferring How does the variety of trees in the tropical rain forest compare with the variety of trees in a deciduous forest? Can you suggest any advantages of having a wide variety of species?

N o one knows exactly how many species live on Earth. So far, more than 1.7 million species have been identified. The number of different species in an area is called its **biodiversity.** It is difficult to estimate the total biodiversity on Earth because many areas of the planet have not been thoroughly studied. Some experts think that the deep oceans alone could contain 10 million new species! Protecting this diversity is a major environmental issue today.

Factors Affecting Biodiversity

Biodiversity varies from place to place on Earth. **Factors that affect biodiversity in an ecosystem include area, climate, and diversity of niches.**

Area Within an ecosystem, a large area will contain more species than a small area. For example, suppose you were counting tree species in a forest. You would find far more tree species in a 10-square-meter area than in a 1-square-meter area.

GUIDE FOR READING

◆ What factors affect an area's biodiversity?

◆ Which human activities threaten biodiversity?

◆ How can biodiversity be protected?

Reading Tip Before you read, use the headings to make an outline on biodiversity.

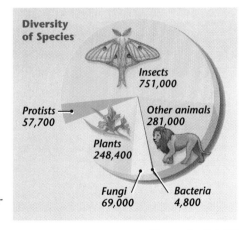

Diversity of Species

Insects
751,000

Protists —
57,700

Other animals
281,000

Plants
248,400

Fungi
69,000

Bacteria
4,800

Figure 10 Organisms of many kinds are part of Earth's biodiversity. *Interpreting Graphs Which group of organisms has the greatest number of species?*

READING STRATEGIES

Vocabulary To help students recall the new terms, suggest that each student compile a set of vocabulary flashcards.

Media and Technology

🎧 **Audiotapes** English-Spanish Summary 3-3

Answers to Self-Assessment

Caption Question

Figure 10 insects

Program Resources

◆ **Teaching Resources** 3-3 Lesson Plan, p. 79; 3-3 Section Summary, p. 80
◆ **Interdisciplinary Exploration Series** "Fate of the Rain Forest," pp. 10–11, 22–23

Objectives

After completing the lesson, students will be able to

◆ identify factors that affect biodiversity;

◆ name some human activities that threaten biodiversity;

◆ list some ways that biodiversity can be protected;

◆ explain the value of biodiversity.

Key Terms biodiversity, keystone species, genes, extinction, endangered species, threatened species, habitat destruction, habitat fragmentation, poaching, captive breeding

1 Engage/Explore

Activating Prior Knowledge

Ask students: **What organisms are native to our area?** (*Answers will vary. Encourage students to consider a wide variety of organism types, including insects, worms, mosses, algae, and bacteria, as well as mammals, birds, fish, reptiles, and amphibians.*) Write the name of each organism on the chalkboard, and after students have finished naming organisms, ask: **Would you say there is very much diversity of species living here?** (*Answers may vary, but in most cases students will say there is.*)

········· **DISCOVER** ·········

Skills Focus inferring
Materials *two labeled cups containing different seed mixtures, paper plate*
Time 20 minutes
Advance Preparation Use a mixture of at least ten types of seeds for Cup A and four or five types for Cup B.
Expected Outcome The average number of different kinds of seeds should be greater for the tropical rain forest.
Think It Over The tropical rain forest has a greater variety of trees than the deciduous forest. The wider variety of tree species supports a wider variety of other organisms that depend on the trees for habitat and food.

2 Facilitate

Factors Affecting Biodiversity

Including All Students

For students who need more help, review the meanings of the terms *area* (length times width), *climate* (the typical weather pattern in an area over a long period of time—Chapter 2, page 59), and *niche* (an organism's unique role in an ecosystem—Chapter 1, page 32). If students have difficulty defining *climate* and *niche* correctly, let them look back at the text definitions in the earlier chapters. **learning modality: verbal**

Building Inquiry Skills: Observing

Materials *books and magazines with photographs of coral reefs*

ACTIVITY

Time 15 minutes

To illustrate the rich diversity of life on coral reefs, encourage small groups of students to examine other photographs similar to Figure 12, choose a "favorite" photo, and list all the organisms shown in the photo and named in its caption or accompanying text. In a follow-up class discussion, list the number of species on the board for each group. **learning modality: visual**

How Diverse Are Tropical Ecosystems?

In Costa Rica, which is half the size of Tennessee, there are 850 species of birds—200 more than in all the rest of North America.

A 10-hectare area of forest in Borneo contains 700 species of trees, as many as all of North America.

A single river in Brazil contains more species than all of the rivers in the United States combined.

Figure 11 Tropical ecosystems tend to be more diverse than those further from the equator.

Figure 12 Coral reefs are the second most diverse ecosystems. *Applying Concepts What is one reason why coral reefs are so diverse?*

Climate In general, the number of species increases from the poles toward the equator. The tropical rain forests of Latin America, southeast Asia, and central Africa are the most diverse ecosystems in the world. These forests cover about 7 percent of Earth's land surface and contain over half of the world's species.

The reason for the great biodiversity in the tropics is not fully understood. Many scientists hypothesize that it has to do with climate. For example, tropical rain forests have fairly constant temperatures and large amounts of rainfall throughout the year. Many plants in these regions have year-round growing seasons. This means that food is available for other organisms year-round.

Niche Diversity Coral reefs make up less than 1 percent of the oceans' area. But reefs are home to 20 percent of the world's saltwater fish species. Coral reefs are the second most diverse ecosystems in the world. Found only in shallow, warm waters, coral reefs are often called the rain forests of the sea. A reef provides many different niches for organisms that live under, on, and among the coral. This enables more species to live in the reef than in a more uniform habitat such as a flat sandbar.

Checkpoint *What is one possible reason that tropical regions have the greatest biodiversity?*

The Value of Biodiversity

Perhaps you are wondering how biodiversity is important. Does it matter whether there are 50 or 5,000 species of ferns in some faraway rain forest? Is it necessary to protect every one of these species?

Background

Facts and Figures Scientists have not yet studied most species of plants, animals, fungi, and microorganisms to determine whether they might be useful to humans. Of approximately 250,000 known plant species, only about 25,000 have been investigated.

Insects are one example of an often overlooked biological resource. Insects play a major role in pollinating crops, controlling weeds, and even in controlling some insects that are pests. And other insects produce unusual chemical compounds for which humans may find some use. For example, scientists have found a compound made by fireflies that has potential as an antiviral agent in humans. A fungicide produced by centipedes to protect their eggs might also protect crops from fungus attack.

There are many reasons why preserving biodiversity is important. The simplest reason is that wild organisms and ecosystems are a source of beauty and recreation.

Economic Value Many plants, animals, and other organisms are essential for human survival. In addition to providing food and oxygen, these organisms supply raw materials for clothing, medicine, and other products. No one knows how many other useful species have not yet been identified.

Ecosystems are economically valuable, too. For example, many companies now run wildlife tours in rain forests, savannas, mountain ranges, and other locations. This ecosystem tourism, or "ecotourism," is an important source of jobs and money for nations such as Brazil, Costa Rica, and Kenya.

Value to the Ecosystem All the species in an ecosystem are connected to one another. Species may depend on each other for food and shelter. A change that affects one species will surely affect all the others.

Some species play a particularly important role. A species that influences the survival of many other species in an ecosystem is called a **keystone species.** If a keystone species disappears, the entire ecosystem may change. For example, the sea stars in Figure 14 are a keystone species in their ecosystem. The sea stars prey mostly on the mussels that live in tide pools. When researchers removed the sea stars from an area, the mussels began to outcompete many of the other species in the tide pool. The sea star predators had kept the population of mussels in check, allowing other species to live. When the keystone species disappeared, the balance in the ecosystem was destroyed.

Figure 13 Ecosystem tours such as safaris can provide income for local people. These tourists are observing giraffes in Botswana.

Figure 14 These sea stars on the Washington coast are an example of a keystone species. By preying on mussels, the sea stars keep the mussels from taking over the ecosystem.

Chapter 3 **E ◆ 99**

The Value of Biodiversity

Building Inquiry Skills: Communicating

Time 20 minutes

ACTIVITY

Divide the class into small groups, and pose the following hypothetical environmental issue for each group to debate: **A chemical for making a new drug has been discovered in a plant species growing in the Amazon rain forest. Several rare species of butterflies depend on the plant for food. To harvest the chemical for human use, the plants have to be cut down and removed from the forest. Should people make use of this new resource, and if so, how?** Encourage each group to try to reach consensus on the issue. After students have debated for a time, let each group report its decision and the reasoning behind it to the rest of the class. **learning modality: verbal**

Demonstration

Materials *model architectural building blocks or photo of arch with keystone*

ACTIVITY

Time 5–10 minutes

Use model architectural building blocks to construct an arch with a keystone. (If such blocks are not available, use a photo of an arch with a keystone.) Point to the keystone, and ask: **What do you predict will happen if I remove this block?** *(Some may predict the arch will fall.)* Remove the keystone to confirm students' predictions. Explain that the block you removed is called a keystone. Ask: **Why is a keystone a good analogy for a keystone species?** *(Because when a keystone species is removed, the entire ecosystem may collapse)* **learning modality: visual**

Program Resources

🎒 **Science Explorer Series** *Earth's Waters,* Chapter 5, describes coral reefs in greater detail.

Answers to Self-Assessment

Caption Question

Figure 12 A coral reef provides many different niches, which enables a wide variety of species to live there.

☑ *Checkpoint*

Because of its unique climate, the tropical rain forest provides food year-round.

Ongoing Assessment

Writing Have each student identify and briefly explain the three major factors that affect an ecosystem's biodiversity.

 Students can save their work in their portfolios.

Gene Pool Diversity

Building Inquiry Skills: Predicting

Ask students: **What is cloning?** (*Making an exact duplicate of an organism—more precisely, using genes taken from an organism's cells to create a new individual that is genetically identical to the original organism*) Pose the following question: **Suppose scientists found an easy and inexpensive way to create large herds of sheep, cattle, and other domestic animals through cloning. Do you think this would be a good idea? Why or why not?** (*Some students may say that cloned herds could have traits that increase our supply of meat, milk, wool, leather, and other products. However, students should realize that entire herds of genetically identical animals could increase susceptibility to disease.*) **learning modality: logical/mathematical**

Extinction of Species

Addressing Naive Conceptions

Materials *large sheet of construction paper, colored markers, source books* **ACTIVITY**

When students consider extinction, they usually think of dinosaurs and other species that became extinct in the distant past. Explain that many species have become extinct in relatively recent times. Let each pair of students research one species that became extinct in the past 300 years. Examples include the quagga, dodo, moa, Tasmanian wolf (thylacine), dusky seaside sparrow, Santa Barbara song sparrow, Greek auk, Hawaii oo, passenger pigeon, Abingdon tortoise, blue pike, Tecopa pupfish, and Sampson's pearly mussel. Suggest that one student in each pair draw a picture of the organism and the other student write a brief, first-person description of it—for example, *I'm a quagga, a variety of zebra. I used to live in huge, wild herds in South Africa, but I was hunted for my hide. I became extinct in 1883.* **learning modality: verbal**

Figure 15 Just as diversity of species is important to an ecosystem, diversity of genes is important within a species. Diverse genes give these potatoes their rainbow of colors.

Gene Pool Diversity

The organisms in a healthy population have a diversity of traits. These traits are determined by genes. **Genes** are the structures in an organism's cells that carry its hereditary information. Every organism receives a combination of genes from its parents. Genes determine the organism's characteristics, from its size and appearance to its ability to fight disease. The organisms in one species share many genes. But each organism also has some genes that differ from those of other individuals. These individual differences make up the total gene "pool" of that species.

Species that lack a diverse gene pool are less able to adapt to disease, parasites, or drought. For example, most agricultural crops, such as wheat and corn, have very little diversity. These species are bred to be very uniform. If a disease or parasite attacks, the whole population could be affected. A fungus once wiped out much of the corn crop in the United States in this way. Fortunately, there are many wild varieties of corn that have slightly different genes. At least some of these plants contain genes that make them more resistant to the fungus. Scientists were able to breed corn that was not affected by the fungus. Keeping a diverse gene pool helps ensure that crop species can survive such problems.

☑ *Checkpoint* *What do an organism's genes determine?*

Extinction of Species

The disappearance of all members of a species from Earth is called **extinction.** Extinction is a natural process. Many species that once lived on Earth, from dinosaurs to dodos, are now extinct. But in the last few centuries, the number of species becoming extinct has increased dramatically.

Once a population drops below a certain level, the species may not be able to recover. For example, millions of passenger pigeons once darkened the skies in the United States. People hunted the birds for sport and food, killing many hundreds of thousands. This was only part of the total population of passenger pigeons. But at some point, there were not enough birds to reproduce and increase the population. Only after the birds disappeared did people realize that the species could not survive without its enormous numbers.

Species in danger of becoming extinct in the near future are considered **endangered species.** Species that could become endangered in the near future are considered **threatened species.**

100 ◆ E

Background

History of Science In the past 100 years, scientists have greatly increased the yields of crops such as corn and wheat by creating highly productive but genetically uniform varieties. With genetic uniformity, however, goes decreased resistance to certain diseases and pests. To restore resistance to these crop varieties, scientists cross them with other, often wild, varieties that retain genetic diversity. Scientists used this approach to create a type of corn that could resist the corn blight fungus described in the student text. They crossed genetically uniform varieties susceptible to the blight with Mexican varieties that possessed the genes needed to be blight resistant. Because the cultivation and domestication of corn (or maize) began in Mexico thousands of years ago, Mexican varieties are ancestral to modern varieties and have greater genetic diversity.

100 ◆ E

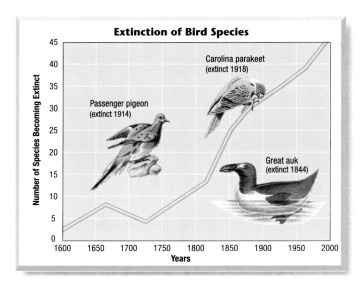

Extinction of Bird Species

Carolina parakeet (extinct 1918)

Passenger pigeon (extinct 1914)

Great auk (extinct 1844)

y-axis: Number of Species Becoming Extinct — 0, 5, 10, 15, 20, 25, 30, 35, 40, 45

x-axis: Years — 1600, 1650, 1700, 1750, 1800, 1850, 1900, 1950, 2000

Figure 16 This graph shows the rate of extinction of bird species in the last 400 years.
Interpreting Graphs How many bird species became extinct in 1750? In 1850? In 1950?

Threatened and endangered species are found on every continent and in every ocean. Some are well-known animals such as Africa's black rhinoceros. Others are little known, such as hutias, rodents that live on only a few Caribbean islands. Ensuring that these species survive is one way to protect Earth's biodiversity.

Causes of Extinction

A natural event, such as an earthquake or volcano, can damage an ecosystem, wiping out populations or even some species. **Human activities can also threaten biodiversity. These activities include habitat destruction, poaching, pollution, and introduction of exotic species.**

Habitat Destruction　The major cause of extinction is **habitat destruction,** the loss of a natural habitat. This can occur when forests are cleared to build towns or create grazing land. Plowing grasslands or filling in wetlands greatly changes those ecosystems. Some species may not be able to survive such changes to their habitats.

　Breaking larger habitats into smaller, isolated pieces, or fragments, is called **habitat fragmentation.** For example, building a road through a forest disrupts habitats. This makes trees more vulnerable to wind damage. Plants may be less likely to successfully disperse their seeds. Habitat fragmentation is also very harmful to large mammals. These animals usually need large areas of land to find enough food to survive. They may not be able to obtain enough resources in a small area. They may also be injured trying to cross to another area.

Figure 17 Building this subdivision caused the habitats in the area to change. Open land was replaced by houses, streets, and yards.
Inferring How would these changes affect species in this area?

Answers to Self-Assessment

☑ *Checkpoint*

Genes determine an organism's traits.

Caption Questions

Figure 16 1750–6; 1850–24; 1950–37
Figure 17 Organisms could no longer meet their food and shelter needs from their surroundings. The number of species probably decreased.

Causes of Extinction, continued

EXPLORING
Endangered Species

Make sure students realize that all of the species shown in this feature are native to the United States. Locate and label the area where each species is found on a large wall map. (Grizzly bear–northern and western U.S.; piping plover–east coastal areas; Eureka Valley primrose–Oregon; whooping crane–central and southwestern U.S.) Encourage interested students to research the names and locations of other endangered species in the United States and add them to the map. Then challenge students to create a large table on the chalkboard listing all the endangered species and the reason why each is endangered. **learning modality: visual**

Real-Life Learning

Point out to students that the tropical fish and parrots sold in reputable pet shops in this country are specifically bred for the pet trade, not imported illegally. Invite a local pet store owner or manager to speak to students about obtaining fish, parrots and other birds, exotic reptiles, and other nonnative species. **learning modality: verbal**

Poaching The illegal killing or removal of wildlife species is called **poaching.** Many endangered animals are hunted for their skin, fur, teeth, horns, or claws. These things are used for making medicines, jewelry, coats, belts, and shoes.

People illegally remove organisms from their habitats to sell them as exotic pets. Tropical fish, tortoises, and parrots are very popular pets, making them valuable to poachers. Endangered plants may be illegally dug up and sold as houseplants. Others are poached to be used as medicines.

Pollution Some species are endangered because of pollution. Substances that cause pollution, called pollutants, may reach animals through the water they drink or air they breathe. Pollutants

EXPLORING Endangered Species

A broad range of species and habitats are represented on the endangered list in the United States.

Grizzly bear ▶ This omnivore needs a large area to obtain food. Shrinking wilderness areas have limited its numbers.

Piping plover The ▶ population of this tiny, active coastal bird is recovering as a result of increased protection of its sand dune nesting sites.

◀ **Eureka valley evening primrose** This flower, which blooms for only one night, must compete for water with exotic plants.

Background

Facts and Figures According to Worldwatch, a research institute that monitors environmental issues, primates are one of the most threatened groups of species on Earth today. Almost half of the world's more than 200 primate species are in danger of extinction.

The declines are due largely to human activity, as forests are lost through logging and clearing for building homes and agriculture. In Malaysia and Indonesia, nearly 80 percent of the forests used by orangutans have been cut down. Japan's macaques are losing living space to cities. Primates are also hunted in various places. Orangutans, gorillas, gibbons, and chimps are trapped for the pet trade.

may also settle in the soil. From there they are absorbed by plants, and build up in other organisms through the food chain. Pollutants may kill or weaken organisms or cause birth defects.

Exotic Species Introducing exotic species into an ecosystem can threaten biodiversity. When European sailors began visiting Hawaii hundreds of years ago, rats from their ships escaped onto the islands. Without any predators in Hawaii, the rats multiplied quickly. They ate the eggs of the nene goose. To protect the geese, people brought the rat-eating mongoose from India to help control the rat population. Unfortunately, the mongooses preferred eating eggs to rats. With both the rats and the mongoose eating its eggs, the nene goose is now endangered.

◀ Steller's sea lion This mammal competes with fishermen for its prey along the Pacific coast.

Schaus swallowtail ▶ butterfly Threatened by habitat loss and pesticide pollution in the Florida Keys, this butterfly was nearly wiped out by Hurricane Andrew.

◀ New Mexico ridgenose rattlesnake Illegal collectors have reduced the population of this rare snake, the largest known group of which lives in a single canyon.

▲ Whooping crane Threatened by habitat destruction and disease, half of the remaining population of this wading bird is in captivity. The species seems to be recovering well since its lowest point in the 1940s.

 Exploring Life Science Videodisc
Unit 6, Side 2, "Can We Save the Tigers?"

Chapter 8

Inquiry Challenge

Materials *plastic chips or paper squares*
Time 10 minutes

Challenge students to work together to devise a model showing how pollutants build up as organisms feed on each other in a food chain. *(Sample model: One student represents a top-level consumer such as a hawk, five students represent first-level consumers such as rabbits, and the rest of the students represent producers such as clover plants. Each "clover plant" holds a plastic chip representing a unit of a toxic chemical sprayed on a field. Each "rabbit" eats several clover plants by taking their chips. Then each "hawk" eats two or three rabbits by taking all of the chips they collected from the clover plants. The two hawks between them will have all of the toxic chemical chips.)* Ask: **Why do you think pollutants build up in organisms?** *(Their bodies cannot break the pollutants down into harmless materials or get rid of them as waste products.)* **cooperative learning**

Including All Students

Encourage students who need additional challenges to research other examples of exotic species that have been introduced to the United States that compete with native species, and what has happened to the native species as a result. Examples include the blue water hyacinth, purple loosestrife, kudzu, leafy spurge, Eurasian milfoil, tamarisk tree, flathead catfish, sea lamprey, green crab, zebra mussel, gypsy moth, brown tree snake, and starling. Let students share their findings in a class discussion. **learning modality: verbal**

Ongoing Assessment

Skills Check Have each student draw a concept map identifying and explaining the four human causes of extinction described in the text.

Portfolio Students can save their concept maps in their portfolios.

Protecting Biodiversity

Real-Life Learning

Take the class on a field trip to visit a zoo with a captive-breeding program or invite a zoologist to speak to the class. Before students visit the zoo or listen to the speaker, instruct them to write down two or three questions about captive breeding and endangered species.
learning modality: verbal

Building Inquiry Skills: Communicating

Time 15 minutes

ACTIVITY

After students read about the California condor, share the following information: In 1973, the federal government listed the gray wolf (timber wolf) as endangered after its population dropped to a few hundred in Minnesota and almost zero in the other lower-48 states. This protected gray wolves from hunting and trapping. In addition, captive breeding programs released more gray wolves into the wild. Biologists estimate that there are now 2,380 wolves in Minnesota and Wisconsin. In 1998 the government recommended removing the gray wolf from the endangered species list. Divide the class into groups to debate the issue of hunting and trapping bans from two viewpoints—that of farmers and ranchers who are losing animals to gray wolf predation, and that of people who support continued protection of the species. **learning modality: verbal**

Demonstration

Materials *aquarium, sand, water, 2 crayfish, several cans and/or boards*

ACTIVITY

Time 15 minutes for initial set-up

Explain that people can help preserve biodiversity by constructing artificial habitats to replace ones that were destroyed or damaged. Share the information in Background below. Then let students help you create an "artificial" habitat: Set up an aquarium with only sand in the bottom, and add two crayfish. Have students observe the crayfish for a day or two. Then add several and/or boards to the aquarium to provide hiding places. Let students continue to observe the crayfish. **learning modality: visual**

Many people are working to preserve the world's biodiversity. Some focus on protecting individual endangered species, such as the giant panda or the gray whale. Others try to protect entire ecosystems, such as the Great Barrier Reef in Australia. **Many programs to protect biodiversity combine scientific and legal approaches.**

Captive Breeding One scientific approach to protecting severely endangered species is captive breeding. **Captive breeding** is the mating of animals in zoos or wildlife preserves. Scientists care for the young to increase their chance of survival. These offspring are then released back into the wild.

A captive breeding program was the only hope for the California condor. California condors are the largest birds in North America. They became endangered as a result of habitat destruction, poaching, and pollution. By the mid-1980s there were fewer than ten California condors in the wild. Fewer than 30 were in zoos. Scientists captured all the wild condors and brought them to the zoos. Soon afterward, the first California condor chick was successfully bred in captivity. Today, there are more than 100 California condors in zoos. Some condors have even been returned to the wild. Though successful, this program has cost more than $20 million. It is not possible to save many species in this costly way.

Laws and Treaties Laws can help protect individual species. Some nations have made it illegal to sell endangered species or products made from them. In the United States, the Endangered Species Act of 1973 prohibits importing or trading products made from threatened or endangered species. This law also requires the development of plans to save endangered species.

Figure 18 Captive breeding programs use a scientific approach to protect endangered species.
A. California condor chicks raised in captivity need to learn what adult condors look like. Here, a scientist uses a puppet to feed and groom a chick.
B. These young green turtles were hatched in the laboratory. Now a researcher is releasing the turtles into their natural ocean habitat.

104 ◆ E

American alligators, Pacific gray whales, and green sea turtles are just a few of the species that have begun to recover as a result of legal protection.

The most important international treaty protecting wildlife is the Convention on International Trade in Endangered Species. Eighty nations signed this treaty in 1973. This treaty lists nearly 700 threatened and endangered species that cannot be traded for profit. Laws like these are difficult to enforce. Even so, they have helped to reduce the poaching of many endangered species, including African elephants, snow leopards, sperm whales, and mountain gorillas.

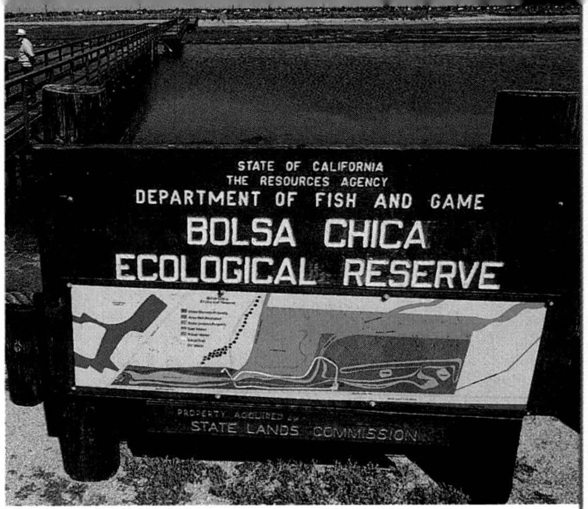

Figure 19 Preserving whole habitats is probably the most effective way to protect biodiversity.

Habitat Preservation The most effective way to preserve biodiversity is to protect whole ecosystems. Preserving whole habitats saves not only endangered species, but also other species that depend on them.

Beginning in 1872 with Yellowstone National Park, the world's first national park, many countries have set aside wildlife habitats as parks and refuges. In addition, private organizations have purchased millions of hectares of endangered habitats throughout the world. Today, there are about 7,000 nature parks, preserves, and refuges in the world.

To be most effective, reserves must have the characteristics of diverse ecosystems. For example, they must be large enough to support the populations that live there. The reserves must contain a variety of niches. And of course, it is still necessary to keep the air, land, and water clean, remove exotic species, and control poaching.

Section 3 Review

1. What are three factors that affect biodiversity?
2. List four possible causes of extinction.
3. Give an example of a legal approach and a scientific approach to preventing extinction.
4. Which are the most diverse ecosystems on Earth?
5. Identify three ways in which biodiversity is important.
6. **Thinking Critically** **Making Generalizations** Explain how the statement "In the web of life, all things are connected" relates to keystone species.

Science at Home

Obtain a map of your community or state. With a family member, identify any city, state, or national parks, reserves, or refuges in your area. Create a travel brochure highlighting one of these areas. Describe the habitats there. Find out whether any endangered or threatened species live in the park. Include their pictures in your brochure.

3 Assess

Section 3 Review Answers

1. Area, climate, and diversity of niches
2. Habitat destruction, poaching, pollution, and exotic species
3. *Legal approach:* Laws such as the Endangered Species Act and the Convention on International Trade in Endangered Species; *Scientific approach:* captive breeding in zoos or wildlife preserves, habitat preservation
4. Tropical rain forests and coral reefs
5. Biodiversity is important for beauty and recreation, economic reasons, the health of ecosystems, and genetic diversity.
6. A keystone species is one that influences the survival of many other species in an ecosystem. If something happens to the keystone species, all other species in the ecosystem are affected.

Science at Home

ACTIVITY

Besides looking at maps, students can contact their state's Environmental Protection Agency, a local chapter of the National Audubon Society, or their town's parks department. Students' brochures should describe the habitats of endangered or threatened species in the area.

Program Resources

◆ **Teaching Resources** 3-3 Review and Reinforce, p. 81; 3-3 Enrich, p. 82

Media and Technology

Interactive Student Tutorial CD-ROM E-3

Exploring Life Science Videodisc Unit 6, Side 2, "It's All Happening at the Zoo"

Chapter 6

Performance Assessment

Writing Have each student identify and briefly describe the four causes of extinction presented in the text.

Portfolio Students can save their work in their portfolios.

SECTION 4 The Search for New Medicines

Objective

After completing the lesson, students will be able to

◆ explain why many rain forest plants are sources of medicines.

Key Term taxol

1 Engage/Explore

Activating Prior Knowledge

Before students read the introductory text on this page, ask: **Where are temperate rain forests located?** (*Along the northwest coast of the United States*) If students have difficulty recalling this information, have them look back at the biome map on page 63 in Chapter 2.

DISCOVER

Skills Focus observing
Materials *black marking pen, strip of filter paper, water, clear plastic cup, tape, pencil*
Time 15 minutes
Tips If filter paper is not available, use paper towels cut into strips.
Expected Outcome Water will carry the dissolved black ink up the strip, where the individual colors will separate out.
Think It Over The specific colors that separate from the black ink will depend on the marker used. Different colors will advance up the strip at different rates: blue the fastest, yellow slightly slower, and red much slower.

SECTION 4 The Search for New Medicines

DISCOVER ACTIVITY

How Are Plant Chemicals Separated?

1. Using a black marking pen, draw a dot about 2 centimeters from the end of a strip of filter paper.
2. Pour a few centimeters of water into a clear plastic cup.
3. Tape the top edge of the filter paper strip to a pencil. Place the pencil across the top of the cup so that the ink dot hangs just below the water surface. If necessary, turn the pencil to adjust the length of the paper.

4. Observe what happens to the black dot.

Think It Over
Observing How many different colors of ink did you separate from the black ink? This process models one method of separating individual chemicals contained in plants.

GUIDE FOR READING

◆ Why are many rain forest plants sources of medicines?

Reading Tip As you read, identify statements that show how biodiversity is related to human health.

Pacific yew tree

Y ou lace up your hiking boots, and sling your collecting bag over your shoulder. It's time to head out for another day of searching in the cool, damp forest. Stepping carefully to avoid mud, you walk beneath the giant evergreens. Their needle-covered branches form a thick roof above your head. Rotting logs covered with ferns, seedlings, and brightly colored fungi line your path. You scan the ground for telltale signs of the object of your search. What are you looking for in this forest? A plant that can save lives!

This ancient forest is the temperate rain forest of the Pacific Northwest. Many of its giant trees are more than 200 years old. Like tropical rain forests, temperate rain forests are diverse ecosystems. They contain many species that are found nowhere else. Some of these species are threatened or endangered, including the bull trout, Olympic salamander, and the life-saving plant you are looking for—the Pacific yew tree.

Plants and Medicines

People have always valued plants for their ability to heal wounds and fight diseases. For example, aspirin was originally made from the bark of the willow tree. The active chemical in aspirin can now be made in a laboratory.

READING STRATEGIES

Reading Tip Some statements that show how biodiversity is related to human health that students might identify include: *People have always valued plants for their ability to heal wounds and fight diseases. Some chemicals rain forest plants produce to protect their leaves and bark can also be used to fight human diseases. Almost half of all medicines sold today contain chemicals originally found in wild organisms.*

Summarizing To ensure that students understand the sequence of events in the development of taxol as an anticancer drug, have them summarize the text in The Story of Taxol and A Threatened Supply of Taxol on pages 107–108. Tell students to write one sentence that summarizes the main idea of each paragraph. When the sentences are read in order, they will provide a summary of the text.

The ability to fight disease is a result of the plants' adaptations to their environment. Plants in many ecosystems produce chemicals that protect them from predators, parasites, and diseases. This is particularly true in rain forests, where so many organisms make their living by eating plants. **Some chemicals that rain forest plants produce to protect their leaves and bark can also be used to fight human diseases.**

Figure 20 Scientists studied Pacific yew tree seedlings to learn more about the cancer-fighting substance taxol. In the closeup, a researcher examines taxol crystals.

The Story of Taxol

The Pacific yew tree is very resistant to diseases and insects. Scientists began studying the bark of the Pacific yew to find out why it was so hardy. They separated chemicals from the bark. During this analysis, the scientists discovered unusual crystals in the bark. These crystals are made from a chemical called **taxol,** the substance that protects the Pacific yew tree.

Scientists next experimented with taxol in the laboratory. They discovered that taxol crystals affect cancer cells in an unusual way. Typically, cancer cells grow and divide very rapidly. This quick growth forms a mass of cells called a tumor. When cancer cells are exposed to taxol, the taxol forms structures that look like tiny cages around each cancer cell. These structures prevent the cancer cells from dividing. As a result, the cancer cannot grow and spread.

After more research, doctors were ready to test taxol on cancer patients. The taxol treatments often were able to shrink certain types of tumors. Sometimes they even stopped the cancer from spreading in the body. Taxol is now used to treat more than 12,000 cancer patients each year.

✓ *Checkpoint* *How is taxol helpful to Pacific yew trees?*

Media and Technology

 Audiotapes English-Spanish Summary 3-4

 Exploring Life Science Videodisc Unit 6, Side 2, "A Question of Balance"

Chapter 2

Answers to Self-Assessment

✓ *Checkpoint*

Taxol makes the trees resistant to diseases and insects.

Program Resources

◆ **Teaching Resources** 3-4 Lesson Plan, p. 83; 3-4 Section Summary, p. 84
◆ **Interdisciplinary Exploration Series** "Fate of the Rain Forest," pp. 12–13

---

2 Facilitate

Plants and Medicines

Real-Life Learning

Materials *packages from herbal teas and dietary supplements*
Time 15 minutes

Tell students that many traditional folk remedies are still used today. As examples, supply empty packages from a variety of herbal teas and dietary supplements such as chamomile, St. John's wort, ginseng, kava kava, echinacea, ginkgo biloba, goldenseal, and cat's claw. Let students examine the labels and identify the herb each product contains and its purported benefits. Point out the notice on each supplement's label that the product is not approved by the FDA for medical use. Also encourage students to ask older family members about traditional remedies that were commonly used in the past. **learning modality: verbal**

Building Inquiry Skills: Observing

Materials *small branches from yew shrubs*
Time 10 minutes

Provide each pair or small group of students with a small branch clipped from a variety of yew (*Taxus*) that is commonly used for landscaping. Let students examine the needles and the thin, scaly bark. Explain that the Pacific yew is related to these shrubs but is a large tree that grows up to 14 m tall with a wide trunk. Before taxol was discovered, wood from the Pacific yew was used to build furniture. **learning modality: kinesthetic**

Ongoing Assessment

Writing Have each student explain how protective chemicals are helpful to plants.

A Threatened Supply of Taxol

Building Inquiry Skills: Calculating

Point out that the text says more than 12,000 cancer patients are treated with taxol each year. Ask: **How many yew trees would have to be cut down to supply the drug to those people?** *(36,000 per year)* **learning modality: logical/ mathematical**

Biodiversity and Medicine

Cultural Diversity

Explain that many scientists are learning about the medicinal qualities of wild organisms from native peoples. These groups often still depend on plants and animals for medicines. For example, cat's claw (Uña de Gato), a traditional herbal medicine in Peru, has a high alkaloid content. Limited studies have found that alkaloids may help bolster the disease-fighting function of white blood cells. **learning modality: verbal**

3 Assess

Section 4 Review Answers

1. Many of these plants produce chemicals that protect them against predators, parasites, and diseases.
2. Temperate rain forests, which are cool, damp, and heavily shaded
3. Taxol encloses each cancer cell in a cage that keeps the cell from dividing.
4. The company would be interested in testing new species to determine whether they might have any medical uses.

Check Your Progress

CHAPTER PROJECT 3

As students observe their plots, encourage them to draw the organisms in detail so they can identify them later using field guides. Remind students to make notes about abiotic factors as well. Check each group's notebook occasionally to make sure students are recording data.

Figure 21 This researcher is pressing leaves as part of a species survey in a forest reserve.

A Threatened Supply of Taxol

The demand for taxol as a cancer treatment has grown rapidly. Now many scientists have become concerned about the supply of Pacific yew trees. It takes the bark of three Pacific yew trees to produce enough pure taxol for one cancer patient's treatment. If the bark is removed from a yew tree, the tree cannot survive. And by the time researchers discovered taxol's value as a cancer-fighting drug, a large portion of the yew trees' temperate rain forests were gone.

Taxol has a very complex chemical structure. Chemists have been working for many years to reproduce this structure. In 1996, chemists successfully created taxol in the laboratory for the first time. This discovery could help protect the remaining Pacific yew trees for future generations.

Biodiversity and Medicine

Almost half of all medicines sold today contain chemicals originally found in wild organisms. What other medicines are growing undiscovered in the forests of the world? So far, only about 2 percent of the world's known plant species have been studied for possible medical use. In 1995 the American Medical Association called for the protection of Earth's biodiversity. Their goal was to preserve the undiscovered medicines that may exist in nature. Governments, scientists, and private companies are working together to find new species all over the world. Perhaps they will find new sources of cancer-fighting drugs.

Section 4 Review

1. What adaptations of rain forest plants make them a likely source of medicines?
2. Describe the ecosystem in which Pacific yew trees are found.
3. How does taxol affect cancer cells?
4. **Thinking Critically Inferring** Suppose a group of scientists is planning an expedition to identify new species in the South American rain forest. Why might a company that manufactures medicines be interested in supporting their expedition?

Check Your Progress

CHAPTER PROJECT 3

Visit your plot regularly to make observations. Use field guides to identify the plants, animals, and other organisms you observe. Record their locations within your plot along with their common and scientific names. By now you should also be planning how to present your findings. Consider using a series of drawings, a flip chart, a computer presentation, or a video of your plot with closeups of the species you have identified. (*Hint:* Be sure to include the data you collected on abiotic factors.)

Background

Integrating Science Taxol was first tested in women with severe ovarian cancer that had not responded to chemotherapy and radiation. Ovarian tumors in 40 percent of the women shrank to half their original size. When taxol was later given to women with breast cancer, more than half the patients experienced partial remission.

Program Resources

◆ **Teaching Resources** 3-4 Review and Reinforce, p. 85; 3-4 Enrich, p. 86

Media and Technology

 Interactive Student Tutorial CD-ROM E-3

SECTION 1 Environmental Issues

Key Ideas

- Three types of environmental issues are resource use, population growth, and pollution.
- Environmental science is the study of the natural processes that occur in the environment and how humans can affect them.
- Making environmental decisions requires balancing different viewpoints and weighing the costs and benefits of proposals.

Key Terms

renewable resources
nonrenewable resources
pollution
development viewpoint
preservation viewpoint
conservation viewpoint

SECTION 2 Forests and Fisheries

Key Ideas

- Because new trees can be planted to replace those that are cut down, forests can be renewable resources.
- Managing fisheries involves setting fishing limits, changing fishing methods, developing aquaculture techniques, and finding new resources.

Key Terms

clear-cutting   fishery
selective cutting   aquaculture
sustainable yield

SECTION 3 Biodiversity

Key Ideas

- Factors that affect biodiversity include area, climate, and diversity of niches.
- Tropical rain forests are the most diverse ecosystems in the world. Coral reefs are the second most diverse ecosystems in the world.
- Diversity of organisms is a source of beauty, inspiration, and recreation. Many species and ecosystems also have economic value. Some species play critical roles in their ecosystems.
- Human activities that threaten biodiversity include habitat destruction, poaching, pollution, and introduction of exotic species.
- Three techniques for protecting biodiversity are regulating capture and trade, captive breeding, and habitat preservation.

Key Terms

biodiversity   threatened species
keystone species   habitat destruction
genes   habitat fragmentation
extinction   poaching
endangered species   captive breeding

SECTION 4 The Search for New Medicines

INTEGRATING HEALTH

Key Ideas

- Many plants make chemicals that protect them from predators, parasites, and disease. These chemicals may fight human diseases.
- The cancer-fighting drug taxol comes from Pacific yew trees, which have been affected by logging of the forests where they grow.
- The possible discovery of other medicines is one reason to protect biodiversity.

Key Term

taxol

USING THE INTERNET   *ACTIVITY*

www.science-explorer.phschool.com

Program Resources

- **Teaching Resources** Chapter 3 Project Scoring Rubric, p. 70; Chapter 3 Performance Assessment, pp. 194–196; Chapter 3 Test, pp. 197–200

Media and Technology

Interactive Student Tutorial CD-ROM E-3

Computer Test Bank E-3

Performance Assessment

Writing Have students explain why it is important to be able to duplicate taxol in a laboratory.

Reviewing Content:
Multiple Choice
1. b **2.** d **3.** a **4.** b **5.** b

True or False
6. true **7.** renewable **8.** true **9.** keystone
10. preservation

Checking Concepts
11. *Sample answers: personal/local issue*—deciding whether to recycle materials; *national/global issue*—setting aside land for wildlife refuges
12. By considering the viewpoints of many different people and weighing the costs and benefits of different solutions
13. Clear-cutting exposes soil to erosion by wind and water, damages streams with eroded silt, and destroys forest habitats. Selective cutting is less damaging to the forest environment and maintains diversity.
14. *Any one:* Set limits on the amount and/or size of fish that can be caught; use nets with a larger mesh size; outlaw fishing methods that kill all the fish in an area rather than selected species; raise fish on farms (aquaculture)
15. Species lose the places where they feed, breed, and nest. If they cannot find a substitute niche, they must move to a new location to survive. If they cannot relocate, they will not survive.
16. Each student's editorial should demonstrate understanding of the viewpoint he or she has chosen: development (using resources freely to benefit people), preservation (not disturbing the environment), or conservation (using resources without destroying them).

Thinking Visually
17. **a.** Economic value; **b., c.** Captive breeding, Habitat preservation; **d., e.** Poaching, Exotic species. Sample title: Facts About Biodiversity

Reviewing Content

 For more review of key concepts, see the Interactive Student Tutorial CD-ROM.

Multiple Choice
Choose the letter of the best answer.

1. The viewpoint that humans should be able to benefit from all of Earth's resources is the
 a. conservation viewpoint.
 b. development viewpoint.
 c. scientific viewpoint.
 d. preservation viewpoint.
2. The most diverse ecosystems in the world are
 a. coral reefs. **b.** deserts.
 c. grasslands. **d.** tropical rain forests.
3. If all members of a species disappear from Earth, that species is
 a. extinct. **b.** endangered.
 c. nonrenewable. **d.** threatened.
4. The illegal removal from the wild or killing of an endangered species is called
 a. habitat destruction.
 b. poaching.
 c. pollution.
 d. captive breeding.
5. Taxol, which comes from Pacific yew trees, is a medicine that is used to fight
 a. heart disease. **b.** cancer.
 c. lung disease. **d.** diabetes.

True or False
If the statement is true, write true. If it is false, change the underlined word or words to make the statement true.

6. The three main types of environmental issues today are resource use, pollution, and <u>population growth</u>.
7. Forests and fisheries are examples of <u>nonrenewable</u> resources.
8. A <u>sustainable yield</u> is a number of trees that can be regularly harvested without affecting the health of the forest.
9. A species that influences the survival of many other species in an ecosystem is called a(n) <u>endangered</u> species.
10. The most effective way to protect biodiversity is through habitat <u>fragmentation</u>.

Checking Concepts

11. Give an example of a personal or local environmental issue and an example of a national or global environmental issue.
12. How are environmental decisions made?
13. Compare the effects of clear-cutting and selective cutting on forest ecosystems.
14. Describe one way to prevent overfishing.
15. Explain how habitat destruction affects species.
16. **Writing to Learn** You are a member of the county land use commission. Hundreds of people are moving to your county every day. You must make a decision regarding how to manage a 5,000-hectare woodland area in your county. Choose one point of view: development, preservation, or conservation. Write an editorial for a newspaper explaining your position.

Thinking Visually

17. **Concept Map** Copy the biodiversity concept map below onto a sheet of paper. Complete it and add a title. (For more on concept maps, see the Skills Handbook.)

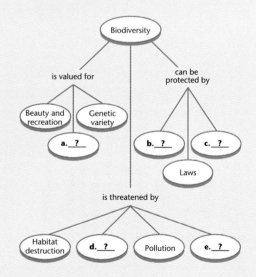

Applying Skills

18.

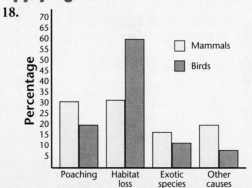

19. Habitat loss is the major cause for both birds and mammals. Poaching is almost as significant for mammals.
20. *Sample answer:* Areas where birds tend to nest and breed, such as wetlands, are particularly threatened by habitat destruction.

Thinking Critically

21. As the number of humans increases, they compete with other species for space, food, water, and other resources. More humans also create more pollution and develop more land,

Applying Skills

One study identifies the reasons that mammal and bird species are endangered or threatened. Use the table to answer Questions 18–20.

Reason	Mammals	Birds
Poaching	31%	20%
Habitat loss	32%	60%
Exotic species	17%	12%
Other causes	20%	8%

18. Graphing Make a bar graph comparing the reasons that mammals and birds are endangered and threatened. Show percents for each animal group on the vertical axis and reasons on the horizontal axis.

19. Interpreting Data What is the major reason that mammals become endangered or threatened? What mainly endangers or threatens birds?

20. Developing Hypotheses Suggest explanations for the differences between the data for mammals and birds.

Thinking Critically

21. Relating Cause and Effect Explain how human population growth affects other species on Earth.

22. Making Generalizations Describe how an exotic species can threaten other species in an ecosystem.

23. Predicting How could the extinction of a species today affect your life 20 years from now?

24. Relating Cause and Effect Explain why many human medicines are made from chemicals that come from plants.

25. Making Judgments Suppose you were given $1 million toward saving an endangered turtle species. You could use the money to start a captive breeding program for the turtles. Or you could use the money to purchase and protect part of the turtle's habitat. How would you spend the money? Explain your answer.

24. Many plants produce chemicals that ward off disease and parasites. These chemicals often have disease-fighting properties in humans.

25. Accept all reasonable responses so long as students support their choices with well-reasoned arguments that include why the method has a greater chance of success or can achieve more for the money invested.

Performance Assessment

Wrap Up
CHAPTER PROJECT 3

Present Your Project Before groups give their presentations to the entire class, meet with each group briefly to review students' plans. Suggest any questions that may not have occurred to them.

Reflect and Record Let each group reconvene to discuss their answers to these questions, then encourage all groups to share their ideas in a class discussion.

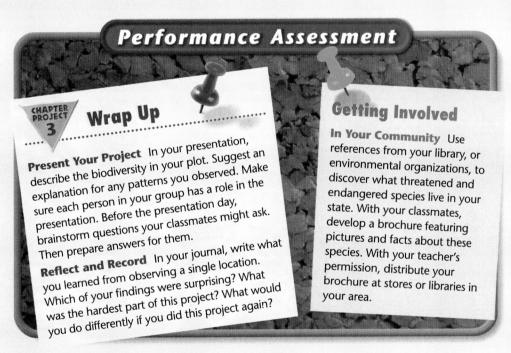

Performance Assessment

CHAPTER PROJECT 3 Wrap Up

Present Your Project In your presentation, describe the biodiversity in your plot. Suggest an explanation for any patterns you observed. Make sure each person in your group has a role in the presentation. Before the presentation day, brainstorm questions your classmates might ask. Then prepare answers for them.

Reflect and Record In your journal, write what you learned from observing a single location. Which of your findings were surprising? What was the hardest part of this project? What would you do differently if you did this project again?

Getting Involved

In Your Community Use references from your library, or environmental organizations, to discover what threatened and endangered species live in your state. With your classmates, develop a brochure featuring pictures and facts about these species. With your teacher's permission, distribute your brochure at stores or libraries in your area.

which in turn destroys natural habitats. Pollution and habitat destruction can threaten the survival of some species.

22. An exotic species may compete with native species for limited resources. If the exotic species has no natural predators in its new habitat, it may outcompete the native species.

23. *Sample answers:* The species might have been the source of a medicine or had another use that is unknown today. The species might have been the source of genes for rare traits that could help other species survive.

Program Resources

◆ **Inquiry Skills Activity Book** Provides teaching and review of all inquiry skills

Getting Involved

In Your Community If students cannot identify threatened or endangered species in their state, let them choose uncommon native species that are particularly interesting to them. Provide nature magazines, field guides, art supplies, and access to photocopying equipment for creating the class brochure.

Land and Soil Resources

Sections	Time	Student Edition Activities	Other Activities
CHAPTER PROJECT 4 **What's in a Package?** p. 113	Ongoing (2 weeks)	Check Your Progress, pp. 119, 134 Wrap Up, p. 137	
1 Conserving Land and Soil pp. 114–120 ◆ Describe major forms of land use. ◆ Identify problems that occur when soil is not properly managed.	3–4 periods/ $1\frac{1}{2}$–2 blocks	**Discover** How Does Mining Affect the Land?, p. 114 **Skills Lab: Controlling Variables** Save That Soil, p. 120	TE Integrating Earth Science, p. 116 TE Building Inquiry Skills: Observing, p. 116 TE Inquiry Challenge, p. 117 IES "Fate of the Rain Forest," pp. 16–19, 26–27
2 Solid Waste pp. 121–129 ◆ Name and describe three ways of dealing with solid waste. ◆ List the four major types of recyclable waste. ◆ Describe methods for managing solid waste.	3–4 periods/ $1\frac{1}{2}$–2 blocks	**Discover** What's in the Trash?, p. 121 **Sharpen Your Skills,** Graphing, p. 123 **Try This** It's in the Numbers, p. 125 **Science at Home,** p. 127 **Real-World Lab: How it Works** Waste, Away!, pp. 128–129	TE Demonstration, p. 122 TE Building Inquiry Skills: Making Models, p. 123 TE Integrating Technology, p. 124 TE Building Inquiry Skills: Calculating, p. 124 TE Real-Life Learning, p. 125 TE Building Inquiry Skills: Communicating, p. 126 ISLM E–4, "Choosing Packing Materials" PTA "Testing Orange Juice"; "Testing Toilet Paper," pp. 1–8
3 *INTEGRATING* **C**HEMISTRY **Hazardous Wastes** pp. 130–134 ◆ List and describe the categories of hazardous wastes. ◆ Explain how hazardous wastes affect human health. ◆ Identify methods for managing hazardous wastes.	2 periods/ 1 block	**Discover** What's Hazardous?, p. 130	TE Building Inquiry Skills: Classifying, p. 131 TE Real-Life Learning, p. 131 TE Integrating Health, p. 132 TE Inquiry Challenge, p. 132 TE Building Inquiry Skills: Communicating, p. 133 TE Using the Visuals: Figure 16, p. 134
Study Guide/Chapter Review pp. 135–137	1 period/ $\frac{1}{2}$ block		ISAB Provides teaching and review of all inquiry skills

 For Standard or Block Schedule The Resource Pro® CD-ROM gives you maximum flexibility for planning your instruction for any type of schedule. Resource Pro® contains Planning Express®, an advanced scheduling program, as well as the entire contents of the Teaching Resources and the Computer Test Bank.

CHAPTER PLANNING GUIDE

Program Resources	Assessment Strategies	Media and Technology
TR Chapter 4 Project Teacher Notes, pp. 92–93 **TR** Chapter 4 Project Overview and Worksheets, pp. 94–97 **TR** Chapter 4 Project Scoring Rubric, p. 98	**SE** Performance Assessment: Chapter 4 Project Wrap Up, p. 137 **TE** Check Your Progress, pp. 119, 134 **TE** Performance Assessment: Chapter 4 Project Wrap Up, p. 137 **TR** Chapter 4 Project Scoring Rubric, p. 98	Science Explorer Internet Site
TR 4-1 Lesson Plan, p. 99 **TR** 4-1 Section Summary, p. 100 **TR** 4-1 Review and Reinforce, p. 101 **TR** 4-1 Enrich, p. 102 **TR** Chapter 4 Skills Lab, pp. 111–112 **SES** Book G, *Earth's Changing Surface,* Chapters 2 and 3	**SE** Section 1 Review, p. 119 **SE** Analyze and Conclude, p. 120 **TE** Ongoing Assessment, pp. 115, 117 **TE** Performance Assessment, p. 119 **TR** 4-1 Review and Reinforce, p. 101	Exploring Earth Science Videodisc, Unit 6 Side 2, "Is Our Soil Endangered?" Audiotapes: English-Spanish Summary 4-1 Transparency 9, "Soil Layers" Interactive Student Tutorial CD-ROM, E-4
TR 4-2 Lesson Plan, p. 103 **TR** 4-2 Section Summary, p. 104 **TR** 4-2 Review and Reinforce, p. 105 **TR** 4-2 Enrich, p. 106 **TR** Chapter 4 Real-World Lab, pp. 113–115	**SE** Section 2 Review, p. 127 **SE** Analyze and Conclude, p. 129 **TE** Ongoing Assessment, pp. 123, 125 **TE** Performance Assessment, p. 127 **TR** 4-2 Review and Reinforce, p. 105	Exploring Earth Science Videodisc, Unit 6 Side 2, "Where Does Your Garbage Go?"; "It Really Isn't Garbage" Audiotapes: English-Spanish Summary 4-2 Transparency 10, "Exploring a Landfill" Interactive Student Tutorial CD-ROM, E-4
TR 4-3 Lesson Plan, p. 107 **TR** 4-3 Section Summary, p. 108 **TR** 4-3 Review and Reinforce, p. 109 **TR** 4-3 Enrich, p. 110	**SE** Section 3 Review, p. 134 **TE** Ongoing Assessment, pp. 131, 133 **TE** Performance Assessment, p. 134 **TR** 4-3 Review and Reinforce, p. 109	Audiotapes: English-Spanish Summary 4-3 Interactive Student Tutorial CD-ROM, E-4
TR Chapter 4 Performance Assessment, pp. 201–203 **TR** Chapter 4 Test, pp. 204–207	**SE** Chapter 4 Review, pp. 135–137 **TR** Chapter 4 Performance Assessment, pp. 201–203 **TR** Chapter 4 Test, pp. 204–207 **CTB** Test E-4	Computer Test Bank, Test E-4 Interactive Student Tutorial CD-ROM, E-4

Key:
SE Student Edition
CTB Computer Test Bank
ISAB Inquiry Skills Activity Book

TE Teacher's Edition
SES Science Explorer Series Text
PTA Product Testing Activities by *Consumer Reports*

TR Teaching Resources
ISLM Integrated Science Laboratory Manual
IES Interdisciplinary Explorations Series

Meeting the National Science Education Standards and AAAS Benchmarks

National Science Education Standards	Benchmarks for Science Literacy	Unifying Themes
Science As Inquiry (Content Standard A) ◆ **Design and conduct a scientific investigation** Students investigate how rainfall can cause erosion. *(Skills Lab)* ◆ **Develop descriptions, explanations, predictions, and models using evidence** Students model landfills to see how they work. *(Real-World Lab)* **Earth and Space Science** (Content Standard D) ◆ **Structure of the Earth system** Soil is a complex system made up of living and nonliving things. *(Section 1)* **Science and Technology** (Content Standard E) ◆ **Evaluate completed technological designs or products** Students analyze product packaging. *(Chapter Project)* ◆ **Understandings about science and technology** A sanitary landfill can prevent waste from polluting the land and water. *(Section 2; Real-World Lab)* **Science in Personal and Social Perspectives** (Content Standard F) ◆ **Personal health** Exposure to hazardous wastes can affect health. *(Section 3)* ◆ **Natural hazards** Poor soil management can result in erosion, nutrient depletion, and desertification. *(Section 1; Skills Lab)* ◆ **Science and technology in society** Solid waste can be buried, burned, or recycled. Hazardous waste is any material that can be harmful if it is not properly disposed of. *(Chapter Project; Sections 2, 3)*	**1B Scientific Inquiry** Students analyze product packaging, investigate how different land surfaces are affected by rainfall, and model different kinds of landfills to see how they work. *(Chapter Project; Skills Lab; Real-World Lab)* **3A Technology and Science** Some farming methods can help reduce soil erosion. A well-designed sanitary landfill contains the waste and prevents it from polluting the surrounding land and water. Scientists have developed several methods of hazardous waste disposal. *(Sections 1, 2, 3; Real-World Lab)* **3C Issues in Technology** Poor soil management can result in erosion, nutrient depletion, and desertification. The basic ways to deal with solid waste are to bury it, burn it, or recycle it. Hazardous waste is any material that can be harmful to human health or the environment if it is not properly stored, transported, treated, or disposed of. *(Sections 1, 2, 3; Chapter Project; Skills Lab)* **4B The Earth** Three uses that change the land are agriculture, development, and mining. A wide range of materials can be recycled. *(Sections 1, 2)*	◆ **Energy** The burning of solid waste is called incineration. Recycling saves energy. *(Sections 1, 2; Skills Lab)* ◆ **Modeling** Students model different land surfaces to see how they are affected by rainfall and different kinds of landfills to see how they work. *(Skills Lab; Real-World Lab)* ◆ **Patterns of Change** Agriculture, development, and mining change the land. A substance that can be broken down and recycled by natural decomposers is biodegradable. Exposure to hazardous wastes may cause severe health problems. *(Sections 1, 2, 3)* ◆ **Scale and Structure** Soil is a complex system made up of living and nonliving things. A well-designed sanitary landfill prevents waste from polluting the land and water. Secure landfills are lined with concrete and many layers of plastic. *(Sections 1, 2, 3; Real-World Lab)* ◆ **Stability** The process of restoring land to a more natural, productive state is called land reclamation. Radioactive wastes contain unstable atoms. *(Sections 1, 2, 3)* ◆ **Systems and Interactions** Some farming methods can help reduce erosion. The basic ways to deal with solid waste are to bury it, burn it, or recycle it. *(Sections 1, 2, 3; Chapter Project)* ◆ **Unity and Diversity** Most recycling focuses on four major categories of products: metal, glass, paper, and plastic. Hazardous wastes can be toxic, explosive, flammable, or corrosive. Radioactive wastes also need special disposal. *(Sections 2, 3)*

Media and Technology

Exploring Earth Science Videodisc

◆ **Section 1** "Is Our Soil Endangered?" examines past and present farming practices and proposes practices for the future.

◆ **Section 2** "Where Does Your Garbage Go?" takes viewers on a field trip to a landfill to observe disposal methods. "It Really Isn't Garbage" describes ways to reuse and recycle plastics.

Interactive Student Tutorial CD-ROM

◆ **Chapter Review** Interactive questions help students to self-assess their mastery of key chapter concepts.

Student Edition Connection Strategies

◆ **Section 1** Integrating Earth Science, p. 116

◆ **Section 2** Integrating Technology, p. 124

◆ **Section 3** Integrating Chemistry, pp. 130–134
Integrating Health, p. 132
Social Studies Connection, p. 133

USING THE INTERNET

www.science-explorer.phschool.com

Visit the Science Explorer Internet site to find an up-to-date activity for Chapter 4 of *Environmental Science.*

ACTIVITY	Time (minutes)	Materials Quantities for one work group	Skills
Section 1			
Discover, p. 114	10	**Consumable** mixture of sand and soil, 10–15 sunflower seeds **Nonconsumable** pan, pencil, tweezers, spoon	Predicting
Skills Lab, p. 120	40	**Consumable** newspaper, loose soil, water, sod **Nonconsumable** 2 blocks, 2 unbreakable pans, "rainmaker"	Developing Hypotheses, Controlling Variables, Observing
Section 2			
Discover, p. 121	20	**Consumable** trash bag, 10–15 items commonly found in household waste, plastic gloves, graph paper **Nonconsumable** ruler	Interpreting Data
Sharpen Your Skills, p. 123	15	**Nonconsumable** protractor, drawing compass	Graphing
Try This, p. 125	10	**Nonconsumable** pieces of plastic products with recycling codes	Classifying
Science at Home, p. 127	home	**Consumable** household trash collected for one week **Nonconsumable** scale, calculator (optional)	Calculating
Real-World Lab, pp. 128–129	40; 20	**Consumable** plastic wrap, heavy-duty plastic bag, 12 small sponge cubes, cheesecloth, water, red food coloring, soil, newspaper **Nonconsumable** measuring cup, small pebbles, 5 rubber bands, 3 transparent wide-mouthed jars, metric ruler, scissors, tweezers	Making Models, Drawing Conclusions
Section 3			
Discover, p. 130	10	**Nonconsumable** labels from common hazardous household products	Forming Operational Definitions

A list of all materials required for the Student Edition activities can be found on pages T14–T15. You can order Materials Kits by calling 1-800-828-7777 or by accessing the Science Explorer Internet site at **www.science-explorer.phschool.com.**

What's in a Package?

The Chapter 4 Project provides an opportunity for students to examine product packaging, determine the various materials used and their functions, and investigate what happens to the materials when the packages are discarded.

Purpose Students will identify the materials used in a package; infer the purpose of each material for the product's producers, retailers, and consumers; find out what happens to each type of material in the community's waste-disposal system; and communicate findings in a display.

Skills Focus After completing the Chapter 4 Project, students will be able to
◆ classify the types of materials used in product packages;
◆ infer the purpose of each material;
◆ draw conclusions about what happens to each type of material when it is discarded;
◆ communicate their findings.

Project Time Line The Chapter 4 Project requires about two weeks to complete. This project is most appropriate as an individual activity, though students could work cooperatively to research what happens to the various materials when they are discarded. As the class studies Section 1, each student should choose a product package and begin analyzing the materials used in it. The major portion of the project involves finding out what happens to each material when the package is discarded and then preparing a class display.

Advance Preparation You may wish to contact the municipal department or private company that handles waste collection and recycling in the students' community, and arrange to have a representative speak to the class when students are ready to research waste disposal. If a visit to the class is not possible, arrange to have a designated representative available to answer students' questions on the phone. Other sources of information include municipal waste department fact sheets and town websites.

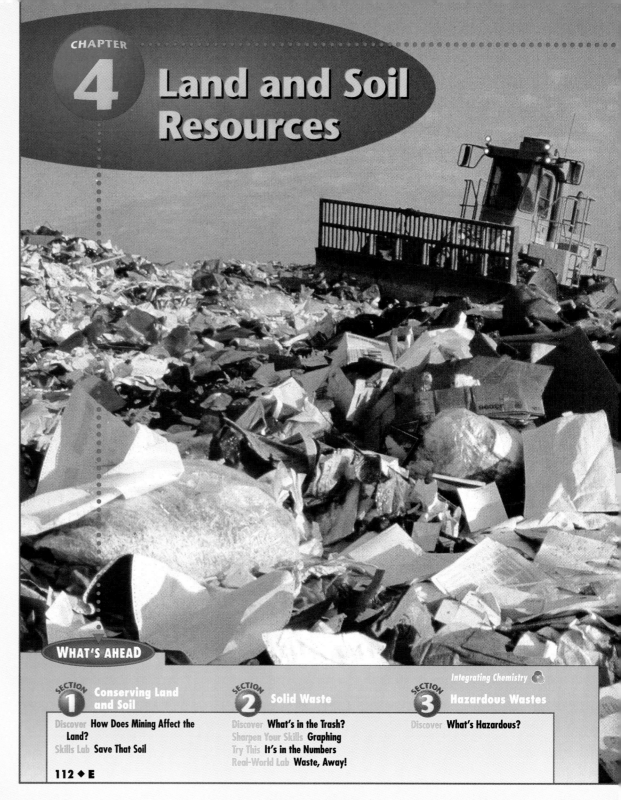

CHAPTER

4 Land and Soil Resources

WHAT'S AHEAD

SECTION 1 Conserving Land and Soil
Discover **How Does Mining Affect the Land?**
Skills Lab **Save That Soil**

SECTION 2 Solid Waste
Discover **What's in the Trash?**
Sharpen Your Skills **Graphing**
Try This **It's in the Numbers**
Real-World Lab **Waste, Away!**

SECTION 3 *Integrating Chemistry* **Hazardous Wastes**
Discover **What's Hazardous?**

112 ◆ E

Possible Materials

◆ Let each student choose a package for the project. Encourage students to choose packages that include two or more different materials. Alternatively, you may wish to collect appropriate packages and assign them to students. CAUTION: *Tell students to make sure the packages are empty before they bring them to school. If students select cans, bottles, and plastic containers for foods, advise them to wash the containers thoroughly with hot, soapy water before bringing them to class. Do not* *allow students to use packaging for raw chicken, ground beef, or any other uncooked meats or fish. Be particularly aware of your school's policy regarding students bringing over-the-counter medicines, vitamin pills, and similar items to school, as empty packages may be misinterpreted by administrators or other teachers.*

◆ Students will need scissors to take their packages apart.
◆ Provide posterboard, tape, colored markers, and other supplies for product displays.

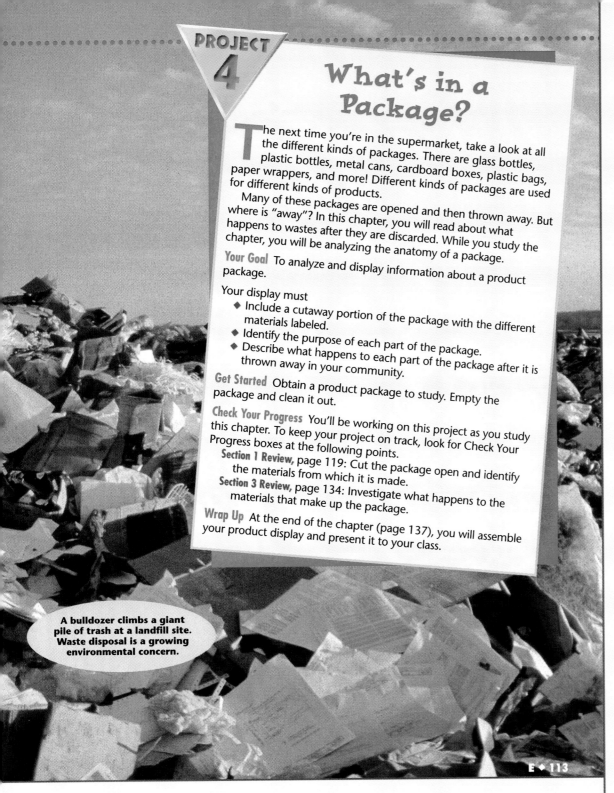

What's in a Package?

The next time you're in the supermarket, take a look at all the different kinds of packages. There are glass bottles, plastic bottles, metal cans, cardboard boxes, plastic bags, paper wrappers, and more! Different kinds of packages are used for different kinds of products.

Many of these packages are opened and then thrown away. But where is "away"? In this chapter, you will read about what happens to wastes after they are discarded. While you study the chapter, you will be analyzing the anatomy of a package.

Your Goal To analyze and display information about a product package.

Your display must

◆ Include a cutaway portion of the package with the different materials labeled.
◆ Identify the purpose of each part of the package.
◆ Describe what happens to each part of the package after it is thrown away in your community.

Get Started Obtain a product package to study. Empty the package and clean it out.

Check Your Progress You'll be working on this project as you study this chapter. To keep your project on track, look for Check Your Progress boxes at the following points.

Section 1 Review, page 119: Cut the package open and identify the materials from which it is made.
Section 3 Review, page 134: Investigate what happens to the materials that make up the package.

Wrap Up At the end of the chapter (page 137), you will assemble your product display and present it to your class.

A bulldozer climbs a giant pile of trash at a landfill site. Waste disposal is a growing environmental concern.

E ◆ 113

Launching the Project Invite students to read the Chapter 4 Project description on page 113. Lead the class in brainstorming types of packaging materials they know of, and list their ideas on the board. Ask students how the materials might be grouped.

Discuss some purposes of packaging materials—for example, keeping the product from spoiling, keeping it from breaking or being damaged during shipment, displaying the product attractively, preventing theft, and making the product convenient for consumers

to store and use. Ask students to suggest which packaging materials might be best for each purpose.

Distribute Chapter 4 Project Overview on pages 94–95 of Teaching Resources, and have students review the project rules and procedures. Encourage students' questions and comments. Also distribute Worksheet 1 on page 96 of Teaching Resources, which lists a wide variety of possible products.

At the end of Section 1, distribute Worksheet 2 on page 97 of Teaching Resources, which provides a format for analyzing a package's components.

Additional information on guiding the project is provided in Chapter 4 Project Teacher Notes on pages 92–93 in Program Resources.

Program Resources

◆ **Teaching Resources** Chapter 4 Project Teacher Notes, pp. 92–93; Chapter 4 Project Overview and Worksheets, pp. 94–97; Chapter 4 Project Scoring Rubric, p. 98

Performance Assessment

The Chapter 4 Project Scoring Rubric on page 98 in Teaching Resources will help you evaluate how well students complete the Chapter 4 Project. You may want to share the scoring rubric with students so they are clear about what will be expected of them. Students will be assessed on

◆ their completeness and accuracy in classifying the types of materials used in a product package;
◆ their ability to infer the purpose of each packaging material;
◆ their thoroughness in researching what happens to each type of material when the package is discarded in their community;
◆ how well they have communicated their findings to the class.

SECTION ① Conserving Land and Soil

Objectives

After completing the lesson, students will be able to
- describe major forms of land use;
- identify problems that occur when soil is not properly managed.

Key Terms development, litter, topsoil, subsoil, bedrock, erosion, nutrient depletion, fallow, crop rotation, desertification, land reclamation

1 Engage/Explore

Activating Prior Knowledge

To determine what students already know about soil, ask: **What is soil made of?** (*Rock that was broken down into very small pieces over time; accept other reasonable responses without comment at this time.*) **What else does soil contain?** (*Students may mention minerals, nutrients, dead and decaying organisms, and living organisms.*)

••••••• DISCOVER ••••••••

Skills Focus predicting
Materials *pan, mixture of sand and soil, 10–15 sunflower seeds, pencil, tweezers, spoon*
Time 10 minutes
Advance Preparation For each student or small group, prepare a model mining site by filling a pan about half full with a mixture of sand and soil, burying 10–15 sunflower seeds in the mixture, then smoothing the surface to hide the seeds. CAUTION: *Students should wash their hands when they finish.*
Tips Let students use any method they wish to locate and extract the seeds.
Expected Outcome The site will have many holes and mounds of dirt.
Think It Over Students should realize that the land is changed significantly when a site is mined. Restoring it is difficult; holes must be filled, the excavated soil replaced and regraded, and the land replanted.

SECTION ① Conserving Land and Soil

DISCOVER •••••••••••••••••••••••••••• ACTIVITY

How Does Mining Affect the Land?

1. You will be given a pan filled with sand and soil representing a mining site. There are at least 10 deposits of "ore" (sunflower seeds) buried in your mining site.

2. Your goal is to locate and remove the ore from your site. You may use a pencil, a pair of tweezers, and a spoon as mining tools.

3. After you have extracted the chunks of ore, break them open to remove the "minerals" inside. **CAUTION:** Do not eat the sunflower seeds.

4. Observe your mining site and the surrounding area after your mining operations are finished.

Think It Over
Predicting How did mining change the land at your mining site? Predict whether it would be easy or difficult to restore the land to its original state. Explain.

GUIDE FOR READING

- How do people use land?
- What kinds of problems occur when soil is not properly managed?

Reading Tip Before you read, use the section headings to make an outline about land and soil conservation. Leave space in the outline to take notes.

L ess than a quarter of Earth's surface is dry land. Except for a small amount formed when volcanoes erupt, new land cannot be created. All the people on Earth must share this limited amount of land to produce their food, build shelter, and obtain other resources. Land is a precious resource. As the American author Mark Twain once said about land, "They don't make it anymore."

Types of Land Use

People use land in many ways. **Three uses that change the land are agriculture, development, and mining.** Examples of these land uses are shown in Figure 1.

READING STRATEGIES

Reading Tip Students' outlines should include the following main heads and subheads: **I.** *Types of Land Use,* **A.** *Agriculture,* **B.** *Development,* **C.** *Mining,* **II.** *Protecting the Soil,* **A.** *Erosion,* **B.** *Nutrient Depletion,* **C.** *Desertification,* **III.** *Restoring the Land.* Students might include *Soil Layers* as the first subhead below *Protecting the Soil.* Encourage students to include vocabulary terms and definitions in their outlines.

Study and Comprehension After students have examined Exploring Soil Conservation on page 117, have them write new captions for the photographs, paraphrasing the text captions in their own words. Tell students to make sure their captions explain what each farming practice involves and how it helps reduce soil erosion.

Agriculture Land is the source of most food. Crops such as wheat, rice, and potatoes require large areas of fertile land. But less than a third of Earth's land can be farmed. The rest is too dry, too wet, too salty, or too mountainous. To provide food for the growing population, new farmland must be created by clearing forests, draining wetlands, and irrigating deserts. When people make these changes, organisms that depended on the natural ecosystem must find new homes.

Many crops are grown to feed livestock such as hogs, chicken, and cattle. Other land serves as pasture or rangeland for grazing animals.

Development People settled the first villages in areas that had good soil and were near a source of fresh water. As population grew, these settlements became towns and cities. People built more houses and paved roads. The construction of buildings, roads, bridges, dams, and other structures is called **development.**

In the United States, about a million hectares of farmland (an area half the size of New Jersey) are developed each year. Development not only reduces the amount of farmland, but can also destroy wildlife habitats.

Mining Mining is the removal of nonrenewable resources such as iron, copper, and coal from the land. Resources just below the surface are strip mined. Strip mining involves removing a strip of land to obtain the minerals and then replacing the strip. Strip mines expose the soil. It can then be blown or washed away more easily. Strip-mined areas may remain barren for years before the soil becomes rich enough to support the growth of plants again.

For resources located deep underground, it is necessary to dig a tunnel, or shaft. The minerals are carried up through the shafts. This process is called underground mining.

☑ *Checkpoint* *Why isn't all land suitable for farming?*

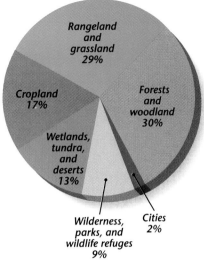

Land Use in the United States

Rangeland and grassland 29%

Forests and woodland 30%

Cropland 17%

Wetlands, tundra, and deserts 13%

Wilderness, parks, and wildlife refuges 9%

Cities 2%

Figure 1 Land in the United States is used in many ways. *Classifying Which of these land uses change the natural ecosystems of the land?*

Figure 2 Three major uses of land are agriculture, development, and mining.

Chapter 4 **E ◆ 115**

Answers to Self-Assessment

Caption Question

Figure 1 Cropland, cities, and rangeland

☑ *Checkpoint*

Much of Earth's land is too dry, too wet, too salty, or too mountainous to be farmed.

2 Facilitate

Types of Land Use

Using the Visuals: Figure 1

Have students answer the caption question in a class discussion. Students should readily recognize that both the cities (an example of development) and the cropland (agriculture) are uses that change natural ecosystems. Some students may also realize that in the rangeland and grassland section of the graph, rangeland—land that is used for grazing domestic animals—is another use that changes natural ecosystems. If students do not make this connection on their own, ask: **Think about the biomes you studied in Chapter 2. Is grassland a type of biome?** *(Yes)* **Is rangeland a type of biome?** *(No)* **How does using land for grazing cattle, sheep, and other animals change the natural ecosystem?** *(Sample answers: Herds can overgraze an area. Large animals may trample native plants, birds' nests on the ground, and animals' burrows or dens. The domestic animals might out-compete native species for space, water, and food.)* **learning modality: logical/mathematical**

Real-Life Learning

After students have examined the photographs in Figure 2 and read the caption, ask: **What examples of these three types of land uses have you seen for yourself? How was the land changed?** *(Answers will vary depending on students' location.)* Use prompting questions to help students describe the changes in detail and consider the effects of those changes on both the land itself and the organisms that lived in the area. **learning modality: verbal**

Ongoing Assessment

Oral Presentation Call on students at random to describe the various kinds of land use and tell how they affect the natural ecosystems of the land.

Protecting the Soil

 Integrating Earth Science

Materials *glass jar with screw-on lid, water, soil sample, hand lens*

Time *Day 1:* 5 minutes; *Day 2:* 10 minutes

To illustrate the materials in topsoil, ask each student to collect and bring in about 500 mL of soil from a location near home. (Advise students to remove any visible living organisms and leave them at the location.) Have each student put his or her sample in a jar, add water to cover the soil well, screw the lid on tightly, then shake the jar gently until the soil and water are thoroughly mixed. (Remind students to wash their hands.) Have students leave their jars undisturbed overnight and examine them the next day. Ask: **What do you see in the jar now?** (*The soil components have settled in layers, with the largest and most dense particles at the bottom and the finest particles at the top; lightweight organic matter is floating on the surface.*)
learning modality: kinesthetic

Building Inquiry Skills: Observing

Materials *small potted plants such as ivy, geraniums, or begonias, hand lens, craft stick, newspaper*

Time 10 minutes

Provide a small potted plant to each group of students. Instruct students to carefully remove the plant from the pot. Then have students examine the roots with a hand lens, paying particular attention to how the roots wrap around and hold onto the soil particles. Instruct students to shake the plant over a sheet of newspaper and gently flick the roots with their fingers to dislodge as much soil as they can. When they examine the roots again, they will see fine particles of soil still clinging to the roots. (Remind students to wash their hands.) When they are done, students should repot the plants with fresh soil. **learning modality: visual**

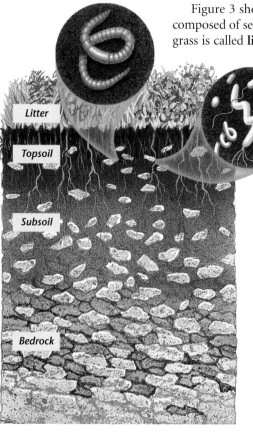

Figure 3 Soil consists of several layers. *Applying Concepts In which layer are most plant roots located? What do the roots absorb there?*

INTEGRATING EARTH SCIENCE Do you think of soil only as something that has to be washed off your hands or swept off the floor? Then you may not realize how much you depend on soil! Soil is a complex system made up of living and nonliving things. It contains the minerals and nutrients that plants need to grow. Soil also absorbs, stores, and filters water. Bacteria, fungi, and other organisms that live in soil break down the wastes and remains of living things. These decomposers recycle the chemical substances that are necessary for life.

Figure 3 shows the structure of fertile soil. Notice that it is composed of several layers. The very top layer of dead leaves and grass is called **litter.** The next layer, **topsoil,** is a mixture of rock fragments, nutrients, water, air, and decaying animal and plant matter. The water and nutrients are absorbed by the many plant roots located in this layer. Below the topsoil is the **subsoil.** The subsoil also contains rock fragments, water, and air, but has less animal and plant matter than the topsoil.

It can take hundreds of years to form just a few centimeters of new soil. All soil begins as the rock that makes up Earth's crust, called **bedrock.** Natural processes such as freezing and thawing gradually break apart the bedrock. Plant roots wedge between rocks and break them into smaller pieces. Chemicals released by lichens slowly break the rock into smaller particles. Animals such as earthworms and moles help grind rocks into even smaller particles. As dead organisms break down, their remains also contribute to the mixture.

Because rich topsoil takes a long time to form, it is important to protect Earth's soil. **Poor soil management can result in three problems: erosion, nutrient depletion, and desertification.**

Erosion The process by which water, wind, or ice moves particles of rocks or soil is called **erosion.** Normally, plant roots hold soil in place. But when soil is exposed to wind and water, erosion occurs more rapidly. Many uses of land, including logging, mining, and farming, expose the soil and can cause erosion. Some farming methods that help reduce erosion are described in *Exploring Soil Conservation.*

Background

Integrating Science In addition to leaving fields fallow and rotating crops, many farmers today use organic farming to reduce nutrient depletion.

Instead of manufactured fertilizers, organic farmers use natural fertilizers such as manure and composted plant matter. Instead of herbicides, they weed with physical methods. And instead of pesticides, they use insect-eating organisms such as praying mantises, ladybugs, birds, and bats.

Nutrient Depletion Plants make their own food through photosynthesis. But plants also require a variety of nutrients from the soil. Just as your body needs iron, zinc, and calcium to grow and function properly, plants need nitrogen, potassium, phosphorus, and other nutrients. Decomposers supply these nutrients to the soil as they break down the remains of dead organisms.

Sometimes, a farmer plants the same crops in a field year after year. As a result, the plants use more nutrients than the decomposers can replace. The soil becomes less fertile, a situation that is called **nutrient depletion.**

One way to prevent nutrient depletion is to periodically leave fields **fallow,** or unplanted with crops. A second way to prevent nutrient depletion is to leave the unused parts of crops, such as cornstalks and watermelon vines, in the fields rather than

EXPLORING Soil Conservation

These farming practices can help reduce soil erosion.

Conservation plowing ▽
Rather than plowing fields and leaving them bare, farmers use machines that break up only the subsoil. This method leaves the dead stalks and weeds from the previous year's crop in the ground to hold the topsoil in place.

◁ **Strip cropping and contour plowing**
Farmers alternate strips of tall crops, such as corn, with short crops, such as squash. The short crops prevent soil from washing out of the tall crop rows, which are less protected. Crops are planted in curving rows that follow the slope, or contour, of the land. Contour plowing can reduce soil erosion as much as 50 percent on gently sloping land.

▲ **Windbreaks**
Rows of trees are planted along the edges of fields. These windbreaks block the wind and also trap eroding soil. Using fruit or nut trees as windbreaks provides an extra benefit for the farmer and wildlife.

Terracing ▷
Steep hillsides are built up into a series of flat "terraces." The ridges of soil at the edges of the terraces slow down runoff and catch eroding soil.

Discuss the various farming practices described in the feature, with particular attention to how each helps to reduce soil erosion. If students live in or have visited an agricultural area, encourage them to describe examples of these farming practices that they have seen. Challenge students to find other photographs of these practices—particularly of terracing, which is not often done in the United States but is common in hilly countries with limited fertile land. **learning modality: verbal**

Inquiry Challenge

Materials *2 deep pans or plastic storage containers, mixture of sand and soil, water*
Time 20 minutes

Challenge small groups of students to create a model showing how either contour plowing or terracing helps reduce soil erosion compared with straight-row plowing or planting on an unterraced hillside. *(Each group should use one container to model the "non-conservation" practice and the other container to model the erosion-reducing practice. Students could compare the results subjectively by describing the amount of erosion they observe in the two containers. To quantify the effects of each practice, students could measure the amount of water that collects at the bottom of the hill in each container and/or the amount of soil that is washed downhill.)* **cooperative learning**

Media and Technology

 Transparencies "Soil Layers," Transparency 9

 Exploring Earth Science Videodisc Unit 6, Side 2, "Is Our Soil Endangered?"

Chapter 5

Answers to Self-Assessment

Caption Question

Figure 3 Topsoil; the roots absorb water and nutrients.

Program Resources

 Science Explorer Series *Earth's Changing Surface*, Chapter 2, describes soil formation and composition, and in Chapter 3, erosion is discussed.

Ongoing Assessment

Drawing Have each student draw and label a simple diagram showing the layers found in the soil.

Portfolio Students can save their drawings in their portfolios.

Protecting the Soil, continued

Using the Visuals: Figure 4

Have students compare this map with the following biome maps in Chapter 2: desert and grassland biomes, Figure 17, page 64, and forest biomes, Figure 19, page 66. Then ask: **Which type of biome is most threatened by desertification?** *(grassland)* **learning modality: visual**

Cultural Diversity

Display a map of Africa and point out the location of the Sahel, just south of the Sahara, the world's largest desert. Explain that the Sahel is a dry grassland. Many parts of the Sahel are experiencing desertification due to repeated droughts and overgrazing. People in the Sahel face continuing food shortages and many other problems caused by the loss of land that can be farmed. Encourage volunteers to find out more about the Sahel and report to the class. **learning modality: verbal**

Restoring the Land

Including All Students

Support students who need more help by encouraging them to relate the text's description of land reclamation to their own direct experience. If students did the Discover at the beginning of the section, ask: **What did your mining site look like when you finished?** *(The site was full of holes and piles of soil.)* Have students recall their predictions about how easy or difficult it would be to restore the land. Then ask: **Now that you've read about restoring the land, were there any problems or costs that you didn't think of earlier?** *(Students may not have realized that the subsoil and topsoil would have to be replaced after the mining operation or that new trees would need to be planted.)* **learning modality: logical/mathematical**

clearing them away. The stalks and vines decompose in the fields, adding nutrients to the soil.

Another method of preventing nutrient depletion is crop rotation. In **crop rotation,** a farmer plants different crops in a field each year. Different types of plants absorb different amounts of nutrients from the soil. Some crops, such as corn and cotton, absorb large amounts of nutrients. The next year, the farmer plants crops that use fewer soil nutrients, such as oats, barley, or rye. The year after that, the farmer sows legumes such as alfalfa or beans to restore the nutrient supply. Another benefit of crop rotation is that it limits the growth of pest populations from year to year.

☑ *Checkpoint* *What causes nutrient depletion?*

Desertification Plants cannot grow without the moisture and nutrients in fertile soil. The advance of desertlike conditions into areas that previously were fertile is called **desertification.** In the past 50 years, desertification has occurred on about five billion hectares of land.

One cause of desertification is climate. During periods of drought, crops fail. Without plant cover, the exposed soil easily blows away. Overgrazing of grasslands by cattle and sheep also exposes the soil. Cutting down trees for firewood can also cause desertification.

Desertification is a very serious problem. People cannot grow crops and graze livestock where desertification has occurred. People may face famine and starvation as a result. In central Africa, where desertification is severe, millions of rural people are moving to the cities because they can no longer support themselves on the land.

Figure 4 Large areas of the world are at risk of desertification. One cause is overgrazing. Without grass to hold the soil in place, the Senegal plain is becoming a barren desert. *Interpreting Maps In which biome are most of the areas at risk of desertification located? (Hint: Refer to Chapter 2.)*

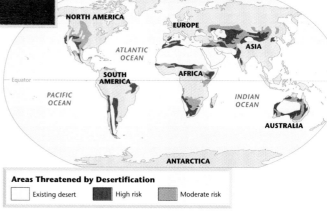

Areas Threatened by Desertification
☐ Existing desert   ■ High risk   ▨ Moderate risk

Figure 5 It's hard to believe that cows now graze on the same hillside that used to be an open mine. Thanks to land reclamation practices, many mining areas are being restored for other uses.

Restoring the Land

Fortunately, it is often possible to restore land damaged by erosion or mining. The process of restoring an area of land to a more natural, productive state is called **land reclamation.** In addition to restoring lands for agriculture, land reclamation can restore habitats for wildlife. Many different types of land reclamation projects are currently underway all over the world. But it is generally more difficult and expensive to restore damaged land and soil than it is to protect them in the first place.

Figure 5 shows an example of land reclamation. When the mining operation in the first scene was completed, the mine operators smoothed out the sides of the mining cuts. Then they carefully replaced the subsoil and topsoil that had been removed before mining. Finally, they planted grass. The former mine is now agricultural land.

Section 1 Review

1. List three ways that people use land.
2. What are three problems that can occur when topsoil is not properly managed?
3. Describe the effects of strip mining on the land.
4. Why is it important to protect topsoil?
5. Describe two methods for reducing soil erosion.
6. **Thinking Critically Relating Cause and Effect** How may human activities be related to desertification?

Check Your Progress
CHAPTER PROJECT 4

Cut your package open so that you can observe its construction. Create a data table identifying each part of the package, the material it is made of, and its purpose. What properties of these materials make them desirable as packaging? (*Hint:* Packaging benefits include protecting a product from breakage, preventing spoilage, making it more attractive, or making it easier to use. Can you think of other benefits of the materials in your package?)

Chapter 4   **E ◆ 119**

Answers to Self-Assessment
Caption Question
Figure 4 the grassland biome

✓ *Checkpoint*
If a farmer plants the same crop in a field year after year, the plants use more nutrients than decomposers in the soil can replace, and the soil becomes less fertile.

---

3 Assess

Section 1 Review Answers

1. Agriculture, development, and mining
2. Erosion, nutrient depletion, and desertification
3. Removing a strip of land exposes the soil to erosion by wind and water. The area may remain barren for years before the soil becomes rich enough again to support plant growth.
4. Topsoil contains the minerals and nutrients that plants need, and it takes a long time for fertile topsoil to form.
5. Students can describe conservation plowing, strip cropping, contour plowing, terracing, and planting windbreaks.
6. To meet the needs of the growing human population, people raise large herds of grazing animals, cut down trees, and carry out strip mining, all of which contribute to desertification.

Check Your Progress
CHAPTER PROJECT 4

CAUTION: *Make sure students handle scissors carefully. Review the safety guidelines in Appendix A.* Give each student a copy of Chapter 4 Project Worksheet 2 on page 97 in Teaching Resources. Explain that the worksheet will help them analyze the packaging materials and infer the purpose of each one. Remind students to keep a sample of each material for use in their product displays.

Performance Assessment

Skills Check Have each student create a concept map that identifies and briefly explains the three major problems that occur when soil is not managed well.

 Students can save their concept maps in their portfolios.

E ◆ 119

Save That Soil

Preparing for Inquiry

Key Concept Plants help reduce erosion by holding soil with their roots.

Skills Objectives Students will be able to
- develop a hypothesis about how different land surfaces are affected by rainfall;
- control all variables except land surface;
- observe erosion by water of two different land surfaces.

Time 40 minutes

Advance Planning Purchase enough aluminum or plastic pans for each group to have two. For each group, cut one piece of sod to fit a pan. Obtain enough loose soil for each group to partially fill one pan.

Guiding Inquiry

Troubleshooting the Experiment

- If students have limited experience with controlling variables, discuss what a variable is.
- Some ways students might devise a "rainmaker" are to punch holes in the bottom of a paper cup or to use a sprinkler top for a soda bottle.
- Before Step 4, ask students how they will control the amount and flow of "rainfall."
- In Step 5, remind students to examine not only the soil left at the upper end of each pan but the runoff water at the lower end. Muddier water indicates more erosion.

Expected Outcome

The loose soil will erode easily and be washed down to the lower end of the pan. The sod will lose very little soil.

Analyze and Conclude

1. "Rainwater" washed away the loose soil much more easily than the soil in the sod.
2. Loose soil is eroded more easily than soil with plants growing in it. A farmer can conserve topsoil by keeping the land planted.

3. The amounts of soil that are eroded can be compared only if the original amount of soil and the amount and kind of "rainfall" were the same.

Extending the Inquiry

Design an Experiment To compare erosion by different kinds of "rainfall," loose soil should be used in both pans.

Save That Soil

I n this lab, you'll decide how to control variables as you investigate the way rainfall causes soil erosion.

Problem

How are different types of land surfaces affected by rainfall?

Materials

newspaper   2 unbreakable pans
2 blocks   sod
loose soil   "rainmaker"
water

Procedure

1. Cover a table with newspaper. Obtain two pans. Insert a block under one end of each pan to raise the two ends to the same height.
2. Read over the rest of the lab. Write a hypothesis that you will test. Pay careful attention to the variables you must control.
3. Place loose soil in the raised end of one pan. Place a small square of sod (soil with grass growing in it) in the raised end of the second pan. One variable is the amount of soil in each pan. Find a way to make the two amounts of soil the same. Record your procedures.
4. Create a "rainmaker" that controls the amount of water and the way it falls on the two soil samples. Then use your rainmaker to test the effect of the same amount of "rain" on the two kinds of soil. Record the results.
5. Review your experiment and your results. Do you see any procedure you wish to change? If so, get your teacher's permission to try the lab again with your revised procedures.

Analyze and Conclude

1. What effects did the "rainwater" produce on each type of soil you tested?
2. This experiment models soil erosion. What can you conclude about actual soil erosion caused by rain? How could a farmer use the information gained from this experiment to conserve topsoil?
3. **Think About It** Why was it essential for you to control the amounts of soil and "rainfall" in the two pans?

Design an Experiment

How does soil erosion caused by a gentle, steady rain compare with that caused by a heavy downpour? Design an experiment to find out. Be sure to control the way you imitate the two types of rain. Obtain your teacher's permission before conducting this experiment.

Safety

Students should wear safety goggles and lab aprons. Review the safety guidelines in Appendix A.

Program Resources

- **Teaching Resources** Chapter 4 Skills Lab, pp. 111–112

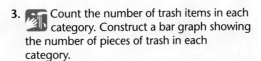

DISCOVER • ACTIVITY

What's in the Trash?

Your teacher will give you a trash bag. The items in the bag represent the most common categories of household waste in the United States.

1. Before you open the bag, predict what the two most common categories are.

2. Put on some plastic gloves. Open the bag and sort the trash items into categories based on what they are made of.

3. Count the number of trash items in each category. Construct a bar graph showing the number of pieces of trash in each category.

Think It Over

Interpreting Data Based on your graph, what are the two most common types of household waste? Was your prediction correct?

How much trash does your family throw away in a year? If it's your job to take the trash out, you might say that it's a large amount. But the amount of trash produced in the United States may be even greater than you think. Consider these facts:

- The average person produces about 2 kilograms of trash daily.
- Every hour, people throw away 2.5 million plastic bottles.
- Every two weeks, people throw away enough glass bottles and jars to fill the World Trade Center towers in New York City.
- Every year, people throw away enough white paper to build a wall 4 meters high that stretches from coast to coast.
- Every year, people throw away 1.6 billion pens, 2.9 million tons of paper towels, and 220 million automobile tires.

You can see why people call the United States a "throw-away society"! Disposable products can be cheap and convenient. But they have created a big problem—what to do with all the trash.

GUIDE FOR READING

- What can be done with solid waste?
- What are the four major types of waste that can be recycled?
- What are the "three R's"?

Reading Tip Before you read, preview *Exploring a Landfill* on page 122. Make a list of any unfamiliar words in the diagram. Look for the meanings of these words as you read.

E ◆ 121

READING STRATEGIES

Reading Tip One word included in *Exploring a Landfill* that may be unfamiliar to students is *groundwater*. Ask students what they think the word means, then let them consult other sources to verify their responses. (*Groundwater refers to fresh water that has seeped down through the soil and collected in permeable rock or soil layers below Earth's surface.*)

Program Resources

- **Teaching Resources** 4-2 Lesson Plan, p. 103; 4-2 Section Summary, p. 104
- **Integrated Science Laboratory Manual** E-4, "Choosing Packing Materials"

Media and Technology

Audiotapes English-Spanish Summary 4-2

SECTION
2 Solid Waste

Objectives

After completing the lesson, students will be able to

- name and describe three ways of dealing with solid waste;
- list the four major types of recyclable waste;
- describe methods for managing solid waste.

Key Terms municipal solid waste, leachate, sanitary landfill, incineration, recycling, biodegradable, resins, composting

1 Engage/Explore

Activating Prior Knowledge

Ask students: **What kinds of things does your family throw away?** (*Used paper, metal cans, glass jars, plastic milk jugs, and so on*) **How does your family get rid of its trash?** (*Trash may be collected in the students' community, or families may bring it to a "dump" themselves. Some families may recycle part of their trash.*)

• • • • • • • DISCOVER • • • • • • • •

Skills Focus interpreting data

Materials *trash bag containing common household wastes (see Advance Preparation below), plastic gloves, graph paper, ruler*

Time 20 minutes

Advance Preparation For each group of students, prepare a trash bag containing the following items: 4 paper items; 2 items of yard waste such as leaves; 1 piece of rubber, cloth, or wood waste; 1 soda can or other metal item; 1 glass jar or bottle; 1 plastic item; 1 food-waste item such as an orange peel.

Tips Have students work on the floor so glass containers do not fall and break.

Expected Outcome Students should sort the items into the seven categories above.

Think It Over Paper and yard waste

2 Facilitate

The Problem of Waste Disposal

Demonstration

Materials *various trash items, bathroom scale, plastic gloves*

Time 10 minutes

Point out the text statement that each day, the average person produces about 2 kg of waste. Tell students that 1 kg equals 2.2 pounds, and let them calculate how many pounds 2 kg equal. *(4.4)* Have a volunteer calculate the daily total for a family of four. *(17.6 lbs)* Have another volunteer help you add trash to the bag until the scale indicates about 17 pounds. Pass the bag around so each student can lift it and get a sense of its weight.

learning modality: kinesthetic

EXPLORING
a Landfill

Ask different volunteers to read the captions aloud. Ask: **What is special about this landfill?** *(It is designed to prevent it from polluting the surrounding environment.)* Then ask: **Why do landfill operators want to reduce the waste's volume before burying it?** *(To keep the landfill from running out of space; to make the landfill last as long as possible.)* **What do you think happens when a town's landfill runs out of space?** *(The town has to build a new landfill; the trash has to be trucked to another town's landfill or maybe even out of state; the town has to find another way to dispose of its trash, perhaps by building an incinerator.)*

learning modality: logical/mathematical

The Problem of Waste Disposal

In their daily activities, people generate many types of waste, including used paper, empty packages, and food scraps. The waste materials produced in homes, businesses, schools, and other places in a community are called **municipal solid waste.** Other sources of solid waste include construction debris and certain agricultural and industrial wastes. **Three methods of handling solid waste are to bury it, to burn it, or to recycle it.** Each method has advantages and disadvantages.

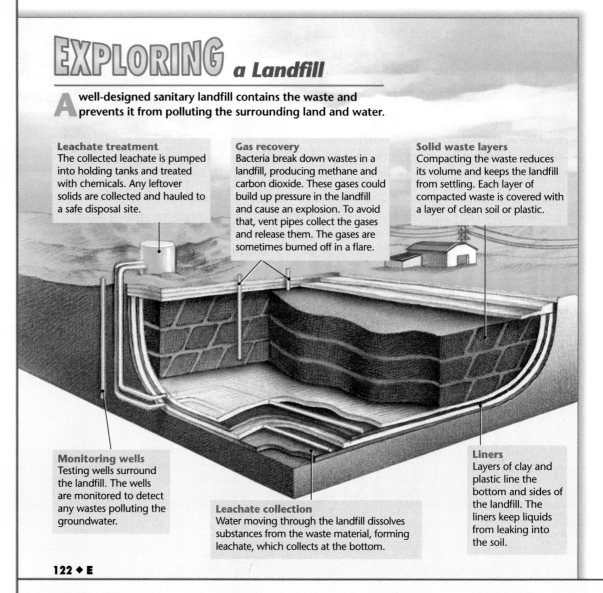

EXPLORING a Landfill

A well-designed sanitary landfill contains the waste and prevents it from polluting the surrounding land and water.

Leachate treatment
The collected leachate is pumped into holding tanks and treated with chemicals. Any leftover solids are collected and hauled to a safe disposal site.

Gas recovery
Bacteria break down wastes in a landfill, producing methane and carbon dioxide. These gases could build up pressure in the landfill and cause an explosion. To avoid that, vent pipes collect the gases and release them. The gases are sometimes burned off in a flare.

Solid waste layers
Compacting the waste reduces its volume and keeps the landfill from settling. Each layer of compacted waste is covered with a layer of clean soil or plastic.

Monitoring wells
Testing wells surround the landfill. The wells are monitored to detect any wastes polluting the groundwater.

Leachate collection
Water moving through the landfill dissolves substances from the waste material, forming leachate, which collects at the bottom.

Liners
Layers of clay and plastic line the bottom and sides of the landfill. The liners keep liquids from leaking into the soil.

122 ◆ E

Background

History of Science Sanitary landfills are a vast improvement over open dumps, but they are not an ideal solution. Many of the materials that fill up landfills are organic and could biodegrade. But little of the paper, grass clippings, and food waste in a sanitary landfill actually decomposes. That's because the soil used to cover the landfill limits the availability of the oxygen needed for the organic wastes to decompose.

One solution is municipal solid waste composting. With this technique, all the organic wastes that a community produces can be composted. As much as three fourths of all household waste by weight could be composted. This would dramatically reduce the volume of waste disposed in sanitary landfills. One drawback of this type of composting is that heavy metals and toxic pesticide residues may be left in the compost.

Landfills Until fairly recently, people usually disposed of waste in open holes in the ground. But these open dumps were dangerous and unsightly. Rainwater falling on the wastes dissolved chemicals from the waste, forming a polluted liquid called **leachate.** Leachate could run off into streams and lakes, or trickle down into the groundwater below the dump.

In 1976, the government banned open dumps. Now much solid waste is buried in landfills that are constructed to hold the wastes more safely. A **sanitary landfill** holds municipal solid waste, construction debris, and some types of agricultural and industrial waste. *Exploring a Landfill* shows the parts of a well-designed sanitary landfill. Once a landfill is full, it is covered with a clay cap to keep rainwater from entering the waste.

However, even well-designed landfills still pose a risk of polluting groundwater. And while capped landfills can be reused in certain ways, including as parks and sites for sports arenas, they cannot be used for other needs, such as housing or agriculture.

Incineration The burning of solid waste is called **incineration** (in sin ur AY shun). Incineration has some advantages over the use of landfills. The burning facilities, or incinerators, do not take up as much space. They do not pose a risk of polluting groundwater. The heat produced by burning solid waste can be used to generate electricity. These "waste-to-energy" plants supply electricity to many homes in the United States.

Unfortunately, incinerators do have drawbacks. Even the best incinerators release some pollution into the air. And although incinerators reduce the volume of waste by as much as 90 percent, some waste still remains. This waste needs to be disposed of somewhere. Finally, incinerators are much more expensive to build than sanitary landfills. Many communities cannot afford to replace an existing landfill with an incinerator.

☑ *Checkpoint* **What is a waste-to-energy plant?**

Figure 6 This waste-to-energy plant generates electricity while disposing of municipal solid waste.

Answers to Self-Assessment

☑ *Checkpoint*

A power plant that uses the heat from burning solid waste to generate electricity

Program Resources

◆ **Product Testing Activities** by *Consumer Reports* "Testing Orange Juice"; "Testing Toilet Paper," pp. 1–8

Sharpen your Skills

Graphing

What happens to trash? Use  the data in the table below to construct a circle graph of methods of municipal solid waste disposal in the United States. Give your circle graph a title. (For help making a circle graph, see the Skills Handbook.)

Method of Disposal	Percentage of Waste
Landfills	56%
Recycling	27%
Incineration	17%

Sharpen your Skills

Graphing

Materials *protractor, drawing compass*
Time 15 minutes

Students should determine the size of each wedge of the circle graph by multiplying 360° by each percentage. *(Landfills = 202°, Recycling = 97°, Incineration = 61°) Sample title:* Methods of Waste Disposal in the U.S.
Extend Have students make a second circle graph to show what would happen if 15% of the total waste were recycled instead of being sent to landfills. *(Landfills = 148°, Recycling = 151°)*
learning modality: logical/mathematical

Building Inquiry Skills: Making Models

Materials *glass or plastic jar, coffee filter, rubber band, soil, food coloring, beaker, water*
Time 10 minutes

Have each group of students make a simple model of leachate, as follows: Put a coffee filter over the mouth of a jar, letting it hang into the jar, and secure it in place with a rubber band. Fill the filter about halfway with soil. Put several drops of food coloring on the soil, then pour water into the jar. When students have finished, ask: **What do you see in the bottom of the jar?** *(Colored water)* **Where did the color come from?** *(The food coloring)* **What does the food coloring represent in this model?** *(Chemicals on the soil's surface)* **In a real landfill, where do chemicals come from?** *(The wastes in the landfill)*
learning modality: kinesthetic

Ongoing Assessment

Skills Check Have each student construct a compare/contrast table that identifies the advantages and disadvantages of sanitary landfills and incinerators.

portfolio Students can save their tables in their portfolios.

Recycling

Materials *various small items of trash, plastic gloves, trowels, resealable plastic bags* **ACTIVITY**
Time 10–15 minutes

Let each group of students select an item of trash and bury the item in a designated spot on the school grounds or in a soil-filled storage bin in the classroom. Then have students dig up their items at the end of this unit, place them in plastic bags, and compare them to see which materials began to decompose and which did not. CAUTION: *Make sure students who are allergic to molds do not sniff or handle decomposing materials. Remind students to wear plastic gloves when handling the trash and wash their hands when they are finished.* **learning modality: kinesthetic**

Building Inquiry Skills: Calculating

Materials *newspapers, metric ruler, calculator (optional)* **ACTIVITY**
Time 10 minutes

Show students a stack of one week's issues of a major daily newspaper that you have collected. Explain that one tree, 10.5 to 12 m tall, produces a stack of newspapers 1.2 m high. Choose a volunteer to measure the height of your stack of papers. Ask: **How many weeks would it take for me to use up one tree just by reading the newspaper?** *(120 cm ÷ height of your stack)* **How many trees would I use up in a year?** *(52 ÷ weeks to use 1 tree)* **If every one of your families also read the newspaper every day, how many trees would we all use up in a year?** *(above answer × [number of students + yourself])* **learning modality: logical/mathematical**

Figure 7 Metal and glass are two frequently recycled materials. **A.** Crumpled aluminum cans ride up a conveyor belt in a recycling center. **B.** A giant mound of crushed glass awaits recycling. *Predicting Without recycling, what might eventually happen to the supply of aluminum?*

Recycling

INTEGRATING TECHNOLOGY The process of reclaiming raw materials and reusing them is called **recycling.** Recycling reduces the volume of solid waste. Recycling enables people to use the materials in wastes again, rather than discarding those materials. As you know, matter in ecosystems is naturally recycled through the water cycle, carbon cycle, and other processes. A substance that can be broken down and recycled by bacteria and other decomposers is **biodegradable** (by oh dih GRAY duh bul).

Unfortunately, many of the products people use today are not biodegradable. Plastic containers, metal cans, rubber tires, and glass jars are examples of products that do not naturally decompose. Instead, people have developed techniques to recycle the raw materials in these products.

A wide range of materials, including motor oil, tires, and batteries, can be recycled. **Most recycling focuses on four major categories of products: metal, glass, paper, and plastic.**

Metal In your classroom, you are surrounded by metal objects that can be recycled. Your desk, scissors, staples, and paper clips are probably made of steel. Another very common metal, aluminum, is used to make soda cans, house siding, window screens, and many other products.

Metals such as iron and aluminum can be melted and reused. Recycling metal saves money and causes less pollution than making new metal. With recycling, no ore needs to be mined, transported to factories, or processed. In addition, recycling metals helps conserve these nonrenewable resources.

Glass Glass is made from sand, soda ash, and limestone mixed together and heated. Glass is one of the easiest products to recycle because glass pieces can be melted down over and over to make new glass containers. Recycled glass is also used to make fiberglass, bricks, tiles, and the reflective paints on road signs.

Recycling glass is less expensive than making glass from raw materials. Because the recycled pieces melt at a lower temperature than the raw materials, less energy is required. Recycling glass also reduces the environmental damage caused by mining for sand, soda, and limestone.

☑ *Checkpoint* *Why is it easy to recycle glass?*

Paper It takes about 17 trees to make one metric ton of paper. Paper mills turn wood into a thick liquid called pulp. Pulp is spread out and dried to produce paper. Pulp can also be made from used paper such as old newspapers. The newspapers must be washed to remove the inks and dyes. The paper is then mixed with more water and other chemicals to form pulp.

Most paper products can only be recycled a few times. Recycled paper is not as smooth or strong as paper made from wood pulp. Each time paper is recycled to make pulp, the new paper is rougher, weaker, and darker.

Plastic When oil is refined to make gasoline and other petroleum products, solid materials called **resins** are left over. Resins can be heated, stretched, and molded into plastic products. Have you ever noticed a symbol like the ones in Figure 8 on a plastic container? This number indicates what type of plastic a container is made of. For example, plastics labeled with a *1* or a *2* are made from plastics that are often recycled. Common products made from these types of plastic include milk jugs, detergent containers, and soda bottles.

Figure 8 These plastic bottles have numbers indicating the type of plastic they are made of. Plastics must be sorted by type before they are recycled.

Chapter 4 **E ◆ 125**

Media and Technology

⊘ **Exploring Earth Science Videodisc**
Unit 6, Side 2, "It Really Isn't Garbage"

Chapter 9

Answers to Self-Assessment

Caption Question
Figure 7 The supply of aluminum would decrease or be used up.

☑ *Checkpoint*
Glass pieces can be melted down over and over to make new glass containers and other products.

TRY THIS

Skills Focus classifying
Materials *pieces of plastic products (see Advance Preparation below)*
Time 10 minutes
Tips Assemble a set of plastic pieces by selecting several examples from each of these recycling categories: **1** (polyethylene terphthalate), soft-drink bottles; **2** (high-density polyethylene), milk and water jugs; **3** (vinyl), shampoo bottles; **4** (low-density polyethylene), ketchup bottles; **5** (polypropylene), squeeze bottles; **6** (polystyrene), fast-food containers and coffee cups; **7** (all other resins and layered multi-materials). To reduce preparation time, assemble one set of plastic pieces and let students take turns sorting the pieces.
Expected Outcome Students should be able to sort the plastics into at least four or five groups according to the plastics' color/clarity and rigidity.
Extend Have students make a compare/contrast table listing the types, descriptions, and uses of the different groups of plastics. **learning modality: logical/mathematical**

Real-Life Learning

Materials *used item that could be reused by converting it into another useful item*
Time 15 minutes

Collect used glass, plastic, and metal containers and paper items such as old greeting cards. Make sure all containers are empty and clean. Give each student one item. Tell students to think of a way to convert the item into something that would be useful at home or in school. Let students describe and/or carry out their ideas. (*Examples: A jar could be made into a pencil holder or a bank for saving change. A used greeting card could be cut to make gift tags.*) **learning modality: kinesthetic**

Ongoing Assessment

Oral Presentation Call on students at random to explain why metal, glass, and plastic should be recycled instead of being discarded in landfills.

E ◆ 125

TRY THIS

It's in the Numbers

Sort pieces of plastic products into groups according to their recycling numbers. Compare and contrast the pieces in each group with each other and with those in other groups.

Classifying Write a sentence describing characteristics of the plastics in each group.

Solid Waste Management

Real-Life Learning

To help students relate the text's concepts on recycling to their own lives, ask: **What ways to recycle have you seen?** (*Students may mention some of the examples described in the text as well as other examples, such as dry cleaners providing bins for customers to return plastic bags or supermarkets offering a slight price reduction if customers bring in their own bags for packing their groceries.*) **Why do some people not recycle?** (*Accept all reasonable answers, such as that recycling takes effort.*) **Can you suggest any ways to increase the number of people who recycle?** (*Accept all reasonable responses.*) **learning modality: verbal**

What Can You Do?

Building Inquiry Skills: Communicating

Challenge students individually or in small 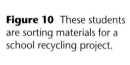 groups to think of a creative way to communicate the "three R's" to their community. For example, students could create posters, public service announcements, skits, rap songs, or poems. At a specified time, have each student or group present its product to the class for critique. Then after students have made their revisions, let them present their products in a community forum, such as a parent-teacher meeting, parents' night at school, or a community civic association meeting. **learning modality: verbal**

Energy Savings in Manufacturing	
Material	**Using Recycled Rather Than Raw Materials**
Aluminum	90–97 %
Glass	4–32 %
Paper	23–74 %

Figure 9 As this table shows, some kinds of recycling save more energy than others.
Interpreting Data Which type of recycling saves the most energy?

When they are recycled, they take on very different forms: as fiber filling for sleeping bags and jackets, carpeting, park benches, shower stalls, floor tiles, trash cans, or dock pilings!

Is Recycling Worthwhile? In addition to conserving resources, recycling saves energy. Figure 9 shows how much energy can be saved by using recycled materials instead of raw materials.

Recycling is not a complete answer to the solid waste problem. Many materials can be recycled. But scientists have not found good ways to recycle other materials, such as plastic-coated paper and plastic foam. There are not enough uses for some recycled products, such as low-quality recycled newspaper. Finally, all recycling processes require energy and create some pollution.

✓ *Checkpoint* **What are some advantages and disadvantages of recycling?**

Solid Waste Management

In the past few decades, people have become more aware of the solid waste problem. Many communities now collect recyclable items along with other household trash. Many supermarkets recycle paper and plastic grocery bags. Many states charge deposit fees on certain glass, metal, and plastic containers. When people return the containers to be recycled, they get their deposit back. This return system encourages people to recycle the containers instead of throwing them away. You might have seen recycling bins for metal and glass drink containers in movie theaters, parks, and other public areas. Consumers can also choose to buy products made with recyclable materials.

Figure 10 These students are sorting materials for a school recycling project.

Background

Facts and Figures The number of U.S. communities with recycling programs increased dramatically during the 1990s. Today, the average American family of four annually recycles more than 450 kg of aluminum and steel cans, plastic containers, glass jars and bottles, newspapers, and cardboard. More than 100 million people now live in areas with curbside-collection recycling programs. In other communities, trash is collected and taken to resource recovery facilities, where it is sorted by hand or separated using technologies that include magnets, screens, and conveyor belts—like the one shown in Figure 7 on page 124. The United States currently recycles about a quarter of its municipal solid waste.

As a result of these efforts, the amount of municipal solid waste that is recycled has increased. But most municipal solid waste in the United States still goes to landfills. Yet as usable land becomes more scarce, it will be even more critical to reduce the need for landfills.

What Can You Do?

The good news is that there are lots of ways individuals can help control the solid waste problem. **These are sometimes called the "three R's"—reduce, reuse, and recycle.** *Reduce* refers to creating less waste in the first place. For example, you can use a cloth shopping bag rather than a disposable paper or plastic bag. *Reuse* refers to finding another use for an object rather than discarding it. For example, you could refill plastic drink bottles with drinking water or juice you mix instead of buying drinks in new bottles. And *recycle* refers to reclaiming raw materials to create new products. You can make sure you recycle at home, and you can also encourage others to recycle. How about starting a used paper collection and recycling program at your school?

One way to significantly reduce the amount of solid waste your family produces is to start a compost pile. **Composting** is the process of helping the natural decomposition processes break down many forms of waste. Compost piles can be used to recycle yard trash such as grass clippings and raked leaves, and food waste such as fruit and vegetable scraps, eggshells, and coffee grounds. Some farms use compost piles to naturally recycle animal manure. Compost is an excellent natural fertilizer for plants.

Figure 11 Many communities have neighborhood compost bins like this one in Brooklyn, in New York City. *Applying Concepts How does composting help solve the solid waste problem?*

Section 2 Review

1. What happens to most solid waste in the United States?
2. List the four major categories of solid waste that are most often recycled.
3. Name and define the "three R's" of solid waste management.
4. Give an example of a way in which communities can reduce their solid waste.
5. What is composting?
6. **Thinking Critically Comparing and Contrasting** Compare the recycling of metal and paper. How are they similar? How are they different?

Science at Home

For one week, have your family collect their household trash in large bags. Do not include food waste. At the end of the week, hold a trash weigh-in. Multiply the total amount by 52 to show how much trash your family produces in a year. Together, can you suggest any ways to reduce your family trash load?

Section 2 Review Answers

1. It goes to landfills.
2. Metal, glass, plastic, paper
3. *Reduce* means creating less waste in the first place. *Reuse* means finding another use for an object instead of discarding it. *Recycle* means reclaiming raw materials to create new products.
4. Answers may vary. *Sample answer:* By creating community composting programs
5. The process of helping the natural decomposition processes break down many forms of waste
6. The recycling of both metals and paper reclaims raw materials for new products. Metals can be recycled many times, whereas paper products can be recycled only a few times before quality is reduced.

Science at Home

If students' families already recycle, tell students to weigh the materials being recycled separately from the other materials. Let students report their findings in class.

Program Resources

◆ **Teaching Resources** 4-2 Review and Reinforce, p. 105; 4-2 Enrich, p. 106

Media and Technology

 Interactive Student Tutorial CD-ROM E-4

Answers to Self-Assessment

Caption Question

Figure 9 Recycling aluminum
Figure 11 It reduces the solid waste discarded in landfills or incinerated.

✓ *Checkpoint*

Reduces need for raw materials and landfill space, saves energy; some products not suitable, some recycled materials not in demand

Performance Assessment

Writing Have each student briefly explain the benefits of recycling compared with discarding waste materials in landfills or burning them in incinerators.

Portfolio Students can save their explanations in their portfolios.

Waste, Away!

Preparing for Inquiry

Key Concept A sanitary landfill prevents groundwater pollution more effectively than a poorly designed landfill or an open dump does.

Skills Objectives Students will be able to
- make models of a sanitary landfill, a poorly designed landfill, and an open dump;
- draw conclusions about the environmental benefits of sanitary landfills.

Time 40 minutes on Day 1; 20 minutes on Day 2

Advance Preparation Cut the cheesecloth and plastic pieces large enough to overlap the top of the jar when they are suspended in it, as shown in the photo. Cut extra pieces in case some tear when students add pebbles to them. Check the plastic pieces to make sure there are no holes in them.

Alternative Materials If supplies are limited, have one third of the groups construct System 1, one third construct System 2, and one third construct System 3.

Guiding Inquiry

Invitation Hold up a transparent drinking glass of clean tap water, then drop a few small pieces of household waste into it. Ask: **Would you want to drink water with trash in it? Why not?** *(Chemicals in the trash pollute the water.)*

Introducing the Procedure
- Invite students to read the entire lab procedure. Answer any questions they have.
- Explain that the models will represent three different types of landfills, but at this point do not discuss which type each model represents.

Troubleshooting the Experiment
- Circulate among the groups as they build the models to make sure the cheesecloth and plastic pieces are draped well down into the jars and are secured tightly with rubber bands.

Waste, Away!

About two thirds of municipal solid waste ends up in a landfill. In this lab, you'll investigate how landfills are constructed to be most effective and safe.

Problem

How do different kinds of landfills work?

Skills Focus

making models, drawing conclusions

Materials

measuring cup	metric ruler	soil
small pebbles	cheesecloth	scissors
plastic wrap	water	newspaper
5 rubber bands	red food coloring	tweezers
heavy-duty plastic bag		
12 small sponge cubes		
3 transparent, wide-mouthed jars		

Procedure

1. Read over the rest of the procedure to preview the three landfill systems you will model. Determine which parts of the models represent potential drinking water, rainfall, solid waste, leachate, and the landfill systems themselves. Write a prediction about the way each system will respond to the test you'll conduct in Part 2.

Part 1 Modeling Three Landfill Systems

2. Obtain 3 identical jars. Label them *System 1, System 2,* and *System 3.* Pour clean, clear water into each jar to a depth of 5 cm.

3. Add equal amounts of small pebbles to each jar. The pebbles should be just below the surface of the water.

4. For System 1, cover the pebble and water mixture with 2.5 cm of soil.

5. For System 2, suspend a piece of cheesecloth in the jar about 5 cm above the water line, as shown in the photograph. Hold the cheesecloth in place with a rubber band around the outside mouth of the jar. Gently pour a handful of small pebbles into the cheesecloth.

6. For System 3, suspend a plastic bag in the jar about 5 cm above the water line. Hold the bag in place with a rubber band around the outside mouth of the jar. Gently pour a handful of small pebbles into the plastic bag.

7. Observe the water and pebbles at the bottom of each system. Record your observations.

Part 2 Testing the Systems

8. Soak 12 identical sponge cubes in water tinted with red food coloring. Use tweezers to place four soaked sponge cubes onto the top surface in each jar.

9. Cover the sponge cubes in Systems 2 and 3 with a thin layer of soil. Leave the sponge cubes in System 1 uncovered.

- In Steps 5 and 6, caution students to add the pebbles gently so they do not tear the cheesecloth and plastic.
- When students draw the systems in Step 10, they should label the following elements: *groundwater* (water at bottom of jar); *soil; liner* (cheesecloth and plastic pieces); and *trash* (colored sponge cubes). Students could also label the pebbles *permeable layer.*

Expected Outcome

The groundwater in Systems 1 and 2 will turn red with "leachate"—food coloring from the sponge cubes. The water may also be cloudy with dissolved soil particles that have washed out of the landfills. The groundwater in System 3 will remain clear, with all of the leachate contained by the plastic liner.

Analyze and Conclude

1. In System 1, an open dump, there is no barrier to separate waste from the soil and keep leachate from seeping into the groundwater. In System 2, a poorly designed landfill, the

10. Make a labeled drawing of each system. Explain what each part of the model represents.
11. Pour 150 mL of water over each system. Then cover each jar with plastic wrap, and hold the wrap in place with a rubber band. Let the systems stand overnight.
12. Observe each landfill system. Note especially any changes in the color or clarity of the "groundwater." Record your observations.

Analyze and Conclude

1. Explain how your models represent three common types of landfills: a well-designed, or sanitary, landfill; a landfill with a poor design; and an open dump. Compare the way the three systems work.
2. Which part of the model represented the leachate? How well did each landfill system protect the groundwater from the leachate?

3. Do you think a community's water supply is protected when waste is placed in landfills that are not immediately above groundwater sources? Explain.
4. **Apply** Based on your results, which landfill system is safest for the environment? Explain your answer.

Design an Experiment

Solid waste can be compacted (crushed into smaller pieces) and have liquid removed before it is placed in a landfill. Does preparing the waste in this way make it safer for the environment? Write a hypothesis, then use the ideas and procedures from this lab to test your hypothesis. Obtain your teacher's permission before trying your experiment.

landfill carries leachate to nearby rivers and streams or to permeable soil layers above groundwater supplies.
4. A well-designed sanitary landfill (like System 3) is safest because it protects groundwater the best.

Extending the Inquiry

Design an Experiment Compacting the waste takes less space and extends the life of the landfill but does not remove harmful substances from the waste. It also keeps the wastes from settling inside the landfill. Removing liquid from the waste could reduce the amount of leachate produced. Students could model reduced-liquid waste by soaking the sponge cubes in food coloring, then squeezing the liquid out and allowing the cubes to dry thoroughly before placing them in the landfill models.

permeable liner contains the waste but allows leachate to seep into the groundwater. In System 3, a well-designed sanitary landfill, the plastic liner contains the leachate and keeps it from seeping into the groundwater.
2. The red-tinted water represented the leachate. Only System 3 protected the groundwater.
3. Locating a landfill in an area that is not immediately above groundwater is safer. However, groundwater can still become contaminated if surface runoff from the

Program Resources

◆ **Teaching Resources** Chapter 4 Real-World Lab, pp. 113–115

Safety

Remind students to wear lab aprons and safety goggles and handle the glass jars carefully. Review the safety guidelines in Appendix A.

SECTION 3 Hazardous Wastes

Objectives

After completing the lesson, students will be able to
- list and describe the categories of hazardous wastes;
- explain how hazardous wastes affect human health;
- identify methods for managing hazardous wastes.

Key Terms hazardous waste, toxic, explosive, flammable, corrosive, radioactive

1 Engage/Explore

Activating Prior Knowledge

Ask students: **What kinds of activities can be hazardous?** (*Sample answers: riding a bicycle in traffic, driving on icy roads, using a chainsaw, climbing a tall ladder*) **When you're involved in a hazardous activity, what do you do to protect yourself?** (*Be very careful, follow safety guidelines, wear protective clothing or equipment, and so forth*)

DISCOVER

Skills Focus forming operational definitions
Materials *labels from common hazardous household products, such as pesticides, herbicides, cleaning agents, nail polish remover and other solvents, spray lacquers*
Time 10 minutes
Tips Tell students to look for the word *Warning* on the labels and carefully read the information that follows it. Keep the labels for use in other activities.
Expected Outcome Students will find warnings such as *Causes eye and skin irritations; Harmful if swallowed; Do not use near fire or flame;* and *Use outdoors or in a well-ventilated area.*
Think It Over Students' definitions should focus on the risk of harm or injury to people and other living organisms.

SECTION 3 Hazardous Wastes

DISCOVER ············ ACTIVITY

What's Hazardous?

1. Your teacher will give you labels from some common hazardous household products.
2. Read the information on each label. Identify the word or words that tell why the product is hazardous.

Think It Over
Forming Operational Definitions Based on your observations of the product labels, write a definition of the term *hazardous.*

GUIDE FOR READING

- ◆ What are the categories of hazardous wastes?
- ◆ How can hazardous wastes affect human health?
- ◆ What techniques can be used to manage hazardous wastes?

Reading Tip Before you read, rewrite the headings in each section as *how, what,* or *where* questions. As you read, look for answers to these questions.

Figure 12 This school in Love Canal was abandoned because of pollution.

In the early 1950s, the city of Niagara Falls, New York, bought an area of land around an old canal. The canal had been filled with chemical wastes from nearby industries. On top of this land, the city built a new neighborhood and elementary school. The neighborhood was named Love Canal.

Then strange things began to happen. Children playing in muddy fields developed skin rashes. Wooden fence posts rotted and turned black. People reported colored liquid seeping into their basements. Babies were born with birth defects. Adults developed epilepsy, liver disease, and nerve disorders. The neighborhood was finally declared a federal emergency disaster area. More than two hundred families were moved away.

What was behind these strange events at Love Canal? Building the neighborhood had caused the clay cover on the old canal dump site to crack. Rainwater seeped into the buried wastes through the cracks. The construction caused chemicals to leak from the underground storage containers. Over time, water mixed with the chemicals to form a dangerous leachate. This leachate polluted the soil and the groundwater and leaked into people's basements.

The Love Canal problem was the first time a federal emergency was declared in an area because of hazardous wastes. It helped people realize that certain chemicals can remain dangerous in soil and water for many years. As a result, new laws were passed to find and clean up other dangerous waste sites.

READING STRATEGIES

Reading Tip Students' questions might include *What are some types of hazardous wastes?, What are the health effects of hazardous wastes?, What problems are involved in the disposal of hazardous wastes?, How do people locate disposal sites?,* and *How can people reduce hazardous waste?*

Vocabulary To help students recall the major categories of hazardous wastes, suggest that each student make a set of cards, each with the name of a category and its symbol (copied from Figure 13) on the front of the card and, on the back, the textbook's definition paraphrased in the student's own words.

Types of Hazardous Wastes

Many people picture hazardous wastes as bubbling chemicals, thick fumes, or oozing slime. But even some harmless-looking, common materials such as window cleaner, radio batteries, and nail polish remover can become hazardous wastes. **Hazardous waste** is any material that can be harmful to human health or the environment if it is not properly disposed of.

Hazardous wastes are created during the manufacture of many household products. Many more are produced as a result of agriculture, industry, military operations, and research at hospitals and scientific laboratories.

Hazardous wastes are classified into four categories: toxic, explosive, flammable, and corrosive. Figure 13 gives some examples of these types of waste. **Toxic** wastes, or poisonous wastes, are wastes that can damage the health of humans and other organisms. **Explosive** wastes are wastes that react very quickly when exposed to air or water, or that explode when they are dropped. Explosive wastes are also called reactive wastes. **Flammable** wastes catch fire easily and can begin burning at fairly low temperatures. **Corrosive** wastes are wastes that dissolve or eat through many materials.

Other wastes that require special disposal are radioactive wastes. **Radioactive** wastes are wastes that contain unstable atoms. These unstable atoms give off radiation that can cause cancer and other diseases. There are two types of radioactive wastes: high-level waste and low-level waste. An example of high-level radioactive waste is the used fuel from nuclear reactors. Low-level radioactive wastes are produced when radioactive minerals such as uranium are mined. They are also produced at some medical and scientific research sites. Radioactive waste can remain dangerous for thousands of years.

Category: Toxic
Examples: Chlorine, PCBs, mercury

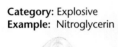

Category: Explosive
Example: Nitroglycerin

Figure 13 Vehicles transporting dangerous materials must use signs like these to alert people of the potential dangers of their loads.

Category: Radioactive
Examples: Uranium, plutonium

Category: Flammable
Example: Kerosene

Category: Corrosive
Examples: Hydrochloric acid, sodium hydroxide

Chapter 4 **E ◆ 131**

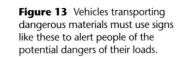

2 Facilitate

Types of Hazardous Wastes

Building Inquiry Skills: Classifying

Materials *labels from common hazardous household products (See Discover activity on page 130.)*
Time 10 minutes

Challenge students to sort the labels into four of the categories described on this page—toxic, explosive, flammable, and corrosive—plus a fifth group for products whose warnings indicate more than one type of hazard. Ask: **How many labels do you have in each group? What kinds of products do those labels represent?** *(Answers will vary, but students may find that many, if not most, hazardous products fall into more than one category.)* **learning modality: verbal**

Real-Life Learning

Time 5 minutes

Encourage students to copy the symbols from Figure 13. Then instruct students to cut out the individual symbols and tape the appropriate ones to hazardous products they find in the classroom, other areas of the school (the art room or shop area, for example), and at home. In a follow-up class discussion, ask: **Were you surprised by the number of hazardous products you found?** *(Students may not have realized that so many common, everyday products contain hazardous substances.)* **learning modality: kinesthetic**

Ongoing Assessment

Writing Have each student name the categories of hazardous wastes and define each category in his or her own words.

Students can save their work in their portfolios.

Health Effects of Hazardous Wastes

Integrating Health

Materials *labels from common hazardous household products (See Discover activity on page 130.)*

Time 10 minutes

Have students examine the labels to look for wording that indicates the specific health hazards of the products. Also point out that labels often include first-aid instructions in case the user needs immediate treatment after exposure to a hazardous ingredient in a product. Encourage students to look for those instructions as well and read them aloud. As students read the first-aid procedures, list on the board the names of any antidotes or medications that people should have in their homes in case of an emergency—for example, syrup of ipecac to induce vomiting. Suggest that students copy the list and check their own homes to see if their families have these materials on hand. **learning modality: verbal**

Disposal of Hazardous Wastes

Inquiry Challenge

Time 15 minutes

Divide the class into small groups, and pose the following problem: **Many years ago, containers of toxic chemicals were buried in a vacant field. Now the containers are leaking, and the wastes are soaking into the soil. How can you make a model to show what is happening?** Let each group discuss possible models, agree on one, draw it on a large sheet of paper, and then describe it to the rest of the class. *(Example: Fill a small jar with colored water, punch a pinhole in the jar's lid, then bury the jar on its side in a dishpan filled with sand.)* Also ask groups to explain what they could do to model how the "wastes" could be cleaned up. If time allows, have students build and demonstrate their models. **cooperative learning**

Health Effects of Hazardous Wastes

INTEGRATING HEALTH A person can be exposed to hazardous wastes by breathing, eating or drinking, or touching them. Many factors determine the effects of a hazardous substance on a person. One factor is how harmful the substance is. Another factor is how much of the substance a person is exposed to. A third factor is how long the exposure lasts. A person may be exposed for a short time, such as a child accidentally drinking antifreeze. Or a person may be exposed for many years, as were the residents of Love Canal. Finally, a person's age, weight, and health all influence how a substance affects that person.

In general, short-term exposure to hazardous wastes may cause irritation or more severe health problems. These health problems can include breathing difficulties, internal bleeding, paralysis, coma, and even death. **Long-term exposure to hazardous wastes may cause diseases, such as cancer, and may damage body organs, including the brain, liver, kidneys, and lungs.** These effects may eventually be life threatening.

Disposal of Hazardous Wastes

It is hard to safely dispose of hazardous wastes. Burying them can pollute the soil or groundwater. Releasing wastes into lakes or rivers can pollute surface water. Burning hazardous wastes can pollute the air. You can see the problem!

Methods of hazardous waste disposal include burial in landfills, incineration, and breakdown by living organisms. Another method involves storing liquid wastes in deep rock layers.

Figure 14 Hazardous wastes can pollute the soil, water, and air. The chemical drums on the left were illegally dumped in a field. Below, environmental scientists in protective gear test the contents of an old storage tank.

Background

History of Science Two federal laws dictate the management of hazardous waste. The Resource Conservation and Recovery Act covers hazardous waste currently being produced. The Comprehensive Environmental Response, Compensation, and Liability Act, commonly known as Superfund, provides for cleanup of abandoned and inactive hazardous waste sites.

The federal government estimates that the United States has more than 300,000 old hazardous waste sites. At many such sites, hazardous chemicals have seeped deep into the soil and polluted groundwater. Sites that pose the greatest threat to public health and the environment are placed on the Superfund National Priorities List; the federal government will assist in their cleanup.

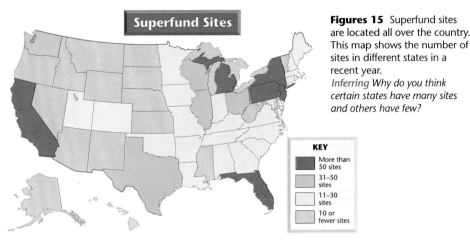

Superfund Sites

KEY
- More than 50 sites
- 31–50 sites
- 11–30 sites
- 10 or fewer sites

Figures 15 Superfund sites are located all over the country. This map shows the number of sites in different states in a recent year.
Inferring Why do you think certain states have many sites and others have few?

Hazardous wastes are most often disposed of in carefully designed landfills. These landfills are lined with clay and plastic to keep chemicals from leaking into the soil and groundwater. A clay and plastic cover prevents rainwater from seeping into the wastes.

Scientists have developed some other methods for disposing of hazardous waste. For example, wastes can be incinerated at very high temperatures. Incineration often breaks down harmful compounds into less harmful ones. Bacteria, algae, and fungi can break down some hazardous chemicals. Another disposal method involves pumping liquid wastes into a layer of sandstone or limestone thousands of meters underground. The wastes spread throughout this soft rock layer. But the wastes cannot move through the thicker, harder layers of rock above and below. A few types of hazardous waste, such as motor oil and lead-acid car batteries, can even be recycled.

Scientists have not been able to develop completely safe methods for disposing of radioactive waste. Some techniques used today are mixing the waste with concrete or sealing it in abandoned mine shafts. High-level radioactive wastes are currently stored in vaults dug hundreds of meters underground or in concrete and steel containers above ground. But these storage areas are temporary. Scientists are still searching for methods that will provide safe, permanent disposal of radioactive wastes.

✓ *Checkpoint* How are most hazardous wastes disposed of?

Locating Disposal Sites

Besides deciding how to dispose of hazardous wastes, communities must also decide *where* to dispose of them. Should there be fewer, larger disposal sites, or many smaller ones? Each answer has costs and benefits.

Social Studies
CONNECTION

In 1980, Congress passed a law creating a hazardous waste site cleanup program called the Superfund. The law determines who should pay for the cleanup. This can include any businesses or people that have ever owned or operated the property, or have ever contributed wastes to it.

In Your Journal

Most industries did not purposely pollute the air, land, and water. In the past, people were largely unaware that some industrial wastes were hazardous, and that these substances could have serious effects many years later. Should these industries still be responsible for paying for the cleanup? If not, where should this money come from? Write a paragraph explaining your opinion.

Social Studies
CONNECTION

For additional information about Superfund, see Background on the previous page.

In Your Journal Accept divergent views on the questions posed in the text, as long as students support their positions with sound reasoning. Encourage students to share their views in a class discussion. **learning modality: verbal**

Locating Disposal Sites

Building Inquiry Skills: Communicating

Time 20–30 minutes

ACTIVITY

Ask students to imagine their community's government has just announced that it wants the residents to vote on whether to allow a private company to build a landfill in the community for hazardous wastes trucked in from all over the state. Residents would receive a tax benefit plus job opportunities if the landfill is built. Then divide the class into small groups, and assign one of the following viewpoints to each group: *We should vote for the landfill because . . .*, or *We should vote against the landfill because. . . .* Allow time for each group to discuss the issue from its assigned viewpoint. Then choose one student from each group to participate in a debate in front of the rest of the class. At the conclusion of the debate, have students vote on the issue. **learning modality: logical/ mathematical**

Answers to Self-Assessment

Caption Question

Figure 15 *Sample answers:* States with many sites may have large-scale industry and/or mining that produced more hazardous wastes than states with fewer sites.

✓ *Checkpoint*
Most are buried in landfills.

Ongoing Assessment

Drawing Have each student draw and label a simple diagram showing how a landfill for hazardous wastes is constructed.

 Students can save their drawings in their portfolios.

Reducing Hazardous Waste

Using the Visuals: Figure 16

Materials *citronella candles*
Time 5 minutes

Burn a citronella candle in the classroom while students are involved in another activity. When the aroma is noticeable, ask: **What's that odor?** (*Some students may be familiar with the odor of citronella candles.*) Point out the photograph's caption. Suggest that students examine labels in stores to find examples of other products that can be used in place of hazardous chemicals. Let them report their findings in class. **learning modality: verbal**

3 Assess

Section 3 Review Answers

1. *Toxic wastes* can affect the health of humans and other organisms. *Explosive wastes* react very quickly when exposed to air or water or explode when they are dropped. *Flammable wastes* catch fire easily and begin burning at fairly low temperatures. *Corrosive wastes* dissolve or eat through many materials.

2. Short-term exposure may cause irritation or more severe health problems such as breathing difficulties, internal bleeding, paralysis, coma, and death. Long-term exposure may cause diseases such as cancer and may damage body organs.

3. One method is to bury hazardous wastes in landfills lined and sealed with plastic and clay. Other disposal methods include incineration at very high temperatures, exposure to organisms that break the wastes down, pumping the wastes deep underground, and recycling them.

4. For the first time in U.S. history, a national emergency was declared because of hazardous wastes. The problem helped people realize how long certain chemicals can remain dangerous in soil and water. As a result, new laws were passed to find and clean up other dangerous waste sites.

Figure 16 The scent of these citronella candles naturally repels insects and creates less hazardous waste than bug spray.

Most people don't want to live or work near a hazardous waste disposal facility. In general, people would prefer to have a single large facility located in an area where few people live. A central facility could treat many different types of hazardous wastes. It would be easier to monitor than many scattered sites. However, transporting hazardous wastes to a distant central facility can be costly, difficult, and dangerous. The greater travel distances increase the risk of an accident that could release hazardous wastes into the environment. It may be safer, cheaper, and easier to transport wastes to small local facilities instead.

Reducing Hazardous Waste

The best way to manage hazardous wastes is to produce less of them in the first place. Industries are eager to develop safe alternatives to harmful chemicals. For example, some brands of furniture polishes are now made from lemon oil and beeswax instead of petroleum oils. Many products such as air fresheners, plastic dishes and countertops, carpets, and curtains used to be made with the chemical formaldehyde, which gradually leaked out of these products into the air. Companies have developed alternatives to formaldehyde to use in their products. For instance, the next time you are in a supermarket or hardware store, look for air fresheners that are labeled "formaldehyde-free."

At home, you can find substitutes for some hazardous household chemicals. For example, instead of using insect spray, use harmless materials that naturally repel insects, such as the citronella candles shown in Figure 16. Many household cleaners also now come in biodegradable forms.

Section 3 Review

1. List and define the four categories of hazardous waste.
2. Describe the short-term and long-term effects of hazardous substances on human health.
3. Describe one method used to dispose of hazardous wastes.
4. What was the significance of the events at Love Canal?
5. Explain why radioactive wastes are particularly difficult to manage.
6. **Thinking Critically Making Judgments** Do you think hazardous wastes should be treated and disposed of at one central facility or at many small local facilities? Give reasons for your answer.

Check Your Progress

CHAPTER PROJECT 4

By now you should be investigating what happens to the different materials in your package when it is thrown away. You will need to find out what types of waste your community recycles, and how it handles other solid waste. (*Hint:* The town engineer or Department of Public Works may be a good source of this information. Be sure to check with your teacher before contacting anyone.)

Program Resources

◆ **Teaching Resources** 4-3 Review and Reinforce, p. 109; 4-3 Enrich, p. 110

Media and Technology

Interactive Student Tutorial CD-ROM E-4

SECTION 1 — How Land is Used

Key Ideas

◆ Land is a nonrenewable resource. All the people on Earth must share this limited resource for agriculture, development, mining, and other uses.

◆ Soil is a complex system that takes a very long time to form.

◆ Poor soil management can cause erosion, nutrient depletion, and desertification.

◆ There are many farming techniques to help prevent erosion and nutrient depletion.

Key Terms

development
litter
topsoil
subsoil
bedrock
erosion

nutrient depletion
fallow
crop rotation
desertification
land reclamation

SECTION 2 — Solid Waste

Key Ideas

◆ Wastes are produced in the making and using of many products.

◆ Three ways of handling solid waste are to bury it, to burn it, or to recycle it.

◆ Most municipal solid waste in the United States is buried in sanitary landfills.

◆ The main types of municipal solid waste that are recycled are metal, glass, paper, and plastic.

◆ Recycling can conserve both resources and energy. However, there are not always many ways to use recycled materials.

◆ One way to help solve the solid waste problem is to practice the "three R's"— reduce, reuse, and recycle.

Key Terms

municipal solid waste
leachate
sanitary landfill
incineration

recycling
biodegradable
resins
composting

SECTION 3 — Hazardous Wastes

 INTEGRATING CHEMISTRY

Key Ideas

◆ Hazardous wastes are materials that can threaten human health and safety or can be harmful to the environment if they are not properly disposed of.

◆ Hazardous wastes include toxic, explosive, flammable, and corrosive wastes. Radioactive wastes also require special disposal.

◆ How a person is affected by a hazardous substance depends on several factors, including the amount of the substance, the length of time the person is exposed, and how the substance enters the person's body.

◆ It is very difficult to find safe ways to dispose of hazardous wastes and good places to store them. A good way to manage hazardous wastes is to produce less of them.

Key Terms

hazardous waste
toxic
explosive

flammable
corrosive
radioactive

USING THE INTERNET

www.science-explorer.phschool.com

Chapter 4 **E ◆ 135**

CHAPTER 4 REVIEW

5. Radioactive wastes can remain dangerous to humans and other organisms for thousands of years.

6. Answers may vary. A central facility might dispose of hazardous waste more efficiently, would not expose as many people to the potential dangers of spills and leaks, and would be easier to monitor than many scattered sites. However, transporting hazardous waste to a central facility would be costly, difficult, and potentially dangerous. Small local facilities could be cheaper and safer.

CHAPTER PROJECT 4

Check Your Progress

Ask the representative you contacted earlier to present information in a class visit. (See page 112.) If a visit is not possible, designate two or three volunteers to call and collect information for the rest of the class. Remind students to take notes during the visit or phone call so they will have all the information they need for their final presentations and displays.

Program Resources

◆ **Teaching Resources** Chapter 4 Project Scoring Rubric, p. 98; Chapter 4 Performance Assessment, pp. 201–203; Chapter 4 Test, pp. 204–207

Media and Technology

Interactive Student Tutorial CD-ROM E-4

Computer Test Bank Test E-4

Performance Assessment

Oral Presentation Call on students at random to give reasons why it is important to dispose of hazardous wastes safely.

E ◆ 135

Reviewing Content:
Multiple Choice
1. a **2.** c **3.** a **4.** c **5.** c

True or False
6. true **7.** topsoil **8.** true **9.** true
10. groundwater

Checking Concepts
11. *Living:* bacteria, earthworms, fungi, insects, plant roots; *Nonliving:* minerals, water, air

12. *Any one:* Contour plowing: Rows of crops along the slope of the land prevent soil from washing away. Terracing: Flat steps cut into a hillside with ridges along their edges slow runoff and catch eroding soil. Conservation plowing: Machines break up the deeper subsoil layer without disturbing the topsoil. Windbreaks: Rows of trees are planted along the edges of fields to block the wind and trap eroding soil.

13. *Any two:* Leaving fields fallow (unplanted with crops); leaving crop wastes in the fields; rotating crops

14. The type of plastic the container is made of and how it can be recycled

15. *Any one:* Institute curbside recycling with trash pickup; place recycling bins in public places

16. Composting is the process of helping the natural decomposition processes break down many forms of waste. Biodegradable materials—yard wastes, food wastes, paper, and so on—can be composted.

17. The substance might have leached out of waste in a landfill and seeped into groundwater, thus contaminating people's water supply.

18. Students should draw on what they learned in Section 3 about hazardous substances in common household products.

Thinking Visually
19. Students' tables should include the following information: Landfills are cheaper to build but may be more expensive to operate; can cause pollution of soil and groundwater; are not attractive while in operation; provide jobs and produce methane that can be captured for use as fuel. Incinerators are

---

Reviewing Content

 For more review of key concepts, see the Interactive Student Tutorial CD-ROM.

Multiple Choice
Choose the letter of the best answer.

1. The advance of desertlike conditions into areas that previously were fertile is called
  a. desertification.
  b. crop rotation.
  c. nutrient depletion.
  d. land reclamation.

2. Water containing dissolved chemicals from a landfill is called
  a. resin.
  b. litter.
  c. leachate.
  d. compost.

3. Solid wastes are burned in the process of
  a. incineration.
  b. composting.
  c. erosion.
  d. recycling.

4. Which of the following is a biogradable waste?
  a. a glass jar   **b.** a metal can
  c. an apple core   **d.** a plastic bag

5. Wastes that contain unstable atoms are called
  a. corrosive.   **b.** flammable.
  c. radioactive.   **d.** explosive.

True and False
If the statement is true, write true. If it is false, change the underlined word or words to make the statement true.

6. Three major types of land use are agriculture, development, and <u>mining</u>.
7. The layer of soil that contains the most animal and plant matter is the <u>subsoil</u>.
8. Fields that are left unplanted with crops are called <u>fallow</u>.
9. Most of the municipal solid waste generated in the United States is disposed of in <u>landfills</u>.
10. Liners prevent the waste in landfills from polluting the <u>air</u>.

Checking Concepts
11. List two living things and two nonliving things that are found in topsoil.
12. Choose one of the following techniques and explain how it can reduce soil erosion: contour plowing, terracing, conservation plowing, or windbreaks.
13. Give examples of two techniques for preventing nutrient depletion.
14. What does the number on a plastic container indicate?
15. Describe one way communities can encourage residents to produce less solid waste.
16. What is composting? What kinds of materials can be composted?
17. Explain how a person might be exposed to a hazardous substance that was buried underground many years ago.
18. **Writing to Learn** Write a public service announcement to inform people about household hazardous wastes. Begin with a "hook" to catch your listener's attention. Be sure to explain what makes a waste hazardous. Also give examples of household hazardous wastes, and tell people what to do with these substances.

Thinking Visually
19. **Compare/Contrast Table** On a separate sheet of paper, copy the table below about ways to dispose of municipal solid waste. Then complete it and add a title. (For more on compare/contrast tables, see the Skills Handbook.)

	Landfill	Incinerator
Cost		
Pollution		
Attractiveness		
Usefulness to Community		

---

more expensive to build but cheaper to operate; can cause air pollution and also create some solid waste that must be disposed of elsewhere; could be more attractive than an operating landfill; provide jobs and could be used to generate electricity. *Sample title:* Landfills versus Incinerators

Applying Skills
20.

Applying Skills

Use the following data on municipal solid waste in the United States to answer Questions 20–22.

Type of Waste	Percent of Total
Paper and cardboard	38%
Food wastes	10%
Yard wastes	13%
Metals	8%
Plastics	9%
Glass	6%
Other wastes	16%

20. **Graphing** Use the data to create a circle graph. (To review circle graphs, see the Skills Handbook.)
21. **Classifying** Which of the types of waste shown are recyclable? Which include wastes that can be composted?
22. **Developing Hypotheses** Why do you think paper makes up the largest percent of solid waste?

Thinking Critically

23. **Making Judgments** Suppose you go to the store to buy some juice. You can choose from juice sold in an aluminum, glass, or plastic container, all for the same price. Which would you choose? Explain your answer.
24. **Applying Concepts** If you owned a large farm on a hill, how would you prevent soil erosion? Explain your answer.
25. **Problem Solving** In strip mining, a layer of soil is removed to expose a resource, such as coal, underneath. What methods could be used to restore this damaged land?
26. **Predicting** Suppose that hundreds of years in the future, people dig into a landfill from around the year 2000. What types of materials might they find? What types of materials might not be present? Explain your answers.
27. **Applying Concepts** Why is it unsafe to bury or incinerate radioactive waste?

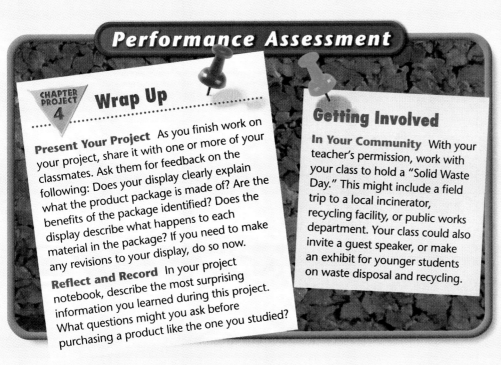

Performance Assessment

CHAPTER PROJECT 4 **Wrap Up**

Present Your Project As you finish work on your project, share it with one or more of your classmates. Ask them for feedback on the following: Does your display clearly explain what the product package is made of? Are the benefits of the package identified? Does the display describe what happens to each material in the package? If you need to make any revisions to your display, do so now.

Reflect and Record In your project notebook, describe the most surprising information you learned during this project. What questions might you ask before purchasing a product like the one you studied?

Getting Involved

In Your Community With your teacher's permission, work with your class to hold a "Solid Waste Day." This might include a field trip to a local incinerator, recycling facility, or public works department. Your class could also invite a guest speaker, or make an exhibit for younger students on waste disposal and recycling.

---

21. Paper and cardboard, metals, plastics, and glass are recyclable. Yard wastes and food wastes can be composted.
22. *Sample answer:* Paper is used to make more products and product packages that are discarded than any other type of material.

Thinking Critically

23. Accept all answers so long as students provide well-reasoned arguments for their choices.
24. Students should suggest contour plowing or terracing, both of which reduce soil erosion caused by water flowing down slopes.
25. The topsoil and subsoil could be replaced in their original order. Then the area could be replanted.
26. For materials that would be found, students should identify metals, plastics, glass,

Program Resources

◆ **Inquiry Skills Activity Book** Provides teaching and review of all inquiry skills

---

and other nonbiodegradable materials. For materials that in theory would not be present, students should mention paper products, yard waste, and other biodegradable materials. Students could also point out that commonly recycled materials might be present, but in low amounts.

27. Radioactive waste remains dangerous for thousands of years. Burying it in an open dump or sanitary landfill or burning it in an incinerator would not protect people and other organisms from the hazards of radioactivity. Burning the waste might pollute the air, and burying the waste could pollute the groundwater or incorporate radioactive substances in the food chain.

Performance Assessment

CHAPTER PROJECT 4 **Wrap Up**

Present Your Project Remind students that their displays should also include a cut-away view of the package and a sample of each material used in it. Having every student present his or her display to the entire class might be time-consuming and tedious. Instead, assign students to small groups or have two poster sessions where half the class displays their projects to the other half.

Reflect and Record Invite students to share their reflections on the project in a class discussion.

Getting Involved

In Your Community This activity presents an excellent opportunity for cooperative learning. Divide the class into groups based on the types of tasks involved. For example, one group could be responsible for contacting possible sites for the visit and presenting choices to the rest of the class, another group could arrange transportation by parents or other adults, a third group could take notes during the visit, and a fourth group could use the notes to summarize the information in a class report or display.

5 Air and Water Resources

Sections	Time	Student Edition Activities		Other Activities
CHAPTER PROJECT 5 **Pollution vs. Purity** p. 139	Ongoing (2 weeks)	Check Your Progress, pp. 153, 158 Wrap Up, p. 161		
1 Air Pollution pp. 140–148 ◆ Identify and describe outdoor and indoor air pollutants. ◆ Explain the importance of ozone in the upper atmosphere. ◆ Describe the greenhouse effect and explain how it affects climate.	3–4 periods/ $1\frac{1}{2}$–2 blocks	**Discover** How Does the Scent Spread?, p. 140 **Try This** How Acid Is Your Rain?, p. 143 **Sharpen Your Skills** Communicating, p. 144 **Science at Home,** p. 147 **Real-World Lab: You and Your Environment** How Does the Garden Grow?, p. 148	TE TE TE TE TE TE IES	Addressing Naive Conceptions, p. 141 Building Inquiry Skills: Observing, p. 142 Real-Life Learning, p. 143 Math Toolbox, p. 145 Inquiry Challenge, p. 145 Integrating Earth Science, p. 146 "Metropolis," pp. 35–36, 40; "Where River Meets Sea," p. 38
2 The Water Supply pp. 149–154 ◆ Identify factors that make most of Earth's water not useful to people. ◆ Identify human sources of water pollution.	2–3 periods/ 1–$1\frac{1}{2}$ blocks	**Discover** How Does the Water Change?, p. 149 **Try This** Getting Clean, p. 150 **Skills Lab: Measuring** Concentrate on This!, p. 154	TE TE TE PTA	Building Inquiry Skills: Graphing, p. 150 Inquiry Challenge, p. 151 Building Inquiry Skills: Making Models, p. 152 "Testing Bottled Water," pp. 1–8
3 🔴 **INTEGRATING TECHNOLOGY** **Finding Pollution Solutions** pp. 155–158 ◆ Describe ways that technology can help control air pollution. ◆ Describe ways that technology can help control water pollution.	1–2 periods/ $\frac{1}{2}$–1 block	**Discover** Can You Remove the Tea?, p. 155 **Sharpen Your Skills** Graphing, p. 156	TE TE TE ISLM IES	Real-Life Learning, p. 157 Cultural Diversity, p. 157 Real-Life Learning, p. 158 E-5, "Pollution Prevention With Rocks" "Where River Meets Sea," pp. 35–37
Study Guide/Chapter Review pp. 159–161	1 period/ $\frac{1}{2}$ block		ISAB	Provides teaching and review of all inquiry skills

For Standard or Block Schedule The Resource Pro® CD-ROM gives you maximum flexibility for planning your instruction for any type of schedule. Resource Pro® contains Planning Express®, an advanced scheduling program, as well as the entire contents of the Teaching Resources and the Computer Test Bank.

CHAPTER PLANNING GUIDE

Program Resources	Assessment Strategies	Media and Technology
TR Chapter 5 Project Teacher Notes, pp. 116–117 **TR** Chapter 5 Project Overview and Worksheets, pp. 118–121 **TR** Chapter 5 Project Scoring Rubric, p. 122	**SE** Performance Assessment: Chapter 5 Project Wrap Up, p. 161 **TE** Check Your Progress, pp. 153, 158 **TE** Performance Assessment: Chapter 5 Project Wrap Up, p. 161 **TR** Chapter 5 Project Scoring Rubric, p. 122	Science Explorer Internet Site
TR 5-1 Lesson Plan, p. 123 **TR** 5-1 Section Summary, p. 124 **TR** 5-1 Review and Reinforce, p. 125 **TR** 5-1 Enrich, p. 126 **TR** Chapter 5 Real-World Lab, pp. 135–136 **SES** Book D, *Human Biology and Health,* Chapters 5, 6 **SES** Book I, *Weather and Climate,* Chapter 4	**SE** Section 1 Review, p. 147 **SE** Analyze and Conclude, p. 148 **TE** Ongoing Assessment, pp. 141, 143, 145 **TE** Performance Assessment, p. 147 **TR** 5-1 Review and Reinforce, p. 125	Exploring Earth Science Videodisc, Unit 4 Side 2, "The Greenhouse Effect" and "Changes in Climate" Exploring Physical Science Videodisc, Unit 4 Side 2, "A Better Cool" Audiotapes, English-Spanish Summary 5-1 Transparencies 11, "Temperature Inversion"; 12, "The Ozone Cycle"; 13, "The Greenhouse Effect"; 14, "Exploring Climate Predictions" Interactive Student Tutorial CD-ROM, E-5
TR 5-2 Lesson Plan, p. 127 **TR** 5-2 Section Summary, p. 128 **TR** 5-2 Review and Reinforce, p. 129 **TR** 5-2 Enrich, p. 130 **TR** Chapter 5 Skills Lab, pp. 137–139 **SES** Book H, *Earth's Waters,* Chapter 3	**SE** Section 2 Review, p. 153 **SE** Analyze and Conclude, p. 154 **TE** Ongoing Assessment, p. 151 **TE** Performance Assessment, p. 153 **TR** 5-2 Review and Reinforce, p. 129	Exploring Earth Science Videodisc, Unit 2 Side 2, "What's in Our Tap?" Audiotapes, English-Spanish Summary 5-2 Interactive Student Tutorial CD-ROM, E-5
TR 5-3 Lesson Plan, p. 131 **TR** 5-3 Section Summary, p. 132 **TR** 5-3 Review and Reinforce, p. 133 **TR** 5-3 Enrich, p. 134	**SE** Section 3 Review, p. 158 **TE** Ongoing Assessment, p. 157 **TE** Performance Assessment, p. 158 **TR** 5-3 Review and Reinforce, p. 133	Exploring Life Science Videodisc, Unit 2 Side 1, "Xeriscape" Audiotapes, English-Spanish Summary 5-3 Interactive Student Tutorial CD-ROM, E-5
TR Chapter 5 Performance Assessment, pp. 208–210 **TR** Chapter 5 Test, pp. 211–214	**SE** Chapter 5 Review, pp. 159–161 **TR** Chapter 5 Performance Assessment, pp. 208–210 **TR** Chapter 5 Test, pp. 211–214 **CTB** Test E-5	Interactive Student Tutorial CD-ROM, E-5 Computer Test Bank, Test E-5

Key: **SE** Student Edition **TE** Teacher's Edition **TR** Teaching Resources
CTB Computer Test Bank **SES** Science Explorer Series Text **ISLM** Integrated Science Laboratory Manual
ISAB Inquiry Skills Activity Book **PTA** Product Testing Activities by *Consumer Reports* **IES** Interdisciplinary Explorations Series

Meeting the National Science Education Standards and AAAS Benchmarks

National Science Education Standards	Benchmarks for Science Literacy	Unifying Themes
Science As Inquiry (Content Standard A) ◆ **Design and conduct a scientific investigation** Students investigate how pollutants affect seed growth. *(Real-World Lab)* ◆ **Use appropriate tools and techniques to gather, analyze, and interpret data** Students compare concentrations of a pollutant. *(Skills Lab)* ◆ **Communicate scientific procedures and explanations** Students communicate the importance of protecting air or water quality. *(Chapter Project)* **Earth and Space Science** (Content Standard D) ◆ **Structure of the Earth system** Air is a mixture of nitrogen, oxygen, carbon dioxide, water vapor, and other gases. Earth has a limited supply of fresh water. *(Sections 1, 2)* **Science and Technology** (Content Standard E) ◆ **Understandings about science and technology** Technology can help control pollution. *(Chapter Project; Sections 1, 2, 3)* **Science in Personal and Social Perspectives** (Content Standard F) ◆ **Personal health** Pollution can affect the health of humans. *(Sections 1, 2)* ◆ **Risks and benefits** Small changes in people's behavior can help reduce pollution. *(Chapter Project; Section 3)*	**1B Scientific Inquiry** Students investigate how pollutants affect seed growth and compare different concentrations of a pollutant in water. *(Real-World Lab; Skills Lab)* **3A Technology and Science** Technology can help control pollution. *(Section 3)* **3B Designs and Systems** The engines of motor vehicles release emissions into the air. Most pollution is the result of human activities, including agriculture, industry, construction, and mining. *(Chapter Project; Sections 1, 2)* **3C Issues in Technology** In the United States, laws help to reduce pollution. *(Section 3)* **4B The Earth** Air is a mixture of nitrogen, oxygen, carbon dioxide, water vapor, and other gases. Earth has a limited supply of fresh water. *(Sections 1, 2)* **6E Physical Health** Pollution can affect the health of humans. *(Sections 1, 2)* **7D Social Trade-Offs** Important human activities can cause air and water pollution. *(Chapter Project; Sections 1, 2)* **12D Communication Skills** Students communicate about air or water quality to younger students. *(Chapter Project)*	◆ **Energy** Obtaining and using energy resources can result in pollution. The theory of global warming predicts that increases in carbon dioxide will cause the average temperature to rise. The addition of heat can have a negative effect on a body of water. *(Chapter Project; Sections 1, 2)* ◆ **Modeling** Most scientists base their climate predictions on computer models. Students use models to observe the effects of pollutants on seed growth and compare the concentrations of a pollutant in water. *(Section 1; Real-World Lab; Skills Lab)* ◆ **Patterns of Change** Pollution can affect the health of humans and other living things. The theory of global warming predicts that increases in carbon dioxide will cause the average temperature to rise. *(Sections 1, 2)* ◆ **Scale and Structure** The ozone layer is a layer of the upper atmosphere about 30 kilometers above Earth's surface. Pollution can affect areas far from its source. *(Sections 1, 2)* ◆ **Stability** Earth's supply of fresh water is renewable. *(Section 2)* ◆ **Systems and Interactions** The engines of motor vehicles release emissions that cause air pollution. Most pollution is the result of human activities, including agriculture, industry, construction, and mining. Technology can help reduce pollution. *(Chapter Project; Sections 1, 2, 3)*

Media and Technology

Exploring Earth Science Videodiscs
◆ **Section 1** "The Greenhouse Effect" models how trapped heat from the sun can create global warming. "Changes in Climate" considers natural and human factors that influence climate change.
◆ **Section 2** "What's in Our Tap?" tours a water treatment plant.

Exploring Physical Science Videodiscs
◆ **Section 1** "A Better Cool" discusses freon and ozone.

Exploring Life Science Videodiscs
◆ **Section 3** "Xeriscape" illustrates a landscaping technique that uses native plants to conserve water.

Interactive Student Tutorial CD-ROM
◆ **Chapter Review** Interactive questions help students to self-assess their mastery of key chapter concepts.

Student Edition Connection Strategies

◆ **Section 1** Language Arts Connection, p. 141
Integrating Health, p. 142
Math Toolbox, p. 145
Integrating Earth Science, p. 146

◆ **Section 3** Integrating Technology, pp. 155–158

USING THE INTERNET

www.science-explorer.phschool.com

Visit the Science Explorer Internet site to find an up-to-date activity for Chapter 5 of *Environmental Science*.

ACTIVITY	Time (minutes)	Materials Quantities for one work group	Skills
Section 1			
Discover, p. 140	5	**Nonconsumable** bottle of perfume (for teacher only)	Inferring
Try This, p. 143	10	**Consumable** rainwater, pH paper, pH chart, lemon juice **Nonconsumable** two plastic cups	Measuring
Sharpen Your Skills, p. 144	15	No special materials are required.	Communicating
Science at Home, p. 147	home	**Consumable** petroleum jelly **Nonconsumable** 2 empty glass jars	Predicting, Observing
Real-World Lab, p. 148	30; 5 x 5 days	**Consumable** potting soil, 20 radish seeds, detergent solution, day-old tap water, acid solution, oil solution, salt solution, masking tape **Nonconsumable** 2 plastic petri dishes with lids, metric ruler, wax pencil	Controlling Variables, Measuring, Interpreting Data
Section 2			
Discover, p. 149	5	**Consumable** water, milk **Nonconsumable** flashlight, clear plastic cup, plastic dropper	Observing
Try This, p. 150	10; 5 x 3 days	**Consumable** water, food coloring, sugar **Nonconsumable** plastic cup, spoon, graduated cylinder	Making Models
Skills Lab, p. 154	40	**Consumable** food coloring, water **Nonconsumable** 9 small test tubes, marker, plastic dropper, test tube rack	Measuring, Calculating, Observing
Section 3			
Discover, p. 155	10	**Consumable** cooled herbal tea, paper filter, crushed charcoal **Nonconsumable** 2 plastic cups, funnel	Developing Hypotheses
Sharpen Your Skills, p. 156	20	**Consumable** graph paper **Nonconsumable** 2 pens or pencils of different colors	Graphing

A list of all materials required for the Student Edition activities can be found on pages T14–T15. You can order Materials Kits by calling 1-800-828-7777 or by accessing the Science Explorer Internet site at **www.science-explorer.phschool.com.**

Pollution vs. Purity

Chapter 5 focuses on the causes and effects of air and water pollution and on methods of protecting air and water quality. The Chapter 5 Project will give students an opportunity to explore chapter concepts in greater depth and to convey their understanding to others.

Purpose For the Chapter 5 Project, students will research a specific topic related to air or water quality, then create a book, game, video, or other educational tool to communicate their findings and ideas to younger students. The project is suitable as either an individual or a small-group activity.

Skills Focus After completing the Chapter 5 Project, students will be able to
◆ relate the causes and effects of specific forms of air or water pollution;
◆ make judgments about ways that individuals can help reduce those forms of pollution;
◆ communicate information about air or water quality to younger students using age-appropriate materials and methods.

Project Time Line The Chapter 5 Project requires about two weeks to complete, depending on the amount of time you allot for the research phase of the project. As students study Sections 1 and 2, they will choose a specific topic for study, conduct their research, and organize the information they gather. During Section 3, students will design and create the final product. At the conclusion of the chapter, students will present their products to younger students and evaluate the products' appeal and effectiveness in conveying information about air or water quality.

Possible Materials
◆ Provide appropriate materials for creating the final products that students have chosen—posterboard and art supplies for making board games, video cameras for creating videos, and the like. Encourage students to use materials from home as well.

Advance Preparation Check your school and town libraries to make sure

CHAPTER

5 Air and Water Resources

WHAT'S AHEAD

SECTION
1 Air Pollution

Discover **How Does the Scent Spread?**
Sharpen Your Skills **Communicating**
Try This **How Acid Is Your Rain?**
Real-World Lab **How Does the Garden Grow?**

SECTION
2 The Water Supply

Discover **How Does the Water Change?**
Try This **Getting Clean**
Skills Lab **Concentrate on This!**

SECTION
3 *Integrating Technology* **Finding Pollution Solutions**

Discover **Can You Remove the Tea?**
Sharpen Your Skills **Graphing**

students will have access to ample research materials for the project. Contact teachers of younger students to arrange for your students to present their final products at the conclusion of the chapter. Try to provide a range of age/grade possibilities so your students can choose among them.

Launching the Project Invite students to read the Chapter 5 Project description on page 139. Then ask: **What kinds of things did you enjoy doing in school when you were younger? What made learning fun?** Encourage students

to keep these ideas in mind as they work on this project, particularly when they plan their final products.

Distribute Chapter 5 Project Overview on pages 118–119 of Teaching Resources, and have students review the project rules and procedures. Invite questions and comments. Emphasize that the final product should be designed for their specific target audience. Advise students to think about the target audience's age range, skills, interests, and previous learning when they develop the final

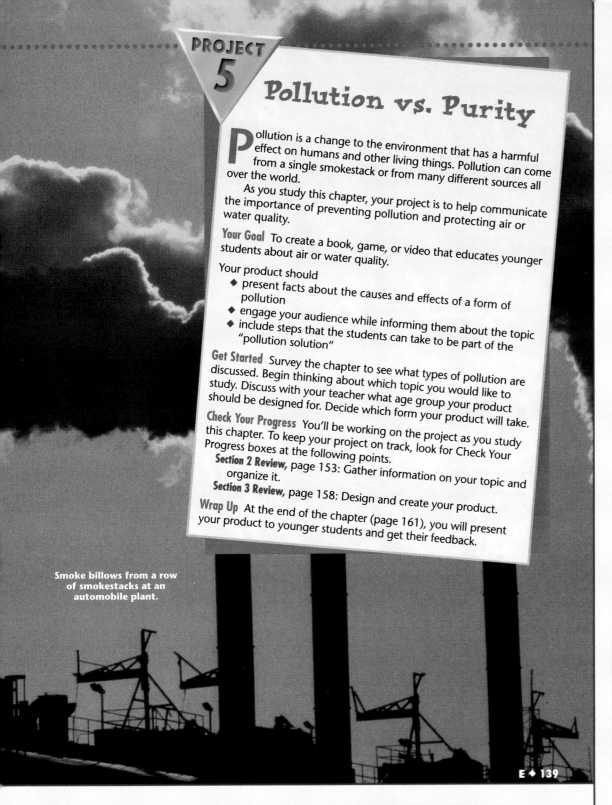

Pollution vs. Purity

Pollution is a change to the environment that has a harmful effect on humans and other living things. Pollution can come from a single smokestack or from many different sources all over the world.

As you study this chapter, your project is to help communicate the importance of preventing pollution and protecting air or water quality.

Your Goal To create a book, game, or video that educates younger students about air or water quality.

Your product should
- present facts about the causes and effects of a form of pollution
- engage your audience while informing them about the topic
- include steps that the students can take to be part of the "pollution solution"

Get Started Survey the chapter to see what types of pollution are discussed. Begin thinking about which topic you would like to study. Discuss with your teacher what age group your product should be designed for. Decide which form your product will take.

Check Your Progress You'll be working on the project as you study this chapter. To keep your project on track, look for Check Your Progress boxes at the following points.
Section 2 Review, page 153: Gather information on your topic and organize it.
Section 3 Review, page 158: Design and create your product.

Wrap Up At the end of the chapter (page 161), you will present your product to younger students and get their feedback.

Smoke billows from a row of smokestacks at an automobile plant.

E ♦ 139

---

product. Encourage students to consider students in special-needs classes, as well as younger students.

If you prefer to have students do the project as a small-group activity, divide the class into groups of two to four students each. Let the groups meet briefly to brainstorm ideas for specific topics and products. Whether the project is done individually or in groups, monitor students' choices of topics, products, and target audiences.

When students are ready to make their final

Program Resources

- **Teaching Resources** Chapter 5 Project Teacher Notes, pp. 116–117; Chapter 5 Project Overview and Worksheet, pp. 118–121; Chapter 5 Project Scoring Rubric, p. 122

---

products, distribute Chapter 5 Project Worksheet 1, which provides guidelines for creating a board game, video, or skit. At the end of the chapter, distribute Worksheet 2, which provides a format for students to obtain the younger students' feedback on the products' appeal and effectiveness.

Additional information on guiding the project is provided in Chapter 5 Project Teacher Notes on pages 116–117 of Teaching Resources.

Performance Assessment

The Chapter 5 Project Scoring Rubric on page 122 in Teaching Resources will help you evaluate how well students complete the Chapter 5 Project. You may want to share the scoring rubric with students so they are clear about what will be expected of them. Students will be assessed on
- their ability to identify the causes and effects of one specific type of air or water pollution and organize the information;
- their ability to create an age-appropriate product to teach younger students about air or water quality and present the product to the target audience;
- their participation in their group, if they worked in groups.

Objectives

After completing the lesson, students will be able to
- identify and describe outdoor and indoor air pollutants;
- explain the importance of ozone in the upper atmosphere;
- describe the greenhouse effect and explain how it affects climate.

Key Terms air pollution, emissions, photochemical smog, ozone, temperature inversion, acid rain, ozone layer, chlorofluorocarbons, greenhouse effect, global warming

1 Engage/Explore

Activating Prior Knowledge

Encourage students to describe specific examples of air pollution that they have seen, such as smog hanging over a city, smoke coming from factory smokestacks, and grime or pollen settling on cars parked outdoors. Ask: **What kinds of materials pollute the air we breathe?** (*Accept all responses without comment at this time.*)

DISCOVER

Skills Focus inferring
Materials *bottle of perfume*
Time 5 minutes
Tips Make sure students are evenly spaced throughout the room so the scent will reach different students at different times.
Expected Outcome Students closest to you will smell the perfume first, and those standing farthest away will smell it last.
Think It Over Students will see a "wave" of raised hands traveling from you to the farthest parts of the room. Students should infer that molecules of perfume traveled across the room in the air.

SECTION
1 Air Pollution

DISCOVER  ACTIVITY

How Does the Scent Spread?

1. Choose a place to stand so that you and your classmates are evenly spread around the room.
2. Your teacher will open a bottle of perfume in one corner of the room.
3. Raise your hand when you first smell the perfume.

Think It Over
Inferring Describe the pattern you observed as people raised their hands. How do you think the smell traveled across the room?

GUIDE FOR READING

- What causes photochemical smog?
- How is the ozone layer important?
- What are climate predictions based on?

Reading Tip As you read, make a list of different types of air pollution. Write a sentence about the effect of each type.

Figure 1 The air supply aboard the space station *Mir* was threatened by a collision during docking.

June 25, 1997, began as an ordinary day aboard the Russian space station *Mir*. The three crew members were busy with their usual tasks. One checked on the various scientific experiments. Another was exercising. The third cosmonaut was skillfully guiding a supply ship as it docked with *Mir*.

Suddenly, the crew members heard a frightening sound—the crumpling of collapsing metal. The space station jolted from side to side. The pressure gauges indicated an air leak! One crew member hurried to prepare the emergency evacuation vehicle. Meanwhile, the other two managed to close the airtight door between the damaged area and the rest of the space station. Fortunately, the pressure soon returned to normal. A disaster had been avoided. There was no need to abandon ship.

Closing the door preserved the most valuable resource on *Mir*—the air. Although you probably don't think about the air very often, it is just as important on Earth as it is on a space station. Air is a resource you use every minute of your life.

What's in the Air?

Though you can't see, taste, or smell it, you are surrounded by air. Air is a mixture of nitrogen, oxygen, carbon dioxide, water vapor, and other gases. Almost all living things depend on these gases to carry out their life processes.

Nitrogen, oxygen, and carbon dioxide cycle between the atmosphere and living things. These cycles ensure that the air supply on Earth will not run out. But they don't guarantee that the air will always be clean. A change to the atmosphere that has harmful effects is called **air pollution.** Substances that cause pollution are called pollutants. Pollutants can be particles, such as

---

READING STRATEGIES

Reading Tip Students could list the following types of air pollution: emissions (particles and gases) from factories, power plants, and automobiles; photochemical smog; acid rain; cigarette smoke; carbon monoxide from incomplete burning of fuels; radon; and chlorofluorocarbons. Their sentences should describe or explain the source of each type.

Caption Writing Distribute photocopies of Figure 4, and suggest that each student write a new caption that identifies each source of indoor pollution shown. Then have each student add another source of air pollution to the drawing. Have students exchange cartoons and expand the caption to include the pollution source that was added.

ash, or gases, such as chlorine. Air pollution can affect the health of humans and other living things. Pollution can even impact the climate of the whole planet.

What causes air pollution? If you're like many people, you probably picture a factory smokestack, belching thick black smoke into the sky. Until the mid-1900s, factories and power plants that burned coal produced most of the air pollution in the United States. Particles and gases that are released into the air are called **emissions**. Today, there is an even larger source of emissions that cause air pollution: motor vehicles such as cars, trucks, and airplanes. The engines of these vehicles release gases such as carbon monoxide, an invisible toxic gas.

Though most air pollution is the result of human activities, there are some natural causes as well. For example, an erupting volcano sends an enormous load of soot, ash, sulfur, and nitrogen oxide gases into the atmosphere.

☑ *Checkpoint* **What are some examples of air pollutants?**

Smog

Have you ever heard a weather forecaster talk about a "smog alert"? A smog alert is a warning about a type of air pollution called photochemical smog. **Photochemical smog** is a thick, brownish haze formed when certain gases in the air react with sunlight. When the smog level is high, it settles as a haze over a city. Smog can make people's eyes burn and irritate their throats.

The major sources of photochemical smog are the gases emitted by automobiles and trucks. Burning gasoline in a car engine releases some gases into the air. These gases include hydrocarbons (compounds containing hydrogen and carbon) and nitrogen oxides. The gases react in the sunlight and produce a form of oxygen called **ozone**. Ozone, which is toxic, is the major chemical found in smog.

Language **Arts**
CONNECTION

People sometimes coin, or invent, a word to express a specific idea. For example, Londoners coined the word *smog* to describe the heavy gray air formed when coal smoke mixed with ocean fog.

In Your Journal

Can you guess the meaning of these coined words?

◆ brunch   ◆ chortle
◆ squinched   ◆ liger

Try coining a few descriptive words of your own. Exchange your words with a classmate and see if you can guess the meanings of the other's words.

Figure 2 A haze of photochemical smog hangs over this city's skyline. *Interpreting Photographs What is the source of the smog?*

E ◆ 141

Program Resources

◆ **Teaching Resources** 5-1 Lesson Plan, p. 123; 5-1 Section Summary, p. 124
◆ **Interdisciplinary Exploration Series** "Metropolis," pp. 35–36, 40; "Where River Meets Sea," p. 38

Media and Technology

 Audiotapes English-Spanish Summary 5-1

Answers to Self-Assessment

☑ *Checkpoint*

Air pollutants include particles such as ash and gases such as chlorine and carbon monoxide.

Caption Question

Figure 2 The source of smog is the gases emitted by automobiles and trucks in the city.

2 *Facilitate*

What's in the Air?

Addressing Naive Conceptions

Materials *drawing compass, calculator*
Time 10–15 minutes

Ask: **Which gas do you think is most common in the air we breathe?** *(Accept all responses without comment.)* Then provide the following data: nitrogen 78%; oxygen 21%; argon 0.9%; other gases, including carbon dioxide and water vapor, 0.1%. Ask: **Was your prediction correct, or were you surprised?** *(Students may have thought that oxygen is the most common gas or that carbon dioxide is present in a much higher proportion.)* Challenge each student to use these data to create a circle graph. *(Nitrogen 281°, oxygen 75.5°, argon 3°, other gases 0.5°)* **learning modality: logical/mathematical**

Smog

Language **Arts**
CONNECTION

To clarify how the word smog was created, write *smoke + fog* on the board, erase *oke* and *f*, and write *= smog*.

In Your Journal As a class, discuss suggestions for each word. (*Brunch:* a meal midway between breakfast and lunch; *chortle:* to chuckle and snort; *squinch:* to squint or squeeze and pinch; *liger:* the offspring of a lion and a tiger) The word *chortle* was coined by British author Lewis Carroll, who coined many terms in his famous poem "Jabberwocky." Students may enjoy identifying other coined words in the poem. **learning modality: verbal**

Ongoing Assessment

Oral Presentation Call on students to each name one source of particles or gases that contribute to air pollution.

E ◆ 141

Smog, continued

Integrating Health

Some respiratory problems, such as asthma, bronchitis, and emphysema are caused or worsened by breathing polluted air. A local hospital, nursing association, or pediatric practice may be able to provide pamphlets or a speaker on these topics. Encourage students to use the information they receive to make posters that include a labeled diagram of the respiratory system (or parts of it) and a brief description of how the system is affected. **learning modality: verbal**

Acid Rain

Building Inquiry Skills: Observing

Materials *plastic cup, scissors, piece of nylon stocking fabric, tape, hand lens*
Time 10–15 minutes for setup plus follow-up observations

Have students examine nylon stocking fabric with a hand lens and draw what they see. Also have students pull and twist the fabric to test its strength and flexibility. Then have each student make an "acid rain tester" by cutting out the bottom of a plastic cup and taping a piece of stocking over the opening. Take students outdoors to hang the testers where they will be exposed to air and rain. At the end of a week, have students reexamine the fabric, compare it with their original drawings, retest its strength and flexibility, and look for broken fibers and other signs of damage. Encourage students to consider what could have caused any damage. Point out that polluting gases in the air, such as sulfur oxides and nitrogen oxides, also affect the nylon. **learning modality: visual**

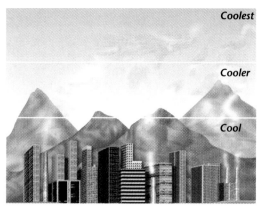
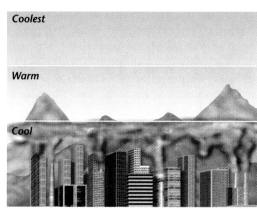

Figure 3 Normally, pollutants rise high in the air and blow away (left). But during a temperature inversion, a layer of warm air traps pollutants close to the ground (right).

Temperature Inversion Pollutants usually blow away from the place where they are produced. Normally, air close to the ground is heated by Earth's surface. As the air warms, it rises into the cooler air above it. The pollutants are carried higher into the atmosphere where they blow away. But certain weather conditions cause a condition known as a temperature inversion. During a **temperature inversion,** a layer of warm air prevents the rising air from escaping. The polluted air is trapped and held close to Earth's surface. The smog becomes more concentrated and dangerous.

Health Effects of Smog The effects of smog can be more serious than itchy, watery eyes and a scratchy throat. The ozone in smog can cause lung problems and harm the body's defenses against infection. When smog levels reach a certain point, a city issues a smog alert. During a smog alert, you should avoid exercising outdoors. People who have asthma or other conditions that affect their breathing should be particularly careful.

Checkpoint *What happens during a temperature inversion?*

Acid Rain

Another type of air pollution is caused by power plants and factories that burn coal and oil. These fuels produce nitrogen oxides and sulfur oxides when they are burned. These gases react with water vapor in the air, forming nitric acid and sulfuric acid. The acids return to Earth's surface dissolved in precipitation. Precipitation that is more acidic than normal is called **acid rain.** Acid rain can be in the form of snow, sleet, or fog as well as rain.

As you can imagine, acid falling from the sky has some negative effects. When acid rain falls into a pond or lake, it changes

---

Background

Facts and Figures Ordinary rainwater contains dissolved carbon dioxide and other compounds of natural origin that form weak acid solutions. Normally, the pH of rainwater is about 5 to 6. But rain in the northeastern United States usually has a pH of about 4. Sometimes the rain in this region is at least as acidic as vinegar, which has a pH of 3.

One factor that makes acid rain such a complex problem is that it occurs far from the source of the gases that cause it. For example, gases from coal-burning power plants in England are blown eastward and cause acid rain in Sweden and Norway. In the United States, midwestern and eastern states produce much of the acid rain that falls in New England and southeastern Canada.

the conditions there. Many fish, and particularly their eggs, cannot survive in more acidic water. Acid rain that falls on the ground can damage plants by affecting the nutrient levels in the soil. Whole forests have been destroyed by acid rain. Fortunately, some of the effects of acid rain are reversible. Badly damaged lakes have been restored by adding substances such as lime that neutralize the acid.

Acid rain doesn't just affect living things. The acid reacts with stone and metal in buildings and statues. Automobiles rust more quickly in areas with acid rain. These effects are not reversible.

Indoor Air Pollution

You might think that you could avoid air pollution by staying inside. But in fact, the air inside buildings can be polluted, too. Many substances can cause indoor air pollution. Some, such as dust, pet hair, and air fresheners, bother only those people who are allergic to them. Other pollutants have more widespread effects. Asbestos, a building material common in older buildings, can cause lung disease. Products such as oil-based paints, glues, and cleaning supplies may give off toxic fumes. Read the label whenever you use any of these products. You may need to open a window or use the chemical outdoors.

If you have been near someone smoking a cigarette, you know how the smell stays in your clothes and hair even after you leave the room. The smoke reached your lungs every time you inhaled near the smoking person. Research has shown that cigarette smoke can damage the lungs and heart. Now smoking is banned in many places such as restaurants, airports, and stadiums.

How Acid Is Your Rain?

In this activity you will test whether rain in your area is more or less acidic than lemon juice (citric acid).

1. Collect some rainwater in a clean plastic cup.
2. Indoors, dip a piece of pH paper into the cup. Compare the color of the paper to the chart on the package to find the pH. (The lower the pH of a substance, the more acidic it is.)
3. Pour a little lemon juice into a plastic cup. Repeat Step 2 with the lemon juice.

Measuring What is the pH of the rainwater? How does it compare to the pH of the lemon juice?

Figure 4 Air inside buildings can be polluted, too. *Observing How many sources of pollution can you spot in this room?*

Skills Focus measuring
Materials *rainwater, 2 plastic cups, pH paper, pH chart, lemon juice*
Time 10 minutes
Tips You might want to collect rainwater ahead of time for this activity.
Expected Outcome Rainwater is normally slightly acidic (pH 5–6); a pH lower than 5 indicates acid rain. Lemon juice's pH is 2.
Extend Have students measure the pH of tap water and compare it with their pH measurements of rainwater and lemon juice. **learning modality: logical/mathematical**

Indoor Air Pollution

Real-Life Learning

Materials *containers of various products such as oil-based paints, glues, and cleaning supplies that give off toxic fumes*
Time 10 minutes

Display the products for students to examine their labels. (CAUTION: *Instruct students to not open any container.*) Have volunteers read aloud cautionary statements on the labels. Then ask: **How could you use these products safely?** (*Instructions may vary. Usually such products can be used safely outside or in well-ventilated areas.*) **How should such products be stored?** (*They should be stored in a secure area, away from small children and pets, and the containers should be closed tightly.*) **How should such products be disposed of?** (*Most such products should be taken to a hazardous waste site.*) **learning modality: verbal**

Program Resources

Science Explorer Series *Human Biology and Health,* Chapters 5 and 6, provide more information on the respiratory system, asthma, and allergies.

Media and Technology

Transparencies "Temperature Inversion," Transparency 11

Answers to Self-Assessment

☑ Checkpoint

A layer of warm air prevents cooler air below it from rising, trapping polluted air close to Earth's surface.

Caption Question

Figure 4 *Samples:* Smoking, dusting, burning wood in the fireplace, cat hair, bird feathers, flower pollen, carpet fumes

Ongoing Assessment

Drawing Have each student draw and label a diagram to explain how acid rain forms.

Students can save their drawings in their portfolios.

Indoor Air Pollution, continued

Including All Students

For students who need additional help with language skills, write *carbon dioxide* and *carbon monoxide* on the board and ask: **What difference do you see between these terms?** *(The prefixes di- and mon-; draw a box around each prefix.)* **What do these word parts mean?** *(Di- means "two," mon- means "one.")* **What do you think *dioxide* and *monoxide* mean?** *("Two oxygens" and "one oxygen")* Write CO_2 and CO below the terms, and draw a simple diagram of each molecule. Explain that CO_2, a harmless gas, has two oxygen atoms in each molecule, while CO has only one. CO is deadly because it is absorbed by red blood cells more easily than oxygen (O_2) is. When a person breathes CO, it replaces the O_2 in the body, causing suffocation. Stress the value of detectors in preventing CO poisoning. **learning modality: verbal**

Sharpen your Skills

Communicating

Time 15 minutes

Tips Have students work in groups of three. Establish a time limit of 30 or 45 seconds for the announcement. Let each group tape-record its announcement.

Expected Outcome Play the announcements in class, and have students assess each one for the elements cited in the text, including "listener appeal."

Extend Let the class choose the most effective announcement. Arrange to have it broadcast over the school's PA system.

learning modality: verbal

Figure 5 Installing a carbon monoxide detector in a home can save lives. Because carbon monoxide has no color or odor, it cannot be detected by sight or smell.

Sharpen your Skills

Communicating

Write a radio public service announcement to inform people about either carbon monoxide or radon. Think about how the announcement could catch your listeners' attention. Describe the source and effects of the pollutant. Suggest how listeners can protect themselves.

Carbon Monoxide One particularly dangerous type of indoor air pollution is carbon monoxide. Carbon monoxide is a colorless, odorless gas that forms when wood, coal, oil, or gas are incompletely burned. When carbon monoxide builds up in an enclosed space such as a basement, apartment, or house, it can be deadly. Because carbon monoxide cannot be detected by sight or smell, its victims have no warning that the level is dangerously high. Any home heated by wood, coal, oil, or gas should have a carbon monoxide detector. The detector sounds a warning alarm when the gas is present.

Radon Another type of pollution that is difficult to detect is radon. Radon is a colorless, odorless gas that is radioactive. It is formed naturally by certain types of rocks underground. Radon can enter homes through cracks in basement walls or floors. Research indicates that breathing radon gas over many years may cause lung cancer and other health problems. But the level of radon necessary to cause these effects is unknown. To be safe, many homeowners have installed ventilation systems to prevent radon from building up in their homes.

☑ *Checkpoint* *Why is it important to install carbon monoxide detectors in homes?*

The Ozone Layer

If you have ever had a sunburn, you have experienced the painful effects of the sun's ultraviolet radiation. But did you know that such burns would be even worse without the protection of the ozone layer? The **ozone layer** is a layer of the upper atmosphere about 30 kilometers above Earth's surface. Actually, the concentration of ozone in this layer is very low—only a few parts per million.

Background

Integrating Science The ozone layer is located in the upper atmosphere, in the stratosphere. In 1985, meteorologists brought a strange discovery to the attention of other scientists: there was a "hole" in the ozone layer. They had observed a large area in the stratosphere over Antarctica where the ozone layer had become much thinner. The area of the hole in the mid-1990s was about 23.3 million km^2, roughly as big as North America. There is also evidence of a smaller hole in the ozone layer above the Arctic.

CFCs are the primary cause of the depletion of the stratospheric ozone layer. Ultraviolet radiation from the sun breaks the CFCs apart, forming chlorine. Chlorine reacts with ozone, thereby destroying the ozone molecules.

Yet even the small amount of ozone in the ozone layer protects people from the effects of too much ultraviolet radiation. These effects include sunburn, eye diseases, and skin cancer.

Since you read earlier that ozone is a pollutant, the fact that ozone can be helpful may sound confusing. The difference between ozone as a pollutant and ozone as a helpful gas is its location. Ozone close to Earth's surface in the form of smog is harmful. Higher in the atmosphere, where people cannot breathe it, ozone protects us.

The Source of Ozone Ozone is constantly being made and destroyed. When sunlight strikes an ozone molecule, the energy of the ultraviolet radiation is partly absorbed. This energy causes the molecule to break apart into an oxygen molecule and an oxygen atom, as shown in Figure 6. The oxygen atom soon collides with another oxygen molecule. They react to form a new ozone molecule. Each time this cycle occurs, some ultraviolet energy is absorbed. That energy does not reach Earth's surface.

The Ozone Hole In the late 1970s, scientists observed that the amount of ozone in the ozone layer seemed to be decreasing. What was to blame for this loss of ozone?

One problem was a group of gases containing chlorine and fluorine, called **chlorofluorocarbons,** or "CFCs." CFCs had been used instead of smelly, toxic ammonia in refrigerators and air conditioners. CFCs were also used in fire extinguishers and aerosol spray cans. Then scientists discovered that CFCs react with ozone molecules. The CFCs block the cycle that absorbs ultraviolet radiation. In 1990, many nations signed an agreement to ban the use of almost all CFCs by the year 2000. Unfortunately, the CFC molecules are very stable. They have remained in the atmosphere for a long time. But scientists predict that if the ban is maintained, the ozone layer will gradually recover.

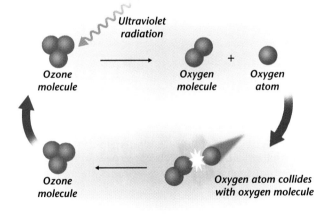

Ozone molecule → Oxygen molecule + Oxygen atom
Ozone molecule ← Oxygen atom collides with oxygen molecule
Ultraviolet radiation

Math TOOLBOX

Concentration

Levels of pollutants are often written as concentrations. A concentration is a ratio that compares the amount of one substance to a certain amount of another substance. For example, suppose that the concentration of ozone in a part of the atmosphere is 3 parts per million. This means that there are 3 molecules of ozone in 1,000,000 molecules of air. This ratio can also be written in three other ways:

3 : 1,000,000 or

3 to 1,000,000 or

$$\frac{3}{1,000,000}$$

Figure 6 When ultraviolet radiation from the sun strikes an ozone molecule, some energy is absorbed by the ozone molecule. This energy causes the ozone molecule to split into an oxygen molecule and a free oxygen atom. *Interpreting Diagrams What happens when the free oxygen atom collides with an oxygen molecule?*

Math TOOLBOX

Materials *graph paper ruled in tenths of an inch*
Time 10 minutes

Give each student a sheet of graph paper ruled in tenths of an inch, and have students calculate the total number of small squares in an 8- by 10-inch block on the sheet. *(8,000)* Tell students to darken any four small squares on the sheet. Ask: **What is the concentration of black squares?** *(4 parts per 8,000)* Have four volunteers come to the board and write the four ways to express this ratio. *(4 parts per 8,000; 4:8,000; 4 to 8,000; and 4/8,000)* For students who need an additional challenge, ask: **How many parts per thousand is that?** *(0.5)* **per million?** *(500)* **per billion?** *(500,000)* **learning modality: logical/ mathematical**

Inquiry Challenge

Materials *clay or other materials of students' choice; flashlight or lamp*
Time 10 minutes

Challenge pairs of students to create a model to demonstrate the ozone cycle. *(Sample model: Shape three balls from clay to represent oxygen atoms. Stick the three balls together to represent an ozone molecule. Shine light at the ozone molecule and detach one oxygen atom. Then there is an oxygen molecule and a single oxygen atom. To create an ozone molecule, stick the single ball to the two attached balls, returning to the first step in the cycle.)* **cooperative learning**

Answers to Self-Assessment

☑ *Checkpoint*

Carbon monoxide cannot be seen or smelled, so detectors are needed to warn people when it is present at dangerous levels.

Caption Question

Figure 6 An ozone molecule is formed.

Ongoing Assessment

Writing Have each student explain how ozone forms in the atmosphere and why this process protects organisms on Earth.

 Students can save their work in their portfolios.

E ◆ 145

Integrating Earth Science

Materials *2 small glass aquaria; 2 thermometers; 2 rulers; string; paper cup cut in half lengthwise; tape; glass aquarium cover or plastic wrap*
Time 10 minutes

Put two glass aquaria on a sunny windowsill, and lay a ruler across each one. Suspend a thermometer from each ruler with the numbered side facing toward the classroom and away from the window. Shade each thermometer by taping a cup half behind it. Ask a volunteer to read both thermometers and record these starting temperatures on the board. Then cover one aquarium with a glass cover or a piece of plastic wrap taped to the sides. At regular intervals, have other volunteers take new readings and record the temperatures and times on the board. In a follow-up class discussion, ask: **What happened to the air temperature in the uncovered aquarium?** *(It should have increased a bit at first, then stayed the same.)* **What happened to the air temperature in the covered aquarium?** *(It kept increasing.)* **What does the air inside the aquaria represent in this model?** *(The air near Earth's surface)* **What does the cover on the aquarium represent?** *(The gases that trap heat and keep it from escaping into space)* **What is this process called?** *(The greenhouse effect)* **learning modality: logical/mathematical**

EXPLORING
Climate Predictions

Point out that the questions posed in the captions are ones that scientists ask as they study Earth's climate and try to predict long-term changes. Emphasize that there are no "right" answers to questions such as these. In a class discussion or in small groups, let students offer their own ideas in response to the questions. **learning modality: verbal**

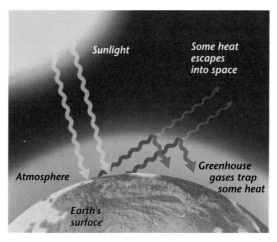

Figure 7 When energy in the form of sunlight strikes Earth's surface, it changes to heat. Certain gases in the atmosphere trap some of the heat, preventing it from escaping back into space. This trapping of heat is known as the greenhouse effect.
Applying Concepts What gases in the atmosphere trap heat near Earth's surface?

Some changes to the atmosphere affect the climate of the whole planet. To understand why, you need to know more about the atmosphere.

The Greenhouse Effect Think about the sun shining through a window on a cool day. The window lets light enter the room. The light strikes objects in the room and is converted to heat. But the closed windows trap the warm air inside, so the room becomes warmer.

In the atmosphere, water vapor, carbon dioxide, and certain other gases act like windows. These gases allow sunlight to reach Earth's surface, but they prevent the heat from escaping back into space. The trapping of heat near Earth's surface is called the **greenhouse effect**. Without the greenhouse effect, Earth would be much colder—about 33°C colder on average.

Global Warming Since the 1800s, coal and oil have been the main sources of energy in most of the world. As you have read, burning these substances produces carbon dioxide. During this time, the amount of carbon dioxide in the atmosphere has increased from 280 parts per million to 350 parts per million. This amount is increasing more quickly every year.

Does increasing carbon dioxide cause the greenhouse effect to become stronger? One theory, called **global warming,** predicts that the increase in carbon dioxide will cause the average temperature to continue to rise. Scientists have estimated that the increase in the next century could be as much as 3 to 8 Celsius degrees. Although that may not sound like a big change, it could have a huge impact. Parts of the Antarctic ice cap would melt, raising the level of the oceans. The temperature change would affect climate patterns all over the world. This would affect where crops are grown. There might also be more severe storms.

Predicting Climate Change It is difficult to predict how Earth's climate will be affected by changes in the atmosphere. The systems that create climate are very complex. Scientists have studied these systems for less than a century, a very short time to learn about processes that can occur over thousands of years. **Most scientists base their climate predictions on computer models that calculate the effects of changes in the atmosphere.** As *Exploring Climate Predictions* shows, making these predictions requires many types of information.

Background

History of Science In June 1992, the United Nations Conference on Environment and Development met to discuss international environmental problems, including pollution and deterioration of Earth's atmosphere. As a result, more than 165 nations have signed a climate change treaty to curb carbon dioxide emissions and thus reduce the greenhouse effect.

Media and Technology

 Exploring Earth Science Videodisc
Unit 4, Side 2, "The Greenhouse Effect"

Chapter 5

 Exploring Earth Science Videodisc
Unit 4, Side 2, "Changes in Climate"

Chapter 6

EXPLORING Climate Predictions

Many factors affect the complex systems that create climate. Good predictions must consider as many of these factors as possible.

Emissions
Power plants, factories, and vehicles produce gases that increase the greenhouse effect. Will there be more emissions in the future, or will ways be found to reduce them? Will people change their habits to use less energy?

Oceans
Carbon dioxide cycles between the atmosphere and the oceans, where it dissolves in the water. If ocean temperatures change, will more or less carbon dioxide be dissolved?

Forests
Plants take in carbon dioxide during photosynthesis. As forests are cut down, more carbon dioxide stays in the atmosphere. But if Earth continues to get warmer, more plants may grow. They will remove more carbon dioxide from the air. Which effect will be greater?

Clouds
If Earth gets warmer, more water will evaporate. More water vapor in the air would increase the greenhouse effect. But there would also be more clouds, which reflect sunlight away from Earth's surface. Will the result be warmer or cooler air?

 Section 1 Review

1. How does photochemical smog form?
2. How does the ozone layer protect people?
3. How do scientists make climate predictions?
4. Give three examples of indoor air pollutants and list their sources.
5. **Thinking Critically Predicting** One possible result of global warming is that melting ice could cause ocean levels to rise. What effects might this have?

Science at Home

What particles are in your air? With a family member, set up two particle collectors. Smear petroleum jelly on the inside of two clean, empty glass jars. Place one inside your home and the other outside. Make sure both jars are in locations where they will not be disturbed. Predict what you will find if you leave the jars in place for a few days. Compare the particles in each jar. How similar are they? Can you identify any of the particles?

 Outside Wed. 11/5

---

3 Assess

Section 1 Review Answers

1. Hydrocarbons and nitrogen oxides react in sunlight to produce ozone, the major chemical in photochemical smog.
2. The ozone layer absorbs some of the harmful ultraviolet energy in sunlight and prevents it from reaching Earth's surface.
3. Most scientists base their climate predictions on computer models that calculate the effects of changes in the atmosphere.
4. *Any three:* dust, pet hair, and air fresheners; asbestos from building materials; oil-based products; gases and particles in cigarette smoke; carbon monoxide from burning wood, coal, oil, or gas as fuel; radon gas that enters buildings from rocks underground
5. *Sample answer:* Rising ocean levels would flood coastal areas, destroying cities, farms, and habitats.

Science at Home

Materials *2 clean, empty glass jars; petroleum jelly* **ACTIVITY**

Suggest that students place the inside jar in a busy room, such as the kitchen or living room, and the outside jar in their yard or close to a driveway or street. Depending on the time of year, students may observe pollen grains as well as dust, pet hair, soot, and the like.

Media and Technology

 Transparencies "The Greenhouse Effect," 13, and "Exploring Climate Predictions," 14

 Interactive Student Tutorial CD-ROM E-5

 Exploring Physical Science Videodisc Unit 4, Side 2, "A Better Cool"

 Chapter 9

Answers to Self-Assessment

Caption Question

Figure 7 Water vapor, CO_2, and others

Program Resources

◆ **Teaching Resources** 5-1 Review and Reinforce, p. 125; 5-1 Enrich, p. 126
 Science Explorer Series *Weather and Climate* discusses climate change.

Performance Assessment

Drawing Have each student draw and label a diagram to explain one of the following processes: the formation of photochemical smog, the formation of acid rain, the ozone cycle, or the greenhouse effect.

Portfolio Students can save their diagrams in their portfolios.

You and Your Environment

How Does the Garden Grow?

Preparing for Inquiry

Key Concept Pollutants in water reduce seed germination and injure growing plants.

Skills Objectives Students will be able to
◆ measure given amounts of plain water and a polluted solution as the manipulated variable in an experiment;
◆ control all other variables;
◆ interpret data on seed germination and plant growth.

Time *Day 1:* 30 minutes; *Days 2–6:* 5 minutes each

Advance Planning Let tap water stand uncovered for 24–48 hours to allow chlorine to dissipate. Prepare each polluted solution by mixing 5 mL of the pollutant with 100 mL water (for acid use vinegar, for oil use vegetable oil).

Guiding Inquiry

Troubleshooting the Experiment
◆ Advise students to make sure the hypothesis is a testable statement.
◆ Monitor students' choices of places to put the two dishes.

Expected Outcome
All or most seeds in the control dish should germinate within two or three days and grow well. Some or all seeds in the pollutant dish will fail to germinate, and any sprouts will not grow well.

Analyze and Conclude
1. Answers will vary. Pollutants usually reduce the number of seeds that germinate.
2. Yes; seedlings in the pollutant dish did not grow as well as those in the control dish.
3. Answers will depend on hypotheses.
4. *Sample answer:* Fewer seeds would germinate, and the seedlings that did sprout would not grow into healthy plants.

You and Your Environment

HOW DOES THE GARDEN GROW?

Air pollution doesn't just affect the air. It can affect rain, which then falls on the land, harming organisms living there. In this lab you will investigate how pollutants affect plants.

Problem

How do pollutants affect seed growth?

Skills Focus

controlling variables, measuring, interpreting data

Materials

2 plastic petri dishes with lids   wax pencil
potting soil   acid solution
20 radish seeds   oil solution
detergent solution   salt solution
day-old tap water   masking tape
metric ruler

Procedure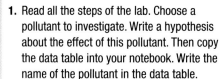

1. Read all the steps of the lab. Choose a pollutant to investigate. Write a hypothesis about the effect of this pollutant. Then copy the data table into your notebook. Write the name of the pollutant in the data table.
2. Write your initials on the lids of the petri dishes. Then write "Control" on one lid. Label the other lid with the name of your pollutant.
3. Fill each dish with potting soil. Do not pack down the soil.

4. Pour 10 mL of water into the control dish. Pour 10 mL of the pollutant solution into the pollutant dish. Lightly scatter 10 seeds on the soil surface in each dish.
5. Cover each dish with the correct lid. Tape the lids firmly in place. Store the dishes where they will receive light and will not be moved. Wash your hands with soap.
6. Once a day for the next five days, observe the seeds (do not open the lids). Record your observations in the data table. Use a metric ruler to measure the length of any roots or shoots that develop. If you do not observe any change, record that observation.

Analyze and Conclude

1. How many seeds germinated each day in the control dish? In the pollutant dish? How many seeds total germinated in each dish?
2. Did the seedlings grown under the two conditions differ? If so, how?
3. Did your results support your hypothesis? Explain.
4. **Apply** Predict what the effect would be if the pollutant you investigated reached a vegetable garden or farm.

Design an Experiment

Do you think the pollutant you studied has the same effect on all types of plants? Write a hypothesis, and design an experiment to test it. With your teacher's approval, carry out your plan.

	DATA TABLE			
Date	Number of Seeds That Germinated		Condition of Seedlings	
	Control	Pollutant	Control	Pollutant

Extending the Inquiry

Design an Experiment Students' plans should involve controlling all variables except the types of plants.

Program Resources

◆ **Teaching Resources** Chapter 5 Real-World Lab, pp. 135–136

Safety

Students should wear safety goggles and wash their hands well with soap after handling the seeds and soil. Review the safety guidelines in Appendix A.

SECTION 2 The Water Supply

DISCOVER • ACTIVITY

How Does the Water Change?

1. Shine a flashlight through a clear plastic cup of water.
2. Add 6 drops of milk to the water and stir.
3. Shine the flashlight through the cup again. Note any differences.

Think It Over

Observing Where in the cup of water is the milk located? Could you easily separate the milk from the water?

Most of Earth's surface is covered by some form of water. Oceans cover nearly three fourths of Earth's surface. Around the poles are vast sheets of ice. From space you cannot even see many parts of Earth because they are hidden behind clouds of tiny water droplets. It's hard to believe that water is a scarce resource in much of the world.

A Limited Supply

How can water be scarce when there is so much of it on Earth's surface? **The reason is that most of the water on Earth—about 97 percent—is salt water. Salt water cannot be used for drinking or watering crops.** People need fresh water for these purposes.

In addition, about three quarters of the fresh water on Earth is in the form of ice. This water is not available for people to use. Finally, the supplies of liquid fresh water that do exist are not always close to where people live. For example, many cities in the southwestern United States draw their drinking water from rivers hundreds of kilometers away. About half the people in the United States use **groundwater,** water stored in layers of soil and rock beneath Earth's surface.

> ### GUIDE FOR READING
>
> ◆ Why is fresh water a limited resource?
>
> ◆ What are the major sources of water pollution?
>
> *Reading Tip* As you read, identify sentences that support this statement: *Water is a scarce resource that must be protected.*

Figure 8 A view from space shows the abundance of water on Earth.

E ◆ 149

READING STRATEGIES

Reading Tip Students should identify the following sentences at a minimum: *Most of the water on Earth...is salt water. About three quarters of the fresh water on Earth is in the form of ice. The supplies of liquid fresh water that do exist are not always close to where people live. ...many places... never receive enough rain to meet their water needs.* Students may also identify related sentences that provide more details.

Program Resources

◆ **Teaching Resources** 5-2 Lesson Plan, p. 127; 5-2 Section Summary, p. 128

 Science Explorer Series *Earth's Waters,* Chapter 3, discusses the water supply and water pollution.

Media and Technology

🎧 **Audiotapes** English-Spanish Summary 5-2

SECTION 2 The Water Supply

Objectives

After completing the lesson, students will be able to

◆ identify factors that make most of Earth's water not useful to people;

◆ identify human sources of water pollution.

Key Terms groundwater, drought, water pollution, sewage, fertilizer, pesticide, sediments

1 Engage/Explore

Activating Prior Knowledge

Display a world map or globe, and ask: **How much of Earth's surface is covered by oceans?** (*Nearly 75%; accept all reasonable estimates.*) **Where else does some form of water exist?** (*In glaciers and polar ice, in freshwater lakes and rivers, in soil, deep underground in aquifers, and in the air as vapor. Record students' responses on the board, but do not comment on any omissions at this time.*)

• • • • • • • DISCOVER • • • • • • • •

Skills Focus observing
Materials *flashlight, clear plastic cup, water, plastic dropper, milk*
Time 5 minutes
Tips In Step 3, encourage students to shine the light downward at the cup and from different angles.
Expected Outcome The mixture will appear cloudy; solid particles in the milk will reflect the light so the beam does not pass easily through the cup.
Think It Over The milk is scattered evenly throughout the water and cannot be easily separated from it. (Students may realize that the milk's solid particles can be separated by evaporating the mixture.)

E ◆ 149

2 Facilitate

A Limited Supply

Building Inquiry Skills: Graphing

Materials *drawing compass, calculator (optional)*
Time 10–15 minutes

Provide students with the following data: salt water 97%; ice caps and glaciers 2.3%; groundwater 0.67%; other fresh water (lakes, rivers, soil, atmosphere) 0.03%. Then have each student use these data to create a circle graph. *(Salt water 349.2°, ice caps and glaciers 8.3°, groundwater 2.4°, other fresh water 0.1°; the "other" section should be only as wide as a pencil line.)* Students will readily see that usable fresh water—groundwater plus other fresh water—is only a small portion of all the water on Earth.
learning modality: logical/mathematical

TRY THIS

Skills Focus making models
Materials *15 mL water, plastic cup, spoon, graduated cylinder, food coloring, half teaspoon sugar*
Time 10 minutes plus 5 minutes for follow-up observations on several days
Tips Supply room-temperature water, not hot water, as hot water will produce a super-saturated solution.
Expected Outcome Sugar crystals and a tint from the food coloring will remain in the cup. These materials represent dissolved substances that are left behind when water evaporates in the water cycle. The liquid water changes to water vapor.
Extend Let students repeat the activity using other substances in the water, such as milk, salt, and baking soda. **learning modality: visual**

Figure 9 People obtain and store water in many ways. At left, a tower holds the water supply of a community in Bucks County, Pennsylvania. At right, women in the Yucatán in Mexico draw water from a well.

TRY THIS

Getting Clean

In this activity you will see how Earth's fresh water is purified in the water cycle.

1. Pour 15 mL of water into a plastic cup.
2. Add a few drops of food coloring and half a teaspoon of sugar. Stir until the sugar is dissolved.
3. Put the cup in the sunlight in a place where it will not be disturbed.
4. Check on the cup twice a day until all the water has evaporated. Observe what remains in the cup.

Making Models What do the sugar and food coloring represent? What happens to the water in this activity?

Renewing the Supply Fortunately, Earth's supply of fresh water is renewable. Water continually moves between the atmosphere and Earth's surface in the water cycle. Water evaporates from oceans, lakes, and rivers, becoming water vapor in the atmosphere. As the water evaporates, any dissolved substances are left behind. The pure water vapor condenses into tiny droplets which form clouds. When the droplets become large and heavy enough, they fall as precipitation.

Water Shortages Water shortages occur when people use water in an area faster than the water cycle can replace it. This is more likely to happen during a **drought,** a period when less rain than normal falls in an area. During a drought, people have to limit their water use. All unnecessary water uses may be banned. If the drought is severe, crops may die from lack of water.

Due to growing populations, many places in the world never receive enough rain to meet their water needs. They must obtain water from distant sources or by other means. For example, the desert nation of Saudi Arabia obtains more than half its fresh water by removing salt from ocean water.

☑ *Checkpoint* **What is a drought?**

Water Pollution

When fresh water supplies are scarce, pollution can be devastating. Any change to water that has a harmful effect on people or other living things is called **water pollution.** Some pollutants, such as iron and copper, make water unpleasant to drink or wash in. Other pollutants, such as mercury or benzene, can cause sickness or even death.

Background

Facts and Figures Scientists estimate that Earth has enough fresh water to meet the needs of its human population. However, Earth's usable water is not always found where and when it is needed. In many regions, there is a substantial amount of precipitation. But usable runoff in rivers and streams can vary greatly over the course of a year. For example, in India, 90% of the precipitation occurs during a wet season from June to September. During the rest of the year, there may be little runoff available for human use.

In other regions, longer periods of recurring drought are the problem. Droughts are frequent in the Sahel, a vast belt of semiarid grassland that lies south of the Sahara in Africa.

Most pollution is the result of human activities. Many activities—including agriculture, industry, construction, and mining—produce wastes that can end up in water.

If you did the Discover activity, you saw that a few drops of milk quickly spread throughout a cup of water. You could not tell where the milk first entered the water. In the same way, pollutants dissolve and move throughout a body of water. This is how pollution can affect areas far from its source.

Sewage The water and human wastes that are washed down sinks, toilets, and showers are called **sewage.** If sewage is not treated to kill disease-causing organisms, they quickly multiply. If untreated sewage mixes with water used for drinking or swimming, these organisms can make people very ill.

Even treated sewage can pollute. The wastes in the sewage can feed bacteria living in the water. As the bacteria multiply, they use up the oxygen in the water. Other organisms that need the oxygen, such as fish, cannot survive.

Agricultural Wastes Animal wastes and farm chemicals are also sources of pollution. Two examples are fertilizers and pesticides. **Fertilizers** are chemicals that provide nutrients to help crops grow better. But rain can wash fertilizers into ponds, where they cause algae to grow quickly. The algae soon cover the pond, blocking light from reaching plants in the pond. **Pesticides** are chemicals that kill crop-destroying organisms such as beetles or worms. However, pesticides can also harm other animals such as birds that feed in the sprayed fields.

Because agricultural chemicals are usually spread over a large, open area, it is hard to keep them from polluting nearby water. Even low levels of chemicals in the water can build up to harmful concentrations as they move through the food chain.

Figure 10 This plane is spraying crops with pesticides. *Relating Cause and Effect How might pesticides sprayed on a field affect fish that live in a nearby pond?*

E ◆ 151

Water Pollution

Including All Students
Some students may need more help in organizing the information on water pollution. Create a table on the chalkboard with these headings: *Type of Pollution, Examples of Pollutants, Effects.* Encourage students to review each subsection under the heading, Water Pollution, and then volunteer to help fill in the table. When the table is complete, students can make a copy of it to use as a study guide. **learning modality: verbal**

Inquiry Challenge
Materials *long tray or plastic box, sod, powdered drink mix, water, sprinkling can*
Time 15–20 minutes

Challenge small groups of students to create a model showing how agricultural chemicals that are spread on the ground can reach and pollute nearby bodies of fresh water. *(Sample model: Elevate one end of a tray slightly. Use sod to make a hill that slopes gently from the high end of the tray to the low end. Pour water into the low end to represent a lake. Scatter powdered drink mix over the sod to represent fertilizer or pesticide. Sprinkle water on the sod to represent rain. The lake will become tinted with the color of the drink mix.)* **cooperative learning**

Program Resources
◆ **Product Testing Activities by *Consumer Reports*** "Testing Bottled Water," pp. 1–8

Media and Technology
 Exploring Earth Science Videodisc
Unit 2, Side 2,
"What's in Our Tap?"

Chapter 5

Answers to Self-Assessment

☑ *Checkpoint*
A drought is a period when less rain than normal falls in an area.

Caption Question
Figure 10 The pesticides might be carried into the pond in runoff, poisoning the fish directly or poisoning organisms on which the fish depend for food.

Ongoing Assessment

Skills Check Have each student create a concept map that identifies the two types of agricultural pollutants described in the text, defines each term, and describes how the pollutant affects other organisms.
 Students can save their concept maps in their portfolios.

Water Pollution,
continued

Real-Life Learning

Encourage students to share with the class any observations they have made of examples of water pollution in their community. Have students describe the extent of the pollution and suggest possible sources for it. Then challenge all students to brainstorm ways to reduce each example of pollution. Encourage volunteers to write letters to the appropriate officials, identifying the incidents of pollution and offering suggestions for reducing the pollution. **learning modality: verbal**

Building Inquiry Skills: Making Models

ACTIVITY

Materials *plastic margarine tub or other small bowl, water, cooking oil, plastic dropper, 2 paper towels, graduated cylinder or small plastic cup calibrated in mL*

Time 15 minutes

To demonstrate how difficult it is to clean up an oil spill, have each student fill a small bowl halfway with water, add 25 mL of cooking oil, and then try to remove the oil using a dropper and a paper towel. Tell students to wipe out the small cup with one paper towel, discard that towel, and then put the oil they recover back into the cup so they can see how much they remove from the water. After students have worked for about 10 minutes, ask: **How much oil have you removed?** (*Answers will vary, but students probably will have recovered very little oil.*) **Is there still oil on the water? How can you tell?** (*Yes; the water surface still has an oily sheen.*) Remind students that unlike the cooking oil they are using in this model, crude oil is thick and sticky. (Soak up any remaining oil and oily water with paper towels, and place all disposable materials from the activity in a plastic bag for trash pickup.) **learning modality: kinesthetic**

Figure 11 Industrial processes and mining are two sources of chemical pollutants. At left, a chemical plant spills wastes into a river. At right, dissolved copper from a mine turns a stream turquoise.

Industry and Mining Chemical plants, paper and textile mills, and factories that use metals produce wastes that can pollute water. Mining sites are another source of metal wastes. Chemicals and metals can harm the living things in the polluted bodies of water. In addition, humans that drink the water or feed on these organisms are exposed to the pollution.

Sediments When water runs off bare ground, it turns a muddy brown color. This color is due to particles of rock, silt, and sand called **sediments.** Water that flows through places where the ground is disturbed, such as building sites and mines, can pick up large loads of sediments.

As sediments wash into bodies of water, the particles cover up the food sources, nesting sites, and eggs of organisms. By blocking sunlight in the water, the sediments prevent algae and plants from growing. This affects other organisms that rely on the algae and plants for food.

Oil and Gasoline One of the most dramatic forms of water pollution is an oil spill. You may have seen news reports showing beaches covered with tarry black oil, or of volunteers cleaning globs of oil from the feathers of birds. It can take many years for an area to recover from such a spill.

152 ♦ E

Background

Integrating Science To monitor water pollution, scientists sometimes observe the effects of pollution on organisms such as mollusks, birds, and fish. For example, analysis of mussels taken from coastal waters provides U.S. government scientists clues about toxic compounds in the water. In the Great Lakes region, Canadian scientists test the eggs of herring gulls for toxins.

Surprisingly, a species of tropical fish is used to monitor water pollution in England's Stour River. The fish normally emit 300–500 electric pulses per minute as a sensory aide. In polluted water, the fish increase the pulses to 1,000 per minute. Scientists keep the fishes in separate tanks, pump river water through the tanks, and then observe whether the fishes' emissions increase.

Another pollution problem is caused by oil and gasoline that leak out of underground storage tanks. Think of how many gas stations there are in your area. Each one has storage tanks below the street level to hold the gasoline. In the past, these tanks were often made of steel. Over time, they rusted and developed small holes. As the gasoline leaked out, it soaked into the soil and polluted the groundwater. The pollution was sometimes carried very far away from the leaking tank. Controlling this type of pollution has been difficult because the sources are hidden underground.

Heat Pollution is usually thought of as a substance added to water. But the addition of heat can also have a negative effect on a body of water. Sometimes factories or power plants release water that has been used to cool machinery. This heated water changes the temperature of the stream or lake into which it is released. This temperature change can kill plants, animals, and other organisms in the body of water. If you have ever kept an aquarium, you know that fish can only survive within a small temperature range. Today most power plants have cooling towers that release steam rather than hot water. In the next section, you will read about some other methods of preventing both water and air pollution.

Figure 12 A sheen of oil swirls around a maple leaf in a puddle.
Observing What characteristics of oil make it difficult to clean up?

Section 2 Review

1. Why isn't most of the water on Earth's surface available for people to use?
2. Name four types of human activities that can be sources of water pollution.
3. Explain why finding the source of water pollution can be difficult.
4. What is sewage? Why should sewage be treated before being released to the environment?
5. **Thinking Critically Relating Cause and Effect** In what way can heat pollute a body of water?

Check Your Progress
CHAPTER PROJECT 5

By now you should be gathering information to include in your product. Consider including the story of a historical event related to your topic in order to get your audience's interest. As you collect information, begin putting it in a logical order. Using an outline or a storyboard can help you organize your thoughts. (*Hint:* Be sure to keep your topic well focused. Air and water quality are very broad topics! Focusing your topic will help you stay on task and manage your time.)

Program Resources

◆ **Teaching Resources** 5-2 Review and Reinforce, p. 129; 5-2 Enrich, p. 130

Media and Technology

Interactive Student Tutorial CD-ROM E-5

Answers to Self-Assessment

Caption Question
Figure 12 Oil is thick, sticky, and "tarry."

---

3 Assess

Section 2 Review Answers

1. Most of the water on Earth is salty, and much of the fresh water is ice.
2. Agriculture, industry, construction, mining
3. The source may be far from the polluted water. Pollutants can dissolve and move throughout a body of water. Sources such as gasoline tanks may be hidden underground.
4. Sewage is the water and human wastes that are washed down sinks, toilets, and showers. Sewage contains disease-causing organisms that can mix with water used for drinking or swimming and make people ill.
5. Heated water from factories or power plants raises the temperature of bodies of water into which it is released. The temperature increase can kill plants, animals, and other organisms.

Check Your Progress
CHAPTER PROJECT 5

Students may need some help in narrowing their choices of topics to ones that will be suitable for their target audiences and for which there are adequate resource materials available. To help students organize the information they collect, review outlining procedures with the class.

Performance Assessment

Oral Presentation Call on students at random to name a type of water pollution. Call on other students to give examples and effects.

Concentrate on This!

Preparing for Inquiry

Key Concept Very low concentrations of pollutants may not be visible to the eye.

Skills Objectives Students will be able to
- measure given amounts of water and food coloring representing a pollutant;
- calculate the pollutant's concentration at different dilutions;
- observe solutions to determine whether the pollutant can be detected by sight.

Time 40 minutes

Alternative For students with physical disabilities that would make it difficult to measure the drops accurately, do Steps 2–8 as a small-group demonstration.

Guiding Inquiry

Troubleshooting the Experiment
- Students may need some help with the math calculations.

Expected Outcome
See Sample Data Table below.

Analyze and Conclude
1. The tint becomes lighter until it disappears (usually in Test Tube 5 or 6).
2. Yes; the food coloring molecules are so widely scattered that no tint is visible.
3. A "part" is one drop of food coloring.
4. *Million:* Tube 6; *billion:* Tube 9
5. *Sample answer:* Pollutants are often present in very low concentrations.

Extending the Inquiry

Design an Experiment Students may answer the first question by doing a calculation. *(5 ppm)* Make sure students' plans include one tube with a concentration of 5 ppm and one with a concentration of 10 parts per 10 million (1 ppm).

Concentrate on This!

Many pollutants have harmful effects even at very low concentrations. In this lab you will compare different concentrations of a pollutant in water.

Problem

Can you detect a pollutant in water at a very low concentration?

Materials

9 small test tubes	test tube rack
marker	food coloring
plastic dropper	water

Procedure

1. Read through the entire procedure. Write a prediction about the results you expect. Then copy the data table into your notebook.
2. Label nine test tubes 1 through 9.
3. Use a plastic dropper to add 9 drops of water to each test tube. Try to make all the drops about the same size.
4. Add 1 drop of food coloring to Test Tube 1. Record the total number of drops now in the test tube. Swirl the test tube gently to mix.
5. The concentration of food coloring in Test Tube 1 is 1 drop in 10 drops, or 1 part per 10. Record that concentration in the data table.
6. Now use the dropper to transfer 1 drop of the mixture from Test Tube 1 into Test Tube 2. Swirl Test Tube 2 to mix its contents.
7. Record the concentration in Test Tube 2. [*Hint:* The drop you just added had a concentration of 1 part per 10. When you dilute (water down) that drop to 1/10 of its strength, the new concentration is 1 part per (10 × 10).]
8. For test tubes 3 through 9, add 1 drop from the previous test tube. Record each new concentration in the data table.
9. Observe the water in each test tube. Record your observation. If you do not observe any color in a test tube, write "colorless."

Analyze and Conclude

1. How does the appearance of the water change from test tubes 1 through 9?
2. Food coloring consists of molecules of dye. Are there any food coloring molecules remaining in Test Tube 9? Explain.
3. What is meant by a "part" in this lab?
4. Which test tube has a concentration of 1 part per million? Which test tube has a concentration of 1 part per billion?
5. **Think About It** Why is parts per million a useful form of measurement when discussing environmental issues?

Design an Experiment

Which is more concentrated, a mixture with 5 parts per million, or 10 parts per 10 million? How different do the two mixtures appear? Use the ideas from this lab to design a plan to find out. Check your plan with your teacher.

DATA TABLE

Test Tube	Total Drops Added	Concentration of Food Coloring	Color
1			
2			

Sample Data Table

Test Tube	Total Drops Added	Concentration of Food Coloring	Color
1	10	1:10	very dark
2	10	1:100	dark
3	10	1:1,000	light
4	10	1:10,000	very light
5	10	1:100,000	hint of color
6	10	1:1,000,000	colorless
7	10	1:10,000,000	colorless
8	10	1:100,000,000	colorless
9	10	1:1,000,000,000	colorless

Program Resources

- **Teaching Resources** Chapter 5 Skills Lab, pp. 137–139

Safety

Students should wear aprons and safety goggles. Review the safety guidelines in Appendix A.

Finding Pollution Solutions

DISCOVER ·········•••••••••••••••·········ACTIVITY

Can You Remove the Tea?

1. Pour some cooled herbal tea into a plastic cup. Observe the color of the tea.

2. Place a paper filter in a funnel. Fill it halfway with crushed charcoal. Put the funnel on top of another plastic cup.

3. Slowly pour the tea through the funnel so that it collects in the cup.

4. Observe the filtered liquid.

Think It Over

Developing Hypotheses Suggest an explanation for any changes you observe in the tea after pouring it through the funnel.

O nly 50 years ago, the French Broad River in North Carolina was a river to avoid. Its color changed daily, depending on the dyes being used at a nearby blanket factory. Towns dumped raw sewage into the water. Sediment and fertilizers from farms washed into the river with every rainfall. The few fish were unhealthy and covered with sores. Mostly, the river was a home for wastes and bacteria—certainly not a place for people to play. Today, however, the river is a popular white-water rafting spot. Fish thrive in the clear water. The blanket factory and other plants have stopped releasing wastes into the river. The towns have sewage treatment plants. And ponds catch the runoff from farm fields before it reaches the river.

This story shows that pollution problems can be solved. People near the river still carry out the same activities—farming, building houses, and even making blankets. But by changing the way they do these things, they have stopped the pollution.

In the United States, laws regulate the amount of certain pollutants that can be released into the environment. Laws also state how these pollutants must be handled. The major federal laws that control air and water quality are the Clean Air Act and the Clean Water Act. These laws also encourage the development of new technology to reduce pollution.

GUIDE FOR READING

◆ How can technology help control air pollution?

◆ How can technology help control water pollution?

Reading Tip Before you read, use the section headings to make an outline. Leave space in your outline to take notes.

Rafters enjoying the clean water of the French Broad River

READING STRATEGIES

Reading Tip Students' outlines should include the following headings: *I. Reducing Air Pollution; A. Emissions Controls; B. CFC Substitutes; II. Cleaning Up the Water; A. Sewage Treatment; B. Oil and Gasoline; C. Industrial and Agricultural Chemicals; III. What Can You Do?* Suggest that students also include the vocabulary terms below the appropriate headings.

Program Resources

◆ **Teaching Resources** 5-3 Lesson Plan, p. 131; 5-3 Section Summary, p. 132

◆ **Interdisciplinary Exploration Series** "Where River Meets Sea," pp. 35–37

Media and Technology

 Audiotapes English-Spanish Summary 5-3

INTEGRATING TECHNOLOGY

SECTION 3 Finding Pollution Solutions

Objectives

After completing the lesson, students will be able to

◆ describe ways that technology can help control air pollution;

◆ describe ways that technology can help control water pollution.

Key Terms scrubber, catalytic converter, primary treatment, secondary treatment

1 Engage/Explore

Activating Prior Knowledge

Ask students: **What happens to the waste water from your family's home?** *(Students' houses or apartment buildings may be connected to a municipal sewage system or have a private septic system. If students do not know, encourage them to find out.)*

········· DISCOVER ·········

Skills Focus developing hypotheses

Materials *cooled herbal tea, 2 plastic cups, paper filter, funnel, crushed charcoal*

Time 10 minutes

Tips Use a tea that has a distinct color, and brew a strong solution. Using powdered iced tea mix in cool water is effective.

Expected Outcome The filtered tea will be lighter in color than the unfiltered tea.

Think It Over The charcoal and paper filter trapped tiny particles in the tea, making its color lighter.

2 Facilitate

Reducing Air Pollution

Sharpen your Skills

Graphing

Materials *graph paper, 2 pens or pencils of different colors*

Time *20 minutes*

Tips Point out that chlorine is the active ingredient in ordinary household bleach. If students question how chlorine gets into the atmosphere, let them review the last paragraph on page 145. Explain that when CFC molecules drift high into the atmosphere, the sun's ultraviolet radiation destroys them, releasing chlorine in the process. This chlorine affects the ozone layer.

Expected Outcome *Sample paragraph:* With the ban, the chlorine level in 2005 is predicted to be less than 1.5 times the level in 1985. Without the ban, the 2005 level would be 5 times the 1985 level and nearly 3 times the 2005 level with the ban. Although the level increased from 1985 to 1995 with the ban, it is expected to decrease through 2005.

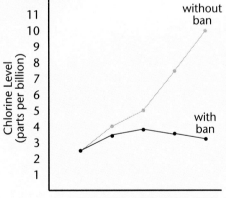

Extend Suggest that students calculate the percentage of increase or decrease each year with and without the ban. Also ask: **Why is a line graph, not a bar graph, appropriate for these data?** (*A line graph shows changes in one thing over time; a bar graph compares different things at the same point in time.*) **learning modality: logical/ mathematical**

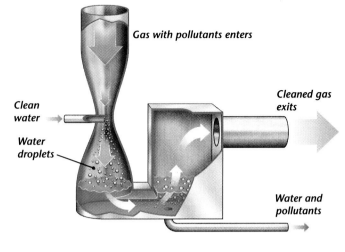

Figure 13 A smokestack scrubber removes pollutants such as sulfur dioxide from emissions. The dirty gas passes through a tube containing water droplets. Pollutants dissolve in the water, leaving clean gas to flow out of the chamber. The dirty water still must be properly disposed of.

Sharpen your Skills

Graphing ACTIVITY

The table below shows a scientist's predictions of chlorine levels in the atmosphere with and without the ban on CFCs. Make a line graph of the data, using two different colors. Write a short paragraph describing the results.

Year	Chlorine Level (parts per billion)	
	With Ban	Without Ban
1985	2.5	2.5
1990	3.5	4.0
1995	3.8	5.0
2000	3.6	7.5
2005	3.4	10.0

Reducing Air Pollution

The Clean Air Act has resulted in the development of technology to control air pollution. **The major role of technology in controlling air pollution is to reduce emissions.**

Emissions Controls At one time, industries dealt with emissions by building tall smokestacks. The stacks released wastes high in the air, where they could blow away. But the pollutants still ended up somewhere. Now factories place devices in the stacks to treat emissions. For example, a filter can trap particles of ash. The device in Figure 13, called a **scrubber,** removes pollutants from emissions using a stream of water droplets. Pollutants dissolve in the water and fall into a container.

Cars and trucks now contain pollution control devices. For example, a **catalytic converter** is a device that reduces emissions of carbon monoxide, hydrocarbons, and nitrogen oxides. This device causes the gases to react, forming less harmful carbon dioxide and water.

Laws can ensure that people use pollution-control devices. For example, in many states, cars must pass emissions tests. The state of California's strict emissions-testing laws have helped reduce the smog problem in Los Angeles in recent years.

CFC Substitutes When a pollutant is banned by law, people must find substitutes for the banned substance. For example, in 1990 many nations agreed to stop using most CFCs by the year 2000. Scientists immediately began to search for substitutes for these chemicals. Refrigerators and air conditioners were redesigned to use less harmful substances. Researchers developed new ways to make products such as plastic foam without using CFCs. As a result of this work, fewer CFCs should enter the atmosphere after 2000 than in the past.

Background

History of Science Mexico City, one of the world's largest cities, has the worst air pollution of any city. In 1990, the city instituted a plan to improve air quality. According to the plan, vehicles equipped with catalytic converters and burning unleaded fuel would replace older vehicles. The city also implemented periodic checks of exhaust emissions and driving restrictions for periods when air quality is especially bad.

Although levels of lead, sulfur dioxide, and carbon monoxide in the air have been reduced, the city's plan has not been a complete success. Critics charge that the city government does not enforce the laws that combat air pollution strictly enough. Unfortunately, Mexico City's air quality in 1996 was worse than it had been a decade earlier.

Cleaning Up the Water

Technology can also help control water pollution. **Two ways to reduce water pollution are to treat wastes so that they are less harmful, and to find substitutes for pollutants.**

Sewage Treatment   Most communities treat wastewater before returning it to the environment. A typical sewage plant handles the waste in several steps. **Primary treatment** removes solid materials from the wastewater. During primary treatment, the water passes through filters. Then it is held in tanks where heavy particles settle out. **Secondary treatment** involves using bacteria to break down wastes. Finally, the water is treated with chlorine to kill disease-causing organisms.

The town of Arcata, California, treats sewage in a creative way. Wastewater flows into ponds containing algae that begin to break down the sewage. Then the water flows into artificial marshes lined with cattails and bulrushes. These plants and the bacteria in the marsh filter and clean the water. These marshes are also habitats for many mollusks, fish, and birds. Trails for walking and biking encourage people to enjoy the marshes as well. After two months in this system, the wastewater is cleaner than the bay into which it is released!

Oil and Gasoline   Oil is a pollutant that nature can handle in small amounts. Bacteria that break down oil live in the ocean. When oil is present, the bacteria multiply quickly as they feed on it. As the oil disappears, the bacteria population dies down. But in the case of a very large spill, many organisms are affected before the balance in the ecosystem is restored.

Gasoline or oil that leaks from an underground tank is hard to clean up. If the pollution has not spread far, the soil around the tank can be removed. But pollution that reaches groundwater may be carried far away. Groundwater can be pumped to the surface, treated, and then returned underground. This can take many years.

Figure 14 A bicyclist in Arcata, California, may not even be aware that this peaceful marsh is also a sewage treatment system.
Applying Concepts What are the two major sewage treatment steps?

Figure 15 Workers struggle to clean oil from a rocky beach.

Chapter 5   **E ◆ 157**

Answers to Self-Assessment

Caption Question

Figure 14 The two steps are primary treatment, which removes solid materials, and secondary treatment, which uses bacteria to break down wastes.

Cleaning Up the Water

Real-Life Learning

Take the class on a field trip to visit your community's wastewater treatment plant. Before the visit, have students brainstorm a list of questions they would like to have answered. Ask the plant guide to pay particular attention to those questions during the tour. **learning modality: visual**

Cultural Diversity

Time 15–30 minutes

Point out to students that emission controls, wastewater treatment plants, and other technological devices to reduce air and water pollution are very expensive. Individuals and businesses in the United States and other developed countries are more able to afford these devices than those in developing countries, where people must work very hard simply to supply their most basic needs. In developing countries, pollution control may seem like a luxury. As one example, share the information in Background on the previous page. Then pose the following question to the class: **Imagine you're a taxi driver in Mexico City. You have to work twelve hours a day, seven days a week, just to earn enough money to pay for your family's food, clothing, housing, and other basic needs. Now city officials tell you that you have to replace your old taxi with a newer one that doesn't release so much pollution. How would you feel? What would you do?** Divide the class into small groups, and let students discuss the issue from the viewpoints of both the taxi driver and the officials who are trying to improve air quality. Have students share their ideas in a follow-up class discussion. **learning modality: verbal**

Ongoing Assessment

Drawing Have each student draw a flowchart to identify and describe the steps in the sewage treatment process. Students can save their flowcharts in their portfolios.

Figure 16 These teens are planting trees in a park in Austin, Texas. Planting trees is one way to improve air quality. Trees absorb carbon dioxide from the air and produce oxygen.

Industrial and Agricultural Chemicals Instead of releasing wastes to the environment, industries can recycle their wastes to recover useful materials. Once such programs are underway, companies often find they save money as well as reduce pollution. Others change their processes to produce less waste or less harmful waste. For example, some industries use natural fruit acids as cleaning agents rather than toxic solvents. Likewise, many farmers are finding alternatives to toxic pesticides and fertilizers for their crops.

What Can You Do?

You may not think there is much you can do to reduce air and water pollution. But in fact, some small changes in people's behavior can make a big difference.

You can help reduce air pollution by reducing certain types of energy use. Much air pollution is a result of fuels that are burned to provide electricity and transportation. Using less energy conserves fuel resources and also reduces pollution. When you take public transportation, walk, or ride a bicycle, there is one fewer car on the road. This means there are fewer emissions that contribute to smog and the greenhouse effect. In the next chapter, you will read how you can use less energy for these purposes.

It is also easy to prevent water pollution at home. Some common household water pollutants are paint and paint thinner, motor oil, and garden chemicals. You can avoid causing water pollution by never pouring these chemicals down the drain. Instead, save these materials for your community's next hazardous household waste collection day.

 Section 3 Review

1. What role does technology usually play in controlling air pollution?
2. In what two basic ways can technology help control water pollution?
3. Describe one smokestack device that can help reduce emissions from factories.
4. Explain how small oil spills can be cleaned up naturally.
5. **Thinking Critically Making Generalizations** Explain how laws can play a part in reducing pollution.

Check Your Progress **CHAPTER PROJECT 5**

Now you are ready to make your finished product using the information you have gathered. Keep in mind the age group of your audience when you are considering word choice, number and style of pictures, music, and other parts of your product. (*Hint:* Don't forget to include steps that members of your audience can take to be part of the solution. Make sure these suggestions are appropriate for their age.)

SECTION 1 Air Pollution

Key Ideas

◆ Air pollutants can be in the form of particles or gases.

◆ The major sources of photochemical smog are the gases emitted by motor vehicles.

◆ Sources of indoor air pollution include smoke, dust, pet hair, asbestos, and other substances. Two dangerous pollutants that are very difficult to detect are carbon monoxide and radon.

◆ Certain gases in Earth's atmosphere prevent heat from escaping back into space.

◆ The ozone layer protects people and other living things from the effects of too much ultraviolet radiation.

◆ Most scientists base their climate predictions on computer models that calculate the effects of changes in the atmosphere.

Key Terms

air pollution	acid rain
emissions	ozone layer
photochemical smog	chlorofluorocarbons
ozone	greenhouse effect
temperature inversion	global warming

SECTION 2 The Water Supply

Key Ideas

◆ Most of Earth's water—about 97 percent—is salt water.

◆ People and many other organisms require fresh water to carry out their life processes.

◆ Although there are some natural sources of water pollution, most pollution is the result of human activities. Agriculture, industry, construction, and mining all produce wastes that can end up in water.

Key Terms

groundwater	fertilizer
drought	pesticide
water pollution	sediments
sewage	

SECTION 3 Finding Pollution Solutions
INTEGRATING TECHNOLOGY

Key Ideas

◆ The major role of technology in controlling air pollution is to reduce emissions.

◆ Two basic ways to reduce water pollution are to treat wastes so that they are less harmful, and to find substitutes for pollutants.

Key Terms

scrubber	primary treatment
catalytic converter	secondary treatment

USING THE INTERNET

ACTIVITY

www.science-explorer.phschool.com

Chapter 5 **E ◆ 159**

Program Resources

◆ **Teaching Resources** Chapter 5 Project Scoring Rubric, p. 122; Chapter 5 Performance Assessment pp. 208–210; Chapter 5 Test, pp. 211–214

Media and Technology

Interactive Student Tutorial CD-ROM E-5

Computer Test Bank Test E-5

Reviewing Content:

Multiple Choice
1. b 2. b 3. c 4. b 5. b

True or False
6. true 7. true 8. upper 9. salt
10. bacteria

Checking Concepts

11. Photochemical smog can cause breathing and lung problems and harm the body's defenses against infection.
12. Coal and oil produce nitrogen oxides and sulfur oxides when they are burned. These gases react with water vapor in the air to form nitric acid and sulfuric acid. The acids return to Earth's surface dissolved in precipitation.
13. Water vapor and carbon dioxide act like windows, allowing sunlight to reach Earth's surface but preventing the heat from escaping back into space.
14. A drought is a period when less rain than normal falls on an area. During a drought, people have to limit their water use. If the drought is severe, people may have to travel long distances to get water, and crops may die.
15. Runoff from rain can wash fertilizers into lakes, rivers, ponds, and streams, where they cause an overgrowth of algae.
16. Motor vehicles can be equipped with catalytic converters, which reduce carbon monoxide emissions.
17. Bacteria that normally live in the ocean feed on the oil and break it down.
18. Students' newscasts should focus on the points presented in *Exploring Climate Predictions,* page 147.

Thinking Visually

19. **a.** outdoor **b.** and **c.** *Any two:* carbon monoxide, radon, pet hair/feathers, asbestos, fumes from carpets or furniture **d.** and **e.** *Any two:* smog, acid rain, ash, carbon monoxide, nitrogen oxide, ozone, nitric acid, sulfuric acid. Sample title: Air Pollution

Applying Skills

20. *Beginning:* 328 ppm; *Year 20:* 363 ppm
21. By 35 ppm
22. *Sample answers:* In the summer, more plants are growing and removing

Reviewing Content

For more review of key concepts, see the Interactive Student Tutorial CD-ROM.

Multiple Choice
Choose the letter of the best answer.

1. Particles and gases released into the air are
   a. sewage.   b. emissions.
   c. scrubbers.   d. acid rain.
2. A deadly gas formed when fuels are incompletely burned is
   a. ozone.
   b. carbon monoxide.
   c. photochemical smog.
   d. CFCs.
3. Which gas is thought to be the cause of global warming?
   a. radon   b. ozone
   c. carbon dioxide   d. carbon monoxide
4. The water and waste materials washed down toilets and sinks are called
   a. pesticides.
   b. sewage.
   c. industrial chemicals.
   d. fertilizers.
5. A technology that reduces carbon monoxide emissions from vehicles is a
   a. scrubber.
   b. catalytic converter.
   c. filter.
   d. CFC substitute.

True or False
If the statement is true, write true. If it is false, change the underlined word or words to make the statement true.

6. Most photochemical smog is produced by <u>motor vehicles</u>.
7. The presence of a layer of warm air that traps pollutants close to Earth's surface is called a <u>temperature inversion</u>.
8. Ozone in the <u>lower</u> atmosphere protects people from ultraviolet radiation.
9. About 97 percent of Earth's water is <u>fresh</u> water.
10. Oil in the ocean will eventually be broken down by <u>fish</u>.

Checking Concepts

11. Describe some possible health effects of photochemical smog.
12. How does acid rain form?
13. What role do water vapor and carbon dioxide play in the greenhouse effect?
14. What is a drought? What effects could a drought have on people?
15. Explain how fertilizers from a farm might pollute a nearby river.
16. What is one way to reduce emissions from cars and trucks?
17. How can a small oil spill in the ocean be naturally cleaned up?
18. **Writing to Learn** Write a television newscast explaining how one of the following factors is related to climate predictions: clouds, forests, oceans, emissions.

Thinking Visually

19. **Concept Map** Copy the concept map below about air pollution onto a separate sheet of paper. Then complete it and add a title. (For more on concept maps, see the Skills Handbook).

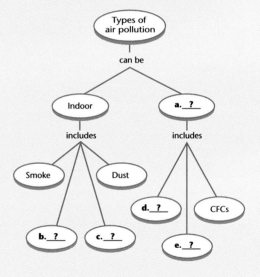

carbon dioxide from the air. Also, more heating fuels are burned in the winter, so carbon dioxide emissions increase.

Thinking Critically

23. Both radon and carbon monoxide are gases that pollute indoor air and are difficult to detect. Carbon monoxide forms when wood, coal, oil, or gas is incompletely burned. Radon is formed naturally by certain types of rocks underground and is radioactive. Carbon monoxide can kill people if it reaches certain

levels. Radon is thought to cause cancer over long periods of time.
24. More ultraviolet light would be blocked and prevented from reaching Earth's surface. Sunburn and cases of eye diseases and cancer caused by ultraviolet radiation would decrease.
25. In cities; the major sources of photochemical smog are the gases emitted by motor vehicles, which are more concentrated in cities than in rural areas.

Applying Skills

Use the graph to answer Questions 20–22.

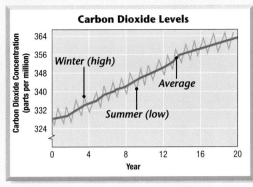

Carbon Dioxide Levels

Carbon Dioxide Concentration (parts per million)

364
356
348
340
332
324

Winter (high)

Average

Summer (low)

0   4   8   12   16   20

Year

20. Interpreting Data What was the average level of carbon dioxide in the atmosphere at the beginning of the study? What was the average level of carbon dioxide in Year 20 of the study?

21. Calculating How much did the average level of carbon dioxide increase during the study period?

22. Developing Hypotheses In each year of the study, the winter level of carbon dioxide was higher than the summer level. Suggest an explanation for this.

Thinking Critically

23. Comparing and Contrasting How are radon and carbon monoxide alike? How are they different?

24. Predicting What effect might a sudden increase in the amount of ozone in the ozone layer have?

25. Making Generalizations Would you expect the levels of photochemical smog to be worse in cities or in rural areas? Explain your answer.

Performance Assessment

CHAPTER PROJECT 5 Wrap Up

Present Your Project Share your finished project with a group of younger students. As the children view or play with the product, notice what parts they find most interesting. After they are finished, ask them what they liked and didn't like about the product. What do they remember most?

Reflect and Record In your project notebook, write a short evaluation of your product. What parts of the product do you feel worked best? Which ones were most difficult? What challenges did you face in communicating information in the form you chose to work with?

Getting Involved

In Your School Conduct a school air-quality audit. With your classmates, create a plan for evaluating your school's air quality. Check your plan with your teacher before beginning. You might survey the school for possible sources of pollutants, including dangerous gases and substances that could cause allergies. You could also measure the air temperature in different areas at different times of the day. Prepare a summary of your findings.

Program Resources

◆ **Inquiry Skills Activity Book** Provides teaching and review of all inquiry skills

---

Performance Assessment

CHAPTER PROJECT 5 Wrap Up

Present Your Project
Before they present their final products to younger students, let students present them to another group of students as a "trial run." Encourage students to offer positive comments and tactful suggestions for improvement. This practice session will also give you an opportunity to assess students' work. Distribute Chapter 5 Project Worksheet 2, page 121 in Teaching Resources, so students can elicit feedback from the younger students.

Reflect and Record Encourage students to incorporate comments from Worksheet 2 into their self-evaluations.

Getting Involved

In Your School This activity is well-suited for cooperative learning, with different students or groups surveying different areas of the school. Encourage students to devise some sort of air-particle detector, such as a loop of clear tape attached to an index card, or a plastic petri dish or microscope slide covered with a thin layer of petroleum jelly. Arrange to have students present their summary to the school principal, maintenance supervisor, or other official.

Sections	Time	Student Edition Activities	Other Activities
CHAPTER PROJECT 6 **Energy Audit** p. 163	Ongoing (2–3 weeks)	Check Your Progress, pp. 170, 178, 185 Wrap Up, p. 193	
1 Fossil Fuels pp. 164–170 ◆ Explain how fuels provide energy. ◆ List the three major fossil fuels. ◆ Explain why fossil fuels are considered nonrenewable resources.	2–3 periods/ 1–1½ blocks	**Discover** What's in a Piece of Coal?, p. 164 **Sharpen Your Skills** Graphing, p. 166	TE Inquiry Challenge, p. 166 TE Building Inquiry Skills: Classifying, p. 167 TE Building Inquiry Skills: Observing, p. 168 TE Building Inquiry Skills: Calculating, p. 169
2 Renewable Sources of Energy pp. 171–180 ◆ Explain how the sun provides energy and describe ways to collect this energy. ◆ Identify and describe various sources of energy not dependent on fossil fuels.	4–5 periods/ 2–2½ blocks	**Discover** Can You Capture Solar Energy?, p. 171 **Real-World Lab: How It Works** Cooking With Sunshine, p. 179	TE Integrating Technology, p. 172 TE Real-Life Learning, p. 173 TE Building Inquiry Skills: Making Models, p. 175 TE Demonstration, p. 177 IES "Fate of the Rain Forest," pp. 16–19 ISLM E-6, "Solar Heating"
3 *INTEGRATING CHEMISTRY* **Nuclear Energy** pp. 181–185 ◆ Describe nuclear fission and nuclear fusion reactions. ◆ Explain how a nuclear power plant produces electricity.	1–2 periods/ ½–1 block	**Discover** Why Do They Fall?, p. 181 **Try This** Shoot the Nucleus, p. 182 **Sharpen Your Skills** Calculating, p. 183	TE Building Inquiry Skills: Making Models, p. 182 TE Real-Life Learning, p. 184 TE Inquiry Challenge, p. 184
4 Energy Conservation pp. 186–190 ◆ List two ways to ensure that there will be enough energy for the future. ◆ Identify things that individuals can do to conserve energy.	2–3 periods/ 1–1½ blocks	**Skills Lab: Designing Experiments** Keeping Comfortable, p. 186 **Discover** Which Bulb Is More Efficient?, p. 187 **Science at Home,** p. 190	TE Building Inquiry Skills: Calculating, p. 188 TE Building Inquiry Skills: Observing, p. 189
Study Guide/Chapter Review pp. 191–193	1 period/ ½ block		ISAB Provides teaching and review of all inquiry skills

For Standard or Block Schedule The Resource Pro® CD-ROM gives you maximum flexibility for planning your instruction for any type of schedule. Resource Pro® contains Planning Express®, an advanced scheduling program, as well as the entire contents of the Teaching Resources and the Computer Test Bank.

CHAPTER PLANNING GUIDE

Program Resources	Assessment Strategies	Media and Technology
TR Chapter 6 Project Teacher Notes, pp. 140–141 TR Chapter 6 Project Overview and Worksheet, pp. 142–145 TR Chapter 6 Project Scoring Rubric, p. 146	SE Performance Assessment: Chapter 6 Project Wrap Up, p.193 TE Check Your Progress, pp. 170, 178, 185 TE Performance Assessment: Chapter 6 Project Wrap Up, p. 193 TR Chapter 6 Project Scoring Rubric, p. 146	🌐 Science Explorer Internet Site
TR 6-1 Lesson Plan, p. 147 TR 6-1 Section Summary, p. 148 TR 6-1 Review and Reinforce, p. 149 TR 6-1 Enrich, p. 150 SES Book H, *Earth's Waters,* Chapter 5	SE Section 1 Review, p. 170 TE Ongoing Assessment, pp. 165, 167, 169 TE Performance Assessment, p. 170 TR 6-1 Review and Reinforce, p. 149	📀 Exploring Earth Science Videodisc, Unit 6 Side 2, "Our Passion for Driving"; "Power for the People" 🎧 Audiotapes, English-Spanish Summary 6-1 📽 Transparency 15, "An Electric Power Plant" 💿 Interactive Student Tutorial CD-ROM, E-6
TR 6-2 Lesson Plan, p. 151 TR 6-2 Section Summary, p. 152 TR 6-2 Review and Reinforce, p. 153 TR 6-2 Enrich, p. 154 TR Chapter 6 Real-World Lab, pp. 163–164 SES Book I, *Weather and Climate,* Chapter 2 SES Book H, *Earth's Waters,* Chapter 4 SES Book F, *Inside Earth,* Chapter 3	SE Section 2 Review, p. 178 SE Analyze and Conclude, p. 179 TE Ongoing Assessment, pp. 173, 175, 177 TE Performance Assessment, p. 178 TR 6-2 Review and Reinforce, p. 153	📀 Exploring Physical Science Videodisc, Unit 4 Side 2, "Wired to the Sun" 🎧 Audiotapes, English-Spanish Summary 6-2 📽 Transparencies 16, "Exploring a Solar House"; 17, "A Geothermal Power Plant" 💿 Interactive Student Tutorial CD-ROM, E-6
TR 6-3 Lesson Plan, p. 155 TR 6-3 Section Summary, p. 156 TR 6-3 Review and Reinforce, p. 157 TR 6-3 Enrich, p. 158	SE Section 3 Review, p. 185 TE Ongoing Assessment, p. 183 TE Performance Assessment, p. 185 TR 6-3 Review and Reinforce, p. 157	🎧 Audiotapes, English-Spanish Summary 6-3 📽 Transparencies 18, "Nuclear Fission"; 19, "A Nuclear Power Plant"; 20, "Nuclear Fusion" 💿 Interactive Student Tutorial CD-ROM, E-6
TR Chapter 6 Skills Lab, pp. 165–167 TR 6-4 Lesson Plan, p. 159 TR 6-4 Section Summary, p. 160 TR 6-4 Review and Reinforce, p. 161 TR 6-4 Enrich, p. 162	SE Analyze and Conclude, p. 186 SE Section 4 Review, p. 190 TE Ongoing Assessment, p. 189 TE Performance Assessment, p. 190 TR 6-4 Review and Reinforce, p. 161	🎧 Audiotapes, English-Spanish Summary 6-4 💿 Interactive Student Tutorial CD-ROM, E-6
TR Chapter 6 Performance Assessment, pp. 215–217 TR Chapter 6 Test, pp. 218–221	SE Chapter 6 Review, pp. 191–193 TR Chapter 6 Performance Assessment, pp. 215–217 TR Chapter 6 Test, pp. 218–221 CTB Test E-6	💿 Interactive Student Tutorial CD-ROM, E-6 💾 Computer Test Bank, Test E-6

Key: **SE** Student Edition **TE** Teacher's Edition **TR** Teaching Resources
CTB Computer Test Bank **SES** Science Explorer Series Text **ISLM** Integrated Science Laboratory Manual
ISAB Inquiry Skills Activity Book **PTA** Product Testing Activities by *Consumer Reports* **IES** Interdisciplinary Explorations Series

Meeting the National Science Education Standards and AAAS Benchmarks

National Science Education Standards	Benchmarks for Science Literacy	Unifying Themes
Science As Inquiry (Content Standard A) ◆ **Design and conduct a scientific investigation** Students investigate how solar energy can be used to cook food and compare how well different materials stop heat transfer. *(Real-World Lab; Skills Lab)* ◆ **Use appropriate tools and techniques to gather, analyze, and interpret data** Students evaluate energy use in their school. *(Chapter Project)* **Physical Science** (Content Standard B) ◆ **Transfer of energy** Fuel provides energy as the result of a chemical change. Nuclear reactions convert matter into energy. Certain materials can slow the transfer of heat. *(Sections 1, 3, 4; Skills Lab)* **Science and Technology** (Content Standard E) ◆ **Understandings about science and technology** The energy stored in fuels can be used to generate electricity. Technologies to capture and use solar energy, wind and water power, and alternative fuels help meet energy needs. Nuclear fission can be used to generate electricity. People have developed technologies that improve efficiency and reduce energy use. *(Sections 1, 2, 3, 4; Science & History)* **Science in Personal and Social Perspectives** (Content Standard F) ◆ **Science and technology in society** Students evaluate the benefits and costs of hydroelectric dams. *(Science and Society)*	**1B Scientific Inquiry** Students evaluate energy use in their school, investigate how solar energy can be used to cook food, and compare how well different materials stop heat transfer. *(Chapter Project; Real-World Lab; Skills Lab)* **3A Technology and Science** People have developed technologies that improve energy efficiency and reduce energy use. *(Section 4; Science & History)* **3B Designs and Systems** Control rods are used to control fission reactions in nuclear reactors. Certain materials can slow the transfer of heat. *(Section 3; Skills Lab)* **3C Issues in Technology** Students suggest ways to save energy in their school. Students evaluate the benefits and costs of hydroelectric dams. Reducing energy use is called energy conservation. *(Chapter Project; Science and Society; Section 4)* **8C Energy Sources and Use** The three major fossil fuels are coal, oil, and natural gas. The sun, wind, water, tides, biomass material, Earth's interior, and hydrogen are renewable sources of energy. Controlled nuclear fission reactions can be used to generate electricity. *(Sections 1, 2, 3; Real-World Lab)*	◆ **Energy** Students evaluate energy use in their school. A fuel is a substance that provides a form of energy as the result of a chemical reaction. The sun, wind, water, tides, biomass material, Earth's interior, and hydrogen are renewable sources of energy. Nuclear reactions convert matter into energy. Reducing energy use is called energy conservation. *(Chapter Project; Sections 1, 2, 3, 4; Real-World Lab; Skills Lab; Science & History)* ◆ **Patterns of Change** Over time, heat and pressure changed dead organisms into fossil fuels. When a neutron hits a nucleus, the nucleus splits apart into two smaller nuclei and three neutrons. *(Sections 1, 3)* ◆ **Scale and Structure** Hydrocarbons are energy-rich chemical compounds that contain carbon and hydrogen atoms. The central core of an atom that contains protons and neutrons is called a nucleus. *(Sections 1, 3)* ◆ **Stability** A renewable source of energy is one that is constantly being supplied. Radioactive wastes remain dangerous for many thousands of years. *(Sections 2, 3)* ◆ **Systems and Interactions** Electric power plants generate electricity by converting energy from one form to another. People have developed technologies that improve energy efficiency and reduce energy use. *(Sections 1, 4; Science and Society)* ◆ **Unity and Diversity** Energy sources can be renewable or nonrenewable. Fission and fusion are two types of nuclear reactions. *(Sections 1, 2, 3)*

Media and Technology

Exploring Earth Science Videodiscs

◆ **Section 1** "Our Passion for Driving" examines the impact of the automobile on the environment. "Power for the People" shows the advantages and disadvantages of fossil fuels and explores the use of alternate power sources.

Exploring Physical Science Videodiscs

◆ **Section 2** "Wired to the Sun" tours a solar-powered home.

Interactive Student Tutorial CD-ROM

◆ **Chapter Review** Interactive questions help students to self-assess their mastery of key chapter concepts.

Student Edition Connection Strategies

◆ **Section 1** Integrating Physics, pp. 164–165
Integrating Technology, pp. 167, 168

◆ **Section 2** Integrating Technology, p. 172
Social Studies Connection, p. 175
Science and Society, p. 180

◆ **Section 3** Integrating Chemistry, pp. 181–185

◆ **Section 4** Science & History, pp. 188–189

USING THE INTERNET

www.science-explorer.phschool.com

Visit the Science Explorer Internet site to find an up-to-date activity for Chapter 6 of *Environmental Science*.

Activity	Time (minutes)	Materials Quantities for one work group	Skills
Section 1			
Discover, p. 164	10	**Nonconsumable** lignite coal, hand lens	Observing
Sharpen Your Skills, p. 166	15	**Nonconsumable** drawing compass, protractor, calculator (optional)	Graphing
Section 2			
Discover, p. 171	10; 5	**Consumable** 500 mL water **Nonconsumable** 2 sealable clear plastic bags, 2 thermometers	Developing Hypotheses
Real-World Lab, p. 179	40	**Consumable** glue, tape, marshmallows, 3 sheets aluminum foil, 3 sheets oaktag paper **Nonconsumable** scissors, 3 thermometers, 3 dowels or pencils, clock or watch	Predicting, Designing Experiments, Forming Operational Definitions
Section 3			
Discover, p. 181	10	**Nonconsumable** 15 dominoes	Inferring
Try This, p. 182	10	**Nonconsumable** 12 marbles	Making Models
Sharpen Your Skills, p. 183	5	**Nonconsumable** calculator (optional)	Calculating
Section 4			
Skills Lab, p. 186	40	**Consumable** ice water, hot water **Nonconsumable** thermometers, beakers, watch or clock, containers and lids made of paper, plastic foam, plastic, glass, and metal	Measuring, Designing Experiments
Discover, p. 187	20	**Nonconsumable** 60-watt incandescent light bulb and 15-watt compact fluorescent light bulb in packages, lamp, thermometer, clock or watch	Inferring
Science at Home, p. 190	home	No special materials are required.	Observing

A list of all materials required for the Student Edition activities can be found beginning on page T14. You can order Materials Kits by calling 1-800-828-7777 or by accessing the Science Explorer Internet site at **www.science-explorer.phschool.com.**

Energy Audit

Chapter 6 covers the sources and uses of energy and ways to conserve energy. The Chapter 6 Project is designed to provide real-life application of chapter concepts.

Purpose The Chapter 6 Project will give students an opportunity to examine energy uses in their school and suggest ways to reduce the school's energy consumption. Each student group will choose one area of the school to study, identify the types of energy used in that area, and determine the amount of each type of energy used. As students collect and record data, they will consider ways to reduce each type of energy use. Each group will prepare a written report that describes the students' findings and lists their ideas for reducing energy uses in the area they studied. The class as a whole will then prepare a proposal for conserving energy throughout the school.

Skills Focus After completing the Chapter 6 Project, students will be able to

- create a data table for recording the types and amounts of energy uses in the area selected for study;
- make observations and record data;
- interpret data and draw conclusions as the basis for recommending ways to reduce energy use;
- communicate findings and recommendations in a written report.

Project Time Line The Chapter 6 Project requires two to three weeks to complete, depending on how long a period of time you want to have students collect and evaluate numerical data, including the school's utility bills and readings of electric meters and fuel gauges. Most observations can be made during a class period. For purposes of comparison, making observations of the same area on different days and at different times of day should help students detect average and unusual uses, such as increased use of heating fuel during a cold spell.

Possible Materials
No special materials are required. Students will find it helpful to use calculators.

Energy Resources

WHAT'S AHEAD

SECTION **1** **Fossil Fuels**

Discover **What's in a Piece of Coal?**
Sharpen Your Skills **Graphing**

SECTION **2** **Renewable Sources of Energy**

Discover **Can You Capture Solar Energy?**
Real-World Lab **Cooking With Sunshine**

Integrating Chemistry
SECTION **3** **Nuclear Energy**

Discover **Why Do They Fall?**
Try This **Shoot the Nucleus**
Sharpen Your Skills **Calculating**

Advance Preparation

- Discuss with your school principal what students will be doing in this project, and obtain approval for students to enter areas that are usually off-limits to them, such as the utility room, or the cafeteria's kitchen. If necessary, arrange to have the school custodian or another adult accompany students to these areas.
- Obtain copies of the school's utility and fuel bills for students' use in determining the amounts of energy used.

Launching the Project Invite students to read the Chapter 6 Project description on page 163. Lead students in brainstorming a list of areas in the school that they could study.

Take the class on a tour of the school building and grounds. Encourage students to keep track of the different energy uses they observe—electricity for lighting, fuel oil or natural gas for heating, electricity or natural gas for cooking, gasoline for the school buses, and the like.

Distribute Chapter 6 Project Overview on

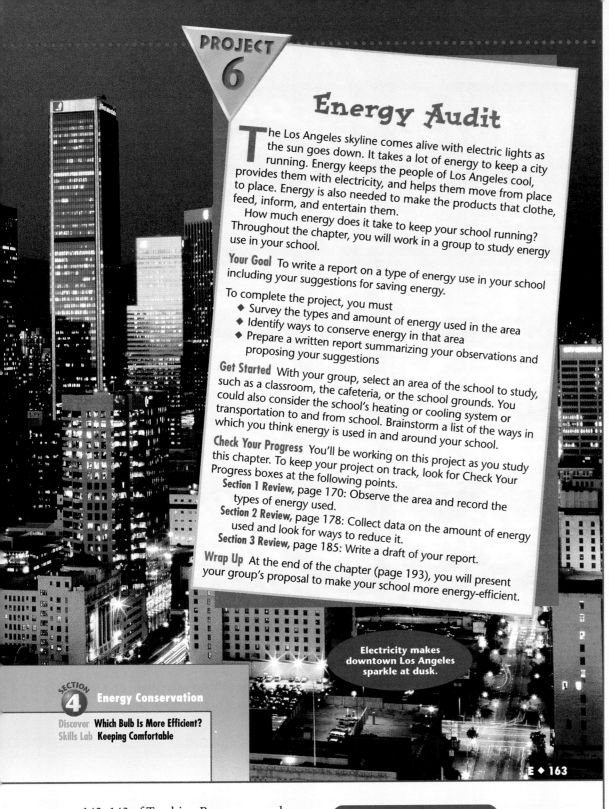

Energy Audit

The Los Angeles skyline comes alive with electric lights as the sun goes down. It takes a lot of energy to keep a city running. Energy keeps the people of Los Angeles cool, provides them with electricity, and helps them move from place to place. Energy is also needed to make the products that clothe, feed, inform, and entertain them.

How much energy does it take to keep your school running? Throughout the chapter, you will work in a group to study energy use in your school.

Your Goal To write a report on a type of energy use in your school including your suggestions for saving energy.

To complete the project, you must
- Survey the types and amount of energy used in the area
- Identify ways to conserve energy in that area
- Prepare a written report summarizing your observations and proposing your suggestions

Get Started With your group, select an area of the school to study, such as a classroom, the cafeteria, or the school grounds. You could also consider the school's heating or cooling system or transportation to and from school. Brainstorm a list of the ways in which you think energy is used in and around your school.

Check Your Progress You'll be working on this project as you study this chapter. To keep your project on track, look for Check Your Progress boxes at the following points.

Section 1 Review, page 170: Observe the area and record the types of energy used.

Section 2 Review, page 178: Collect data on the amount of energy used and look for ways to reduce it.

Section 3 Review, page 185: Write a draft of your report.

Wrap Up At the end of the chapter (page 193), you will present your group's proposal to make your school more energy-efficient.

Electricity makes downtown Los Angeles sparkle at dusk.

E ◆ 163

---

pages 142–143 of Teaching Resources, and have students review the project rules and procedures. Also distribute Chapter 6 Project Worksheet 1 on pages 144–145 of Teaching Resources. This worksheet provides instructions on how to read electric and gas meters and provides equivalents for converting different energy units (kilowatt-hours, gallons, and so forth) into the common unit of BTUs.

Divide the class into groups of three or four, and let the groups meet briefly to choose

areas to study. Monitor the groups' choices to avoid duplication. As an alternative, you could assign an area to each group.

Tell students that each group's members may divide the project responsibilities among themselves in any way they wish. However, emphasize that *every* group member should take part in identifying the types and amounts of energy uses in the area the group has chosen, recording and analyzing data, and developing the written report, and should be prepared to answer questions about the project.

Additional information on guiding the project is provided in Chapter 6 Project Teacher Notes on pages 140–141 of Teaching Resources.

Program Resources

- **Teaching Resources** Chapter 6 Project Teacher Notes, pp. 140–141; Chapter 6 Project Overview and Worksheet, pp. 142–145; Chapter 6 Project Scoring Rubric, p. 146

Performance Assessment

The Chapter 6 Project Scoring Rubric on page 146 in Teaching Resources will help you evaluate how well students complete the Chapter 6 Project. You may want to share the scoring rubric with students so they are clear about what will be expected of them. Students will be assessed on
- their ability to identify and evaluate all the types of energy used in the area studied;
- their ability to make recommendations for reducing those energy uses and to communicate their findings and recommendations to others;
- their participation in their group.

E ◆ 163

Objectives

After completing the lesson, students will be able to
◆ explain how fuels provide energy;
◆ list the three major fossil fuels;
◆ explain why fossil fuels are considered nonrenewable resources.

Key Terms combustion, fossil fuels, hydrocarbons, reserves, petroleum, refinery, petrochemicals

1 Engage/Explore

Activating Prior Knowledge

Ask students: **What is energy?** *(Answers will vary depending on students' prior science learning. Responses may include "strength," "power," "something that makes something else happen," and the like. If necessary, point out that the scientific definition of energy is "the capacity to do work.")*

········· **DISCOVER** ·········

Skills Focus observing
Materials *lignite coal, hand lens*
Time 10 minutes
Tips Lignite—the second stage of coal formation after peat—is the only form of coal that may contain recognizable plant remains.
Expected Outcome Students may or may not find fossils of plant remains in the coal samples. If fossils are present, they will be more noticeable with a hand lens.
Think It Over The lignite's texture, layering, and fossils (if present) can be seen more clearly with a hand lens. If fossils are visible, students should be able to infer that coal is made of plant remains.

SECTION
1 Fossil Fuels

DISCOVER ·······························**ACTIVITY**····

What's in a Piece of Coal?

1. Observe a chunk of coal. Record your observations in as much detail as possible, including color, texture, and shape.

2. Now use a hand lens to observe the coal more closely.

3. Examine your coal for fossils, imprints of plant or animal remains.

Think It Over
Observing What did you notice when you used the hand lens compared to your first observations? What do you think coal is made of?

GUIDE FOR READING

◆ How do fuels provide energy?
◆ What are the three major fossil fuels?
◆ Why are fossil fuels considered nonrenewable resources?

Reading Tip As you read, make a table comparing coal, oil, and natural gas. Describe each fuel and note how it is obtained and used.

The blackout happened on a November afternoon in 1965, just as evening rush hour was beginning. One small part in one power plant stopped working. To replace the lost power, the automatic controls shifted electricity from another source. This overloaded another part of the system, causing it to shut down. The problem kept growing. Within minutes, much of the Northeast was without electricity! Lights went out, plunging buildings into darkness. Thousands of people were trapped in dark elevators. Traffic signals stopped working, causing huge traffic jams. Electric stoves, radios, clocks—nothing worked. It took 13 hours to restore the power. During that time, more than 30 million people were reminded just how much their lives depended on electricity.

Producing electricity is an important use of energy resources. Other uses include transportation and heating. As you read about Earth's energy resources, think about how each is used to meet people's energy needs.

Fuels and Energy

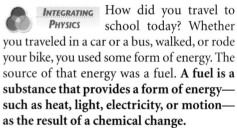 **INTEGRATING PHYSICS** How did you travel to school today? Whether you traveled in a car or a bus, walked, or rode your bike, you used some form of energy. The source of that energy was a fuel. **A fuel is a substance that provides a form of energy—such as heat, light, electricity, or motion—as the result of a chemical change.**

◄ Electric power lines stretch against the evening sky.

READING STRATEGIES

Reading Tip Students' tables should consist of columns for coal, oil, and natural gas. The comparisons should be listed down the side: description, method of obtaining fuel, and use. Students may wish to add further rows to compare advantages and disadvantages or other criteria.

Caption Writing Distribute photocopies of Figure 1. Have each student number the steps shown in the diagram based on the caption description, then write an accompanying key that briefly explains what happens in each numbered step.

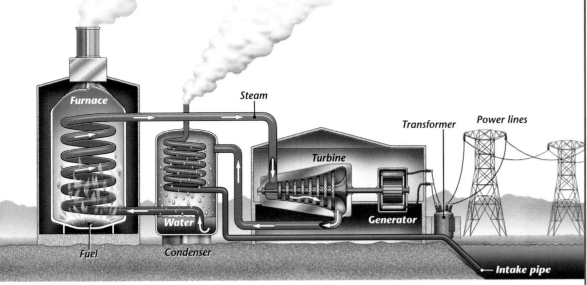

Steam · Transformer · Power lines · Furnace · Turbine · Generator · Water · Fuel · Condenser · Intake pipe

Energy can be converted from one form to another. To see how, rub your hands together quickly for several seconds. Did you feel them become warmer? When you moved your hands, they had mechanical energy, the energy of motion. The friction of your hands rubbing together converted some of this mechanical energy to thermal energy, which you felt as heat.

Combustion Fuels contain stored chemical energy, which can be released by burning. The process of burning a fuel is called **combustion.** For example, the fuel used by most cars is gasoline. When gasoline is burned in a car engine, it undergoes a chemical change. The gasoline combines with oxygen, producing carbon dioxide and water. The combustion of gasoline also converts some of the stored chemical energy into thermal energy. This thermal energy is converted to mechanical energy that moves the car.

Production of Electricity The energy stored in fuels can be used to generate electricity. In most power plants, the thermal energy produced by burning fuel is used to boil water, making steam, as shown in Figure 1. The mechanical energy of the steam turns the blades of a turbine. The shaft of the turbine is connected to a generator. The generator consists of powerful magnets surrounded by coils of copper wire. As the shaft rotates, the magnets turn inside the wire coil, producing an electric current. The electric current flows through power lines to homes and industries.

☑ *Checkpoint* *What are three energy conversions that might occur in a power plant?*

Figure 1 Electric power plants generate electricity by converting energy from one form to another. In the furnace, fuel is burned, releasing thermal energy. This energy is used to boil water and make steam. The mechanical energy of the moving steam turns the blades of a turbine. The turbine turns the shaft of the generator, producing an electric current.

Answers to Self-Assessment

☑ *Checkpoint*

When fuel is burned, chemical energy is converted to thermal energy (heat). Some of the thermal energy is converted to the mechanical energy of moving steam. In a power plant, the mechanical energy is then converted to electrical energy.

---

2 *Facilitate*

Fuels and Energy

 Integrating Physics

After students have read about energy conversion and rubbed their hands together, give some other examples of energy conversions and challenge students to infer the energy changes that are occurring. Some examples include a toaster (*Electrical energy is changed to heat energy.*), light bulb (*Electrical energy is changed to light and heat energy.*), power saw (*Electrical energy is changed to mechanical and heat energy.*), and candle (*Chemical energy is changed to light and heat energy.*). **learning modality: logical/mathematical**

Real-Life Learning

Invite a local auto mechanic or students who are particularly interested in automobiles to bring in and explain diagrams showing how an internal combustion engine works. Suggest that students who need an additional challenge create posters based on the diagrams. Ask: **Besides cars, trucks, buses, and other automobiles, what other devices contain an internal combustion engine?** (*Gasoline-powered lawnmowers, snowblowers, chainsaws, portable generators, and the like*) **learning modality: visual**

Ongoing Assessment

Oral Presentation Call on students at random to identify the energy conversions shown in Figure 1 in the order in which they occur.

What Are Fossil Fuels?

Sharpen your Skills

Graphing

Materials *drawing compass, protractor, calculator (optional)*

Time 15 minutes

Tips To determine the number of degrees for each use, students should first divide each percentage by 100. Then they should multiply each of those numbers by 360° and round off so the three sections total 360°.

Expected Outcome *Transportation 96°; Industry 137°; Homes and businesses 127°*

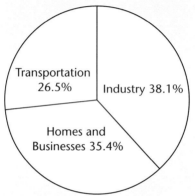

Transportation 26.5%

Industry 38.1%

Homes and Businesses 35.4%

Extend Let students brainstorm specific types of energy uses included in each "end use" category—for example, oil for heating, electricity for refrigeration and lighting, gasoline for automobiles, and so on. **learning modality: logical/mathematical**

Inquiry Challenge

Materials *clay, soil, sand, pebbles, leaves, colored paper, books or heavy weights*

Time 20 minutes

Challenge students to devise a model showing how fossil fuels form over time. *(Models might include trapping materials such as leaves or pieces of colored paper in layers of soft material such as clay or soil, and then compressing the materials under heavy weights.)* Ask: **What happens to buried materials to turn them into fossil fuels?** *(Over time, heat and pressure change the materials into hydrocarbons.)* **learning modality: kinesthetic**

Sharpen your Skills

Graphing

ACTIVITY

Use the data in the table below to make a circle graph showing the uses of energy in the United States. (To review circle graphs, see the Skills Handbook.)

End Use of Energy	Percent of Total Energy
Transportation	26.5
Industry	38.1
Homes and businesses	35.4

What Are Fossil Fuels?

Most of the energy used today comes from organisms that lived hundreds of millions of years ago. As these plants, animals, and other organisms died, their remains piled up. Layers of sand, rock, and mud buried the dead organisms. Over time, heat and pressure changed the material into other substances. **Fossil fuels** are the energy-rich substances formed from the remains of once-living organisms. **The three major fossil fuels are coal, oil, and natural gas.**

Fossil fuels are made of hydrocarbons. **Hydrocarbons** are energy-rich chemical compounds that contain carbon and hydrogen atoms. During combustion, the carbon and hydrogen combine with oxygen in the air to form carbon dioxide and water. This process releases energy in the forms of heat and light.

Fossil fuels have more hydrocarbons per kilogram than most other fuels. For this reason, they are an excellent source of energy. Combustion of one kilogram of coal, for example, provides twice as much heat as burning one kilogram of wood. Oil and natural gas provide three times the energy of wood.

✓ *Checkpoint* Why do fossil fuels yield more energy than other fuels?

Coal

Coal is a solid fossil fuel formed from plant remains. People have burned coal to produce heat for thousands of years. But coal was only a minor source of energy compared to wood until the 1800s. As Europe and the United States entered the Industrial Revolution, the need for fuel increased rapidly.

Figure 2 Coal is formed from the remains of trees and other plants that grew in swamps hundreds of millions of years ago.

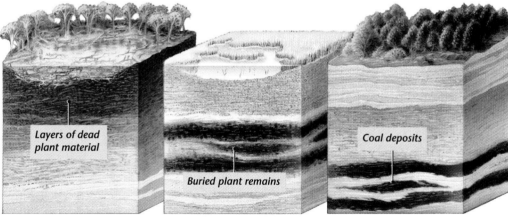

Layers of dead plant material

Buried plant remains

Coal deposits

200 million years ago　　**50 million years ago**　　**Present**

Background

Integrating Science "Black lung"—a form of pneumoconiosis (a general term for lung disease caused by breathing dust)—is caused by breathing coal dust over many years. The buildup of dust in the lungs damages the lungs' air sacs where gas exchange occurs. Scarring reduces the elasticity of lung tissue and makes it less able to absorb oxygen. As a result, the heart must pump harder, which damages the heart and can lead to death from heart failure. Black lung causes permanent damage to the lungs and is incurable.

In the early 1900s, scientists established the link between coal dust levels in mines and black lung disease. Continuing efforts to reduce coal dust levels in mines led to a reduction in the number of cases of black lung. The level of coal dust allowed in mines is now limited by federal law.

United States Coal Reserves

KEY
- Major deposit
- Minor deposit

As forests were cut down, firewood became more expensive. It became worthwhile to find, mine, and transport coal. Coal fueled the huge steam engines that powered trains, ships, and factories during the Industrial Revolution.

Today, coal provides 23 percent of the energy used in the United States. The major use of coal is to fuel electric power plants.

Coal Mining Before it can be used to produce energy, coal has **INTEGRATING TECHNOLOGY** to be removed from the ground, or mined. Some coal is located very deep underground or is mixed with other materials, making it too difficult to obtain. Known deposits of coal (and other fossil fuels) that can be obtained using current technology are called **reserves.**

A century ago, miners had to break the coal apart with hand tools. Today they use machines to chop the coal into chunks and lift it to the surface. The coal is then cleaned to remove rocks, sand, and other materials that do not burn. Removing them also makes the coal lighter, reducing the cost of transporting it.

Coal as an Energy Source Coal is the most plentiful fossil fuel in the United States. It is fairly easy to transport, and provides a lot of energy when burned. But coal also has some disadvantages. Coal mining can increase erosion. Runoff from mines can cause water pollution. Finally, burning most types of coal results in more air pollution than other fossil fuels.

In addition, coal mining can be a dangerous job. Thousands of miners have been killed or injured in accidents in the mines. Many more suffer from "black lung," a disease caused by years of breathing coal dust. Fortunately, the mining industry has been working hard to improve conditions. New safety procedures and better equipment, including robots and drills that produce less coal dust, have made coal mining safer.

Figure 3 The map shows the locations of coal reserves in the United States. In the photograph, a miner obtains hard coal from a shaft deep underground. *Interpreting Maps Which states have major deposits of coal?*

Figure 4 A farmer in Ireland turns over blocks of soft peat. Peat is formed in the early stages of the process of coal formation.

✓ *Checkpoint*
Fossil fuels contain hydrocarbons, which release more energy than other substances when they are burned.

Answers to Self-Assessment

Caption Question
Figure 3 Montana, North and South Dakota, Wyoming, Utah, Colorado, New Mexico, Texas, Nebraska, Iowa, Kansas, Missouri, Oklahoma, Arkansas, Illinois, Indiana, Kentucky, Michigan, Ohio, Pennsylvania, West Virginia, Tennessee, Alabama

Coal

Building Inquiry Skills: Classifying

Materials *samples of peat moss, lignite, bituminous coal, and anthracite; 2 small plastic bags; hand lenses*

ACTIVITY

Time 10 minutes

CAUTION: *Rinse the coal thoroughly to remove any dust. Make sure students wash their hands after handling the samples.* Give each group hand lenses, a plastic bag containing a sample of peat moss, and a second bag containing the three types of coal. Let students examine the samples, noting similarities and differences between them. Explain that peat is the decayed remains of plants—the early stage of coal formation. Then list the following names and characteristics on the board, and challenge students to identify each coal sample. *Lignite:* dark brown; layered; may contain recognizable fragments of plant remains
Bituminous coal: denser than lignite; black; may have bands
Anthracite: the hardest of all coal types; black; shiny **learning modality: kinesthetic**

 Integrating Technology

Encourage students to look closely at the photographs on this page. You may wish to show some pictures of coal miners in the past and the labor-intensive methods and equipment they used. Point out that many years ago, young people students' own age—and even younger—worked in coal mines. Encourage students to describe what they think it was like to work in a coal mine years ago. **learning modality: visual**

Oil

Building Inquiry Skills: Observing

Materials *2 small paper cups, 30 mL dark molasses, paper towel, aluminum pan*

Time 10 minutes

CAUTION: *If you are concerned about spills, have a few volunteers perform this activity as a demonstration for the other students.* Give each student or group a paper towel, a small paper cup containing about 30 mL of dark molasses, and an empty cup. Explain that molasses is very similar to crude oil in consistency. Invite students to pour the molasses from one cup to the other over the pan, try to pick some up with the paper towel, and touch some between the thumb and index finger. Students will find that the molasses is too thick to pour readily, is not absorbed by the towel, and is sticky. Ask: **How easy do you think it would be to clean up crude oil that spilled on a beach?** *(Extremely difficult)* **learning modality: kinesthetic**

Using the Visuals: Figure 5

Let students answer the caption question, then ask: **Which of the named nations has the smallest oil reserve?** *(United States)* **Does this mean the United States is the nation with the smallest oil reserves in the world?** *(No, it has the eleventh largest. All nations other than those named have smaller reserves than the United States.)* **learning modality: logical/ mathematical**

Integrating Technology

Ask students: **Do you know of any other examples where sound waves are used to locate objects or materials?** *(Students may know how sonar is used to map the ocean floor. If they do not, they can read about it in* Earth's Waters *of the Science Explorer Series; see Program Resources on the next page.)* **learning modality: verbal**

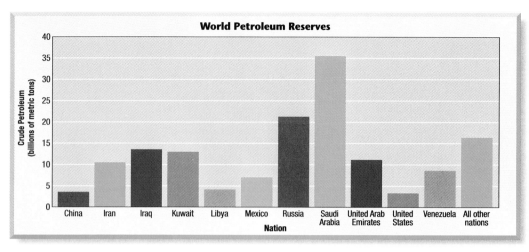

World Petroleum Reserves

(Bar graph: Crude Petroleum (billions of metric tons) vs. Nation. Approximate values — China: 3.5, Iran: 10.5, Iraq: 13.5, Kuwait: 13, Libya: 4, Mexico: 7, Russia: 21, Saudi Arabia: 35.5, United Arab Emirates: 11, United States: 3, Venezuela: 8.5, All other nations: 16)

Figure 5 Known petroleum deposits, called reserves, are located in many parts of the world. *Interpreting Graphs Which two nations have the largest reserves?*

Oil

Oil is a thick, black, liquid fossil fuel. It formed from the remains of small animals, algae, and protists that lived in oceans and shallow inland seas hundreds of millions of years ago. **Petroleum** is another name for oil, from the Latin words *petra* (rock) and *oleum* (oil). Most oil deposits are located underground in tiny holes in sandstone or limestone. The oil fills the holes somewhat like water trapped in the holes of a sponge.

Petroleum accounts for more than one third of the energy produced in the world. Fuel for most cars, airplanes, trains, and ships comes from petroleum. Many homes are heated by oil.

The United States consumes about one third of all the oil produced in the world. But only three percent of the world's supply is located in this country. The difference must be purchased from countries with large oil supplies.

Locating Oil Deposits Because it is usually located deep below

INTEGRATING TECHNOLOGY

the surface, finding oil is difficult. Scientists can use sound waves to test an area for oil without drilling. This technique relies on the fact that sound waves bounce off objects and return as echoes. Scientists send pulses of sound down into the rocks below ground. Then they measure how long it takes the echoes to return. The amount of time depends on whether the sound waves must travel through solid rock or liquid oils. This information can indicate the most likely places to find oil. However, only about one out of every six wells drilled produces a usable amount of oil.

Figure 6 An oil rig bobs up and down as it pumps oil from a Texas oil field.

Background

Facts and Figures In addition to refined petroleum, gasoline contains many different additives. These include antiknock compounds, metal deactivators and antioxidants, antirust and anti-icing agents, detergents, lubricants, and dyes.

For many years, tetraethyl lead was added to gasoline to improve its combustion characteristics. Lead reduces or eliminates "knocking" caused by premature ignition in high-compression engines and lubricates close-fitting engine parts where oil tends to wash away or burn off. However, because lead is highly toxic, the government phased out and finally banned the use of lead as a gasoline additive. As a result, the amount of lead in the atmosphere decreased by about 98 percent between 1970 and 1996.

Refining Oil When oil is first pumped out of the ground, it is called crude oil. Crude oil can be a runny or a thick liquid. In order to be made into useful products, crude oil must undergo a process called refining. A factory where crude oil is separated into fuels and other products by heating is called a **refinery.**

In addition to gasoline and heating oil, many products you use every day are made from crude oil. **Petrochemicals** are compounds that are made from oil. Petrochemicals are used in plastics, paints, medicines, and cosmetics.

☑ *Checkpoint* How is petroleum used?

Natural Gas

The third major fossil fuel is natural gas, a mixture of methane and other gases. Natural gas forms from the same organisms as petroleum. Because it is less dense than oil, natural gas often rises above an oil deposit, forming a pocket of gas in the rock.

Pipelines transport the gas from its source to the places where it is used. If all the gas pipelines in the United States were connected, they would reach to the moon and back—twice! Natural gas can also be compressed into a liquid and stored in tanks as fuel for trucks and buses.

Natural gas has several advantages. It produces large amounts of energy, but lower levels of many air pollutants than coal or oil. It is also easy to transport once the network of pipelines is built. One disadvantage of natural gas is that it is highly flammable. A gas leak can cause a violent explosion and fire.

Gas companies help to prevent dangerous explosions from leaks. If you use natural gas in your home, you probably are familiar with the "gas" smell that alerts you whenever there is unburned gas in the air. You may be surprised to learn that natural gas actually has no odor at all. What causes the strong smell? The gas companies add a chemical with a distinct smell to the gas before it is piped to homes and businesses so that any leaks will be noticed.

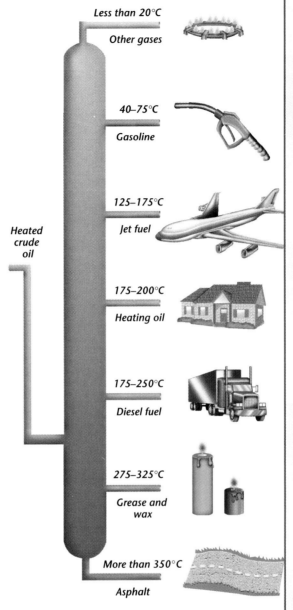

Figure 7 Crude oil is refined to make many different products. In the refining process, heat causes the different molecules in crude oil to separate. Different substances vaporize at specific temperatures.

Less than 20°C — Other gases
40–75°C — Gasoline
125–175°C — Jet fuel
175–200°C — Heating oil
175–250°C — Diesel fuel
275–325°C — Grease and wax
More than 350°C — Asphalt

Heated crude oil

Program Resources

 Science Explorer Series *Earth's Waters*, Chapter 5 describes sonar.

Media and Technology

 Exploring Earth Science Videodisc
Unit 6, Side 2, "Power for the People"

Chapter 2

Answers to Self-Assessment

Caption Question

Figure 5 Saudi Arabia and Russia

☑ *Checkpoint*

Petroleum is refined to make fuels and other products, including plastics.

Natural Gas

Building Inquiry Skills: Calculating

Materials *calculator*
Time 5 minutes

Point out the text statement "If all the gas pipelines in the United States were connected, they would reach to the moon and back—twice!" Have students use the moon's average distance from Earth *(384,392 km)* to calculate the total length of U.S. gas pipelines. *(384,392 × 4 = 1,537,568 km)* They can extend this activity by comparing this distance to another reference, such as the width of their state. **learning modality: logical/mathematical**

Real-Life Learning

Companies that supply natural gas usually publish materials to teach customers about safety issues when dealing with gas appliances and gas lines. Some companies also can provide a representative to speak to your class about gas safety. Contact your local gas company to request materials and, if available, a speaker. **learning modality: verbal**

Fuel Supply and Demand

Building Inquiry Skills: Inferring

Tell students that in 1973, 36 percent of all the oil used in the United States was imported from other countries; in 1993, 51 percent of the oil used was imported. Ask: **What do those percentages tell you?** (*The United States became more dependent on imported oil.*) **Why do you think that happened?** (*The country's oil consumption increased, but production did not increase enough to keep up with the demand.*) **learning modality: logical/mathematical**

Ongoing Assessment

Skills Check Have each student create a simple, three-column table listing the advantages and disadvantages of each type of fossil fuel.

 Students can save their tables in their portfolios.

3 Assess

Section 1 Review Answers

1. Fuels contain stored chemical energy. When they are burned, the chemical energy is converted into other forms of energy.

2. *Coal* is a solid fossil fuel formed from decaying plant matter that was changed by heat and pressure. *Oil* is a thick, black liquid fossil fuel formed from the remains of small animals, algae, and protists. *Natural gas* is a mixture of methane and other gases formed from the same organisms as oil.

3. Because fossil fuels take hundreds of millions of years to form, they can be easily used up faster than they can be replaced.

4. *Advantages:* produces lower levels of many air pollutants; is easy to transport. *Disadvantage:* is highly flammable, so a leak can cause a violent explosion and fire.

5. *Sample answers:* Not all oil deposits have been located; countries may not want to reveal the size of their oil reserves.

Check Your Progress
CHAPTER PROJECT 6

Point out that the school's meters and gauges show the amount of fuel used for the entire building. To estimate the amount used in each area, students can count the number of rooms in the school (including the cafeteria, gym, auditorium, and so forth) and divide the total amount of fuel used by the number of rooms. Students should suggest whether energy use in this area is above or below average.

Performance Assessment

Writing Have each student explain why it is important for the United States to become less dependent on fossil fuels.

Figure 8 During the gasoline crisis, people frequently had to wait in long lines to buy gas. *Relating Cause and Effect What caused the gasoline shortage?*

Fuel Supply and Demand

The many advantages of using fossil fuels as an energy source have made them essential to modern life. **But remember that fossil fuels take hundreds of millions of years to form. For this reason, fossil fuels are considered a nonrenewable resource.** For example, Earth's known oil reserves took 500 million years to form. One fourth of this oil has already been used. If fossil fuels continue to be used more rapidly than they are formed, the reserves will eventually be used up.

Many of the nations that consume large amounts of fuel have very limited reserves of their own. They have to buy oil, natural gas, and coal from the regions that have large supplies. The uneven distribution of fossil fuel reserves has often been a cause of political problems in the world. For example, in the 1970s, a group of oil-exporting nations decided to reduce their oil exports to the United States. As the supply of gasoline fell, prices rose very rapidly. People sometimes waited in line for hours to buy gasoline. This shortage reminded Americans of their dependence on oil imported from other nations.

New sources of energy are needed to replace the decreasing fossil fuel reserves. The rest of this chapter will describe some other sources of energy, as well as ways to make current fuel resources last longer.

Section 1 Review

1. Explain how fuels provide energy.
2. Name the three major fossil fuels and briefly describe each.
3. Explain why fossil fuels are classified as nonrenewable resources.
4. List two advantages and one disadvantage of natural gas as an energy source.
5. **Thinking Critically Applying Concepts** Why is it impossible to know exactly how large the world's oil reserves are?

Check Your Progress
CHAPTER PROJECT 6

With your team, observe your selected area of the school. Determine which types of energy use take place in this area: heating, cooling, lighting, mechanical devices, electronic equipment, or moving vehicles. Record the specific types and amounts of energy use in a data table. To find the amounts, you will need to collect data from electric meters or fuel gauges. (*Hint:* Observe your area at several different times of the day, since the pattern of energy use may vary.)

Program Resources

◆ **Teaching Resources** 6-1 Review and Reinforce, p. 149; 6-1 Enrich, p. 150

Media and Technology

Interactive Student Tutorial CD-ROM E-6

Answers to Self-Assessment

Caption Question

Figure 8 A group of oil-exporting nations reduced oil exports to the United States.

DISCOVER

Can You Capture Solar Energy?

1. Pour 250 milliliters of water into each of two sealable, clear plastic bags.

2. Measure and record the water temperature in each bag. Seal the bags.

3. Put one bag in a dark or shady place. Put the other bag in a place where it will receive direct sunlight.

4. Predict what the temperature of the water in each bag will be after 30 minutes.

5. Measure and record the ending temperatures.

Think It Over

Developing Hypotheses How did the water temperature in each bag change? What could account for these results?

A s the sun rises over the rim of the canyon where your family is camping, you feel its warmth on your face. The night's chill disappears quickly. A breeze stirs, carrying with it the smell of the campfire. Maybe you'll take a morning dip in the warm water of a nearby hot spring.

This relaxing scene is far from the city, with its bustling cars and trucks, factories and power plants. But there are energy resources all around you here, too. The sun warms the air, the wind blows, and heat from inside Earth warms the waters of the spring. These sources of energy are all renewable—that is, they are constantly being supplied. You can see why people are trying to find ways to use these renewable resources instead of fossil fuels. As you read about each source of renewable energy, think about how it could help meet people's energy needs.

Energy From the Sun

The warmth you feel on a sunny day is **solar energy,** energy from the sun. **The sun constantly gives off energy in the form of light and heat.** Solar energy is the source, directly or indirectly, of most other renewable energy resources. In one day, Earth receives enough solar energy to meet the energy needs of the entire world for 40 years. Solar energy does not cause pollution, and it will not run out for billions of years.

So why hasn't solar energy replaced fossil fuels? One reason is that solar energy is only available when the sun is shining. A backup energy source must be available on cloudy days and at night. Another problem is that

> **GUIDE FOR READING**
>
> ◆ How does the sun provide energy?
>
> ◆ What are some renewable sources of energy?
>
> *Reading Tip* Before you read, preview the headings in this section. Predict some sources of energy that are renewable.

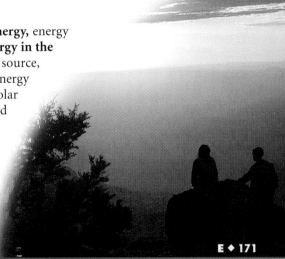

E ◆ 171

Objectives

After completing the lesson, students will be able to
◆ explain how the sun provides energy and describe ways to collect this energy;
◆ identify and describe various sources of energy not dependent on fossil fuels.

Key Terms solar energy, passive solar system, active solar system, hydroelectric power, biomass fuel, gasohol, geothermal energy

1 Engage/Explore

Activating Prior Knowledge

Ask: **Besides coal, oil, and natural gas, what other sources of energy do you know of?** *(Answers will depend on students' prior learning. They may mention the renewable sources covered in this section and "atomic" [nuclear] energy, covered in the next section.)*

DISCOVER

Skills Focus developing hypotheses

Materials *500 mL water, 2 sealable clear plastic bags, 2 thermometers*
Time 10 minutes for setup; 5 minutes for follow-up
Tips Provide room-temperature water for Step 1. If your classroom does not have a sunny window, arrange to place bags in another location where there is direct sunlight.
Expected Outcome Specific temperatures will vary.
Think It Over The water temperature stayed the same in the dark/shaded bag, while the water temperature increased in the bag placed in sunlight. The water in that bag absorbed heat energy from the sun.

Solar Technologies

 Integrating Technology

Materials *several examples of solar cells and small solar-powered motors (available from home-electronics stores)*

ACTIVITY

Let students examine the solar cells and motors. Encourage them to use the cells and motors to make simple devices that will operate when placed in sunlight— for example, a solar-powered toy boat or car. Ask: **What energy conversions are taking place?** *(Solar energy to electrical energy to mechanical energy)* **learning modality: kinesthetic**

Figure 9 Aimed at the sun, these mirrors provide power to an electric plant in New South Wales, Australia. *Inferring How does the shape of these mirrors make them more effective?*

although Earth receives a lot of energy from the sun every day, this energy is very spread out. To obtain enough power, it is necessary to collect this energy from a huge area.

Solar Technologies

 INTEGRATING TECHNOLOGY Improving technologies to capture and use solar energy will help meet future energy needs. Some current solar technologies are described below.

Solar Plants One way to capture the sun's energy involves using giant mirrors. In a solar plant, rows of mirrors focus the sun's rays to heat a tank of water. The water boils, making steam that can be used to generate electricity.

Solar Cells Solar energy can be converted directly into electricity in a solar cell. A solar cell consists of a "sandwich" of very thin layers of the element silicon and other materials. The upper and lower parts of the sandwich have a negative and a positive terminal, like a battery. When light hits the cell, electrons move across the layers, producing an electric current.

The amount of electricity produced by solar cells depends on the area of the cell and the amount of light available. Solar cells are used to power calculators, lights, telephones, and other small devices. However, it would take more than 5,000 solar cells the size of your palm to produce enough electricity for a typical American home. Building solar cells on a large scale is very expensive. As a result, solar cells are used mostly in areas where fossil fuels are difficult to transport.

✓ *Checkpoint* What are solar cells made of and how do they work?

Background

Integrating Science The solar cells described in the student text are made of crystalline silicon and are also known as photovoltaic (PV) cells. Although suitable for use in calculators and watches, these cells are not very efficient at converting solar energy to electricity and are expensive to produce. A new kind of solar cell made from a thin film of semiconductor material may prove to be more efficient and less expensive.

Media and Technology

Transparencies "Exploring a Solar House," Transparency 16

Exploring Physical Science Videodisc
Unit 4, Side 2, "Wired to the Sun"
Chapter 7

Solar Heating Systems Solar energy can be used to heat buildings. As shown in *Exploring a Solar House,* there are two types of solar heating systems: passive and active.

A **passive solar system** converts sunlight into thermal energy without using pumps or fans. If you have ever stepped into a car on a sunny day, you have experienced passive solar heating. Solar energy passes through the car's windows as light. The sun's rays heat the seats and other parts of the car, which then transfer heat to the air. The heated air is trapped inside, so the car gets warmer. The same principle can be used to heat a home.

An **active solar system** captures the sun's energy, then uses fans and pumps to distribute the heat. Light strikes the black metal surface of a solar collector. There, it is converted to thermal energy. Water is pumped through pipes in the solar collector to absorb the thermal energy. The heated water flows to a storage tank. Pumps and fans distribute the heat throughout the building.

EXPLORING *a Solar House*

This solar house uses passive and active heating systems and solar cells to convert solar energy into heat and electricity.

Passive Interior Heating
Sunlight that passes through the windows is absorbed by the walls and floors and converted to heat. At night shades covering the windows prevent the heat from flowing back outside.

Solar Cells
Active solar cells on the roof generate an electric current. A battery stores energy for night use.

Window Design
Large windows on the south and west sides act as passive solar collectors. They let sunlight enter during the winter. Overhangs shade the windows during the summer.

Solar Water Heater
Cool water is pumped from a storage tank to an active solar collector on the roof. Sunlight heats the water in the collector panels. Then the water is returned to the tank. From there it is piped to the different rooms. Air moves over the pipes and is heated.

Backup Heat Source
The house has a wood stove to provide backup heat, especially on cloudy days.

E ◆ 173

Answers to Self-Assessment

Caption Question

Figure 9 The curved shape concentrates the sun's rays by reflecting them toward the center of the dish.

✓ *Checkpoint*

They are made of layers of silicon and other materials. When light hits the cell, electrons move across the layers, producing an electric current.

EXPLORING

a Solar House

After students have reviewed the figure, ask: **Which of these solar systems do you have in your own home?** (*Most students will probably identify the two passive systems, passive interior heating and window design.*) If any students say that their homes are equipped with active solar systems, invite those students to describe the devices and their operation to the rest of the class. **learning modality: verbal**

Real-Life Learning

Materials *2 thermometers, large glass jar*
Time 10 minutes

Give students an opportunity to directly observe passive solar heating. On a sunny day, take the class outdoors to a place that receives direct sunlight, but away from pavement. Have students read the two thermometers and note the temperatures. Then put one thermometer in an upside-down glass jar and the other thermometer in open air. Have students compare the temperatures after several minutes. Ask: **Why is the temperature higher inside the glass jar?** (*The glass allows light to pass into the jar but traps heat inside the jar.*) **learning modality: logical/mathematical**

Ongoing Assessment

Oral Presentation Call on students at random to each describe one example of technology that captures solar energy for use by people.

Capturing the Wind

Using the Visuals: Figure 10

Tell students that people have used windmills for over a thousand years. Display a photograph of a large "old-fashioned" windmill, and have students compare it with the modern windmills shown in the photograph. Ask: **How are modern windmills different from old windmills?** *(Modern windmills are more streamlined, do not have a building as the base, have fewer blades, and the blades are metal instead of wood.)* **Why do you think wind farms use streamlined windmills like these instead of the old-fashioned type?** *(Modern windmills are stronger and also more sensitive to light winds.)* Encourage interested students to find out about the history and technology of windmills. **learning modality: visual**

The Power of Flowing Water

Social Studies CONNECTION

Use Figure 11 to help students understand how a water wheel is used to capture energy. Ask: **What energy conversion takes place at the mill?** *(Kinetic energy is converted to mechanical energy.)*

In Your Journal Remind students that a news story focuses on factual information, particularly the "five Ws"—*Who, What, Where, When,* and *Why.* Divide the class into groups of three to write the stories, with each student writing about one of the three topics mentioned in the text. Have groups share their stories by reading them aloud. **cooperative learning**

Figure 10 This wind farm in the Mojave Desert is one of many in the state of California. *Making Generalizations What are some advantages of wind power?*

Capturing the Wind

The sun is one source of renewable energy. **Other renewable sources of energy include wind, water, tides, biomass material, Earth's interior, and hydrogen.**

Wind energy is actually an indirect form of solar energy. The sun heats Earth's surface unevenly. As a result of this uneven heating, different areas of the atmosphere have different temperatures and air pressure. The differences in pressure cause winds as air moves from one area to another.

Wind can be used to turn a turbine and generate electricity. Wind power plants or "wind farms" consist of many windmills. Together, the windmills generate large amounts of power.

Although wind now provides less than one percent of the world's electricity, it is the fastest-growing energy source. Wind energy is free and does not cause pollution. In places where fuels are difficult to transport, such as Antarctica, wind energy is the major source of power. In the remote grasslands of Mongolia, electricity is obtained from more than 70,000 wind turbines.

Wind energy is not ideal for all locations. Few places have winds that blow steadily enough to be a worthwhile energy source. Wind generators are noisy and can be destroyed by very strong winds. But as fossil fuels become more scarce and expensive, wind generators will become more important.

☑ Checkpoint How can wind be used to generate electricity?

The Power of Flowing Water

Solar energy is also the indirect source of water power. Recall that in the water cycle, energy from the sun heats water on Earth's surface, forming water vapor. The water vapor condenses and falls back to Earth as rain and snow. As the water flows over the land into lakes and oceans, it provides another source of energy.

Background

History of Science The first known windmills were used in Persia (now Iran) in the seventh century A.D. By the twelfth century, their use had spread throughout Europe. They were used for irrigation and to grind grain. In the late 1800s, thousands of windmills were in use in the rural United States.

Program Resources

Science Explorer Series *Weather and Climate,* Chapter 2, provides more detailed information on how solar energy creates wind. *Earth's Waters,* Chapter 4, provides information about tidal action.

Flowing water can turn a turbine and generate electricity in the same way as steam or wind. A dam across a river blocks the flow of water, creating an artificial lake called a reservoir. Water flows through tunnels at the bottom of the dam. As the water moves through the tunnels, it turns turbines connected to a generator.

Hydroelectric power is electricity produced by flowing water. This type of power is the most widely used source of renewable energy in the world today. Once a dam and power plant are built, producing the electricity is inexpensive. Another benefit is that hydroelectric power does not create air pollution. Unlike wind or solar energy, flowing water provides a steady supply of energy.

But hydroelectric power does have limitations. In the United States, for example, most of the suitable rivers have already been dammed. And dams can have negative effects on the environment. You can read more about the pros and cons of hydroelectric dams in *Science and Society* on page 180.

Tidal Energy

Another source of moving water is the tides. The gravity of the moon and sun causes the water on Earth's surface to regularly rise and fall on its shores. Along some coastlines, enormous amounts of water move into bays at the high tide. The water flows out to sea again when the tide goes out.

A few tidal power plants have been built to take advantage of this regular motion. A low dam across the entrance to a shallow bay holds water in the bay at high tide. As the tide goes out, water flowing past turbines in the dam generate electricity, as in a hydroelectric power plant.

Only a few coastal areas in the world are suitable for building tidal power plants. A dam across a bay also blocks boats and fish from traveling up the river. For these reasons, tidal power will probably never become a major source of energy.

✓ *Checkpoint* How are tidal power plants similar to hydroelectric power plants? How are they different?

Figure 11 Flowing water provides the power to turn the water wheel of this historic mill in Tennessee.

Social Studies CONNECTION

Early settlers in the eastern United States often built mills along streams. The mills captured the power of flowing water at dams or waterfalls, where the water turned water wheels connected to machines. Saw mills sawed logs into boards, and grist mills ground wheat into flour. A mill site often formed the center of a new town.

In Your Journal

Suppose you are writing a news story about an old mill. Describe the mill's early importance to the settlers, how a town grew up around it, and how it is used today.

Building Inquiry Skills: Making Models

Materials *large, empty thread spool; 8 self-adhesive index tabs or duct tape and tabs cut from heavy acetate; unsharpened pencil or dowel*
Time 15 minutes

Let students make model waterwheels by attaching tabs around the outside of a thread spool with the tabs parallel to the spool's axis. They can insert a pencil through the spool's hole, making sure the spool turns freely. Allow students to test their waterwheels under a running faucet. Holding the wheel above the stream so the water hits the lower tabs demonstrates an "undershot" waterwheel. Holding the wheel below the stream so the water hits the upper tabs demonstrates an "overshot" wheel. The water-driven turbines used in hydroelectric power plants today are more complicated—and much more efficient—than old waterwheels, but they operate in much the same way. **learning modality: kinesthetic**

Tidal Energy

Real-Life Learning

If students live in or have visited a coastal area, invite them to describe what they have seen and felt as tides moved in and out. Prompt their descriptions by asking questions such as the following: **How far did the waterline move from low tide to high tide?** *(Answers will vary.)* **What did the water flow feel like to you when the tide was coming in or going out?** *(Answers will vary, but students should be able to describe feeling the force of the water against their legs or bodies.)* Point out that it is this force of moving water that is tapped by tidal power plants. **learning modality: verbal**

Answers to Self-Assessment

Caption Question

Figure 10 The wind itself doesn't cost anything and is renewable; wind power is available in remote places where it would be difficult to transport fossil fuels.

Answers to Self-Assessment

✓ *Checkpoint*

p. 174: Wind can be used to turn a turbine.
p. 175: Both use moving water as the energy source and have turbines that generate electricity. A hydroelectric plant uses fresh water in a river or stream; a tidal plant uses ocean tides. Hydroelectric plants are built on rivers; tidal plants are built in bays.

Ongoing Assessment

Writing Have each student describe one advantage of water power over wind power in generating electricity.

Biomass Fuels

Building Inquiry Skills: Predicting

Ask students: **Would burning wood or plant wastes in an open fire be a good way to make use of biomass fuels? Why, or why not?** (*No; open burning allows heat to escape and releases pollutants into the atmosphere.*) **How do you think biomass materials must be burned in order to be efficient and nonpolluting fuels?** (*In some sort of closed incinerator that captures harmful waste products and captures all or most of the heat*) **What else would have to be part of the equipment to generate electricity with the heat of the burning fuel?** (*Water to make steam to drive a turbine*) **learning modality: logical/mathematical**

Including All Students

For students who need help with language skills, write the two words on the board, draw boxes around *gas* in *gasoline* and *ohol* in *alcohol,* draw a plus sign between the two boxes, and ask: **What word do these two parts make when you put them together?** (*gasohol*) **limited English proficiency**

Biomass Fuels

The oldest fuel used for heat and light is wood. As trees carry out photosynthesis, they use the sun's energy to convert carbon dioxide and water into more complicated molecules. Burning wood breaks down these molecules again and releases energy.

Wood is one of a group of fuels, called **biomass fuels,** made from living things. Other biomass fuels include leaves, food wastes, and even manure. As fossil fuel supplies shrink, people are taking a closer look at biomass fuels. For instance, when oil prices rose in the early 1970s, Hawaiian sugar-cane farmers thought of a way to use sugar-cane wastes. They began burning the wastes to generate electricity instead of discarding the wastes in landfills. Now almost one fourth of the electricity used on the island of Kauai comes from biomass material.

Biomass materials can be also converted into other fuels. For example, corn, sugar cane, and other crops can be used to make alcohol. Adding the alcohol to gasoline forms a mixture called **gasohol.** Gasohol can be used as fuel for cars. When bacteria decompose wastes, they convert the wastes into methane gas. The methane produced in some landfills is used to heat buildings.

Alcohol and methane are renewable resources. But producing them in large quantities is more expensive than using fossil fuels. And though wood is renewable, it takes time for new trees to grow and replace those that have been cut down. As a result, biomass fuels are not widely used today in the United States. But as fossil fuels become scarcer, biomass fuels may play a larger role in meeting energy needs.

Figure 12 This corn field is a rich source of biomass fuel. After the corn is harvested, the stalks and leaves can be burned to provide energy. *Comparing and Contrasting How are biomass fuels similar to energy sources such as wind and water? How are these fuels different?*

176 ◆ E

Background

Facts and Figures Besides reducing our dependence on fossil fuels, using biomass fuels helps reduce our waste-disposal problems. In one case in California, the Mesquite Lake Resource Recovery Project, an electric power plant burns cow manure to produce enough electricity for thousands of homes. The manure would otherwise pose a disposal problem because of its high salt content and the presence of seeds that make it undesirable for use as fertilizer.

Some problems are associated with the use of biomass materials. Growing the crops often used as biomass fuels takes up land that could be used for growing food crops. And removing all the stalks, leaves, and roots from a field for use as biomass fuel means that these crop wastes will not decay and enrich the soil. Unprotected soil is also more susceptible to erosion.

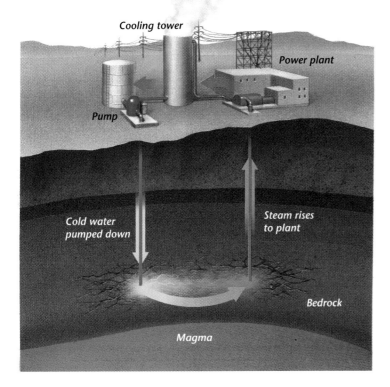

Figure 13 A geothermal power plant uses heat from Earth's interior as an energy source. Cold water is piped deep into the ground, where it is heated by magma. The resulting steam can be used for heat or to generate electricity.

Cooling tower

Power plant

Pump

Cold water pumped down

Steam rises to plant

Bedrock

Magma

Tapping Earth's Energy

Below Earth's surface is a thick layer of very hot, liquid rock called magma. In some places, magma is found very close to the surface. It may even erupt out of the ground as volcanic lava. The intense heat from Earth's interior that warms the magma is called **geothermal energy.**

In certain regions, such as Iceland and New Zealand, the magma heats underground water to the boiling point. The hot water and steam are valuable sources of energy. In Reykjavik, Iceland, 90 percent of homes are heated by water warmed underground in this way. Geothermal energy can also be used to generate electricity, as shown in Figure 13.

Geothermal energy is an unlimited source of cheap energy. But it has disadvantages, just like every other energy source. There are only a few places where magma comes close to Earth's surface. Elsewhere, a very deep well is required to tap this energy. Drilling deep wells is very expensive. Even so, geothermal energy is likely to play a part in meeting energy needs in the future.

✓ *Checkpoint* How can geothermal energy be used to generate electricity?

Using the Visuals: Figure 13

Have students work in pairs to create cycle diagrams of the process shown in the figure. Ask: **What do you think the cooling tower is used for?** (*After the steam has been used to turn turbines in the power plant, it is cooled to turn it into liquid water.*) **learning modality: visual**

Including All Students

Support students who need more help in comprehending the term *geothermal.* Write the term *geothermal* on the board and draw a vertical line between the two word parts. Invite volunteers to look up the meaning of each part in a dictionary and read the meanings aloud (*geo,* "Earth"; *thermal,* "heat"). Ask: **What does "geothermal" mean?** (*Earth-heat, or heat inside Earth*) **limited English proficiency**

Hydrogen Power

Demonstration

Materials *electrolysis apparatus, matches*
Time 10 minutes

 Use an electrolysis apparatus to show students that hydrogen can be obtained by passing an electric current through water. (If you are not familiar with the electrolysis setup and procedure, ask a physical science teacher to show you or to do the demonstration for the class.) At the end of the demonstration, emphasize that more energy is used in producing the electricity needed for electrolysis than is provided by the hydrogen. **learning modality: visual**

Program Resources

Science Explorer Series *Inside Earth,* Chapter 3, provides more information on geothermal energy.

Media and Technology

Transparencies "A Geothermal Power Plant," Transparency 17

Answers to Self-Assessment
Caption Question

Figure 12 They all derive their energy from the sun and are renewable. Using biomass materials to produce alcohol and methane is expensive, and though they are renewable, it takes time for them to grow.

✓ *Checkpoint*

Geothermal energy can be used to produce steam to turn a turbine.

Ongoing Assessment

Writing Have each student briefly describe the two different ways in which biomass materials can be used as fuels.

 Students can save their work in their portfolios.

3 Assess

Section 2 Review Answers

1. Energy from the sun
2. Winds are created by uneven heating of the atmosphere by the sun. Flowing water is part of the water cycle, which is driven by the sun's energy.
3. Active solar systems convert solar energy to thermal energy and then use fans and pumps to distribute the heat. Passive solar systems convert solar energy to thermal energy but do not distribute it.
4. *Any three:* wood, leaves, food wastes, manure, sugar-cane wastes, corn, alcohol, methane
5. Geothermal energy is available only where magma is close to Earth's surface.
6. Accept a variety of responses. Students should support their answers with reasons that take into account the geographic features of their area.

Check Your Progress
CHAPTER PROJECT 6

Check each group's data table to make sure students are collecting and recording data. Provide some copies of the school's fuel and utility bills so students can determine the amount and actual cost of each type of energy used. If a group is studying energy used for transportation, encourage them to survey other students about transportation to school. They also may need to contact your district's central office or the private company that owns and operates the school buses for information.

Figure 14 The object fascinating these three astronauts is a bubble of water—the harmless by-product of the hydrogen fuel cells used on the space shuttle.

Hydrogen Power

Now that you have read about so many energy sources, consider a fuel with this description: It burns cleanly, forming only water as a by-product. It creates no smoke, smog, or acid rain. It can be handled and transported through pipelines, much like natural gas. This fuel exists on Earth in large supply.

This ideal-sounding fuel is real—it's hydrogen. However, there is an obstacle. Almost all the hydrogen on Earth is combined with oxygen in the form of water. Pure hydrogen can be obtained by passing an electric current through water. But it takes more energy to obtain the hydrogen than is produced by burning it again.

Scientists aren't ruling out hydrogen as a good fuel for the future. At present, hydroelectric plants decrease their activity when the demand for electricity is low. Instead, they could run at full power all the time, using the excess electricity to produce hydrogen. Similarly, solar power plants often generate more electricity than is needed during the day. This extra electricity could be used to produce hydrogen. If a way can be found to produce hydrogen cheaply, it could someday be an important source of energy.

Section 2 Review

1. What is solar energy?
2. How are the energy of wind and flowing water each related to solar energy?
3. How are active and passive solar heating systems different?
4. List three examples of biomass fuels.
5. What limits the use of geothermal energy?
6. **Thinking Critically Predicting** Which of the renewable sources of energy do you think is most likely to be used in your community in 100 years? Give reasons to support your answer.

Check Your Progress
CHAPTER PROJECT 6

Continue to collect data on how much energy is used in your group's area of the school. Begin to brainstorm ideas for reducing energy usage in this area. For example, is there a way to use some electrical devices for shorter periods of time? (*Hint:* Interviewing some adults who are responsible for the operation of the school building may give you some good ideas. Be sure to check with your teacher before interviewing anyone.)

Performance Assessment

Skills Check Have each student create a compare/contrast table that includes at least five of the renewable energy sources discussed in this section and identifies one advantage and one disadvantage of each source.

 Students can save their tables in their portfolios.

Program Resources

◆ **Teaching Resources** 6-2 Review and Reinforce, p. 153; 6-2 Enrich, p. 154

Media and Technology

 Interactive Student Tutorial CD-ROM E-6

How It Works

Cooking With Sunshine

In the future, will you cook your meals with sunshine instead of electricity? That's certainly a possibility. In this lab, you'll investigate how solar energy can be used to cook food.

Problem

What is the best shape for a solar cooker?

Skills Focus

predicting, designing experiments, forming operational definitions

Suggested Materials

scissors	glue	3 thermometers
3 dowels	tape	marshmallows
3 sheets of aluminum foil		clock or watch
3 sheets of oaktag paper		

Procedure

Part 1 Capturing Solar Energy

1. Read over the entire lab. Then predict which shape will produce the largest temperature increase when placed in the sun.
2. Glue a sheet of aluminum foil, shiny side up, to each sheet of oaktag paper. Before the glue dries, gently smooth out any wrinkles in the foil.
3. Bend one sheet into a V shape. Bend another sheet into a U shape. Leave the last sheet flat.
4. Place the aluminum sheets in direct sunlight, using wood blocks or books to hold the U- and V-shapes in position.
5. Tape a dowel to each thermometer. Record the starting temperature on each thermometer.
6. Use the dowels to hold the thermometer bulbs in the center of the aluminum shapes. After 15 minutes, record the final temperature on each thermometer.

Part 2 Designing a Solar Cooker

7. Use the results from Step 6 to design a solar cooker that can toast a marshmallow. Prepare a written description of your plan for your teacher's approval. Include an operational definition of a "well-toasted" marshmallow.
8. After your teacher has approved your plan, test your design by placing a marshmallow on a wooden dowel. Record the time it takes to toast the marshmallow.

Analyze and Conclude

1. What was the role of the aluminum foil in this investigation? What other materials could you have used instead? Explain.
2. Which of the three shapes—V, U, or flat—produced the largest increase in temperature? Propose an explanation for this result.
3. What other variables might have affected your results? Explain.
4. **Apply** What are some possible advantages of a solar cooker based on this design? What are some possible disadvantages?

More to Explore

Try adapting your design to heat water. Show your new design to your teacher before trying it.

Extending the Inquiry

More to Explore Have students use a small volume of water. Encourage them to consider the kind of material to use for the water container.

Safety

Students should wear safety goggles and use caution in handling glass thermometers. Review the safety guidelines in Appendix A.

Cooking With Sunshine

Preparing for Inquiry

Key Concept A solar cooker that focuses the sun's rays in its center works best.

Skills Objectives Students will be able to

◆ predict which of three designs will produce the greatest temperature increase in a solar cooker;

◆ design an experiment to test how the shape of a solar cooker affects how it functions;

◆ form an operational definition of a "well-toasted" marshmallow.

Time 40 minutes

Advance Planning Identify a sunny area for the solar cookers.

Guiding Inquiry

Introducing the Procedure

◆ Have students work in groups of three.
◆ If needed, review the meaning of "operational definition."

Troubleshooting the Experiment

◆ In Step 3, make sure students have the foil side on the inside of the U or V.
◆ In Step 6, make sure students hold the thermometers with their bulbs at the same distance from the foil.

Expected Outcome

Specific temperatures will vary, but the U-shaped cooker should produce the largest temperature increase and the flat cooker the smallest increase.

Analyze and Conclude

1. The foil reflected the sun's rays. Other reflective materials such as mirrors or shiny metal could be used.
2. The U shape; it reflects the sun's rays into the center of the cooker.
3. Variables include time of day, distance between the thermometer bulbs and the cookers' surface, and air movement.
4. *Advantages:* simple design, ease of use, inexpensive, no polluting fumes. *Disadvantages:* cannot be used on a cloudy day or at night; slow; not efficient for cooking large items.

Hydroelectric Dams: Are They All Here to Stay?

Purpose

Evaluate the benefits and costs of removing hydroelectric dams, and recommend removing, adapting, or relicensing a dam.

Role-Play

Time 40 minutes

◆ After students have read the feature, ask: **Why should people try to protect fish species?** (*Accept a variety of reasons, including the economic value of commercial fishing.*) **Why are hydroelectric dams an important source of energy?** (*They reduce use of fossil fuels, produce electricity at low cost, and don't cause pollution.*)

◆ Point out that there are *three* possible recommendations: relicense the dam, remove it, or find ways to enable fish to bypass it. Let students discuss the issue freely.

◆ Divide the class into small groups, with each group member representing a different viewpoint—for example, the company that owns the dam, local industries that rely on the electricity produced by the dam, fisheries, ecologists, and citizens. Provide time for the groups to discuss the options.

Extend Suggest that students research the costs of electricity produced by hydroelectric dams and by burning fossil fuels. They could also investigate the effectiveness of fish ladders.

You Decide

◆ Students' answers to Identify the Problem and Analyze the Options should use the points in the text.

◆ In response to Find a Solution, students may rely on issues raised in their discussions or present new ideas. Each student should give a well-reasoned rationale for his or her recommendation.

Hydroelectric Dams: Are They All Here to Stay?

There are hundreds of hydroelectric dams on United States rivers. These dams provide electricity for millions of people. Hydroelectric dams provide clean, inexpensive, and renewable energy. They are a good source of power.

Recently, however, people have learned that dams can have negative effects on river ecosystems. Some people have even suggested removing certain dams. But is this wise? When do the benefits of dams outweigh the problems?

The Issues

How Do Dams Affect the Environment? Because dams change water depth and flow, they can alter the temperature of a river. The water may become too cold or too warm for fish that normally live there. A change in temperature can also reduce the number of algae in a river. This affects other organisms in the river food web.

Some species of fish, such as salmon, herring, and menhaden, hatch in rivers but then travel to the ocean. To breed, they must return to the river. Dams can block the movement of these fish populations. For example, the Columbia River Basin, which has more than 50 dams, once contained more than 10 million salmon. Today it is home to only 2 million salmon.

What Are the Effects of Removing Dams? Some people say that the only way to restore ecosystems is to remove dams. However, these dams supply a small but important part of the nation's electricity. Removing them could force the United States to use more nonrenewable fossil fuels. Fossil fuels also produce more pollution than hydroelectric plants.

The reservoirs behind hydroelectric dams supply water for irrigation and drinking. These supplies would be difficult to replace. In addition, a series of dams on a river can reduce flooding downstream during heavy rains.

What Can People Do? Removing dams might restore some river ecosystems. For example, Edwards Dam on the Kennebec River in Maine is scheduled to be removed to allow several threatened fish species to spawn. But Edwards Dam provides only a small percent of Maine's electric power. This small amount is easier to replace than the power provided by a much larger dam.

There are other ways to protect migrating fish. Fish ladders, for example, are step-like waterways that help fish pass over dams. Fish can even be carried around dams in trucks. Still, these methods are costly and not always successful.

The government issues licenses for hydroelectric dams. In considering license renewals, officials examine environmental impact as well as energy production.

You Decide

1. Identify the Problem
In your own words, explain some of the major issues surrounding hydroelectric dams.

2. Analyze the Options
Examine the pros and cons of removing dams. What are the benefits? What are the costs? Who will be affected by the change?

3. Find a Solution
The license of a nearby dam is up for review. The dam provides electricity, but also blocks the migration of fish. What do you recommend? Explain.

Background

History of Science In November 1997, the Federal Energy Regulatory Commission for the first time refused to renew the license for a hydroelectric dam—the Edwards Dam on the Kennebec River in Maine. The dam produced only a very small amount of electricity, but prevented salmon and other anadromous fish from spawning in the river.

The owners of hydroelectric dams upstream on the Kennebec will contribute $4.75 million toward the costs of removing the dam and restoring 17 miles of spawning grounds in exchange for having their deadlines extended to install fish ladders on the upstream dams.

SECTION 3 Nuclear Energy

DISCOVER ···················· ACTIVITY
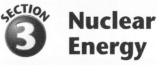

Why Do They Fall?

1. Line up 15 dominoes to form a triangle, as shown.

2. Knock over the first domino so that it falls against the second row of dominoes. Observe the results.

3. Set up the dominoes again, but then remove the dominoes in the third row from the lineup.

4. Knock over the first domino again. Observe what happens.

Think It Over

Inferring Suppose each domino produced a large amount of energy when it fell over. Why might it be helpful to remove the dominoes as you did in Step 3?

Wouldn't it be great if people could use the same method as the sun to produce energy? In a way, they can! The kind of reactions that power the sun involve the central cores of atoms. The central core of an atom that contains the protons and neutrons is called the **nucleus** (plural nuclei). The reactions that involve nuclei, called nuclear reactions, involve tremendous amounts of energy. Two types of nuclear reactions are fission and fusion.

Fission Reactions and Energy

Nuclear reactions convert matter into energy. In 1905, Albert Einstein developed a formula that described the relationship between energy and matter. You have probably seen this famous equation, $E = mc^2$. In the equation, the E represents energy and the m represents mass. The c, which represents the speed of light, is a very large number. This equation states that when matter is changed into energy, an enormous amount of energy is released.

   Nuclear fission is the splitting of an atom's nucleus into two smaller nuclei. The fuel for the reaction is a large atom that has an unstable nucleus, such as uranium-235 (U-235). A neutron is shot at the U-235 atom at high speed. **When the neutron hits the U-235 nucleus, the nucleus splits apart into two smaller nuclei and two or more neutrons.** The total mass of all these particles is a bit less than the mass of the original nucleus. The small amount of mass that makes up the difference has been converted into energy—a lot of energy, as described by Einstein's equation.

GUIDE FOR READING

♦ What happens during fission and fusion reactions?

♦ How does a nuclear power plant produce electricity?

Reading Tip As you read, create a Venn diagram to compare and contrast nuclear fission and nuclear fusion.

Figure 15 Albert Einstein, shown here in 1930, described the relationship between energy and matter.

E ◆ 181

INTEGRATING CHEMISTRY

SECTION 3 Nuclear Energy

Objectives

After completing the lesson, students will be able to
♦ describe nuclear fission and nuclear fusion reactions;
♦ explain how a nuclear power plant produces electricity.

Key Terms nucleus, nuclear fission, reactor vessel, fuel rods, control rods, meltdown, nuclear fusion

1 Engage/Explore

Activating Prior Knowledge

Ask several students to come to the board, draw what they think an atom looks like, and label its parts. Encourage the rest of the class to discuss the drawings and suggest corrections or additions. You can return to the diagrams later in the section.

········ DISCOVER ········

Skills Focus inferring
Materials *15 dominoes*
Time 10 minutes
Tips Make sure students place the dominoes with less than a domino-length space between rows.
Expected Outcome In Step 2, all 15 dominoes will topple as those in one row fall back against those in the next row. With the third row removed in Step 4, the last two rows will remain standing.
Think It Over Removing the third row would stop the production of energy after a certain point.

READING STRATEGIES

Reading Tip Review the format of a Venn diagram: two overlapping circles with likenesses noted in the overlap area and differences noted in the outer areas.

Vocabulary To help students differentiate between fission and fusion, explain that the term *fusion* comes from the root "fuse." Ask students to explain what it means to fuse things together.

Program Resources

♦ **Teaching Resources** 6-3 Lesson Plan, p. 155; 6-3 Section Summary, p. 156

Media and Technology

 Audiotapes English-Spanish Summary 6-3

Fission Reactions and Energy

Building Inquiry Skills: Making Models

Materials *sheet of paper*
Time 5 minutes

Give each student a sheet of paper, and tell the class to think of the paper as the nucleus of a U-235 atom. To model the nucleus splitting into two smaller nuclei and three neutrons, have students tear the paper into five pieces—two larger and three smaller—and label the two larger pieces "smaller nucleus" and the three smaller pieces "neutron." Then have students tear a tiny piece off each "smaller nucleus" and set these tiny pieces aside. Explain that the tiny pieces represent the tiny amount of matter that is converted into energy in a fission reaction. **learning modality: kinesthetic**

TRY THIS

Skills Focus making models

Materials *12 marbles*
Time 10 minutes
Tips Caution students not to walk around during this activity so they do not step on the marbles.
Expected Outcome The single marble represents a neutron being shot at an atom's nucleus. When it strikes the cluster, it scatters the marbles, similar to the breaking apart of the nucleus when it is struck by a neutron.
Extend After students have read about nuclear fusion on pages 184–185, challenge them to adapt this activity to model fusion. **learning modality: kinesthetic**

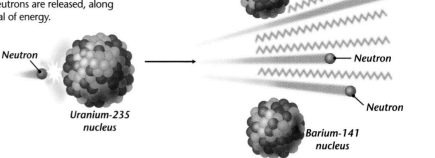

Figure 16 In a nuclear fission reaction, a neutron "bullet" strikes a U-235 nucleus. As a result, the nucleus splits into two smaller nuclei. More neutrons are released, along with a great deal of energy.

TRY THIS

Shoot the Nucleus

In an open area of your classroom, make a model of a nuclear fission reaction. Place a handful of marbles on the floor in a tight cluster, so that they touch one another. Step back about a half-meter from the marbles. Shoot another marble at the cluster.

Making Models What does the marble you shot at the cluster represent? What effect did the marble have on the cluster? How is this similar to a nuclear fission reaction?

Meanwhile, the fission reaction has produced three more neutrons. If any of these neutrons strikes another nucleus, the fission reaction is repeated. More neutrons and more energy are released. If there are enough nuclei nearby, the process continues over and over in a chain reaction, just like a row of dominoes falling. In a nuclear chain reaction, the amount of energy released increases rapidly with each step in the chain.

What happens to all the energy released by these fission reactions? If a nuclear chain reaction is not controlled, the released energy causes a huge explosion. The explosion of an atomic bomb is an uncontrolled nuclear reaction. A few kilograms of matter explode with more force than several thousand tons of a nonnuclear explosive such as dynamite. However, if the chain reaction is controlled, the energy is released as heat, which can be used to generate electricity.

Nuclear Power Plants

Controlled nuclear fission reactions take place inside nuclear power plants. **In a nuclear power plant, the heat released from the reactions is used to change water into steam. As in other types of power plants, the steam then turns the blades of a turbine to generate electricity.** Look at the diagram of a nuclear power plant in Figure 17. In addition to the generator, it has two main parts: the reactor vessel and the heat exchanger.

Reactor Vessel The **reactor vessel** is the section of a nuclear reactor where nuclear fission occurs. The reactor contains rods of U-235, called **fuel rods.** When several fuel rods are placed close together, a series of fission reactions occurs. The reactions are controlled by placing **control rods** made of the metal cadmium between the fuel rods. The cadmium absorbs the neutrons

Background

Integrating Science Investigation of the Chernobyl accident revealed two basic causes. First, the reactor was not housed in a containment building and was extremely unstable at low power. This type of reactor is not used commercially in North America or Western Europe because nuclear engineers consider it too unsafe. Second, many of the plant's operators lacked scientific or technical expertise and made major errors when dealing with the initial problem.

The long-term health effects of the Chernobyl disaster are still being studied. Increases in birth defects and thyroid cancer in children have been documented. Other cancers are not expected to increase until 20 or more years after the accident.

released during the fission reactions. As the cadmium control rods are removed, the fission reactions speed up. If the reactor vessel starts to get too hot, the control rods are moved back in place to slow the chain reaction.

Heat Exchanger Heat is removed from the reactor vessel by water or another fluid that is pumped through the reactor. This fluid passes through a heat exchanger. There, the fluid boils water to produce steam, which runs the electrical generator. The steam is condensed again and pumped back to the heat exchanger.

☑ *Checkpoint* *How are fission reactions controlled?*

The Risks of Nuclear Fission

When it was first demonstrated, people thought that nuclear fission would provide an almost unlimited source of clean, safe energy. Today nuclear power plants generate much of the world's electricity—about 20 percent in the United States and more than 70 percent in France. But these plants have some problems.

In 1986, in Chernobyl, Ukraine, the reactor vessel in a nuclear power plant overheated. The fuel rods generated so much heat that they started to melt, a condition called a **meltdown.** The excess heat increased the steam pressure in the generator. A series of explosions blew parts of the roof off and injured or killed dozens of plant workers and firefighters. Radioactive materials escaped into the environment. Today, the soil in an area the size of Florida remains contaminated with radioactive waste.

Sharpen your Skills

Calculating
ACTIVITY

A single pellet of U-235 the size of a breath mint can produce as much energy as 615 liters of fuel oil. An average home uses 5,000 liters of oil a year. How many U-235 pellets would be needed to supply the same amount of energy?

Figure 17 In a nuclear plant, uranium fuel undergoes fission, producing heat. The heat boils water, and the resulting steam drives the turbines that generate electricity. *Interpreting Diagrams From which part of the power plant is heat released to the environment?*

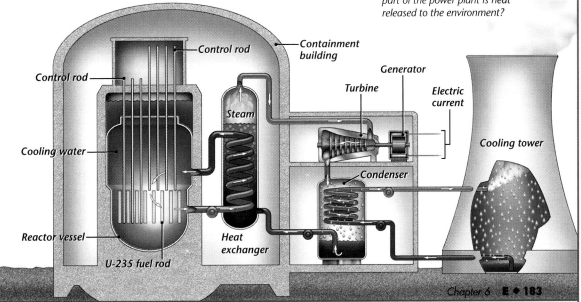

Control rod — Containment building
Control rod
Generator
Turbine
Electric current
Steam
Cooling water
Cooling tower
Condenser
Reactor vessel
Heat exchanger
U-235 fuel rod

Media and Technology

🖳 **Transparencies** "Nuclear Fission," Transparency 18; "A Nuclear Power Plant," Transparency 19

Answers to Self-Assessment

☑ *Checkpoint*
Fission reactions are controlled by placing cadmium control rods between the fuel rods to absorb neutrons.

Caption Question
Figure 17 The cooling tower

Sharpen your Skills

Calculating
Materials *calculator (optional)*
ACTIVITY
Time 5 minutes
Tips If needed, help students determine how to calculate the answer (divide 5,000 by 615).
Expected Outcome About 8 (8.13) pellets would be needed.
Extend Suggest that each student estimate how many homes are in his or her neighborhood, then calculate how many pellets would be needed to supply energy to all those homes for a year.
learning modality: logical/mathematical

The Risks of Nuclear Fission

Building Inquiry Skills: Inferring
Display a large world map, and let volunteers locate Chernobyl (51°N, 30°E, about 130 km north of Kiev). Tell students that the force of the 1986 explosion carried radioactive materials high into the atmosphere, where they spread across the Northern Hemisphere and then settled back to Earth in what is called "fallout." The heaviest fallout occurred in Ukraine, Belarus, Sweden, Norway, Denmark, France, and Switzerland. In addition, Finland, Lithuania, Germany, Poland, the Czech Republic, Slovakia, Austria, Hungary, Italy, and Great Britain suffered moderate fallout. Let students find all these countries on the map. Ask: **What does this tell you about the dangers of nuclear power plants?** *(An accident can affect a huge area.)* **learning modality: visual**

Ongoing Assessment

Oral Presentation Call on students at random to each explain a step in the process of how a nuclear power plant converts nuclear energy to electricity.

Figure 18 One problem with nuclear power is disposal of the used radioactive fuel rods. In this plant in France, the fuel rods are stored in a deep pool of water.

Chernobyl and less-serious accidents at other nuclear power plants have led to public concerns about nuclear plant safety.

The danger of a meltdown is a serious concern. However, a meltdown can be avoided by careful planning. A more difficult problem is the disposal of radioactive wastes produced by power plants. Radioactive wastes remain dangerous for many thousands of years. Scientists must find a way to safely store these wastes for a long period of time. Finally, nuclear power has turned out to be a much more costly source of power than was originally expected. The safety features required for nuclear plants make the plants very expensive.

☑ *Checkpoint* What are three problems with using nuclear fission as an energy source?

The Quest to Control Fusion

A second type of nuclear reaction is fusion. **Nuclear fusion** is the combining of two atomic nuclei to produce a single larger nucleus. **As shown in Figure 19, two kinds of hydrogen nuclei are forced together in a fusion reaction.** One kind (hydrogen-2) has one proton and one neutron, and the other kind (hydrogen-3) has one proton and two neutrons. The tremendous heat and pressure

Figure 19 In a nuclear fusion reaction, two nuclei combine to form a single larger nucleus. *Interpreting Diagrams What is released during a fusion reaction?*

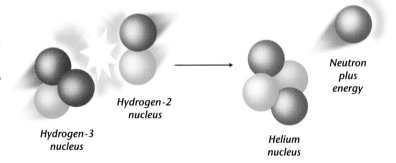

Hydrogen-3 nucleus

Hydrogen-2 nucleus

Helium nucleus

Neutron plus energy

cause them to combine and create a helium nucleus with two protons and two neutrons. This helium nucleus has slightly less mass than the total mass of the two hydrogen nuclei. The difference is converted to energy.

Nuclear fusion would have many advantages as an energy source. Fusion can produce much more energy per atom than nuclear fission. The fuel for a nuclear fusion reactor is also readily available. Water, which is plentiful in Earth's oceans, contains one of the kinds of hydrogen needed for fusion. Fusion should be safer and less polluting than nuclear fission. You can see why scientists are eager to find a way to build a nuclear fusion reactor!

Although some fusion bombs have been exploded, scientists have not yet been able to control a large-scale fusion reaction. The biggest problem is temperature. In the sun, nuclear fusion occurs at 15 million degrees Celsius. Such conditions are almost impossible to create on Earth. Very great pressure would also work to contain a fusion reaction. But no material has been found that could serve as a reactor vessel under such high pressure. Extremely powerful magnetic fields can contain a fusion reaction. However, it takes more energy to generate these fields than the fusion reaction produces.

Although many more years of research are expected, some scientists believe that they will eventually be able to control fusion reactions. If they succeed, the quest for a clean, cheap energy source may be over at last.

Figure 20 Researchers at Los Alamos National Laboratory in New Mexico are studying fusion as an energy source. This machine creates strong magnetic fields that allow fusion to occur for short periods of time.

 Section 3 Review

1. Draw and label a simple diagram of a nuclear fission reaction. Include the following labels: U-235 nucleus, neutrons, smaller nuclei, and energy.
2. How can the energy released in a fission reaction be used to produce electricity?
3. Explain the purpose of control rods.
4. Give two reasons that people have not been able to use nuclear fusion as an energy source.
5. **Thinking Critically Classifying** Is nuclear fission a renewable or nonrenewable energy source? Is nuclear fusion renewable or nonrenewable? Explain.

Check Your Progress CHAPTER PROJECT 6

By now you should begin preparing the written report of your findings about energy use in your group's area of the school. Your report should include the major ways energy is used in your chosen area. You should also include recommendations on how energy use might be reduced.

---

3 Assess

Section 3 Review Answers

1. Students' diagrams should show the U-235 nucleus being struck by one neutron, then splitting to form two smaller nuclei, three neutrons, and energy. (See Figure 16.)
2. The heat energy released by a fission reaction can be used to boil water, producing steam that turns the blades of a turbine to generate electricity.
3. Control rods absorb excess neutrons and control the fission reactions.
4. Fusion reactions cannot be controlled; more energy is needed to produce a fusion reaction than is produced by the reaction itself.
5. Nuclear fission is considered a nonrenewable resource because it depends on uranium, which is a nonrenewable element. Nuclear fusion is considered a renewable resource because Earth's water is abundant and is renewed in natural processes.

Check Your Progress CHAPTER PROJECT 6

Encourage students to make their reports concise, focusing on the major points and, when appropriate, using visual displays (such as a neat copy of the data table). Also suggest that they explain how each recommendation would reduce energy use.

Program Resources

◆ **Teaching Resources** 6-3 Review and Reinforce, p. 157; 6-3 Enrich, p. 158

Media and Technology

Transparencies Transparencies "Nuclear Fusion," Transparency 20

Interactive Student Tutorial CD-ROM E-6

Answers to Self-Assessment

☑ *Checkpoint*

An accident can cause serious damage, injury, and death. Radioactive wastes are difficult to dispose of safely. Nuclear power is costly.

Caption Question

Figure 19 A neutron plus energy

Performance Assessment

Skills Check Have each student create a table that compares the advantages and disadvantages of nuclear fission and nuclear fusion as energy sources.

 Students can save their tables in their portfolios.

Keeping Comfortable

NOTE: This lab is placed before its related section to allow enough time for students to conduct the test in Part 1, then design and carry out their own experiments.

Preparing for Inquiry

Key Concept Different materials lessen the transfer of heat to different degrees.

Skills Objectives Students will be able to

◆ measure temperature changes of water in a paper cup for use as a baseline;

◆ design an experiment to compare how well different materials maintain water temperature by slowing heat transfer.

Time 40 minutes

Advance Planning Prepare hot water and ice water ahead of time, and keep them in insulated containers. CAUTION: *Do not use water hot enough to cause scalding.*

Guiding Inquiry

Helping Design a Plan

◆ Ask: **What is the purpose of doing Part 1 with a paper cup first?** *(To determine a standard for comparing materials)*

Troubleshooting the Experiment

◆ Have students answer the questions in Step 5 in a class discussion before they write their plans. Define *manipulated variable* and *responding variable.*

◆ Make sure students control all variables and record temperatures at regular intervals.

Expected Outcome

The most effective material for stopping heat transfer is plastic foam; the least effective is metal.

Analyze and Conclude

1. Temperatures will vary. Heat flowed from the hot water to the cold water, as shown by the temperature changes.

2. *Rooms:* cold water; *outdoor weather:* hot water; *walls:* paper cup

3. *Most effective:* plastic foam. *Least effective:* metal. Plastic foam kept the

cold water close to its starting temperature for the longest time, while metal let the starting temperature increase the most.

4. Students should realize that other issues, such as the materials' strength, durability, and cost, must be considered.

Extending the Inquiry

More to Explore Students' plans should be similar to those they developed in Part 2.

Keeping Comfortable

Two ways to use less energy are to keep heat out of your home when the weather is hot, and to keep heat in when the weather is cold. In this lab, you will design an experiment to compare how well different materials do this.

Problem

How well do different materials stop heat transfer?

Suggested Materials

thermometers   ice water   hot water
watch or clock   beakers
containers and lids made of paper, plastic foam, plastic, glass, and metal

Design a Plan

Part 1 Measuring Temperature Changes

1. Use a pencil to poke a hole in the lid of a paper cup. Fill the cup about halfway with cold water.

2. Put the lid on the cup. Insert a thermometer into the water through the hole. When the temperature stops dropping, place the cup in a beaker. Add hot water to the beaker until the water level is about 1 cm below the lid.

3. Record the water temperature once every minute until it has increased by 5°C. Use the time it takes for the temperature to increase 1°C as a measure of the effectiveness of the paper cup in preventing heat transfer.

Part 2 Comparing Materials

4. Use the ideas from Part 1 to design a controlled experiment to rank the effectiveness of different materials in preventing heat transfer.

5. Use these questions to help you plan your experiment:

◆ What hypothesis will you test?

◆ Which materials do you predict will be the best and worst at preventing heat transfer? How will you define these terms?

◆ What will your manipulated variable be? What will your responding variable be?

◆ What variables do you need to control? How will you control them?

◆ What step-by-step procedures will you use?

◆ What kind of data table will you use?

6. After your teacher has reviewed your plans, make any necessary changes in your design. Then perform your experiment.

Analyze and Conclude

1. In Part 1, what was the starting temperature of the hot water? What was the starting temperature of the cold water? In which direction did the heat flow? How do you know?

2. If the materials in Part 1 are used to represent your home in very hot weather, which material would represent the rooms in your home? Which would represent the outdoor weather? Which would represent the walls of the building?

3. Which material was most effective at preventing the transfer of heat? Which was the least effective? Explain.

4. **Think About It** Would experiments similar to this one provide you with enough information to choose materials to build a home? Explain.

More to Explore

Create a plan to compare how well the materials would work if the hot water were inside the cup and the cold water were outside. With your teacher's permission, carry out your plan.

Program Resources

◆ **Teaching Resources** Chapter 6 Skills Lab, pp. 165–167

Safety

Students should use caution in handling the thermometers, hot water, and glass containers. Review the safety guidelines in Appendix A.

SECTION 4 Energy Conservation

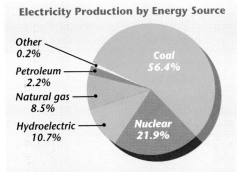

DISCOVER · ACTIVITY

Which Bulb Is More Efficient?

1. Record the light output (listed in lumens) from the packages of a 60-watt incandescent light bulb and a 15-watt compact fluorescent bulb.

2. Place the fluorescent bulb in a lamp socket. **CAUTION:** *Make sure the lamp is unplugged.*

3. Plug in the lamp and turn it on. Hold the end of a thermometer about 8 centimeters from the bulb.

4. Record the temperature after 5 minutes.

5. Turn off and unplug the lamp. When the bulb is cool, remove it. Repeat Steps 2, 3, and 4 with the incandescent light bulb.

Think It Over

Inferring Based on the number of lumens, what is the difference between the amount of light given off by the two types of bulbs? The incandescent bulb uses 5 times as much electricity. Why do you think this might be?

Imagine what would happen if the world ran out of fossil fuels today. Eighty percent of the electric power would disappear. Most buildings would lose their heating and cooling. Forests would disappear as people began to burn wood for heat and cooking. Almost all transportation would stop. Cars, buses, trains, airplanes, and ships would be stranded wherever they ran out of fuel. Since radios, televisions, computers, and telephones depend on electricity, communication would be greatly reduced.

Although fossil fuels won't run out immediately, they also won't last forever. Most people think that it makes sense to start planning now to avoid a fuel shortage in the future. **One approach to the problem is to find new sources of energy. The second way is to make the fuels that are available now last as long as possible while other solutions are being developed.**

Conservation and Efficiency

Reducing energy use is called **energy conservation.** For example, if you walk to the store instead of getting a ride, you are conserving the gasoline needed to drive to the store. Reducing energy use is a solution to energy problems that will help no matter what form of energy is used in the future.

GUIDE FOR READING

◆ What are two ways to make sure there will be enough energy for the future?

◆ How does insulation help conserve energy?

Reading Tip Before you read, list ways to conserve energy. As you read, add to the list.

Electricity Production by Energy Source

Other 0.2%
Petroleum 2.2%
Natural gas 8.5%
Hydroelectric 10.7%
Coal 56.4%
Nuclear 21.9%

Figure 21 Nonrenewable fossil fuels generate over two thirds of the nation's electricity.

Background

Reading Tip To provide structure and prompt students' thinking, suggest that they list types of energy uses (electricity for lights and appliances, oil or natural gas for heating, gasoline for cars, and so forth) as headings across the top of a page and then list ways to reduce each use below the headings.

Program Resources

◆ **Teaching Resources** 6-4 Lesson Plan, p. 159; 6-4 Section Summary, p. 160

Media and Technology

🎧 **Audiotapes** English-Spanish Summary 6-4

SECTION 4 Energy Conservation

Objectives

After completing the lesson, students will be able to
◆ list two ways to ensure that there will be enough energy for the future;
◆ identify things that individuals can do to conserve energy.

Key Terms energy conservation, efficiency, insulation

1 Engage/Explore

Activating Prior Knowledge

Point out the section's title and ask: **What does the term energy conservation mean?** *(Accept all reasonable responses, such as "not wasting energy.")* **What are some examples of wasting energy?** *(Setting a thermostat too high, leaving lights on in an unoccupied room, running a dishwasher with only a small load, and the like.)*

· · · · · · · DISCOVER · · · · · · ·

Skills Focus inferring
Materials *60-watt incandescent light bulb and 15-watt compact fluorescent light bulb in packages, lamp, thermometer, clock or watch*
Time 20 minutes
CAUTION: *Students should use caution when handling the bulbs and lamp plug.*
Tips Compact fluorescent bulbs, widely available in supermarkets and hardware stores, screw into a regular bulb socket.
Expected Outcome The fluorescent bulb will not produce as high a temperature as the incandescent bulb because it uses electricity more efficiently, converting more to light and less to heat.
Think It Over Lumens may vary among bulb brands. Based on 900 lumens for a 60-watt incandescent bulb and 825 lumens for a 15-watt compact fluorescent bulb, the difference is 75 lumens. The incandescent bulb uses more electricity because so much is converted to heat.

E ◆ 187

2 Facilitate

Conservation and Efficiency

Building Inquiry Skills: Calculating

Materials *packages from 60-watt incandescent light bulb and 15-watt compact fluorescent light bulb, calculator (optional)*

ACTIVITY

Time 10 minutes

Explain that the number of watts printed on a light bulb and its package tells how much electrical energy is needed to light the bulb for one second (1 watt = 1 joule per second). Have students examine the packages and identify the wattage of each bulb. *(Incandescent bulb 60 watts, fluorescent bulb 15 watts)* Ask: **How many times more electrical energy does the incandescent bulb use to produce the same amount of light as the fluorescent bulb?** *(4 times as much)* **What is the expected life of each bulb?** *(Answers will depend on brands of bulbs used; examples: incandescent bulb 1,000 hours, fluorescent bulb 10,000 hours)* **How many incandescent bulbs would you need to equal the life of one fluorescent bulb?** *(10)* **How much would 10 incandescent bulbs cost compared with the cost of one fluorescent bulb?** *($7.50 [10 × 75¢] compared with $20.00; prices may vary)* **How much more than 10 incandescent bulbs would the fluorescent bulb cost over its life?** *($12.50)* **Do you think the fluorescent bulb is worth its higher cost?** *(Accept all answers at this point.)* **According to the fluorescent bulb's package, how much would you save in electricity costs by using that one bulb instead of 10 incandescent bulbs for 10,000 hours?** *($45.00)* **What would your total savings be over the life of the fluorescent bulb?** *($45.00 – $12.50, or $32.50)* **So which type of bulb is better, and why?** *(The fluorescent bulb, because it costs less in the long term and conserves electricity.)*
learning modality: logical/ mathematical

188 ◆ E

A way to get as much work as possible out of fuels is to use them efficiently. **Efficiency** is the percentage of energy that is actually used to perform work. The rest of the energy is "lost" to the surroundings, usually as heat. People have developed many ways to increase energy efficiency.

Lighting Lights can use as much as 10 percent of the electricity in your home, but much of that electricity is wasted. An incandescent light bulb converts less than 10 percent of the electricity it uses into light. The rest is given off as heat. You can prove this to yourself by holding your hand close to an incandescent light bulb. But don't touch it! Compact fluorescent bulbs, on the other hand, use only about one fourth as much energy to provide the same amount of light.

☑ *Checkpoint* *Which type of light bulb is more energy-efficient?*

SCIENCE & History

Energy-Efficient Devices

Scientists and engineers have developed many technologies that improve energy efficiency and reduce energy use.

1932 Fiberglass Insulation

Long strands of glass fibers trap air and keep buildings from losing heat. Less fuel is used for heating.

1958 Solar Cells

More than 150 years ago, scientists discovered that silicon can convert light into electricity. The first useful application of solar cells was to power the radio on a satellite. Now solar cells are even used on experimental cars like the one below.

1930   1940   1950

1936 Fluorescent Lighting

Fluorescent bulbs were introduced to the public at the 100th anniversary celebration of the United States Patent Office. Because these bulbs use less energy than incandescent bulbs, most offices and schools use fluorescent lights.

188 ◆ E

Background

Facts and Figures Energy-efficient devices like those shown in the timeline have helped conserve energy. For example, "superinsulated" homes can use from 70 to 95 percent less energy for heating than homes with conventional insulation. These homes are surrounded by an "envelope" of insulation and have airtight construction.

Because of lighter materials and designs that reduce air drag, the fuel efficiency of passenger cars has improved dramatically, from an average of 6.8 km/L in 1981 to 9.1 km/L in 1994.

The National Appliance Energy Conservation Act sets energy-efficiency standards for refrigerators, washing machines, water heaters, and other appliances. As a result of this law, refrigerators built in the mid-1990s use more than 80 percent less energy than those built in the early 1980s.

Heating and Cooling One method of increasing the efficiency of heating and cooling systems is insulation. **Insulation** is a layer of material that helps block the transfer of heat between the air inside and outside a building. You have probably seen insulation made of fiberglass, which looks like fluffy pink cotton candy. The mat of thin glass fibers trap air. **This layer of trapped air helps keep the building from losing or gaining heat from the outside.** A layer of fiberglass 15 centimeters thick insulates a room as well as a brick wall 2 meters thick or a stone wall almost 6 meters thick!

Buildings lose a lot of heat around the windows. Look at the windows in your school or home. Was the building built after 1980? Have the windows been replaced recently? If so, you will most likely see two panes of glass with space between them. The air between the panes of glass acts as insulation.

In Your Journal

Design an advertisement for one of the energy-saving inventions described in this time line. The advertisement may be a print, radio, or television ad. Be sure that your advertisement clearly explains the benefits of the invention.

1967
Microwave Ovens

The first countertop microwave oven for the home was introduced. Microwaves cook food by heating the water the food contains. The microwave oven heats only the food, not the air, racks, and oven walls as in a conventional oven. Preheating is also not required, saving even more energy.

1997
Smart Roads

The Department of Transportation demonstrated that cars can be controlled by computers. Sensors built into the road control all the cars, making traffic flow more smoothly. This uses less energy.

| 1970 | 1980 | 1990 | 2000 |

1981
High-Efficiency Window Coatings

Materials that reflect sunlight were first used to coat windows in the early 1980s. This coating reduces the air conditioning needed to keep the inside of the building cool.

Chapter 6 **E ◆ 189**

Answers to Self-Assessment

☑ *Checkpoint*
A compact fluorescent bulb is more energy-efficient.

Figure 22 A single city bus can transport dozens of people, reducing the number of cars on the roads and saving energy.
Applying Concepts How does riding a bus conserve energy?

Transportation Engineers have improved the energy efficiency of cars by designing better engines and tires. Another way to save energy is to reduce the number of cars on the road. In many communities, public transit systems provide an alternative to driving. Other cities encourage carpooling. If four people travel together in one car, they use much less energy than they would by driving separately. Many cities now set aside lanes for cars containing two or more people.

In the future, cars that run on electricity may provide the most energy savings of all. Electric power plants can convert fuel into electricity more efficiently than a car engine converts gasoline into motion. Therefore, a car that runs on electricity is more energy-efficient than one that runs directly on fuel.

What You Can Do

You can reduce your personal energy use by changing your behavior in some simple ways.

◆ Keep your home cooler in winter and warmer in summer. Instead of turning up the heat, put on a sweater. Use fans instead of air conditioners.

◆ Use natural lighting instead of electric lights when possible.

◆ Turn off the lights or television when you leave a room.

◆ Walk or ride a bike for short trips. Ride buses and trains.

◆ Recycle, especially metal products. Recycling an aluminum can uses only 5 percent of the energy making a new can uses!

The items in this list are small things, but multiplied by millions of people they add up to a lot of energy saved for the future.

Section 4 Review

1. What are two ways to make energy resources last longer?
2. Explain how putting insulation in a building conserves energy.
3. How does carpooling conserve energy?
4. **Thinking Critically Predicting** An office building contains only incandescent lights. The building next door contains fluorescent lights. Predict which building has higher energy bills. Explain your answer.

190 ◆ E

Science at Home

With an adult family member, conduct an energy audit of your home. Look for places where energy is being lost, such as cracks around windows and doors. Also look for ways to reduce energy use, such as running the dishwasher only when it is full. Together, create a list of energy-saving suggestions for your family. Post the list where everyone can see it.

SECTION 1 Fossil Fuels

Key Ideas

◆ A fuel is a substance that provides a form of energy as a result of a chemical change.

◆ Energy can be converted from one form to another.

◆ The three major fossil fuels are coal, oil, and natural gas. These fuels release more energy when they are burned than most other substances do.

◆ Because fossil fuels take hundreds of millions of years to form, they are considered nonrenewable resources.

Key Terms

combustion   petroleum
fossil fuels   refinery
hydrocarbons   petrochemicals
reserves

SECTION 2 Renewable Sources of Energy

Key Ideas

◆ Solar energy is plentiful and renewable, and does not cause pollution. However, a backup energy source is needed.

◆ Because the sun causes winds and drives the water cycle, wind power and water power are considered indirect forms of solar energy.

◆ Biomass fuels, geothermal energy, and hydrogen power are other renewable energy sources that are currently in limited use.

Key Terms

solar energy   biomass fuels
passive solar system gasohol
active solar system   geothermal energy
hydroelectric power

SECTION 3 Nuclear Energy
INTEGRATING CHEMISTRY

Key Ideas

◆ Nuclear reactions include fission reactions and fusion reactions.

◆ In a fission reaction, the impact of a neutron splits an atom's nucleus into two smaller nuclei and two or more neutrons. A large amount of energy is released in the process.

◆ In a nuclear power plant, the thermal energy released from controlled fission reactions is used to generate electricity.

◆ Disadvantages of nuclear power include the risk of a meltdown and radioactive waste.

◆ Scientists have not yet been able to control a major nuclear fusion reaction.

Key Terms

nucleus   control rods
nuclear fission meltdown
reactor vessel   nuclear fusion
fuel rods

SECTION 4 Energy Conservation

Key Ideas

◆ To avoid an energy shortage in the future, people must find new sources of energy and conserve the fuels that are available now.

◆ Insulation keeps a building from losing heat to, or gaining heat from, the outside.

◆ Ways to conserve energy use in transportation include making more efficient vehicles, carpooling, and using public transit.

Key Terms

energy conservation   insulation
efficiency

USING THE INTERNET

ACTIVITY

www.science-explorer.phschool.com

Program Resources

◆ **Teaching Resources** Chapter 6 Project Scoring Rubric, p. 146; Chapter 6 Performance Assessment, pp. 215–217; Chapter 6 Test, pp. 218–221

Media and Technology

 Interactive Student Tutorial CD-ROM E-6

 Computer Test Bank E-6

Reviewing Content:

Multiple Choice

1. b 2. c 3. c 4. a 5. d

True or False

6. petrochemicals 7. true 8. renewable
9. solar cells 10. true

Checking Concepts

11. The coal must be broken out of the surrounding rock and transported to the surface, often from deep underground. Coal creates dust that is unhealthy to breathe.
12. As plants die and decay, their remains pile up and are buried by layers of sand, rock, and mud. Over millions of years, heat and pressure change the decaying remains into coal.
13. Possible answers include overhangs to shade the windows in summer, positioning the house to receive maximum sunlight in winter, solar cells on the roof to provide electricity, and a backup energy source.
14. Wind can turn a turbine, which rotates an electromagnet to create electricity.
15. Very few locations have tides that are large enough to provide a power source.
16. By placing control rods made of cadmium between the fuel rods to limit chain reactions
17. Energy efficiency is the percentage of energy actually used to perform work; *examples:* insulation, fluorescent light bulbs, window coatings, microwave ovens
18. Responses will vary but should include ways of traveling, preparing meals, and obtaining light and heat.

Thinking Visually

19. Students' tables should include similar information to the following. Sample title: Energy Sources
Petroleum: Produces large amount of energy; can be used to produce plastics and other products; Causes air pollution when burned, difficult to find, must be refined.
Solar: Free, renewable, does not cause pollution; Not available on cloudy days or at night, is very spread out.
Wind: Free; renewable; does not cause pollution; Not available in many places;

Reviewing Content

 For more review of key concepts, see the Interactive Student Tutorial CD-ROM.

Multiple Choice
Choose the letter of the best answer.

1. Which of the following is *not* a fossil fuel?
a. coal
b. wood
c. oil
d. natural gas

2. Wind and water energy are both indirect forms of
a. nuclear energy.
b. electrical energy.
c. solar energy.
d. geothermal energy.

3. Which of the following is *not* a biomass fuel?
a. methane
b. gasohol
c. hydrogen
d. sugar-cane wastes

4. The particle used to start a nuclear fission reaction is a(n)
a. neutron.
b. nucleus.
c. proton.
d. atom.

5. A part of a nuclear power plant that undergoes a fission reaction is called a
a. turbine.
b. control rod.
c. heat exchanger.
d. fuel rod.

True or False
If the statement is true, write true. If it is false, change the underlined word or words to make the statement true.

6. Products made from petroleum are called <u>hydrocarbons</u>.
7. The process of burning a fuel for energy is <u>combustion</u>.
8. Geothermal energy is an example of a <u>nonrenewable</u> energy source.
9. Solar energy is harnessed to run calculators using <u>solar satellites</u>.
10. Most of the energy used in the United States today comes from <u>fossil fuels</u>.

Checking Concepts

11. Explain why coal mining is a difficult task.
12. Describe how coal forms.
13. Describe three features of a solar home. (Your answer may include passive or active solar systems.)
14. Explain how wind can be used to generate electricity.
15. What factors limit the use of tides as an energy source?
16. How is a nuclear fission reaction controlled in a nuclear power plant?
17. Define *energy efficiency.* Give three examples of inventions that increase energy efficiency.
18. **Writing to Learn** Suppose you had no electricity. Write a journal entry describing a typical weekday, including your meals, classes, and after-school activities. Explain how you might get things done without electricity.

Thinking Visually

19. **Compare/Contrast Table** Copy the table about types of energy onto a separate sheet of paper. Then complete the table and add a title. The first line is filled in as an example. (For more on compare/contrast tables see the Skills Handbook.)

Energy Type	Advantages	Disadvantages
Coal	Produces large amount of energy; easy to transport	Causes air pollution when burned; difficult to mine
Petroleum		
Solar		
Wind		
Water		
Geothermal		
Nuclear		

---

generators are noisy and can be destroyed by very strong winds
Water: Free, renewable, does not cause pollution; Most of the suitable rivers in the United States have already been dammed, dams can have negative effect on the environment
Geothermal: Free, renewable, does not cause pollution; Available in only a few places, drilling deep wells is expensive.
Nuclear: Produces huge amount of energy; Creates radioactive waste, risk of meltdown, costly

Applying Skills

20. It increased from 5,353 units to 8,070 units.
21. *1973:* 1%; *1995:* 8%
22. *Renewable:* hydroelectric; *nonrenewable:* coal, gas, nuclear, oil. Renewable energy (hydroelectric power) was not very important to the world's energy production in 1995, representing only 3% of the total energy units produced.
23. oil

Applying Skills

The table below shows how the world's energy production changed between 1973 and 1995. Use the information in the table to answer Questions 20–23.

Source of Energy	Energy Units Produced 1973	Energy Units Produced 1995
Coal	1,498	2,179
Gas	964	1,775
Hydroelectric	107	242
Nuclear	54	646
Oil	2,730	3,228
TOTAL Energy Units	5,353	8,070

20. Interpreting Data How did the total energy production change between 1973 and 1995?

21. Calculating What percentage of the total world energy production did nuclear power provide in 1973? In 1995?

22. Classifying Classify the different types of energy according to whether they are renewable or nonrenewable. How important was renewable energy to the world's energy production in 1995?

23. Drawing Conclusions Which energy source was the most important in the world in 1995?

Critical Thinking

24. Comparing and Contrasting Discuss how the three major fossil fuels are alike and how they are different.

25. Classifying State whether each of the following energy sources is renewable or nonrenewable: coal, solar power, methane, hydrogen. Give a reason for each answer.

26. Making Judgments Write a short paragraph explaining why you agree or disagree with the following statement: "The United States should build more nuclear power plants to prepare for the future shortage of fossil fuels."

Performance Assessment

Wrap Up
Present Your Project Share your report with another group. The group should review the report for clarity, organization, and detail. Make revisions based on feedback from the other group. As a class, discuss each group's findings. Prepare a class proposal with the best suggestions for conserving energy in your school.

Reflect and Record In your project notebook, explain what types of energy use were the hardest to measure. What other information would you have liked to have when making your recommendations? Record your overall opinion of energy efficiency in your school.

Getting Involved
In Your Community Find out what major sources of energy provide electricity to your area. Create a public-service announcement or poster informing people about these energy sources and explaining the importance of energy conservation. Be sure to include some practical suggestions of what families can do to conserve.

Critical Thinking

24. *Likenesses:* All form from the remains of organisms, contain hydrocarbons, and produce a large amount of energy when burned. *Differences:* Coal forms from plant remains; oil and natural gas form from the remains of small animals, algae, and protists. Coal is solid, oil is liquid, and natural gas is a gas. Natural gas causes less air pollution than coal and oil.

25. Coal is nonrenewable because it takes so long to form. Solar power is renewable because its supply is unlimited. Methane is renewable

Program Resources

◆ **Inquiry Skills Activity Book** Provides teaching and review of all inquiry skills

because it is produced as wastes decompose. Hydrogen is renewable because it can be obtained from water, which is abundant on Earth.

26. Accept both "agree" and "disagree" responses. Students should support their views with explanations that cite the advantages and disadvantages of nuclear power as an energy source.

Performance Assessment

Wrap Up
Present Your Project Encourage groups to give each other specific suggestions for improving the reports and to avoid making overly general criticisms. In the whole-class discussion, give each group an opportunity to summarize its findings, then focus on the groups's suggestions for reducing energy use. Ask students for their ideas about how the proposal should be organized and presented. You may want to have a group of volunteers compile the final proposal and present it to the entire class for further discussion.
Reflect and Record Specific responses to the questions and issues raised in this paragraph will vary. Allow time for students to share the answers and ideas they recorded.

Getting Involved
In Your Community To avoid having students deluge your area's electric company with telephone requests for information, choose a volunteer to contact the company's public relations department or invite someone to speak to the class. Provide art materials for making posters, tape recorders for creating radio announcements, and video cameras for creating television announcements. Let students present their posters and announcements to the rest of the class.

African Rain Forests

This Interdisciplinary Exploration presents the central theme of rain forest diversity from four different curriculum perspectives: science, mathematics, social studies, and language arts. The four explorations are designed to capture students' interest and help them see how the content they are studying in science relates both to other school subjects and to interesting real-world events. The unit is particularly suitable for team teaching.

1 Engage/Explore

Activating Prior Knowledge

Help students recall what they learned about rain forests in Chapter 2, Ecosystems and Biomes, by asking: **Where are Earth's tropical rain forests located?** *(South and Central America, southeast Asia, Indonesia, and Africa)* **What other kind of rain forest is there? Where is it located?** *(Temperate rain forest; along the northwestern coast of the United States)* Let students look back at the rain forest biome map on page 63 in Chapter 2 to verify their responses.

Introducing the Unit

Draw students' attention to the map on this page. Ask: **Where are the African rain forests located?** *(At or close to the equator)* **What is the climate like in a tropical rain forest?** *(Warm, humid, and rainy)* **Why do you think the nations in east Africa have no tropical rain forests?** *(East Africa's climate must not be humid and rainy enough for rain forests.)* Invite students to read the text on this page to see whether their response is correct. *(The text describes east Africa as both drier and more heavily populated than central Africa.)* Then ask: **How great is the biodiversity in tropical rain forests compared with the biodiversity in other biomes?** *(Tropical rain forests are the most diverse biomes on Earth.)*

African Rain Forests
Preserving Diversity

What forest—

is home to a beetle with wings larger than a sparrow's?
contains a frog that's 30 cm long?
is home to gorillas, chimpanzees, and pygmy hippos?

▲ Ball python

▲ Comet moth

African Rain Forests

Major areas of tropical rain forest, shown in green on the map, cover only 7 percent of Africa.

194 ◆ E

It's an African rain forest. Thousands of plants and animals live here, from colorful orchids to fruit bats, tree frogs, and elephants.

The rain forests of Africa grow in a band near the equator. About 80 percent of the rain-forested area is in central Africa, in the vast basin of the great Congo River. Some parts of the central African rain forest are so dense and hard to reach that explorers have never visited them. East Africa, which is drier and more heavily populated, has only scattered areas of rain forest.

The rain forest regions of the world have similar life forms and niches. But the rain forests of different continents have very different species.

Bonobo chimpanzee ▶

Program Resources

◆ **Teaching Resources** Interdisciplinary Explorations, Science, pp. 168–171; Mathematics, pp. 172–174; Social Studies, pp. 175–176; Language Arts, pp. 177–179

Layers of the Rain Forest

From above, the rain forest may look like a mass of broccoli. But it's really many forests in one—like different levels in an apartment building.

Each layer from the forest floor to the emergent, or top, layer varies in climate and is home to different plants and animals. The emergent layer captures the most rain, sunlight, heat, and wind. Colobus monkeys swing from vines and branches. Vast numbers of birds live in the trees.

Over time, African rain forest plants and animals have developed unusual adaptations to life at different layers of the forest. Some monkeys living in the canopy have long, muscular legs. They can run and leap through the branches. Guenons and baboons have strong teeth and jaws that allow them to crunch fruits, nuts, and seeds. Other monkeys have shorter tails but longer front legs. They live mainly on the forest floor.

In the understory, small animals such as frogs and squirrels "fly." They have tough membranes that stretch between their front and hind legs and allow them to glide from branch to branch.

The forest floor is dark, humid, and still. Termites feed on dead leaves and brush. Many plants have large leaves that allow them to catch the dim light. Some animals, such as frogs and insects, grow to gigantic sizes. Others are little, like the pygmy hippo that runs through the forest.

Science Activity

Design a rain forest animal that is adapted to life at a certain level of the rain forest. Consider how your animal lives, how it travels, and what food it eats. Outline its characteristics and explain how each adaptation helps the animal survive. Draw a sketch.

The emergent layer is formed by a few taller trees that poke through the canopy. Some of these trees are as much as 70 meters high—about as tall as a 17-story building. Colobus monkeys (above) live at this level.

The canopy, from 10 to 40 meters high, is the dense "roof" of the rain forest. The crowns of trees capture sunlight to use in photosynthesis. Rainwater and sunlight filter through thick vegetation. Epiphytic orchids grow to the top of the canopy (below).

The understory has trees and plants that need little light. Pythons lurk in the vegetation. On the forest floor live other animals like the pygmy hippo and the gorilla.

70 meters
60 meters
50 meters
40 meters
30 meters
20 meters
10 meters
0 meters

E ◆ 195

2 Facilitate

◆ Suggest that students make a table to compare the three layers' features, with the names of the layers in the left column and the headings *Height, Rainfall, Light,* and *Sample Organisms* across the top. This can be done as a cooperative learning activity, with the class divided into groups of three and each student in the group filling in the row for one layer.

◆ Challenge students to identify specific phrases in the text and captions that describe adaptations of rain forest animals and plants. As students identify adaptations, list each on the board and ask: **How does this adaptation help the organism survive?** *(Some answers are explicitly stated in the text; others must be inferred.)*

Science Activity

Let students work individually or in pairs. Encourage them to refer to the list on the board and to think of other characteristics that would help animals survive in a specific layer of the rain forest. Students could create a bulletin board display, with an enlarged version of the text's illustration in the center and each student's sketch posted next to the appropriate layer.

Teaching Resources The following worksheets correlate with this page: Dwarf Rain Forest Animals, p. 168; Classifying the Great Apes, pp. 169–170; Bat Adaptations, p. 171.

3 Assess

Activity Assessment

Students' designs will vary. Give each student or pair an opportunity to describe the animal to the rest of the class. During these presentations, assess students' understanding of the conditions in each rain forest layer and the adaptations needed for survival there.

Background

History In less space than the area of Texas, Madagascar contains some 200,000 species of plants and animals, making it one of the most biologically diverse countries in the world. Separated from the African continent by plate tectonics, the island has been an isolated area of speciation for more than 100 million years. Most of the species that evolved on the island are found nowhere else on Earth.

People have lived on Madagascar for only about 2,000 years, but during that time the island has lost 80 percent of its rain forests and about 50 percent of its native species. Except for a few patches, the forests that once covered the island's eastern half have been cleared to create farms and housing for Madagascar's 15 million people.

2 Facilitate

♦ Ask students: **What do you think evergreens are?** (*Trees that keep their leaves all year long*) **What are trees that shed their leaves in autumn called?** (*Deciduous trees; if students cannot recall the term, let them turn back to page 66 in Chapter 2.*) **What are conifers?** (*Trees that produce seeds in cones and have leaves shaped like needles; see page 67.*)

♦ Have students compare the tree heights listed in the table with the figure of forest layers on the previous page. Ask: **Which trees' tops are found in each forest layer?** (*Emergent layer: kapok and teak; canopy: African oil palm, African yellowwood, ebony, and raffia palm; understory: Cape fig*)

Math Activity

Have each student make his or her own graph. Some students may want to sequence the trees from shortest to tallest (or vice versa) on the horizontal axis. **Teaching Resources** The following worksheets correlate with this page: Modeling Rain Forest Layers, p. 172; Giant Rain Forest Animals, p. 173; Comparing Tree Heights, p. 174.

3 Assess

Activity Assessment

Students' graphs should look like the one shown here.
♦ *Greatest:* kapok; *least:* Cape fig
♦ 63 m
♦ 29 m

Reaching for Sunlight

Most rain forest trees are evergreens with broad leathery leaves. Some, like the African yellowwood, are conifers. Because the forest is so dense, trees must grow tall and straight to reach sunlight at the top of the canopy.

Along rivers, the floor and understory of the rain forest are a tangle of plants. Early explorers traveling the rivers assumed that the entire rain forest had similar thick vegetation, or jungle. In fact, the rain forest floor is surprisingly bare.

The canopy trees block the sunlight from plants below. Shaded by the dense canopy, the understory and forest floor are humid and dark. Water drips from the leaves of the canopy high overhead. Young trees have the best chance to grow when trees fall, opening up sunny clearings.

West Africa's tropical forests contain many valuable trees. African mahogany and teak are used to make furniture, tools, and boats. Oil from the oil palm is used in soaps, candles, and some foods. Trees such as ebony that can tolerate shade, grow slowly and develop dark, hard, long-lasting wood.

Math Activity

The table on this page gives the height of some of the trees in the rain forest. Use the information in the table to make a bar graph. On the horizontal axis, label the trees. Use the vertical axis to show the height of the trees.

♦ Which tree has the greatest maximum height? The least maximum height?

♦ What is the height difference between the tallest and the shortest trees?

♦ What is the average height of all the trees shown in the graph?

Trees of the Rain Forest

Tree	Maximum Height
African oil palm	18 m
African yellowwood	20 m
Cape fig	7 m
Ebony	30 m
Kapok	70 m
Raffia palm	12 m
Teak	46 m

African oil palms ▲ grow in Nigeria.

◀ This African sculpture is made of wood from the African rain forest.

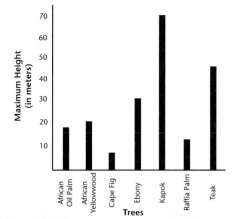

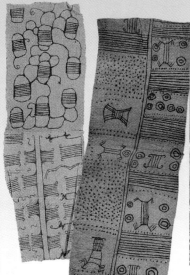

The Mbuti (above) hunt and fish along the Congo River. Their clothing is made of bark cloth (left).

Ituri Forest People

The native peoples of the African rain forest live as they have for thousands of years—by hunting and gathering. The forest supplies them with everything they need—food, water, firewood, building materials, and medicines.

One group of rain forest dwellers is the Mbuti people. The Mbuti live in the Ituri forest of the Democratic Republic of the Congo. Many of the Mbuti are quite small. The men hunt game, such as gazelle and antelope. The women gather wild fruits, nuts, and greens. Their traditional Mbuti clothing is made of tree bark and is wrapped around the waist. The bark is beaten to make it soft. Then it's decorated with geometric designs.

Most Mbuti live as nomads, with no single settled home. Every few months they set up new hunting grounds. They build temporary dome-shaped huts of branches and leaves. Hunting groups of about 10 to 25 families live together. They divide the hunting area among the family groups. On occasion, larger groups gather for ceremonies with dances and ritual music.

Modern Africa has brought changes to the forest people, especially for those who live near the edges of the rain forest. For a few months

of the year, some Mbuti work as laborers for farmers who live in villages at the edge of the forest. When their work is finished, the Mbuti return to the Ituri forest. Most forest people prefer not to cultivate their own land. Since the farmers don't hunt, they trade their goods for meat. In exchange for meat, the Mbuti receive goods such as iron tools, cooking pots, clothes, bananas, and other farm produce.

Social Studies Activity

List the goods that forest people and farmers might have to trade. Assume that no modern conveniences, such as tractors and stoves, are available. Write a paragraph or two explaining how goods might be exchanged. Assign a value to the farmers' goods and the Mbuti goods, depending upon each group's needs. For example, decide how much meat a farmer should pay for medicines from the rain forest. How would the trading process change if money were exchanged?

Background

History Anthropologists use the term Pygmies to refer to human groups in which the average stature of adult males is less than 150 cm. The Mbuti, averaging less than 137 cm, are the shortest Pygmies in Africa.

The Mbuti have traded goods with their farming neighbors, the Bantu, for over 2,000 years. Although they have adopted a few Bantu customs, Mbuti culture has remained essentially unchanged. Groups are not

governed by chiefs or tribal councils; group discussion is the usual means of settling any disputes. Mbuti technology meets the needs of hunter-gatherers. For example, some groups hunt with net and spear, while others use bow and arrow. Special songs honoring the forest are important in Mbuti rites of passage associated with puberty, marriage, and death. Values are reinforced in music, dance, and mime. Family bonds are strong and lasting.

---

2 Facilitate

◆ Have students find the Democratic Republic of the Congo (formerly Zaire) on the map on page 194. Point out that the Democratic Republic of the Congo and the Republic of the Congo are separate nations.

◆ Ask: **What does the first sentence mean by "gathering"?** (*Collecting items from the forest*) Encourage students to imagine what their lives would be like if everything they needed for survival had to be obtained from hunting and gathering. Ask: **What things that you have now would you not have as hunter-gatherers? How would you prepare and cook food? Where would you sleep? What would you do if you became ill? How would you spend most of your time?** To extend this activity, suggest that students write brief, first-person stories describing a typical Mbuti day for someone their own age.

Social Studies Activity

Students can work in pairs, with one student acting as a Mbuti and the other a neighboring farmer. Give volunteers an opportunity to role-play a trading session for the rest of the class.
Teaching Resources The following worksheets correlate with this page: Reading a Map of Madagascar, p. 175; Peoples of the Rain Forest, page 176.

3 Assess

Activity Assessment

Students' paragraphs or role-plays will vary. Accept a variety of reasonable responses to the question about money. Students should realize that money would have no immediate value to either the Mbuti or the farmers; its value lies only in its potential use in another exchange.

2 Facilitate

◆ You can enhance comprehension by reading this selection aloud yourself or by asking your most proficient readers to take turns reading paragraphs aloud for the class. The "drama" of an oral presentation—with its vocal inflections, pauses, word emphasis, gestures, and facial expressions—should enable less capable readers to understand the selection more easily and help them appreciate its touches of humor and richly descriptive narrative.

◆ After the passage has been read, ask students: **Why did Durrell use the word *magical* to describe his experience?** *(He had never seen the rain forest and its wildlife from that viewpoint before.)* Ask students if they have ever ridden in an airplane or been on a mountain or in a tall building where they could look down on things they usually see only from ground level. If they have, encourage them to describe the experience.

Language Arts Activity

To make the task more manageable, set a four- or six-page limit for the pamphlet. (Six pages can be created by folding a standard sheet of paper into thirds.) Although students do not need to do any research to complete the activity successfully, you may want to provide a variety of source materials to prompt their ideas. Use materials that are generously illustrated with colored photographs of the rain forest and its wildlife. Allow students to photocopy or print photographs and incorporate them into their pamphlets. Have students share their pamphlets by posting them on the bulletin board. Save the source materials for students' use in Tie It Together on the next page.

Teaching Resources The following worksheets correlate with pages 198–199: Word Meanings, p. 177; The Aye-Aye, pp. 178–179.

Climbing the Canopy

Much of the rain forest is still a mystery because it's so difficult for scientists to study the canopy. Native forest people sometimes climb these tall trees using strong, thick vines called lianas as support. But rain forest scientists have had to find different methods. Naturalist Gerald Durrell, working in the African rain forest, was lucky enough to find another way to observe the canopy. He describes it here:

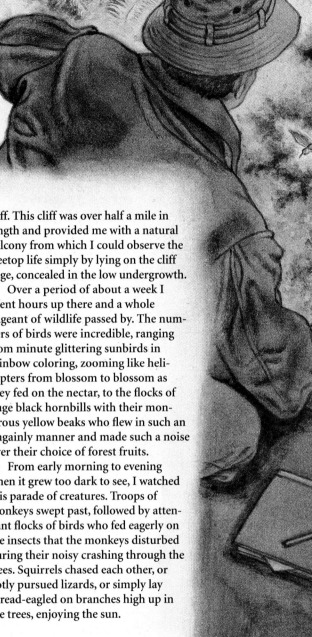

While the canopy is one of the most richly inhabited regions of the forest it is also the one that causes the naturalist the greatest frustration. There he is, down in the gloom among the giant tree trunks, hearing the noises of animal life high above him and having half-eaten fruit, flowers, or seeds rained on him by legions of animals high in their sunlit domain—all of which he cannot see. Under these circumstances the naturalist develops a very bad temper and a permanent crick in the neck.

However, there was one occasion when I managed to transport myself into the forest canopy, and it was a magical experience. It happened in West Africa when I was camped on the thickly forested lower slopes of a mountain called N'da Ali. Walking through the forest one day I found I was walking along the edge of a great step cut out of the mountain. The cliff face, covered with creepers, dropped away for about 50 yards, so that although I was walking through forest, just next to me and slightly below was the canopy of the forest growing up from the base of the cliff. This cliff was over half a mile in length and provided me with a natural balcony from which I could observe the treetop life simply by lying on the cliff edge, concealed in the low undergrowth.

Over a period of about a week I spent hours up there and a whole pageant of wildlife passed by. The numbers of birds were incredible, ranging from minute glittering sunbirds in rainbow coloring, zooming like helicopters from blossom to blossom as they fed on the nectar, to the flocks of huge black hornbills with their monstrous yellow beaks who flew in such an ungainly manner and made such a noise over their choice of forest fruits.

From early morning to evening when it grew too dark to see, I watched this parade of creatures. Troops of monkeys swept past, followed by attendant flocks of birds who fed eagerly on the insects that the monkeys disturbed during their noisy crashing through the trees. Squirrels chased each other, or hotly pursued lizards, or simply lay spread-eagled on branches high up in the trees, enjoying the sun.

Background

History Gerald Durrell (1925–1995) first developed his love of animals and ambition to be a naturalist during his childhood on the island of Corfu, off the west coast of Greece. Long hours spent observing wildlife led Durrell to collect many local animals as pets—to the consternation of his family.

Durrell's first job was as a student keeper at England's Whipsnade Zoo. After joining several collecting expeditions abroad, he began organizing them himself. After trips to remote parts of Africa and other continents, it struck Durrell that zoos should encourage the breeding of threatened species. In the 1950s, he founded the Jersey Wildlife Preservation Trust and Zoological Garden to raise, study, and breed rare species. Durrell wrote the first of his many books, *The Overloaded Ark*, when he was only 22.

Language Arts Activity

◆ Besides being an experienced naturalist and writer, Gerald Durrell is also a careful observer. In this selection, he describes in detail the "magical experience" of being in the canopy. Reread Durrell's description. Now work with a partner to write and design a pamphlet that will persuade visitors to come to an African rain forest. For your pamphlet, write strong, lively descriptions of what you might see, hear, and experience. Be persuasive.

Tie It Together

Celebrate Diversity

Rain forests have the greatest biodiversity—variety of plant and animal life—of any ecosystem on Earth. Many species have yet to be discovered! Plan a display for your school to celebrate biodiversity in the rain forests. Include drawings, photos, and detailed captions.

◆ On a large map, locate and label Earth's tropical rain forests. Divide into groups to choose one rain forest region to research, such as Africa, Brazil, Costa Rica, Hawaii, Indonesia, or Borneo.

◆ Have your group study several animal and plant species in its chosen rain forest. You might choose monkeys, butterflies, birds, orchids, or medicinal plants.

◆ For each species, describe its appearance, where it occurs in the rain forest, its role in the ecosystem, and how it is useful to humans.

British conservationist Gerald Durrell wrote about his adventures with wildlife around the world. He established a zoo on the British island of Jersey and worked to preserve threatened species. In the photo, Durrell holds an anteater.

3 Assess

Activity Assessment

Students' pamphlets will vary widely. Evaluate students' work on the basis of their ability to evoke sensory images of the rain forest and to make a visit seem appealing to the pamphlet's readers.

Tie It Together

Time 4 class periods (2 for research, 2 for designing and creating the display)
Tips Have students work in groups of three or four. Monitor each group's choices of plant and animal species to make sure the group's research will be well-focused and not too wide-ranging. Arrange with your school office for a suitable display area, such as the school entryway, a heavily trafficked hallway, the library, or the cafeteria.
Extend After students have displayed their work in their own school, encourage them to post the displays in areas accessible to the general public—the town library, for example.

Developing scientific thinking in students is important for a solid science education. To learn how to think scientifically, students need frequent opportunities to practice science process skills, critical thinking skills, as well as other skills that support scientific inquiry. The *Science Explorer* Skills Handbook introduces the following key science skills:

◆ Science Process Skills
◆ SI Measuring Skills
◆ Skills for Conducting a Scientific Investigation
◆ Critical Thinking Skills
◆ Information Organizing Skills
◆ Data Table and Graphing Skills

The Skills Handbook is designed as a reference for students to use whenever they need to review a science skill. You can use the activities provided in the Skills Handbook to teach or reinforce the skills.

Think Like a Scientist

Observing

ACTIVITY

Before students look at the photograph, remind them that an observation is only what they can see, hear, smell, taste, or feel. Ask: **Which senses will you use to make observations from this photograph?** *(Sight is the only sense that can be used to make observations from the photograph.)* **What are some observations you can make from the photograph?** *(Answers may vary. Sample answers: The boy is wearing sneakers, sport socks, shorts, and a tee shirt; the boy is sitting in the grass holding something blue against his knee; the boy is looking at his knee; there is a soccer ball laying beside the boy.)* List the observations on the chalkboard. If students make any inferences or predictions about the boy at this point, ask: **Can you be sure your statement is factual and accurate from just observing the photograph?** Help students understand how observations differ from inferences and predictions.

Inferring

ACTIVITY

Review students' observations from the photograph. Then ask: **What inferences can you**

Think Like a Scientist

Although you may not know it, you think like a scientist every day. Whenever you ask a question and explore possible answers, you use many of the same skills that scientists do. Some of these skills are described on this page.

Observing

When you use one or more of your five senses to gather information about the world, you are **observing.** Hearing a dog bark, counting twelve green seeds, and smelling smoke are all observations. To increase the power of their senses, scientists sometimes use microscopes, telescopes, or other instruments that help them make more detailed observations.

An observation must be factual and accurate—an exact report of what your senses detect. It is important to keep careful records of your observations in science class by writing or drawing in a notebook. The information collected through observations is called evidence, or data.

Inferring

When you explain or interpret an observation, you are **inferring,** or making an inference. For example, if you hear your dog barking, you may infer that someone is at your front door. To make this inference, you combine the evidence—the barking dog—and your experience or knowledge—you know that your dog barks when strangers approach—to reach a logical conclusion.

Notice that an inference is not a fact; it is only one of many possible explanations for an observation. For example, your dog may be barking because it wants to go for a walk. An inference may turn out to be incorrect even if it is based on accurate observations and logical reasoning. The only way to find out if an inference is correct is to investigate further.

Predicting

When you listen to the weather forecast, you hear many predictions about the next day's weather—what the temperature will be, whether it will rain, and how windy it will be. Weather forecasters use observations and knowledge of weather patterns to predict the weather. The skill of **predicting** involves making an inference about a future event based on current evidence or past experience.

Because a prediction is an inference, it may prove to be false. In science class, you can test some of your predictions by doing experiments. For example, suppose you predict that larger paper airplanes can fly farther than smaller airplanes. How could you test your prediction?

 Use the photograph to answer the questions below.

Observing Look closely at the photograph. List at least three observations.

Inferring Use your observations to make an inference about what has happened. What experience or knowledge did you use to make the inference?

Predicting Predict what will happen next. On what evidence or experience do you base your prediction?

---

make from your observations? *(Students may say that the boy hurt his knee playing soccer and is holding a coldpack against his injured knee.)* **What experience or knowledge helped you make this inference?** *(Students may have experienced knee injuries from playing soccer, and they may be familiar with coldpacks like the one the boy is using.)* **Can anyone suggest another possible explanation for these observations?** *(Answers may vary. Sample answer: The boy hurt his knee jogging, and he just happened to sit beside a soccer ball his sister*

left in the yard.)* **How can you find out whether an inference is correct?** *(by further investigation)*

Predicting

ACTIVITY

After coming to some consensus about the inference that the boy hurt his knee, encourage students to make predictions about what will happen next. *(Students' predictions may vary. Sample answers: The boy will go to the doctor. A friend will help the boy home. The boy will get up and continue playing soccer.)*

Classifying

Could you imagine searching for a book in the library if the books were shelved in no particular order? Your trip to the library would be an all-day event! Luckily, librarians group together books on similar topics or by the same author. Grouping together items that are alike in some way is called **classifying.** You can classify items in many ways: by size, by shape, by use, and by other important characteristics.

Like librarians, scientists use the skill of classifying to organize information and objects. When things are sorted into groups, the relationships among them become easier to understand.

Classify the objects in the photograph into two groups based on any characteristic you choose. Then use another characteristic to classify the objects into three groups. **ACTIVITY**

Making Models

Have you ever drawn a picture to help someone understand what you were saying? Such a drawing is one type of model. A model is a picture, diagram, computer image, or other representation of a complex object or process. **Making models** helps people understand things that they cannot observe directly.

Scientists often use models to represent things that are either very large or very small, such as the planets in the solar system, or the parts of a cell. Such models are physical models—drawings or three-dimensional structures that look like the real thing. Other models are mental models—mathematical equations or words that describe how something works.

This student is using a model to demonstrate what causes day and night on Earth. What do the flashlight and the tennis ball in the model represent? **ACTIVITY**

Communicating

Whenever you talk on the phone, write a letter, or listen to your teacher at school, you are communicating. **Communicating** is the process of sharing ideas and information with other people. Communicating effectively requires many skills, including writing, reading, speaking, listening, and making models.

Scientists communicate to share results, information, and opinions. Scientists often communicate about their work in journals, over the telephone, in letters, and on the Internet. They also attend scientific meetings where they share their ideas with one another in person.

On a sheet of paper, write out clear, detailed directions for tying your shoe. Then exchange directions with a partner. Follow your partner's directions exactly. How successful were you at tying your shoe? How could your partner have communicated more clearly? **ACTIVITY**

E ◆ 201

On what did you base your prediction? *(Scientific predictions are based on knowledge and experience.)* Point out that in science, predictions can often be tested with experiments.

Classifying **ACTIVITY**

Encourage students to think of other common things that are classified. Then ask: **What things at home are classified?** *(Clothing might be classified by placing it in different dresser drawers; glasses, plates, and silverware are grouped in different parts of the kitchen; screws, nuts, bolts, washers, and nails might be separated into small containers.)* **What are some things that scientists classify?** *(Scientists classify many things they study, including organisms, geological features and processes, and kinds of machines.)* After students have classified the different fruits in the photograph, have them share their criteria for classifying them. *(Some characteristics students might use include shape, color, size, and where they are grown.)*

Making Models **ACTIVITY**

Ask students: **What are some models you have used to study science?** *(Students may have used human anatomical models, solar system models, maps, stream tables.)* **How did these models help you?** *(Models can help you learn about things that are difficult to study, either because they are too big, too small, or complex.)* Be sure students understand that a model does not have to be three-dimensional. For example, a map in a textbook is a model. Ask: **What do the flashlight and tennis ball represent?** *(The flashlight represents the sun, and the ball represents Earth.)* **What quality of each item makes this a good model?** *(The flashlight gives off light, and the ball is round and can be rotated by the student.)*

Communicating **ACTIVITY**

Challenge students to identify the methods of communication they've used today. Then ask: **How is the way you communicate with a friend similar to and different from the way scientists communicate about their work to other scientists?** *(Both may communicate using various methods, but scientists must be very detailed and precise, whereas communication between friends may be less detailed and precise.)* Encourage students to communicate like a scientist as they carry out the activity. *(Students' directions should be detailed and precise enough for another person to successfully follow.)*

E ◆ 201

Making Measurements

Measuring in SI

Review SI units in class with students. Begin by providing metric rulers, graduated cylinders, balances, and Celsius thermometers. Use these tools to reinforce that the meter is the unit of length, the liter is the unit of volume, the gram is the unit of mass, and the degree Celsius is the unit for temperature. Ask: **If you want to measure the length and width of your classroom, which SI unit would you use?** *(meter)* **Which unit would you use to measure the amount of matter in your textbook?** *(gram)* **Which would you use to measure how much water a drinking glass holds?** *(liter)* **When would you use the Celsius scale?** *(To measure the temperature of something)* Then use the measuring equipment to review SI prefixes. For example, ask: **What are the smallest units on the metric ruler?** *(millimeters)* **How many millimeters are there in 1 cm?** *(10 mm)* **How many in 10 cm?** *(100 mm)* **How many centimeters are there in 1 m?** *(100 cm)* **What does 1,000 m equal?** *(1 km)*

Length

(Students should state that the shell is 4.6 centimeters, or 46 millimeters, long.) If students need more practice measuring length, have them use meter sticks and metric rulers to measure various objects in the classroom.

Liquid Volume

(Students should state that the volume of water in the graduated cylinder is 62 milliliters.) If students need more practice measuring liquid volume, have them use a graduated cylinder to measure different volumes of water.

Making Measurements

When scientists make observations, it is not sufficient to say that something is "big" or "heavy." Instead, scientists use instruments to measure just how big or heavy an object is. By measuring, scientists can express their observations more precisely and communicate more information about what they observe.

Measuring in SI

The standard system of measurement used by scientists around the world is known as the International System of Units, which is abbreviated as SI (in French, *Système International d'Unités*). SI units are easy to use because they are based on multiples of 10. Each unit is ten times larger than the next smallest unit and one tenth the size of the next largest unit. The table lists the prefixes used to name the most common SI units.

Common SI Prefixes		
Prefix	**Symbol**	**Meaning**
kilo-	k	1,000
hecto-	h	100
deka-	da	10
deci-	d	0.1 (one tenth)
centi-	c	0.01 (one hundredth)
milli-	m	0.001 (one thousandth)

Length To measure length, or the distance between two points, the unit of measure is the **meter (m).** One meter is the approximate distance from the floor to a doorknob. Long distances, such as the distance between two cities, are measured in kilometers (km). Small lengths are measured in centimeters (cm) or millimeters (mm). Scientists use metric rulers and meter sticks to measure length.

Common Conversions

1 km = 1,000 m
1 m = 100 cm
1 m = 1,000 mm
1 cm = 10 mm

The larger lines on the metric ruler in the picture show centimeter divisions, while the smaller, unnumbered lines show millimeter divisions. How many centimeters long is the shell? How many millimeters long is it?

cm 1 2 3 4 5 6 7

Liquid Volume To measure the volume of a liquid, or the amount of space it takes up, you will use a unit of measure known as the **liter (L).** One liter is the approximate volume of a medium-sized carton of milk. Smaller volumes are measured in milliliters (mL). Scientists use graduated cylinders to measure liquid volume.

Common Conversion

1 L = 1,000 mL

The graduated cylinder in the picture is marked in milliliter divisions. Notice that the water in the cylinder has a curved surface. This curved surface is called the *meniscus.* To measure the volume, you must read the level at the lowest point of the meniscus. What is the volume of water in this graduated cylinder?

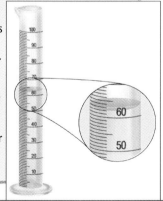

Mass To measure mass, or the amount of matter in an object, you will use a unit of measure known as the **gram (g)**. One gram is approximately the mass of a paper clip. Larger masses are measured in kilograms (kg). Scientists use a balance to find the mass of an object.

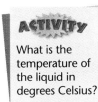

The electronic balance displays the mass of an apple in kilograms. What is the mass of the apple? Suppose a recipe for applesauce called for one kilogram of apples. About how many apples would you need?

Temperature
To measure the temperature of a substance, you will use the **Celsius scale**. Temperature is measured in degrees Celsius (°C) using a Celsius thermometer. Water freezes at 0°C and boils at 100°C.

ACTIVITY
What is the temperature of the liquid in degrees Celsius?

Mass (*Students should state that the mass of the apple is 0.1 kilograms. They would need 10 apples to make 1 kilogram.*) If students need practice determining mass, have them use a balance to determine the mass of various common objects, such as coins, paper clips, and books.

Temperature (*Students should state that the temperature of the liquid is 35°C.*) If students need practice measuring temperature, have them use a Celsius thermometer to measure the temperature of various water samples.

Converting SI Units

Review the steps for converting SI units and work through the example with students. Then ask: **How many millimeters are in 80 centimeters?** (*Students should follow the steps to calculate that 80 centimeters is equal to 800 millimeters.*)

Have students do the conversion problems in the activity. (**1.** *600 millimeters = 0.6 meters;* **2.** *0.35 liters = 350 milliliters;* **3.** *1,050 grams = 1.05 kilograms*) If students need more practice converting SI units, have students make up conversion problems and trade with a partner.

Converting SI Units

To use the SI system, you must know how to convert between units. Converting from one unit to another involves the skill of **calculating**, or using mathematical operations. Converting between SI units is similar to converting between dollars and dimes because both systems are based on multiples of ten.

Suppose you want to convert a length of 80 centimeters to meters. Follow these steps to convert between units.

1. Begin by writing down the measurement you want to convert—in this example, 80 centimeters.
2. Write a conversion factor that represents the relationship between the two units you are converting. In this example, the relationship is *1 meter = 100 centimeters*. Write this conversion factor as a fraction, making sure to place the units you are converting from (centimeters, in this example) in the denominator.

3. Multiply the measurement you want to convert by the fraction. When you do this, the units in the first measurement will cancel out with the units in the denominator. Your answer will be in the units you are converting to (meters, in this example).

Example

80 centimeters = ____?____ meters

$$80 \text{ centimeters} \times \frac{1 \text{ meter}}{100 \text{ centimeters}} = \frac{80 \text{ meters}}{100}$$

$$= 0.8 \text{ meters}$$

Convert between the following units.
1. 600 millimeters = _?_ meters
2. 0.35 liters = _?_ milliliters
3. 1,050 grams = _?_ kilograms

E ◆ 203

Conducting a Scientific Investigation

Posing Questions

Before students do the activity on the next page, walk them through the steps of a typical scientific investigation. Begin by asking: **Why is a scientific question important to a scientific investigation?** *(It is the reason for conducting a scientific investigation and how every investigation begins.)* **What is the scientific question in the activity at the bottom of the next page?** *(Is a ball's bounce affected by the height from which it is dropped?)*

Developing a Hypothesis

Emphasize that a hypothesis is a prediction about the outcome of a scientific investigation, but it is *not* a guess. Ask: **On what information do scientists base their hypotheses?** *(Their observations and previous knowledge or experience)* Point out that a hypothesis does not always turn out to be correct. Ask: **In that case, do you think the scientist wasted his or her time? Explain your answer.** *(No, because the scientist probably learned from the investigation and maybe could develop another hypothesis that could be supported.)*

Designing an Experiment

Have a volunteer read the Experimental Procedure in the box. Then call on students to identify the manipulated variable *(amount of salt added to water)*, the variables that are kept constant *(amount and starting temperature of water, placing containers in freezer)*, the responding variable *(time it takes water to freeze)*, and the control *(Container 3)*.

Ask: **How might the experiment be affected if Container 1 had only 100 mL of water?** *(It wouldn't be a fair comparison with the containers that have more water.)* **What if Container 3 was not included in the experiment?** *(You wouldn't have anything to compare the other two containers to know if their freezing times were faster or slower than normal.)* Help students understand the importance of

Conducting a Scientific Investigation

In some ways, scientists are like detectives, piecing together clues to learn about a process or event. One way that scientists gather clues is by carrying out experiments. An experiment tests an idea in a careful, orderly manner. Although all experiments do not follow the same steps in the same order, many follow a pattern similar to the one described here.

Posing Questions

Experiments begin by asking a scientific question. A scientific question is one that can be answered by gathering evidence. For example, the question "Which freezes faster—fresh water or salt water?" is a scientific question because you can carry out an investigation and gather information to answer the question.

Developing a Hypothesis

The next step is to form a hypothesis. A **hypothesis** is a prediction about the outcome of the experiment. Like all predictions, hypotheses are based on your observations and previous knowledge or experience. But, unlike many predictions, a hypothesis must be something that can be tested. A properly worded hypothesis should take the form of an *If . . . then . . .* statement. For example, a hypothesis might be *"If I add salt to fresh water, then the water will take longer to freeze."* A hypothesis worded this way serves as a rough outline of the experiment you should perform.

keeping all variables constant except the manipulated variable. Also be sure they understand the role of the control. Then ask: **What operational definition is used in this experiment?** *("Frozen" means the time at which a wooden stick can no longer move in a container.)*

Designing an Experiment

Next you need to plan a way to test your hypothesis. Your plan should be written out as a step-by-step procedure and should describe the observations or measurements you will make.

Two important steps involved in designing an experiment are controlling variables and forming operational definitions.

Controlling Variables In a well-designed experiment, you need to keep all variables the same except for one. A **variable** is any factor that can change in an experiment. The factor that you change is called the **manipulated variable.** In this experiment, the manipulated variable is the amount of salt added to the water. Other factors, such as the amount of water or the starting temperature, are kept constant.

The factor that changes as a result of the manipulated variable is called the responding variable. The **responding variable** is what you measure or observe to obtain your results. In this experiment, the responding variable is how long the water takes to freeze.

An experiment in which all factors except one are kept constant is a **controlled experiment.** Most controlled experiments include a test called the control. In this experiment, Container 3 is the control. Because no salt is added to Container 3, you can compare the results from the other containers to it. Any difference in results must be due to the addition of salt alone.

Forming Operational Definitions
Another important aspect of a well-designed experiment is having clear operational definitions. An **operational definition** is a statement that describes how a particular variable is to be measured or how a term is to be defined. For example, in this experiment, how will you determine if the water has frozen? You might decide to insert a stick in each container at the start of the experiment. Your operational definition of "frozen" would be the time at which the stick can no longer move.

EXPERIMENTAL PROCEDURE

1. Fill 3 containers with 300 milliliters of cold tap water.

2. Add 10 grams of salt to Container 1; stir. Add 20 grams of salt to Container 2; stir. Add no salt to Container 3.

3. Place the 3 containers in a freezer.

4. Check the containers every 15 minutes. Record your observations.

Interpreting Data

The observations and measurements you make in an experiment are called data. At the end of an experiment, you need to analyze the data to look for any patterns or trends. Patterns often become clear if you organize your data in a data table or graph. Then think through what the data reveal. Do they support your hypothesis? Do they point out a flaw in your experiment? Do you need to collect more data?

Drawing Conclusions

A conclusion is a statement that sums up what you have learned from an experiment. When you draw a conclusion, you need to decide whether the data you collected support your hypothesis or not. You may need to repeat an experiment several times before you can draw any conclusions from it. Conclusions often lead you to pose new questions and plan new experiments to answer them.

Is a ball's bounce affected by the height from which **ACTIVITY** it is dropped? Using the steps just described, plan a controlled experiment to investigate this problem.

E ◆ 205

Interpreting Data

Emphasize the importance of collecting accurate and detailed data in a scientific investigation. Ask: **What if the students forgot to record the times that they made their observations in the experiment?** *(They wouldn't be able to completely analyze their data to draw valid conclusions.)* Then ask: **Why are data tables and graphs a good way to organize data?** *(They often make it easier to compare and analyze data.)* You may wish to have students review the Skills Handbook pages on Creating Data Tables and Graphs at this point.

Drawing Conclusions

Help students understand that a conclusion is not necessarily the end of a scientific investigation. A conclusion about one experiment may lead right into another experiment. Point out that in scientific investigations, a conclusion is a summary and explanation of the results of an experiment.

Tell students to suppose that for the Experimental Procedure described on this page, they obtained the following results: Container 1 froze in 45 minutes, Container 2 in 80 minutes, and Container 3 in 25 minutes. Ask: **What conclusions can you draw about this experiment?** *(Students might conclude that the more salt that is added to fresh water, the longer it takes the water to freeze. The hypothesis is supported, and the question of which freezes faster is answered—fresh water.)*

You might wish to have students work in pairs to **ACTIVITY** plan the controlled experiment. *(Students should develop a hypothesis, such as "If I increase the height from which a ball is dropped, then the height of its bounce will increase." They can test the hypothesis by dropping balls from varying heights (the manipulated variable). All trials should be done with the same kind of ball and on the same surface (constant variables). For each trial, they should measure the height of the bounce (responding variable).)* After students have designed the experiment, provide rubber balls and invite them to carry out the experiment so they can collect and interpret data and draw conclusions.

Thinking Critically

Comparing and Contrasting

Emphasize that the skill of comparing and contrasting often relies on good observation skills, as in this activity. *(Students' answers may vary. Sample answer: Similarities—both are dogs and have four legs, two eyes, two ears, brown and white fur, black noses, pink tongues; Differences—smooth coat vs. rough coat, more white fur vs. more brown fur, shorter vs. taller, long ears vs. short ears.)*

Applying Concepts

Point out to students that they apply concepts that they learn in school in their daily lives. For example, they learn to add, subtract, multiply, and divide in school. If they get a paper route or some other part-time job, they can apply those concepts. Challenge students to practice applying concepts by doing the activity. *(Antifreeze lowers the temperature at which the solution will freeze, and thus keeps the water in the radiator from freezing.)*

Interpreting Illustrations

Again, point out the need for good observation skills. Ask: **What is the difference between "interpreting illustrations" and "looking at the pictures"?** *("Interpreting illustrations" requires thorough examination of the illustration, caption, and labels, while "looking at the pictures" implies less thorough examination.)* Encourage students to thoroughly examine the diagram as they do the activity. *(Students' paragraphs may vary, but should describe the internal anatomy of an earthworm, including some of the organs in the earthworm.)*

Thinking Critically

Has a friend ever asked for your advice about a problem? If so, you may have helped your friend think through the problem in a logical way. Without knowing it, you used critical-thinking skills to help your friend. Critical thinking involves the use of reasoning and logic to solve problems or make decisions. Some critical-thinking skills are described below.

Comparing and Contrasting

When you examine two objects for similarities and differences, you are using the skill of **comparing and contrasting.** Comparing involves identifying similarities, or common characteristics. Contrasting involves identifying differences. Analyzing objects in this way can help you discover details that you might otherwise overlook.

ACTIVITY
Compare and contrast the two animals in the photo. First list all the similarities that you see. Then list all the differences.

Applying Concepts

When you use your knowledge about one situation to make sense of a similar situation, you are using the skill of **applying concepts.** Being able to transfer your knowledge from one situation to another shows that you truly understand a concept. You may use this skill in answering test questions that present different problems from the ones you've reviewed in class.

ACTIVITY
You have just learned that water takes longer to freeze when other substances are mixed into it. Use this knowledge to explain why people need a substance called antifreeze in their car's radiator in the winter.

Interpreting Illustrations

Diagrams, photographs, and maps are included in textbooks to help clarify what you read. These illustrations show processes, places, and ideas in a visual manner. The skill called **interpreting illustrations** can help you learn from these visual elements. To understand an illustration, take the time to study the illustration along with all the written information that accompanies it. Captions identify the key concepts shown in the illustration. Labels point out the important parts of a diagram or map, while keys identify the symbols used in a map.

Bristles · Blood vessels · Reproductive organs · Hearts · Brain · Mouth · Digestive tract · Nerve cord · Intestine · Waste-removal organs

▲ **Internal anatomy of an earthworm**

ACTIVITY
Study the diagram above. Then write a short paragraph explaining what you have learned.

Relating Cause and Effect

If one event causes another event to occur, the two events are said to have a cause-and-effect relationship. When you determine that such a relationship exists between two events, you use a skill called **relating cause and effect.** For example, if you notice an itchy, red bump on your skin, you might infer that a mosquito bit you. The mosquito bite is the cause, and the bump is the effect.

It is important to note that two events do not necessarily have a cause-and-effect relationship just because they occur together. Scientists carry out experiments or use past experience to determine whether a cause-and-effect relationship exists.

> **ACTIVITY**
> You are on a camping trip and your flashlight has stopped working. List some possible causes for the flashlight malfunction. How could you determine which cause-and-effect relationship has left you in the dark?

Making Generalizations

When you draw a conclusion about an entire group based on information about only some of the group's members, you are using a skill called **making generalizations.** For a generalization to be valid, the sample you choose must be large enough and representative of the entire group. You might, for example, put this skill to work at a farm stand if you see a sign that says, "Sample some grapes before you buy." If you sample a few sweet grapes, you may conclude that all the grapes are sweet—and purchase a large bunch.

> **ACTIVITY**
> A team of scientists needs to determine whether the water in a large reservoir is safe to drink. How could they use the skill of making generalizations to help them? What should they do?

Making Judgments

When you evaluate something to decide whether it is good or bad, or right or wrong, you are using a skill called **making judgments.** For example, you make judgments when you decide to eat healthful foods or to pick up litter in a park. Before you make a judgment, you need to think through the pros and cons of a situation, and identify the values or standards that you hold.

> **ACTIVITY**
> Should children and teens be required to wear helmets when bicycling? Explain why you feel the way you do.

Problem Solving

When you use critical-thinking skills to resolve an issue or decide on a course of action, you are using a skill called **problem solving.** Some problems, such as how to convert a fraction into a decimal, are straightforward. Other problems, such as figuring out why your computer has stopped working, are complex. Some complex problems can be solved using the trial and error method—try out one solution first, and if that doesn't work, try another. Other useful problem-solving strategies include making models and brainstorming possible solutions with a partner.

Relating Cause and Effect

Emphasize that not all events that occur together have a cause-and-effect relationship. For example, tell students that you went to the grocery and your car stalled. Ask: **Is there a cause-and-effect relationship in this situation? Explain your answer.** *(No, because going to the grocery could not cause a car to stall. There must be another cause to make the car stall.)* Have students do the activity to practice relating cause and effect. *(Students should identify that the flashlight not working is the effect. Some possible causes include dead batteries, a burned-out light bulb, or a loose part.)*

Making Generalizations

Point out the importance of having a large, representative sample before making a generalization. Ask: **If you went fishing at a lake and caught three catfish, could you make the generalization that all fish in the lake are catfish? Why or why not?** *(No, because there might be other kinds of fish you didn't catch because they didn't like the bait or they may be in other parts of the lake.)* **How could you make a generalization about the kinds of fish in the lake?** *(By having a larger sample)* Have students do the activity to practice making generalizations. *(The scientists should collect and test water samples from a number of different parts of the reservoir.)*

Making Judgments

Remind students that they make a judgment almost every time they make a decision. Ask: **What steps should you follow to make a judgment?** *(Gather information, list pros and cons, analyze values, make judgment)* Invite students to do the activity, and then to share and discuss the judgments they made. *(Students' judgments will vary, but should be supported by valid reasoning. Sample answer: Children and teens should be required to wear helmets when bicycling because helmets have been proven to save lives and reduce head injuries.)*

Problem Solving

Challenge student pairs to solve a problem about a soapbox derby. Explain that their younger brother is building a car to enter in the race. The brother wants to know how to make his soapbox car go faster. After student pairs have considered the problem, have them share their ideas about solutions with the class. *(Most will probably suggest using trial and error by making small changes to the car and testing the car after each change. Some students may suggest making and manipulating a model.)*

Organizing Information

Concept Maps

Challenge students to make a concept map with at least three levels of concepts to organize information about types of transportation. All students should start with the phrase *types of transportation* at the top of the concept map. After that point, their concept maps may vary. *(For example, some students might place* private transportation *and* public transportation *at the next level, while other students might have* human-powered *and* gas-powered. *Make sure students connect the concepts with linking words. Challenge students to include cross-linkages as well.)*

Compare/ Contrast Tables

Have students make their own compare/contrast tables using two or more different sports or other activities, such as playing musical instruments. Emphasize that students should select characteristics that highlight the similarities and differences between the activities. *(Students' compare/contrast tables should include several appropriate characteristics and list information about each activity for every characteristic.)*

Organizing Information

As you read this textbook, how can you make sense of all the information it contains? Some useful tools to help you organize information are shown on this page. These tools are called *graphic organizers* because they give you a visual picture of a topic, showing at a glance how key concepts are related.

Concept Maps

Concept maps are useful tools for organizing information on broad topics. A concept map begins with a general concept and shows how it can be broken down into more specific concepts. In that way, relationships between concepts become easier to understand.

A concept map is constructed by placing concept words (usually nouns) in ovals and connecting them with linking words. Often, the most general concept word is placed at the top, and the words become more specific as you move downward. Often the linking words, which are written on a line extending between two ovals, describe the relationship between the two concepts they connect. If you follow any string of concepts and linking words down the map, it should read like a sentence.

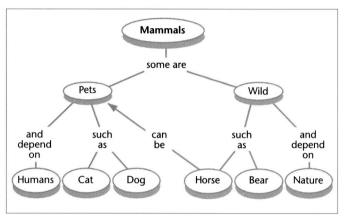

Some concept maps include linking words that connect a concept on one branch of the map to a concept on another branch. These linking words, called cross-linkages, show more complex interrelationships among concepts.

Compare/Contrast Tables

Compare/contrast tables are useful tools for sorting out the similarities and differences between two or more items. A table provides an organized framework in which to compare items based on specific characteristics that you identify.

To create a compare/contrast table, list the items to be compared across the top of a table. Then list the characteristics that will form the basis of your comparison in the left-hand

Characteristic	Baseball	Basketball
Number of Players	9	5
Playing Field	Baseball diamond	Basketball court
Equipment	Bat, baseball, mitts	Basket, basketball

column. Complete the table by filling in information about each characteristic, first for one item and then for the other.

Venn Diagrams

Another way to show similarities and differences between items is with a Venn diagram. A Venn diagram consists of two or more circles that partially overlap. Each circle represents a particular concept or idea. Common characteristics, or similarities, are written within the area of overlap between the two circles. Unique characteristics, or differences, are written in the parts of the circles outside the area of overlap.

To create a Venn diagram, draw two overlapping circles. Label the circles with the names of the items being compared. Write the

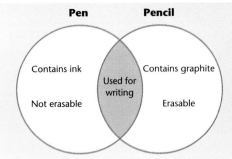

Pen **Pencil**

Contains ink

Used for writing

Contains graphite

Not erasable

Erasable

unique characteristics in each circle outside the area of overlap. Then write the shared characteristics within the area of overlap.

Flowcharts

A flowchart can help you understand the order in which certain events have occurred or should occur. Flowcharts are useful for outlining the stages in a process or the steps in a procedure.

To make a flowchart, write a brief description of each event in a box. Place the first event at the top of the page, followed by the second event, the third event, and so on. Then draw an arrow to connect each event to the one that occurs next.

Preparing Pasta

Boil water

↓

Cook pasta

↓

Drain water

↓

Add sauce

Cycle Diagrams

A cycle diagram can be used to show a sequence of events that is continuous, or cyclical. A continuous sequence does not have an end because, when the final event is over, the first event begins again. Like a flowchart, a cycle diagram can help you understand the order of events.

To create a cycle diagram, write a brief description of each event in a box. Place one event at the top of the page in the center. Then, moving in a clockwise direction around an imaginary circle, write each event in its proper sequence. Draw arrows that connect each event to the one that occurs next, forming a continuous circle.

Steps in a Science Experiment

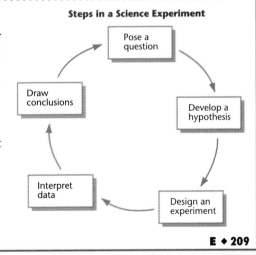

Pose a question

Develop a hypothesis

Design an experiment

Interpret data

Draw conclusions

E ◆ 209

Creating Data Tables and Graphs

Data Tables

Have students create a data table to show how much time they spend on different activities during one week. Suggest that students first list the main activities they do every week. Then they should determine the amount of time they spend on each activity each day. Remind students to give this data table a title. *(Students' data tables will vary. A sample data table is shown below.)*

Bar Graphs

Students can use the data from their data table above to make a bar graph showing how much time they spend on different activities during a week. The vertical axis should be divided into units of time, such as hours. Remind students to label both axes and give their graph a title. *(Students' bar graphs will vary. A sample bar graph is shown below.)*

Creating Data Tables and Graphs

How can you make sense of the data in a science experiment? The first step is to organize the data to help you understand them. Data tables and graphs are helpful tools for organizing data.

Data Tables

You have gathered your materials and set up your experiment. But before you start, you need to plan a way to record what happens during the experiment. By creating a data table, you can record your observations and measurements in an orderly way.

Suppose, for example, that a scientist conducted an experiment to find out how many Calories people of different body masses burn while doing various activities. The data table shows the results.

Notice in this data table that the manipulated variable (body mass) is the heading of one column. The responding variable (for Experiment 1, the number of Calories burned while bicycling) is the heading of the next column. Additional columns were added for related experiments.

CALORIES BURNED IN 30 MINUTES OF ACTIVITY			
Body Mass	Experiment 1 Bicycling	Experiment 2 Playing Basketball	Experiment 3 Watching Television
30 kg	60 Calories	120 Calories	21 Calories
40 kg	77 Calories	164 Calories	27 Calories
50 kg	95 Calories	206 Calories	33 Calories
60 kg	114 Calories	248 Calories	38 Calories

Bar Graphs

To compare how many Calories a person burns doing various activities, you could create a bar graph. A bar graph is used to display data in a number of separate, or distinct, categories. In this example, bicycling, playing basketball, and watching television are three separate categories.

To create a bar graph, follow these steps.

1. On graph paper, draw a horizontal, or *x*-, axis and a vertical, or *y*-, axis.
2. Write the names of the categories to be graphed along the horizontal axis. Include an overall label for the axis as well.
3. Label the vertical axis with the name of the responding variable. Include units of measurement. Then create a scale along the axis by marking off equally spaced numbers that cover the range of the data collected.
4. For each category, draw a solid bar using the scale on the vertical axis to determine the

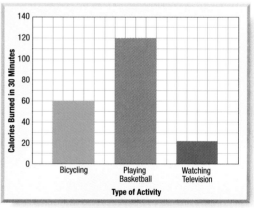

Calories Burned by a 30-kilogram Person in Various Activities

appropriate height. For example, for bicycling, draw the bar as high as the 60 mark on the vertical axis. Make all the bars the same width and leave equal spaces between them.

5. Add a title that describes the graph.

Time Spent on Different Activities in a Week

	Going to Classes	Eating Meals	Playing Soccer	Watching Television
Monday	6	2	2	0.5
Tuesday	6	1.5	1.5	1.5
Wednesday	6	2	1	2
Thursday	6	2	2	1.5
Friday	6	2	2	0.5
Saturday	0	2.5	2.5	1
Sunday	0	3	1	2

Time Spent on Different Activities in a Week

Line Graphs

To see whether a relationship exists between body mass and the number of Calories burned while bicycling, you could create a line graph. A line graph is used to display data that show how one variable (the responding variable) changes in response to another variable (the manipulated variable). You can use a line graph when your manipulated variable is *continuous*, that is, when there are other points between the ones that you tested. In this example, body mass is a continuous variable because there are other body masses between 30 and 40 kilograms (for example, 31 kilograms). Time is another example of a continuous variable.

Line graphs are powerful tools because they allow you to estimate values for conditions that you did not test in the experiment. For example, you can use the line graph to estimate that a 35-kilogram person would burn 68 Calories while bicycling.

To create a line graph, follow these steps.

1. On graph paper, draw a horizontal, or *x*-, axis and a vertical, or *y*-, axis.
2. Label the horizontal axis with the name of the manipulated variable. Label the vertical axis with the name of the responding variable. Include units of measurement.
3. Create a scale on each axis by marking off equally spaced numbers that cover the range of the data collected.
4. Plot a point on the graph for each piece of data. In the line graph above, the dotted lines show how to plot the first data point (30 kilograms and 60 Calories). Draw an imaginary vertical line extending up from the horizontal axis at the 30-kilogram mark. Then draw an imaginary horizontal line extending across from the vertical axis at the 60-Calorie mark. Plot the point where the two lines intersect.

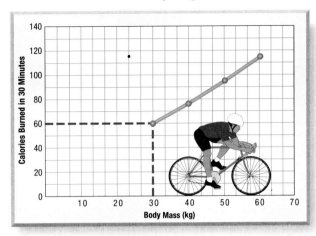

Effect of Body Mass on Calories Burned While Bicycling

5. Connect the plotted points with a solid line. (In some cases, it may be more appropriate to draw a line that shows the general trend of the plotted points. In those cases, some of the points may fall above or below the line.)
6. Add a title that identifies the variables or relationship in the graph.

> **Create line graphs** to display the data from Experiment 2 and Experiment 3 in the data table. **ACTIVITY**

> You read in the newspaper **ACTIVITY** that a total of 4 centimeters of rain fell in your area in June, 2.5 centimeters fell in July, and 1.5 centimeters fell in August. What type of graph would you use to display these data? Use graph paper to create the graph.

Line Graphs

Walk students through the steps involved in creating a line graph using the example illustrated on the page. For example, ask: **What is the label on the horizontal axis? On the vertical axis?** *(Body Mass (kg); Calories Burned in 30 Minutes)* **What scales are used on each axis?** *(3 squares per 10 kg on the x-axis and 2 squares per 20 Calories on the y-axis)* **What does the second data point represent?** *(77 Calories burned for a body mass of 40 kg)* **What trend or pattern does the graph show?** *(The number of Calories burned in 30 minutes of cycling increases with body mass.)*

Have students follow the steps to carry out the first activity. **ACTIVITY** *(Students should make a different graph for each experiment with different y-axis scales to practice making scales appropriate for data. See sample graphs below.)*

Have students carry out the second activity. **ACTIVITY** *(Students should conclude that a bar graph would be best to display the data. A sample bar graph for these data is shown below.)*

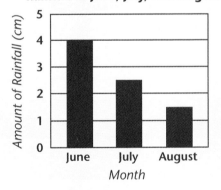

Rainfall in June, July, and August

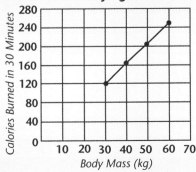

Effect of Body Mass on Calories Burned While Playing Basketball

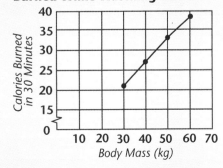

Effect of Body Mass on Calories Burned While Watching Television

Circle Graphs

Emphasize that a circle graph has to include 100 percent of the categories for the topic being graphed. For example, ask: **Could the data in the bar graph titled "Calories Burned by a 30-kilogram Person in Various Activities" (on the previous page) be shown in a circle graph? Why or why not?** *(No, because it does not include all the possible ways a 30-kilogram person can burn Calories.)* Then walk students through the steps for making a circle graph. Help students to use a compass and a protractor. Use the protractor to illustrate that a circle has 360 degrees. Make sure students understand the mathematical calculations involved in making a circle graph.

You might wish to have students work in pairs to complete the activity. *(Students' circle graphs should look like the graph below.)*

ACTIVITY

Circle Graphs

Like bar graphs, circle graphs can be used to display data in a number of separate categories. Unlike bar graphs, however, circle graphs can only be used when you have data for *all* the categories that make up a given topic. A circle graph is sometimes called a pie chart because it resembles a pie cut into slices. The pie represents the entire topic, while the slices represent the individual categories. The size of a slice indicates what percentage of the whole a particular category makes up.

The data table below shows the results of a survey in which 24 teenagers were asked to identify their favorite sport. The data were then used to create the circle graph at the right.

Sports That Teens Prefer

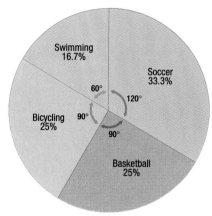

FAVORITE SPORTS

Sport	Number of Students
Soccer	8
Basketball	6
Bicycling	6
Swimming	4

To create a circle graph, follow these steps.

1. Use a compass to draw a circle. Mark the center of the circle with a point. Then draw a line from the center point to the top of the circle.

2. Determine the size of each "slice" by setting up a proportion where x equals the number of degrees in a slice. (NOTE: A circle contains 360 degrees.) For example, to find the number of degrees in the "soccer" slice, set up the following proportion:

$$\frac{\text{students who prefer soccer}}{\text{total number of students}} = \frac{x}{\text{total number of degrees in a circle}}$$

$$\frac{8}{24} = \frac{x}{360}$$

Cross-multiply and solve for x.

$$24x = 8 \times 360$$
$$x = 120$$

The "soccer" slice should contain 120 degrees.

3. Use a protractor to measure the angle of the first slice, using the line you drew to the top of the circle as the 0° line. Draw a line from the center of the circle to the edge for the angle you measured.

4. Continue around the circle by measuring the size of each slice with the protractor. Start measuring from the edge of the previous slice so the wedges do not overlap. When you are done, the entire circle should be filled in.

5. Determine the percentage of the whole circle that each slice represents. To do this, divide the number of degrees in a slice by the total number of degrees in a circle (360), and multiply by 100%. For the "soccer" slice, you can find the percentage as follows:

$$\frac{120}{360} \times 100\% = 33.3\%$$

6. Use a different color to shade in each slice. Label each slice with the name of the category and with the percentage of the whole it represents.

7. Add a title to the circle graph.

In a class of 28 students, 12 students take the bus to school, 10 students walk, and 6 students ride their bicycles. Create a circle graph to display these data.

ACTIVITY

Ways Students Get to School

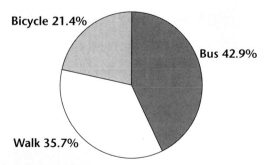

Safety Symbols

These symbols alert you to possible dangers in the laboratory and remind you to work carefully.

Safety Goggles Always wear safety goggles to protect your eyes in any activity involving chemicals, flames or heating, or the possibility of broken glassware.

Lab Apron Wear a laboratory apron to protect your skin and clothing from damage.

Breakage You are working with materials that may be breakable, such as glass containers, glass tubing, thermometers, or funnels. Handle breakable materials with care. Do not touch broken glassware.

Heat-resistant Gloves Use an oven mitt or other hand protection when handling hot materials. Hot plates, hot glassware, or hot water can cause burns. Do not touch hot objects with your bare hands.

Heating Use a clamp or tongs to pick up hot glassware. Do not touch hot objects with your bare hands.

Sharp Object Pointed-tip scissors, scalpels, knives, needles, pins, or tacks are sharp. They can cut or puncture your skin. Always direct a sharp edge or point away from yourself and others. Use sharp instruments only as instructed.

Electric Shock Avoid the possibility of electric shock. Never use electrical equipment around water, or when the equipment is wet or your hands are wet. Be sure cords are untangled and cannot trip anyone. Disconnect the equipment when it is not in use.

Corrosive Chemical You are working with an acid or another corrosive chemical. Avoid getting it on your skin or clothing, or in your eyes. Do not inhale the vapors. Wash your hands when you are finished with the activity.

Poison Do not let any poisonous chemical come in contact with your skin, and do not inhale its vapors. Wash your hands when you are finished with the activity.

Physical Safety When an experiment involves physical activity, take precautions to avoid injuring yourself or others. Follow instructions from your teacher. Alert your teacher if there is any reason you should not participate in the activity.

Animal Safety Treat live animals with care to avoid harming the animals or yourself. Working with animal parts or preserved animals also may require caution. Wash your hands when you are finished with the activity.

Plant Safety Handle plants in the laboratory or during field work only as directed by your teacher. If you are allergic to certain plants, tell your teacher before doing an activity in which those plants are used. Avoid touching harmful plants such as poison ivy, poison oak, or poison sumac, or plants with thorns. Wash your hands when you are finished with the activity.

Flames You may be working with flames from a lab burner, candle, or matches. Tie back loose hair and clothing. Follow instructions from your teacher about lighting and extinguishing flames.

No Flames Flammable materials may be present. Make sure there are no flames, sparks, or other exposed heat sources present.

Fumes When poisonous or unpleasant vapors may be involved, work in a ventilated area. Avoid inhaling vapors directly. Only test an odor when directed to do so by your teacher, and use a wafting motion to direct the vapor toward your nose.

Disposal Chemicals and other laboratory materials used in the activity must be disposed of safely. Follow the instructions from your teacher.

Hand Washing Wash your hands thoroughly when finished with the activity. Use antibacterial soap and warm water. Lather both sides of your hands and between your fingers. Rinse well.

General Safety Awareness You may see this symbol when none of the symbols described earlier appears. In this case, follow the specific instructions provided. You may also see this symbol when you are asked to develop your own procedure in a lab. Have your teacher approve your plan before you go further.

Laboratory Safety

Laboratory safety is an essential element of a successful science class. It is important for you to emphasize laboratory safety to students. Students need to understand exactly what is safe and unsafe behavior, and what the rationale is behind each safety rule.

Review with students the Safety Symbols and Science Safety Rules listed on this and the next two pages. Then follow the safety guidelines below to ensure that your classroom will be a safe place for students to learn science.

◆ Post safety rules in the classroom and review them regularly with students.

◆ Familiarize yourself with the safety procedures for each activity before introducing it to your students.

◆ Review specific safety precautions with students before beginning every science activity.

◆ Always act as an exemplary role model by displaying safe behavior.

◆ Know how to use safety equipment, such as fire extinguishers and fire blankets, and always have it accessible.

◆ Have students practice leaving the classroom quickly and orderly to prepare them for emergencies.

◆ Explain to students how to use the intercom or other available means of communication to get help during an emergency.

◆ Never leave students unattended while they are engaged in science activities.

◆ Provide enough space for students to safely carry out science activities.

◆ Keep your classroom and all science materials in proper condition. Replace worn or broken items.

◆ Instruct students to report all accidents and injuries to you immediately.

Laboratory Safety

Additional tips are listed below for the Science Safety Rules discussed on these two pages. Please keep these tips in mind when you carry out science activities in your classroom.

General Precautions

◆ For open-ended activities like Chapter Projects, go over general safety guidelines with students. Have students submit their procedures or design plans in writing and check them for safety considerations.

◆ In an activity where students are directed to taste something, be sure to store the material in clean, *nonscience* containers. Distribute the material to students in *new* plastic or paper dispensables, which should be discarded after the tasting. Tasting or eating should never be done in a lab classroom.

◆ During physical activity, make sure students do not overexert themselves.

◆ Remind students to handle microscopes and telescopes with care to avoid breakage.

Heating and Fire Safety

◆ No flammable substances should be in use around hot plates, light bulbs, or open flames.

◆ Test tubes should be heated only in water baths.

◆ Students should be permitted to strike matches to light candles or burners *only* with strict supervision. When possible, you should light the flames, especially when working with sixth graders.

◆ Be sure to have proper ventilation when fumes are produced during a procedure.

◆ All electrical equipment used in the lab should have GFI switches.

Using Chemicals Safely

◆ When students use both chemicals and microscopes in one activity, microscopes should be in a separate part of the room from the chemicals so that when students remove their goggles to use the microscopes, their eyes are not at risk.

Science Safety Rules

To prepare yourself to work safely in the laboratory, read over the following safety rules. Then read them a second time. Make sure you understand and follow each rule. Ask your teacher to explain any rules you do not understand.

Dress Code

1. To protect yourself from injuring your eyes, wear safety goggles whenever you work with chemicals, burners, glassware, or any substance that might get into your eyes. If you wear contact lenses, notify your teacher.
2. Wear a lab apron or coat whenever you work with corrosive chemicals or substances that can stain.
3. Tie back long hair to keep it away from any chemicals, flames, or equipment.
4. Remove or tie back any article of clothing or jewelry that can hang down and touch chemicals, flames, or equipment. Roll up or secure long sleeves.
5. Never wear open shoes or sandals.

General Precautions

6. Read all directions for an experiment several times before beginning the activity. Carefully follow all written and oral instructions. If you are in doubt about any part of the experiment, ask your teacher for assistance.
7. Never perform activities that are not assigned or authorized by your teacher. Obtain permission before "experimenting" on your own. Never handle any equipment unless you have specific permission.
8. Never perform lab activities without direct supervision.
9. Never eat or drink in the laboratory.
10. Keep work areas clean and tidy at all times. Bring only notebooks and lab manuals or written lab procedures to the work area. All other items, such as purses and backpacks, should be left in a designated area.
11. Do not engage in horseplay.

First Aid

12. Always report all accidents or injuries to your teacher, no matter how minor. Notify your teacher immediately about any fires.
13. Learn what to do in case of specific accidents, such as getting acid in your eyes or on your skin. (Rinse acids from your body with lots of water.)
14. Be aware of the location of the first-aid kit, but do not use it unless instructed by your teacher. In case of injury, your teacher should administer first aid. Your teacher may also send you to the school nurse or call a physician.
15. Know the location of emergency equipment, such as the fire extinguisher and fire blanket, and know how to use it.
16. Know the location of the nearest telephone and whom to contact in an emergency.

Heating and Fire Safety

17. Never use a heat source, such as a candle, burner, or hot plate, without wearing safety goggles.
18. Never heat anything unless instructed to do so. A chemical that is harmless when cool may be dangerous when heated.
19. Keep all combustible materials away from flames. Never use a flame or spark near a combustible chemical.
20. Never reach across a flame.
21. Before using a laboratory burner, make sure you know proper procedures for lighting and adjusting the burner, as demonstrated by your teacher. Do not touch the burner. It may be hot. And never leave a lighted burner unattended!
22. Chemicals can splash or boil out of a heated test tube. When heating a substance in a test tube, make sure that the mouth of the tube is not pointed at you or anyone else.
23. Never heat a liquid in a closed container. The expanding gases produced may blow the container apart.
24. Before picking up a container that has been heated, hold the back of your hand near it. If you can feel heat on the back of your hand, the container is too hot to handle. Use an oven mitt to pick up a container that has been heated.

Using Glassware Safely

◆ Use plastic containers, graduated cylinders, and beakers whenever possible. If using glass, students should wear safety goggles.

◆ Use only nonmercury thermometers with anti-roll protectors.

◆ Check all glassware periodically for chips and scratches, which can cause cuts and breakage.

Using Chemicals Safely

25. Never mix chemicals "for the fun of it." You might produce a dangerous, possibly explosive substance.

26. Never put your face near the mouth of a container that holds chemicals. Never touch, taste, or smell a chemical unless you are instructed by your teacher to do so. Many chemicals are poisonous.

27. Use only those chemicals needed in the activity. Read and double-check labels on supply bottles before removing any chemicals. Take only as much as you need. Keep all containers closed when chemicals are not being used.

28. Dispose of all chemicals as instructed by your teacher. To avoid contamination, never return chemicals to their original containers. Never simply pour chemicals or other substances into the sink or trash containers.

29. Be extra careful when working with acids or bases. Pour all chemicals over the sink or a container, not over your work surface.

30. If you are instructed to test for odors, use a wafting motion to direct the odors to your nose. Do not inhale the fumes directly from the container.

31. When mixing an acid and water, always pour the water into the container first and then add the acid to the water. Never pour water into an acid.

32. Take extreme care not to spill any material in the laboratory. Wash chemical spills and splashes immediately with plenty of water. Immediately begin rinsing with water any acids that get on your skin or clothing, and notify your teacher of any acid spill at the same time.

Using Glassware Safely

33. Never force glass tubing or thermometers into a rubber stopper or rubber tubing. Have your teacher insert the glass tubing or thermometer if required for an activity.

34. If you are using a laboratory burner, use a wire screen to protect glassware from any flame. Never heat glassware that is not thoroughly dry on the outside.

35. Keep in mind that hot glassware looks cool. Never pick up glassware without first checking to see if it is hot. Use an oven mitt. See rule 24.

36. Never use broken or chipped glassware. If glassware breaks, notify your teacher and dispose of the glassware in the proper broken-glassware container. Never handle broken glass with your bare hands.

37. Never eat or drink from lab glassware.

38. Thoroughly clean glassware before putting it away.

Using Sharp Instruments

39. Handle scalpels or other sharp instruments with extreme care. Never cut material toward you; cut away from you.

40. Immediately notify your teacher if you cut your skin when working in the laboratory.

Animal and Plant Safety

41. Never perform experiments that cause pain, discomfort, or harm to mammals, birds, reptiles, fishes, or amphibians. This rule applies at home as well as in the classroom.

42. Animals should be handled only if absolutely necessary. Your teacher will instruct you as to how to handle each animal species brought into the classroom.

43. If you know that you are allergic to certain plants, molds, or animals, tell your teacher before doing an activity in which these are used.

44. During field work, protect your skin by wearing long pants, long sleeves, socks, and closed shoes. Know how to recognize the poisonous plants and fungi in your area, as well as plants with thorns, and avoid contact with them.

45. Never eat any part of an unidentified plant or fungus.

46. Wash your hands thoroughly after handling animals or the cage containing animals. Wash your hands when you are finished with any activity involving animal parts, plants, or soil.

End-of-Experiment Rules

47. After an experiment has been completed, clean up your work area and return all equipment to its proper place.

48. Dispose of waste materials as instructed by your teacher.

49. Wash your hands after every experiment.

50. Always turn off all burners or hot plates when they are not in use. Unplug hot plates and other electrical equipment. If you used a burner, check that the gas-line valve to the burner is off as well.

Using Sharp Instruments

◆ Always use blunt-tip safety scissors, except when pointed-tip scissors are required.

Animal and Plant Safety

◆ When working with live animals or plants, check ahead of time for students who may have allergies to the specimens.

◆ When growing bacteria cultures, use only disposable petri dishes. After streaking, the dishes should be sealed and not opened again by students. After the lab, students should return the unopened dishes to you. Students should wash their hands with antibacterial soap.

◆ Two methods are recommended for the safe disposal of bacteria cultures. *First method:* Autoclave the petri dishes and discard without opening. *Second method:* If no autoclave is available, carefully open the dishes (never have a student do this) and pour full-strength bleach into the dishes and let stand for a day. Then pour the bleach from the petri dishes down a drain and flush the drain with lots of water. Tape the petri dishes back together and place in a sealed plastic bag. Wrap the plastic bag with a brown paper bag or newspaper and tape securely. Throw the sealed package in the trash. Thoroughly disinfect the work area with bleach.

◆ To grow mold, use a new, sealable plastic bag that is two to three times larger than the material to be placed inside. Seal the bag and tape it shut. After the bag is sealed, students should not open it. To dispose of the bag and mold culture, make a small cut near an edge of the bag and cook in a microwave oven on high setting for at least 1 minute. Discard the bag according to local ordinance, usually in the trash.

◆ Students should wear disposable nitrile, latex, or food-handling gloves when handling live animals or nonliving specimens.

End-of-Experiment Rules

◆ Always have students use antibacterial soap for washing their hands.

A

abiotic factor A nonliving part of an ecosystem. (p. 18)

acid rain Precipitation that is more acidic than normal. (p. 142)

active solar system A method of capturing the sun's energy and distributing it using pumps and fans. (p. 173)

adaptation The behaviors and physical characteristics of species that allow them to live successfully in their environments. (p. 32)

air pollution A change to the atmosphere that has harmful effects. (p. 140)

aquaculture The practice of raising fish and other water organisms for food. (p. 95)

B

bedrock Rock that makes up Earth's crust. (p. 116)

biodegradable Capable of being broken down by bacteria and other natural decomposers. (p. 124)

biodiversity The number of different species in an area. (p. 97)

biogeography The study of where organisms live. (p. 56)

biomass fuel Fuel made from living things. (p. 176)

biome A group of ecosystems with similar climates and organisms. (p. 62)

biotic factor A living part of an ecosystem. (p. 17)

birth rate The number of births in a population in a certain amount of time. (p. 25)

C

canopy A leafy roof formed by tall trees. (p. 63)

captive breeding The mating of endangered animals in zoos or preserves. (p. 104)

carnivore Consumer that eats only animals. (p. 46)

carrying capacity The largest population that an area can support. (p. 27)

catalytic converter A device that reduces carbon monoxide emissions from vehicles. (p. 156)

chlorofluorocarbons Gases containing chlorine and fluorine (also called CFCs). (p. 145)

clear-cutting The process of cutting down all the trees in an area at once. (p. 92)

climate The typical weather pattern in an area over a long period of time. (p. 59)

combustion The burning of a fuel. (p. 165)

commensalism A relationship between two species in which one species benefits and the other is neither helped nor harmed. (p. 37)

community All the different populations that live together in an area. (p. 20)

competition The struggle between organisms for the limited resources in a habitat. (p. 33)

composting Helping the natural decomposition process to break down certain wastes. (p. 127)

condensation The process by which a gas changes to a liquid. (p. 53)

coniferous trees Trees that produce their seeds in cones and have needle-shaped leaves. (p. 67)

conservation viewpoint The belief that people should use natural resources as long as they do not destroy those resources. (p. 88)

consumer An organism that obtains energy by feeding on other organisms. (p. 46)

continental drift The very slow motion of the continents. (p. 56)

control rod Cadmium rod used in a nuclear reactor to absorb neutrons from fission. (p. 182)

controlled experiment An experiment in which all factors except one are kept constant. (p. 205)

corrosive Able to dissolve or break down many other substances, such as an acid. (p. 131)

crop rotation The planting of different crops in a field each year. (p. 118)

D

death rate The number of deaths in a population in a certain amount of time. (p. 25)

deciduous trees Trees that shed their leaves and grow new ones each year. (p. 66)

decomposer An organism that breaks down wastes and dead organisms. (p. 47)

desert An area that receives less than 25 cm of precipitation a year. (p. 64)

desertification The advance of desertlike conditions into areas that previously were fertile. (p. 118)

development The construction of buildings, roads, dams, and other structures. (p. 115)

development viewpoint The belief that humans should be able to freely use and benefit from all of Earth's resources. (p. 88)

dispersal The movement of organisms from one place to another. (p. 57)

drought A period of less rain than normal. (p. 150)

········ **E** ········

ecology The study of how living things interact with each other and their environment. (p. 20)

ecosystem All the living and nonliving things that interact in an area. (p. 16)

efficiency The percentage of energy that is used by a device to perform work. (p. 188)

emigration Leaving a population. (p. 26)

emissions Particles and gases released into the air from a smokestack or motor vehicle. (p. 141)

endangered species A species in danger of becoming extinct in the near future. (p. 100)

energy conservation The practice of reducing energy use. (p. 187)

energy pyramid A diagram that shows the amount of energy that moves from one feeding level to another in a food web. (p. 49)

erosion The process by which water, wind, or ice moves particles of rock or soil. (p. 116)

estimate An approximation of a number based on reasonable assumptions. (p. 24)

estuary A habitat in which the fresh water of a river meets the salt water of the ocean. (p. 71)

evaporation The process by which molecules of a liquid absorb energy and change to the gas state. (p. 52)

exotic species Species that are carried to a new location by people. (p. 58)

explosive Capable of reacting very quickly when exposed to air or water or of exploding when dropped. (p. 131)

extinction The disappearance of all members of a species from Earth. (p. 100)

········ **F** ········

fallow Left unplanted with crops. (p. 117)

fertilizer A chemical that provides nutrients to help crops grow better. (p. 151)

fishery An area with a large population of valuable ocean organisms. (p. 94)

flammable Capable of catching fire easily and burning at low temperatures. (p. 131)

food chain A series of events in which one organism eats another. (p. 47)

food web The pattern of overlapping food chains in an ecosystem. (p. 47)

fossil fuel An energy-rich substance (such as coal, oil, or natural gas) formed from the remains of organisms. (p. 166)

fuel rod Uranium rod that undergoes fission in a nuclear reactor. (p. 182)

········ **G** ········

gasohol A mixture of gasoline and alcohol. (p. 176)

gene A structure in an organism's cells that carries its hereditary information. (p. 100)

geothermal energy Heat from Earth's interior. (p. 177)

global warming The theory that increasing carbon dioxide in the atmosphere will raise Earth's average temperature. (p. 146)

grassland An area populated by grasses that gets 25 to 75 centimeters of rain each year. (p. 65)

greenhouse effect The trapping of heat by certain gases in the atmosphere. (p. 146)

groundwater Water stored in underground layers of soil and rock. (p. 149)

········ **H** ········

habitat The place where an organism lives and that provides the things it needs. (p. 17)

habitat destruction The loss of a natural habitat. (p. 101)

habitat fragmentation The breaking of a habitat into smaller, isolated pieces. (p. 101)

hazardous waste A material that can be harmful if it is not properly disposed of. (p. 131)

herbivore Consumer that eats only plants. (p. 46)

hibernation A low-energy state similar to sleep that some mammals enter in the winter. (p. 67)

host The organism that a parasite lives in or on in parasitism. (p. 38)

hydrocarbon A compound that contains carbon and hydrogen atoms. (p. 166)

hydroelectric power Electricity produced using the energy of flowing water. (p. 175)

hypothesis A prediction about the outcome of an experiment. (p. 204)

immigration Moving into a population. (p. 26)

incineration The burning of solid waste. (p. 123)

insulation Building material that blocks heat transfer between the air inside and outside. (p. 189)

intertidal zone The area between the highest high-tide line and lowest low-tide line. (p. 72)

keystone species A species that influences the survival of many others in an ecosystem. (p. 99)

land reclamation The process of restoring land to a more natural state. (p. 119)

leachate Water that has passed through buried wastes in a landfill. (p. 123)

limiting factor An environmental factor that prevents a population from increasing. (p. 27)

litter Layer of dead leaves and grass on top of the soil. (p. 116)

manipulated variable The one factor that a scientist changes during an experiment. (p. 205)

meltdown A dangerous condition caused by overheating inside a nuclear reactor. (p. 183)

municipal solid waste Waste produced in homes, businesses, and schools. (p. 122)

mutualism A relationship between two species in which both species benefit. (p. 37)

native species Species that have naturally evolved in an area. (p. 58)

natural selection Process by which individuals that are better adapted to the environment are more likely to survive and reproduce than others. (p. 32)

neritic zone The region of shallow ocean water over the continental shelf. (p. 72)

niche An organism's particular role in an ecosystem, or how it makes its living. (p. 32)

nitrogen fixation The process of changing free nitrogen gas into a usable form. (p. 55)

nodules Bumps on the roots of certain plants that house nitrogen-fixing bacteria. (p. 55)

nonrenewable resource A natural resource that is not replaced as it is used. (p. 85)

nuclear fission The splitting of an atom's nucleus into smaller nuclei. (p. 181)

nuclear fusion The combining of two atomic nuclei into a single larger nucleus. (p. 184)

nucleus The central core of an atom that contains the protons and neutrons. (p. 181)

nutrient depletion The situation that arises when more soil nutrients are used than the decomposers can replace. (p. 117)

omnivore A consumer that eats both plants and animals. (p. 46)

ozone A toxic form of oxygen. (p. 141)

ozone layer The layer of the atmosphere that contains a higher concentration of ozone than the rest of the atmosphere. (p. 144)

parasite The organism that benefits by living on or in a host in parasitism. (p. 38)

parasitism A relationship in which one organism lives on or inside another and harms it. (p. 38)

passive solar system A method of converting solar energy into heat without pumps or fans. (p. 173)

permafrost Soil that is frozen all year. (p. 68)

pesticide A chemical that kills crop-destroying organisms. (p. 151)

petrochemical Compound made from oil. (p. 169)

petroleum Liquid fossil fuel; oil. (p. 168)

photochemical smog A thick, brown haze formed when certain gases react in sunlight. (p. 141)

photosynthesis The process in which organisms use water along with sunlight and carbon dioxide to make food. (p. 18)

pioneer species The first species to populate an area. (p. 77)

poaching Illegal hunting of wildlife. (p. 102)

pollution A change to the environment that has a negative effect on living things. (p. 85)

population All the members of one species in a particular area. (p. 19)

population density The number of individuals in a specific area. (p. 23)

precipitation Rain, snow, sleet, or hail. (p. 53)

predation An interaction in which one organism kills and eats another. (p. 34)

predator The organism that does the killing in predation. (p. 34)

preservation viewpoint The belief that all parts of the environment are equally important, no matter how useful they are to humans. (p. 88)

prey An organism that is killed in predation. (p. 34)

primary succession The changes that occur in an area where no ecosystem had existed. (p. 77)

primary treatment The removal of solid materials from wastewater. (p. 157)

producer An organism that can make its own food. (p. 45)

radioactive Containing unstable atoms. (p. 131)

reactor vessel The part of a nuclear reactor where nuclear fission occurs. (p. 182)

recycling The process of reclaiming and reusing raw materials. (p. 124)

refinery A factory where crude oil is separated into fuels and other products. (p. 169)

renewable resource A resource that is naturally replaced in a relatively short time. (p. 85)

reserve A known deposit of fuels. (p. 167)

resin Solid material produced during oil refining that can be used to make plastics. (p. 125)

responding variable The factor that changes as a result of changes to the manipulated variable in an experiment. (p. 205)

sanitary landfill A landfill that holds nonhazardous waste such as municipal solid waste and construction debris. (p. 123)

savanna A grassland close to the equator. (p. 65)

scavenger A carnivore that feeds on the bodies of dead organisms. (p. 46)

scrubber A device that uses water droplets to clean smokestack emissions. (p. 156)

secondary succession The changes that occur after a disturbance in an ecosystem. (p. 78)

secondary treatment The use of bacteria to break down wastes in wastewater. (p. 157)

sediments Particles of rock and sand. (p. 152)

selective cutting The process of cutting down only some trees in an area. (p. 92)

sewage The water and human wastes that are washed down sinks and toilets. (p. 151)

species A group of organisms that are similar and reproduce to produce fertile offspring. (p. 19)

subsoil Layer of soil below topsoil. (p. 116)

succession The series of predictable changes that occur in a community over time. (p. 76)

sustainable yield A regular amount of a renewable resource that can be harvested without reducing the future supply. (p. 92)

symbiosis A close relationship between species that benefits at least one of the species. (p. 37)

taxol Chemical in Pacific yew tree bark that has cancer-fighting properties. (p. 107)

temperature inversion Condition in which a layer of warm air traps polluted air close to Earth's surface. (p. 142)

threatened species A species that could become endangered in the near future. (p. 100)

topsoil An upper layer of soil consisting of rock fragments, organisms, nutrients, water, air, and decaying matter. (p. 116)

toxic Damaging to the health of humans or other organisms; poisonous. (p. 131)

tundra An extremely cold, dry biome. (p. 68)

understory A layer of shorter plants that grow in the shade of a forest canopy. (p. 63)

variable Any factor that can change in an experiment. (p. 205)

water cycle The continuous process by which water moves from Earth's surface to the atmosphere and back. (p. 52)

water pollution A change to water that has a harmful effect. (p. 150)

Index

abiotic factors 18–19
acid rain 142–143
active solar system 173
adaptations 32, 34–35, 195
African rain forests 194–199
agricultural chemicals, water pollution
    from 151, 158
agriculture, land use for 115
air pollution 138–148
    acid rain 142–143
    causes of 141
    global climate change and 146–147
    hydroelectric power and 175
    indoor 143–144
    ozone layer and 144–145
    reducing 156, 158
    smog 141–142
alfalfa, nitrogen fixation and 55
algae
    break down of wastes by 133
    in freshwater biomes 70, 71
aluminum, recycling 124
American Medical Association 108
Antarctica 69, 84, 89
applying concepts, skill of 206
aquaculture 95
Arcata, California, sewage treatment in 157
area, biodiversity and size of 97
asbestos 143
aspirin 106
atoms 52
Australia 56, 58
automobiles
    energy conservation and 187, 188, 190
    smog caused by 141

bacteria
    breakdown of wastes by 133
    as decomposers 47
    nitrogen fixation by 55
ball python 194
bats 13, 35, 37
bay-breasted warbler 33
bedrock 116
biodegradable substances 124
biodiversity 97–105
    extinction of species and 100–103
    factors affecting 97–98
    gene pool diversity 100
    medicine and 108
    protecting 104–105
    value of 98–99
biogeography 56–61
    continental drift 56–57
    limits to dispersal 58–59
    means of dispersal 57–58
biomass fuels 176
biomes 62–75
    boreal forest 67–68
    climate and 62
    deciduous forest 66–67
    desert 64–65
    experiment on 60–61
    freshwater 70–71
    grassland 65–66

    marine 71–73
    mountains and ice 69
    rain forest 63–64
    tundra 68–69
biotic factors 17
birds
    rate of extinction of 101
    of tundra 69
birth rate 25
black lung 167
blackout 164
bonobo chimpanzee 194
boreal forest biome 67–68
breeding, captive 104
Bureau of Land Management (BLM) 10

cadmium control rods 182–183
calculating, skill of 203
California condors 104
California leaf-nosed bat 13
camouflage 34
cancer 107
canopy 63, 195, 198–199
Cape May warbler 33
captive breeding 104
carbon 53
carbon cycle 53–54
carbon dioxide 53–54, 140
    global warming and 146
carbon monoxide 144
    reducing emissions of 156
carnivores 46, 68
carrying capacity 27, 30
catalytic converter 156
catchments 11, 13
certified wood 93
CFCs. See chlorofluorocarbons
chemicals
    used by plants to reduce competition 33
    water pollution from 151, 152
Chernobyl, Ukraine, meltdown at 183–184
chlorofluorocarbons (CFCs) 145, 156
classifying, skill of 201
Clean Air Act 155, 156
Clean Water Act 155
clear-cutting 92, 93
cliff swallows 24
climate 59
    biodiversity and 98
    biomes and 62
    global change of 146–147
    as limit to dispersal 59
    predictions 146, 147
clouds 53, 147
coal 166–167
    acid rain caused by 142–143
    as energy source 167
    formation of 166
    global warming and 146
    mining 167
Colorado River 12–13
coloring
    false 35
    warning 35
combustion 165

comet moth 194
commensalism 37
communicating, skill of 201
communities 20
compare/contrast tables 208
comparing and contrasting, skill of 206
competition 33, 58
composting 127
concentration 145
concept maps 208
condensation 52, 53
coniferous trees 67, 91
conservation
    efficiency and 187–190
    energy 187–190
    recycling and 124, 126
    soil 117
conservation plowing 117
conservation viewpoint 88
consumers 46, 54
    first-level 47, 48, 71
    in food web 47, 48
continental drift 56–57
continental shelf 72
contour plowing 117
controlled experiment 205
controlling variables, skill of 205
control rods 182–183
Convention on International Trade in
    Endangered Species (1973) 105
cooling and energy conservation 189
coral reefs 72, 98
corrosive wastes 131
costs and benefits in environmental
    decisions 89
critical thinking skills 206–207
crop rotation 118
crude oil 169
cycle diagrams 209
cycles of matter 51–55
    carbon cycle 53–54
    nitrogen cycle 54–55
    oxygen cycle 53, 54
    water cycle 52–53, 174

dams 175, 180
data tables 210
death rate 25
deciduous forest biome 66–67
deciduous trees 66
decomposers 46–47
    in food web 48
    in freshwater biomes 70
    nitrogen cycle and 55
    nutrients supplied to soil by 117
decomposition 43
deep-sea gulper 73
deep zone 73
deer mice 25
Denali National Park 67
density, population 23
desert 64–65
    as limit to dispersal 58
    ecosystem of 32
    organisms 31–32, 64–65

Acknowledgments

Illustration

John Edwards & Associates: 50, 59, 72–73, 122, 147, 156, 165, 166, 173, 177, 183, 195
GeoSystems Global Corporation: 11, 63, 64, 66, 68, 118, 133, 167, 194
Andrea Golden: 74t
Biruta Hansen: 20–21, 32
Jared Lee: 143
Martucci Design: 31, 69, 81, 85, 115, 161, 168, 187, 210, 211, 212
Matt Mayerchak: 40, 80, 110, 160, 208, 209
Karen Minot: 97
Morgan Cain & Associates: 45, 142, 145, 146, 169, 182, 184, 186, 202, 203
Ortelius Design Inc.: 57
Judith Pinkham: 90, 120, 128, 179, 186t
Matthew Pippin: 52, 116 (soil)
Pond and Giles: 77, 78, 93
Walter Stuart: 48
Alan Witschonke: 198–199
J/B Woolsey Associates: 22, 26, 33, 36, 47, 53, 54, 74, 101, 116 (spots), 206

Photography

Photo Research Sue McDermott
Cover image Robert Maier/Animals Animals

Nature of Science
Page 10,11t, Courtesy of Elroy Masters; **11b**, Pat O'Hara/DRK Photo; **12tl**, Vireo; **12bl**, Jeff Foott/Tom Stack & Assoc.; **12–13r**, M. Collier/DRK Photo; **13**, Gilbert Grant/Photo Researchers.

Chapter 1
Pages 14–15, Tony Craddock/TSI; **16**, Richard Haynes; **16–17**, Shin Yoshino/Minden Pictures; **17**, Carr Clifton/Minden Pictures; **17 inset top**, Corel Corp.; **17 inset**, S. Nielsen/DRK Photo; **18**, John Cancalosi/Tom Stack & Associates; **19**, Patti Murray/Animals Animals; **23t**, Richard Haynes; **23b**, Michlo Hoshino/Minden Pictures; **24**, C. Allan Morgan/DRK Photo; **25t**, Rob Simpson/Visuals Unlimited; **25b**, Bas van Beek/Leo de Wys; **27**, Mitsuaki Iwago/Minden Pictures; **28t**, Dan Budnick/Woodfin Camp & Associates; **28b**, Russ Lappa; **30**, Gary Griffen/Animals Animals; **31**, J. Alcock/Visuals Unlimited; **33l**, Patti Murray/Animals Animals; **33tr**, Wayne Lankinen/DRK Photo; **33br**, Ron Willocks/Animals Animals; **34l**, Michael Fogden/DRK Photo; **34r**, D. Holden Bailey/Tom Stack & Associates; **35l**, Stephen J. Krasemann/DRK Photo; **35r**, Donald Specker/Animals Animals; **35b**, Jeanne White/Photo Researchers; **37**, Daryl Balfour/TSI; **38**, John Gerlach/DRK Photo; **39**, Tony Craddock/TSI.

Chapter 2
Pages 42–43, Tom McHugh/Steinhart Aquarium/Photo Researchers; **44t**, Richard Haynes; **44b**, Byron Jorjorian/TSI; **45**, Breck P. Kent/Animals Animals/Earth Scenes; **46l**, Stephen J. Krasemann/DRK Photo; **46tr**, John Cancalosi/DRK Photo; **46br**, John Netherton/Animals Animals; **47**, S. Nielsen/DRK Photo; **49**, Stephen J. Krasemann/DRK Photo; **51t**, Richard Haynes; **51b**, R.J. Erwin/DRK Photo; **55**, Dr. Jeremy Burgess/Science Photo Library/Photo Researchers; **56t**, Richard Haynes; **56b**, J. Cancalosi/DRK Photo; **57**, D. Cavagnaro/DRK Photo; **58**, Stephen G. Maka/DRK Photo; **59t**, John Canalosi/DRK Photo; **59b**, Russ Lappa; **61**, Richard Haynes; **62**, Russ Lappa; **63t**, Renee Lynn/TSI; **63m**, Frans Lanting/Minden Pictures; **63b**, Mark Hones/Minden Pictures; **64l**, Joe McDonald/DRK Photo; **64 inset**, Michael Fogden/DRK Photo; **65**, Art Wolfe/TSI; **66l**, Carr Clifton/Minden Pictures; **66 inset**, **67r**, Stephen J. Krasemann/DRK Photo; **67 inset**, Michael Quinton/Minden Pictures; **68, 69**, Michio Hoshino/Minden Pictures; **70l**, David Boyle/Animals Animals; **70r**, Kim Heacox/DRK Photo; **71l**, Stephen G. Maka/DRK Photo; **71r**, Steven David Miller/Animals Animals; **72l**, Anne Wertheim/Animals Animals; **72r**, Gregory Ochocki/Photo Researchers; **73l**, Michael Nolan/Tom Stack & Associates; **73r**, Norbert Wu; **75l,r**, Russ Lappa; **76t,76b**, Tom & Pat Leeson/Photo Researchers; **79**, John Cancalosi/DRK Photo.

Chapter 3
Pages 82–83, Gay Bumgarner/TSI; **84**, Frans Lanting/Minden Pictures; **85l**, Inga Spence/Tom Stack & Associates; **85r**, Charles D. Winters/Photo Researchers; **85b**, Key Sanders/TSI; **86t**, UPI/corbis-Bettmann; **86b**, Corbis-Bettmann; **87t**, UPI/Corbis-Bettmann; **87bl**, Underwood & Underwood/Corbis-Bettmann; **87br**, William Campbell/Peter Arnold; **88**, Jeff Gnass/The Stock Market; **90**, Russ Lappa; **91**, Martin Rogers/Stock Boston; **92**, Gary Braasch/TSI; **94**, Tom Stewart/The Stock Market; **95**, Greg Vaughn/Tom Stack & Associates; **96**, Russ Lappa; **97**, Richard Haynes; **98tl**, Dave Watts/Tom Stack & Associates; **98tm**, Frans Lanting/Minden Pictures; **98tr**, George G. Dimijian/Photo Researchers; **98b**, Fred Bavendam/Minden Pictures; **99t**, Frans Lanting/Minden Pictures; **99b**, Jim Zipp/Photo Researchers; **100**, D. Cavagnaro/DRK Photo; **101**, Randy Wells/TSI; **102l**, John Shaw/Tom Stack & Associates; **102m**, Dan Suzio/Photo Researchers; **102tr**, Stephen J. Krasemann/DRK Photo; **102–103**, Phil A. Dotson/Photo Researchers; **103tm**, Frans Lanting/Minden Pictures; **103m**, David Liebman, **103r**, Lynn M. Stone/DRK Photo; **104l**, Roy Toft/Tom Stack & Associates; **104r**, Frans Lanting/Minden Pictures; **105**, Tom McHugh/Photo Researchers; **106t**, Richard Haynes; **106b**, Greg Vaughn/Tom Stack & Associates; **107l,r**, G. Payne/Liaison International; **108**, D. Cavagnaro/DRK Photo; **109**, Gary Braasch/TSI.

Chapter 4
Pages 112–113, Nick Vedros, Vedros & Assoc./TSI; **114t**, Richard Haynes; **114bl**, Bertrand Rieger/TSI; **114br**, Chad Slattery/TSI; **115**, Jacques Jangoux/TSI; **117tl**, Kevin Horan/TSI; **117tr**, Tom Bean 1994/DRK Photo; **117bl**, Larry Lefever/Grant Heilman Photography; **117br**, Martin Benjamin/The Image Works; **118**, Chris Sattleberger/Panos Pictures; **119l,r**, Wally McNamee/Woodfin Camp & Associates; **120**, Richard Haynes; **121**, Russ Lappa; **123**, Hank Morgan/Science Source/Photo Researchers; **124l**, David Joel/TSI; **124r**, Hank Morgan/Science Source/Photo Researchers; **125**, Russ Lappa; **126**, David Lassman/The Image Works; **127**, Ray Pfortner/Peter Arnold; **128**, David Young Wolff/PhotoEdit; **129**, Richard Haynes; **130t**, Russ Lappa; **130b**, Galen Rowell/Peter Arnold; **131 all**, Russ Lappa; **132l**, Fred Hirschmann/TSI; **132r**, Stephen Agricola/The Image Works; **134**, Russ Lappa, **135**, Fred Hirschmann/TSI.

Chapter 5
Pages 138–139, G. Randall/FPG International; **140t**, Russ Lappa; **140b**, NASA/Liaison International; **141**, Conor Caffrey/SPL/Photo Researchers; **144,147**, Russ Lappa; **149t**, Richard Haynes; **149b**, NASA/The Stock Market; **150l**, Ed Wheeler/The Stock Market; **150r**, Robert Fried/Stock Boston; **151**, Bilderberg/The Stock Market; **152l**, Suzi Moore/Woodfin Camp & Associates; **152r**, Jeffrey Muir Hamilton/Stock Boston; **153**, Randy Duchaine/The Stock Market; **155t**, Richard Haynes; **155b**, Mike Booher/Transparencies, Inc.; **157t**, Courtesy of city of Arcata, CA; **157b**, Stephen Rose/Rainbow; **158**, Bob Daemmrich/Stock Boston; **159t**, Conor Caffrey/SPL/Photo Researchers; **159b**, Randy Duchaine/The Stock Market.

Chapter 6
Pages 162–163, Yamada Toshiro/TSI; **164**, M. L. Sinibaldi/The Stock Market; **167t**, Mike Abrahams/TSI; **167b**, Paul Harris/TSI; **168**, Jbboykin Oil Prod./The Stock Market; **170**, UPI/Corbis-Bettmann; **171**, Chad Ehlers/International Stock; **172**, Nadia MacKenzie/TSI; **174**, A & L Sinibaldi/TSI; **175**, Larry Ulrich/DRK Photo; **176**, Carlie Waite/TSI; **178**, NASA; **179**, Richard Haynes; **180**, Herb Swanson; **181t**, Russ Lappa; **181b**, Photograph by Johan Hagemeyer, courtesy AIP Emilio Segre Visual Archives; **184**, Y. Arthus-Bertrand/Peter Arnold; **185**, U.S. Dept. of Energy/Science Photo Library/Photo Researchers; **187**, Richard Haynes; **188l**, Mitch Kezar/TSI; **188r**, Leonard Lessin/Peter Arnold; **189**, Yves Marcoux/TSI; **190**, Wolf/Monkmeyer; **191l**, Nadia MacKenzie/TSI; **191r**, Yves Marcoux/TSI.

Interdisciplinary Exploration
Page 194tm, Frans Lanting/Minden Pictures; **194tr**, Alan Carey/Photo Researchers; **194bl**, Frans Lanting/Minden Pictures; **194br**, Roy Toft/Tom Stack & Associates; **195t**, Starin/Ardea London Ltd.; **195m**, Peter Steyn/Ardea London Ltd.; **195b**, Tom Brakefield/DRK Photo; **196t**, Dr. Migel Smith/ Earth Scenes; **196b**, Werner Forman Archive/Art Resource; **197l**, Christie's Images; **197r**, Jose Anzel/Aurora; **199**, Corbis-Bettmann

Skills Handbook
Page 200, Mike Moreland/Photo Network; **201t**, Foodpix; **201m**, Richard Haynes; **201b**, Russ Lappa; **204**, Richard Haynes; **206**, Ron Kimball; **207**, Renee Lynn/Photo Researchers.